A Primer on Clinical Experience in Medicine

*Reasoning, Decision Making,
and Communication in Health Sciences*

A Primer on Clinical Experience in Medicine

*Reasoning, Decision Making,
and Communication in Health Sciences*

Milos Jenicek, MD

CRC Press
Taylor & Francis Group
Boca Raton   London   New York

CRC Press is an imprint of the
Taylor & Francis Group, an **informa** business

A PRODUCTIVITY PRESS BOOK

CRC Press
Taylor & Francis Group
6000 Broken Sound Parkway NW, Suite 300
Boca Raton, FL 33487-2742

© 2013 by Taylor & Francis Group, LLC
CRC Press is an imprint of Taylor & Francis Group, an Informa business

No claim to original U.S. Government works

Printed in the United States of America on acid-free paper
Version Date: 20120322

International Standard Book Number: 978-1-4665-1558-1 (Hardback)

Library of Congress Cataloging-in-Publication Data

Jenicek, Milos, 1935-
  A primer on clinical experience in medicine : reasoning, decision making, and communication in health sciences / Milos Jenicek.
       p. ; cm.
  Includes bibliographical references and index.
  ISBN 978-1-4665-1558-1 (alk. paper)
  I. Title.
  [DNLM: 1. Clinical Medicine--methods. 2. Problem Solving. 3. Thinking. WB 102]

616--dc23   2012009122

Visit the Taylor & Francis Web site at
http://www.taylorandfrancis.com

and the CRC Press Web site at
http://www.crcpress.com

To the fresh minds who enter the hospital, wish to understand others, and make themselves understood by all for the benefit of bedridden bodies and souls who expect and deserve so much from us. This book is also dedicated to the experienced minds and hands who help us achieve this goal.

Contents

Foreword

This is a timely book. Educators currently lament a lack of critical thinking at the secondary education level and in postsecondary education. This has translated into medical school entrants who are probably wanting in critical reasoning skills.

The issue was addressed in 2011 at the Harvard Millennium Conference on critical thinking. Teams from across North America met for two days to debate the issue. Pedagogical strategies were considered for the delivery of curricula to promote this fundamental skill at undergraduate, postgraduate, and continuing levels of medical education. The event was almost an anachronism; historically, medicine has probably done better in the past with respect to the underpinnings of thinking and reasoning. Philosophy, logic, and psychology were dominant in some of the earliest medical curricula. At the prestigious School of Medicine in Salerno, Italy, for example, in the Middle Ages, training these thinking skills took up a significant part of the undergraduate curriculum. In recent times, however, there has been a growing emphasis on declarative rather than procedural knowledge, that is, *knowing that* rather than *knowing how*. The electronic movement and manipulation of knowledge are far more disposed to declarative content than to informing us about how to think. Perhaps the Millennium Conference saw this coming and attempted to head it off.

In some ways, at this stage in the evolution of medical science, the notion of critical thinking and decision making (CTDM) might feel almost redundant. Surely, with the advent of increasingly sophisticated technology, the need for human cerebral input might become less rather than more. Take, for example, the case of a patient with undifferentiated abdominal pain: A detailed history and physical examination, coupled with laboratory and plain x-rays will yield a sensitivity of diagnosis in the order of about 30%, whereas a computed tomography (CT) scan delivers a sensitivity of over 90%. Why should clinicians even bother struggling with the formal process of collecting data, CTDM, establishing differential diagnoses, ordering and waiting for the results of laboratory tests (and dealing with their inherent error), and performing baseline imaging when at the push of a button they can triple their own performance? Novitiates to maritime navigation put forward a similar argument: Why should they learn the tedious principles of map reading, the use of a compass, and dead reckoning when they can simply press a button on a handheld global positioning system (GPS) navigation device?

Well, there are three issues to consider here: (1) The first is the cost and consequences of technology. Although GPS devices do emit microwave radiation, it is low and precautions can be taken to distance oneself from the device to reduce exposure. CT scanners, however, are a different matter, and there is growing concern about the amount of radiation to which patients are exposed. Too readily, we go for the effortless and quick answer neglecting to caution patients about their individual accumulating exposure. (2) The second is that technology may not always be available. The navigation device may fall overboard, and the CT scanner may break down or not be available. We will need backup in such circumstances, and, despite the shortcomings of the traditional routes, they do provide reasonable information that we can use. (3) The third, and perhaps the most important, is that we generally need to preserve our reasoning faculties. CT scanners and GPSs are of little value when it comes to making ethical decisions, choosing which politician to vote for, or agreeing with a partner on how best to raise children. The old saw "use it or lose it" applies here. The loss does not come in a Darwinian sense; instead, it arises from creeping cognitive indolence and the comfortable numbness of putting all our eggs in the basket of modern technology. There is a growing imperative to maintain the mental skills that we have painfully acquired over the last few thousand years and use them to maintain cerebral surveillance of the road ahead. Already, there are disquieting rumblings in medical corridors that as new generations of physicians come to rely more on managing information electronically, there has been an abandonment and loss of traditional skills. We should be concerned about this trend. Critical thinking needs preservation and promotion. It is the process by which we evaluate information and necessarily involves the exercise of good thinking habits so that sound reasoning occurs. Like any other skill, once acquired these habits need to be maintained.

In this book, Jenicek instructs us in the art of argumentation. This is not the widely used vernacular version such as having an argument with someone— often polarized with emotion and ending badly; instead, it is used as a vehicle of reasoning. Argumentation is "the act of forming reasons, making inductions, drawing conclusions, and applying them to the case in discussion; the operation of inferring propositions, not known or admitted as true, from facts or principles known, admitted, or proved to be true." It is said that reasoning, tested by argumentation, reflects doubt, and in a world where we are surrounded by uncertainty it would be as well if we understood the basic principles of argumentation; that is, claim, grounds, backing, warrant, qualifiers, and rebuttals. Jenicek illustrates how three distinct areas, medical reasoning, decision making, and multiple aspects of communication (including reading a medical article), can be systematically approached using the argumentation framework.

As he notes, modern medicine is characterized by incomplete information and uncertainty. The best we can usually do is to operate within a bounded rationality, making the best of what we have. We can, at least, impose a structure and discipline on our thinking, reasoning, and decision making that do not add to these shortcomings.

At the end of the day, asks Jenicek, can we afford not to be trained in logic, critical thinking and decision making? Two prominent demands on our thinking in medicine are (1) understanding the nature of the problem (diagnosis) and (2) deciding what to do to fix it (treatment). The second won't work unless the first is correct. So, the emphasis in CTDM lies on getting the right diagnosis in a timely fashion. Our fallibilities in diagnosis mostly lie in faulty reasoning, not in knowledge deficits; critical thinking is mostly about overcoming cognitive bias.

There is burgeoning literature now on the two predominant forms of decision making: (1) intuitive and (2) rational. Two important books have contributed to our understanding: The first book, *Thinking Fast and Slow* (2011), by Nobel laureate Daniel Kahneman, has all but eliminated any residual conjecture about this as the ultimate framework for how we think. Kahneman painstakingly points to the numerous failures that occur in the intuitive mode, where most biases occur. The second book, *Rationality and the Reflective Mind* (2011), by Keith Stanovich, is a cutting-edge work on the psychological workings of the mind. An important feature of critical reasoning is that when the intuitive system goes looking for help in the analytical system, the latter must be up to it; this involves our reflective brain and how well it can reason. How well stocked is its toolbox for reasoning rationally and avoiding cognitive and affective biases, as well as logical fallacies? True reasoning, as Jenicek emphasizes, takes place only in the analytical mode of thinking. Argumentation is a conscious, deliberate, structured way of thinking that engages the reflective mind and decouples us from the pull of intuitive traps. Given that we spend probably 95% of our time in the intuitive mode, we need all the help we can get.

Canada's national media recently issued a challenge: "It's time for a Canadian renaissance in undergraduate education … It ought to produce critical thinkers, scientifically and culturally literate people who can assess evidence, connect the dots and communicate with clarity—the key skills, that, in a fast-changing economy, prepare people for the jobs that haven't been invented yet" (*Globe and Mail*, October 10, 2011).

This book, *A Primer on Clinical Experience in Medicine: Reasoning, Decision Making, and Communication in Health Sciences*, is a primer on how physicians reason, but is also useful to practicing physicians and even teachers who have not undergone formal training in thinking. It is part of the renaissance. In his gentle and engaging way, with occasional humor thrown in, Jenicek takes the reader through the essentials.

Pat Croskerry, MD, PhD
Dalhousie University
Halifax, Nova Scotia, Canada

Author's Welcome and Introduction

Not-So-Random Leading Thoughts

How do and should physicians really think,
make the best possible decisions, and
effectively communicate with peers,
patients and others? Know this before
walking for the first time through the hospital
doors, putting on your scrubs and coat,
hanging a stethoscope around your neck
and turning on your beeper or smartphone.
There is more to clinical propaedeutics
than learning to start an IV line or knowing
how to probe a surgical wound.
How Do Doctors Think?

**Point previously raised by Kathryn Montgomery,
2006 and Jerome Groopman, 2007**

… Everyone who has mixed among mankind
with any capacity of observing them, knows
that the men, who place implicit faith in their
common sense, are, without any exception,
the most wrong-headed and impracticable
persons whom he has ever had to deal.

John Stuart Mill, 1831

and yes,

Common sense appears to be only another
name for the thoughtlessness of the unthinking.

W. Somerset Maugham, 1941

Knowledge may enable you to memorize
the whole *Gray's Anatomy* and Osler's *Principles
and Practice of Medicine*, but only wisdom can
teach you what to do with what you have learned. ...
Knowledge is what you are taught, but
wisdom is what you bring to it.

Robertson Davies, 1984 and 1994

You have to collect evidence where no oath binds the speaker;
to penetrate disguises; to sift conflicting statements;
to reconcile improbabilities. Without the power to experimentalize,
that is, to vary at will the circumstances, so as to disentangle
the essential from the nonessential, or without even the power
to cross-examine, you must come to a conclusion;
often with a moment of deliberation, you must act.

Thomas Laycock, 1812–1876

That is what learning is.
You suddenly understand something
you've understood all your life,
but in a new way.

Doris Lessing, 1919–
Nobel Prize in Literature
Order of Companions of Honour

Introductory Comments

Dear Samantha, John, Claudette, Pierre, Izzy, Hans, Henrik, José, Luis, Mahmoud, Kwang-Ho, Munira, Hiroko, and everyone else, welcome to you as you begin to experience, learn, and practice medicine!

In this action-oriented world, welcome to the field of medicine and other health sciences. We must learn and teach this domain, not only as an array of acts, actions, and activities but also as a set of reasoning, understanding, decision-making, and communication methods. How can you make the most of this new journey?

Military brass must make the best decisions possible in order to win battles and wars. To do so, they are trained in logic, critical thinking, and decision making. Can they perform their jobs without being trained in these three essential skills? Hospitals and their emergency departments and wards are battlefields in the domain of health care and physicians are the hospital brass making decisions to win battles and wars for cures and survival of patients. Can we, ourselves, afford not to be trained in logic, critical thinking, and decision making? We think not, but if you have a counterargument, please say so.

Learning how to use needles, scalpels, and stethoscopes should not be the only components of your first clinical experience. Encounters, thoughts, words, exchange of ideas, decisions, actions, or doing nothing (and knowing why) should also be part of it. Learning how to insert needles in people's skin, catheterize, and pierce other organs or knowing the Krebs cycle by heart are not the only components of propaedeutics in medicine. They are just a starting point perhaps. Learning and understanding clinical problems, making correct decisions, and communicating with others are the very essence of propaedeutics in medicine.

Let us say that you are entering for the first time the hospital, its wards, and its clinics and that you are about to start communicating with your clinical teachers, patients, and various health professionals and hospital administrators. You have not necessarily received formal and structured information about what to expect, how to understand the people you will interact with, and how to otherwise make the most of your first clinical experience. This book should help you in this respect.

When you enter the hospital for the first time and listen to all those busy people in scrubs and coats, you may ask yourself:

- What is going on here?
- What do all these happenings I am witnessing mean?

- What are they saying?
- What do they mean?
- Why are they saying it?
- What should I understand from all I have heard?
- What should I say?
- How can I help?
- What is expected of me?
- What should I expect?
- From among everything I have crammed inside my head since my preclinical days, what should I use and how should I use it?

This book provides answers to these very same questions that certainly crossed the author's mind when as a freshman a long time ago he first walked through the hospital doors. The book is about how doctors and others in the field of health care think, talk, and act. The answers in this book are useful not only for purposeful and contextual thinking and decision making but also for communication and meaningful mutual understanding.

What should you know before seeing your first patient, building his or her medical history, performing the physical examination, and presenting your impressions and recommendations regarding treatment? To be efficient, you must know how your clinical teachers think; you must know how to reason, how to share ideas, and how to make all this compatible for the best benefit of the patient. You must understand physicians, nurses, patients, community care workers, and administrators. You must all speak the same language. The quality of care and patient safety depend on it.

In the forthcoming flood of words and activities from basic sciences, epidemiology, biostatistics, and clinical practice in various specialties to which you will be exposed later on and which you will be expected to understand and enhance, here is a map to help you navigate, increase your self-confidence, contribute in such a way to make your health team happy and, most importantly, help the patient do well. How can you better understand the complexities and intricacies of learning and working for the well-being of the patients and communities who trust you with their physical, mental, social, and spiritual health?

The leading thoughts, some serious some less so, that introduce each chapter are included for a purpose: The old ones remind us that our ideas today are sometimes not quite original, just updated in the current context of medicine. The newer thoughts tell us that we are perhaps going in the right direction. Most of them reflect thinking about the topics that are developed and discussed from one chapter to another. Some make us think twice about what we are learning and doing. They remind us also of many brilliant minds from medicine and elsewhere whose thoughts transcend the technological, social, contextual, and technological contexts of their time. Are there any others to add? Just tell us.

In 1946, British composer Benjamin Britten offered to music lovers his composition titled *The Young Person's Guide to the Orchestra.* He wanted to enable listeners to better understand the tone colors, capacities, roles, harmonies, and interactions of an orchestral piece of music by introducing woodwinds, strings, brass, and percussion one section at a time before being integrated into a fugue. Similarly, the "symphony of medicine" (its parts and the relationships among them) also relies on understanding its sections (domains, specialties, and health professions) and their complementarities, interactions, and overall functioning to achieve desired objectives. In the case of your learning, it is a question of putting together in the best possible way your knowledge, attitudes, and skills. This requires proper understanding of health problems and their management; rational decision making; and communication with patients, peers, and other health professionals in our often complex teams and working environments. For first-year students in health sciences, don't we also need some sort of "young person's guide" to medicine? We believe so.

Medical Propaedeutics

Before any student enters clinics and wards and approaches patients on admission or at the bedside, he or she must know what to expect and what is expected of him or her. In many medical cultures across the world, such an essential step takes place through teaching and learning medical (clinical) propaedeutics. This is a way of acquiring knowledge and some skills required for further learning, but it is not enough for necessary and sufficient proficiency in understanding, decision making, actions, and their evaluation in a particular domain. It is an introductory course into a discipline. In medicine, we may also coin medical propaedeutics as the knowledge, attitudes, and skills necessary for learning but not for proficiency.

In 1851, the *Encyclopedia Americana* defined propaedeutics as "… a term used by the Germans to indicate the knowledge which is necessary or useful for understanding or practicing an art or science, or which unfolds its nature and extent, and the method of learning it. It is applied, therefore, not only to special introductions to particular branches of study but also to auxiliary sciences, logic, philology, etc., and the encyclopedic views of particular branches of science which facilitates the insight into the relations of the parts …."[1]

In short, medical propaedeutics refers to a preliminary instruction, introductory course, or preparatory teaching preceding and pertaining to clinical training and care. In various medical cultures such as those in Europe (Netherlands, Austria, Czech Republic, etc.), South America (Brazil), and the Pacific region (Philippines), this kind of threshold knowledge, that is, "core concepts that once understood, transform perception of a given subject,"[2] includes not only selected elements from basic sciences[3] but also human and physical elements, roles, activities, and functions of a given medical, surgical, or other clinical setting; patient interviews; medical history taking; physical and mental status examinations; and paraclinical explorations and their most basic components and techniques.[4-6] In North America, in addition to the aforementioned types, some type of threshold knowledge, for example, logic and critical thinking, is often required *before* entering training in health sciences. In Dutch, *propedeuse* means a diploma attesting that a student has successfully completed the first year of studies representing the propaedeutic phase (*propedeutische fase*) of his or her undergraduate training.[7]

Currently, medical and surgical propaedeutics includes a selection of fundamental notions from basic sciences, that is, anatomy, pathology, physiology, or genetics; knowledge of the clinical physical environment and its functioning; a basic approach to the patient (history taking, physical examination, recording of clinical data and information in patient charts, taking fluid and tissue samples for laboratory examination as scut work, rules of patient management in routine hospital setting); as well as lectures and introductory textbook readings for major medical specialties such as internal medicine, surgery, psychiatry, and pediatrics. Is this enough for medical propaedeutics? We believe not.

Medical propaedeutics involves more than becoming familiar with and knowing how to take a patient's medical history, examining and/or admitting him or her, or knowing how to draw blood or make a suture. Neophytes in a clinical environment encounter new activities; new ways of thinking by health professionals; new challenges in understanding decisions of others; new ways and tools of communication; new strategies for meeting and interviewing patients; new methods of reading and writing in patient charts; new methods of making progress notes, records, referrals, consults, floor and grand rounds, and journal clubs; various opportunities for case reporting and reading and understanding medical articles and other kinds of scientific writing; and meetings with representatives of medical technology and pharmaceutical products. These are all components of a medical student's new working environment, well beyond learning and understanding the follow up of vital signs; mastering parenteral techniques and tools;

managing the intravenous (IV) line hanging on a stand; comprehending a set of sterilized surgical instruments lying on a mobile tray; or reading flickering monitors for a patient's vital signs.

Beyond the Acquisition of Basic Scientific Knowledge and Clinical Sensorimotor Skills

The acquisition of knowledge and the mastering and use of rules of evidence-based critical reasoning and decision making must be a part of a new physician's knowledge, attitudes, and skills. Why?

The virtue of the best medicine is not only producing, evaluating, and using the best evidence and modern technologies but also flawlessly finding, evaluating, and using them in the daily life of a physician. Isn't this one of the fundamental ways to avoid errors in medicine? We believe so. As a matter of fact, the error-free practice of medicine is an important warrant of its success and the overall quality of medical care. Groopman[8] reminds us that the majority of errors are due to flaws in a physician's thinking, not technical mistakes. Propaedeutics in medical reasoning and decision making should avoid the former. Traditional propaedeutics focuses mainly on the latter.

Slotnick[9] reminds us that "cognitive dimensions encompass what one knows, thinks, and thinks about thinking, knowledge, experience, and insights derived from experience. All of these are essential in helping physicians-in-training and practicing physicians to become progressively more skilful at solving problems …." One wonders if this is a part of the theory of medicine or of its practice. It is probably a part of both.

What Is Clinical Judgment? Entering the World of Reasoning, Decision Making, and Communication

Good clinical judgment has always been an ideal aspired to by everyone in clinical care, and patients expect it from their physicians, nurses, and other health professionals. Especially in the past two generations, several pioneering monographs appeared on this topic, such as the works by Feinstein[10] and White and Stancombe,[11] but surprisingly enough the definition of this term was left mainly to the lexical world. Judgment errors are behind many cases of medical harm and their control is crucial in avoiding damaging the patient.[12,13]

In general, judgment is "the act or faculty of affirming or denying a proposition, whether based on a direct comparison of objects or ideas or derived by a process of reasoning. It is the evaluation of the nature and soundness of some information, giving it a value for subsequent decision making (p. 270)."[14]

In the 1960s, Thorne[15] proposed that "more parsimoniously, clinical judgment properly refers simply to the correctness of the problem-solving thinking of a special class of persons, namely, clinically trained persons with special levels of training, experience and competence. … The competent clinician is operationally defined as one who practices at the highest levels of clinical judgment possible at a time and place."

In *Mosby's Medical Dictionary*,[16] clinical judgment means "the application of information, based on actual observation of a patient combined with subjective and objective data that lead to a conclusion." In the world of informatics in medicine, it is "a framework in which brilliant pieces of understanding are routinely assembled into a working unit of social machinery that is coherent and as error free as possible."[17]

Montgomery[18] situates clinical judgment in a physician–particular patient relationship. For her, clinical judgment refers to "… the ability to work out how general rules—scientific principles, clinical guidelines—apply to one particular patient. … It enables physicians to combine scientific information, clinical skill, and collective experience with similar patients to make sense of the particulars of one patient's illness and to determine the best action to take to cure or alleviate it." Practicing physicians "… are not scientists or artists but practical reasoners, exercising clinical judgment as they see patients and work out what ought to be done for each one of them."

Noreen and Peter Facione[19] emphasized the role of critical thinking underlying clinical judgment. However, is clinical judgment synonymous with critical thinking and reasoning? We believe it is more than that.

In light of our better understanding of medical reasoning and decision making, how can we see and define clinical judgment today? Let us say the following:

Clinical judgment is the capacity to make and choose data and information to produce useful (true or false) claims in clinical practice and research. It also means critical thinking in the practice of medicine based on the "patient/evidence/setting/ethics" fit. Together with elements of knowledge and experience, it relies on the process of integrating meanings and values of clinical and paraclinical observation and data into the making of conclusions and decisions derived from such an integration.

Clinical judgment relies then on the complexity and completeness of data and information and on what the clinician is doing with it in his or her mind.

Beyond the Acquisition of Scientific Evidence, Testimonies, and Narratives-Based and Patient-Centered Medicines

The mastery of all the above and the results of our experiences are considered a necessary element of our understanding of health problems or data and/or information for our decision making about effective preventive or curative actions. Processes of understanding health problems and making decisions rely on the generation and use of multiple experiences. Such experiences appear as statements that constitute crucial parts of modern argumentation, critical thinking, and decision making.

The following distinct steps reflect our clinical doings:

- *Understanding and comprehending* our reasoning about the nature of a health problem and its management, as outlined in Chapter 2
- *Applying* such reasoning to the steps of clinical work summarized in Chapter 3
- *Making decisions* regarding what to do, as proposed in Chapter 4
- *Communicating and sharing* our understanding and decision intentions, actions intended and performed with others (peers, patients, or other care providers), as in Chapter 5

Modern reasoning and decision making in medicine[20-22] are now structurally and methodologically developed enough for pragmatic uses in medical practice and research, which contribute ultimately to patient safety and quality of care.[13] They must be learnt as is anything else and used in the appropriate cases, situations, environments, and settings with clear practical objectives, aims, and purposes. This is what we must do today. In this role, medical reasoning, critical thinking, and decision making must be an integral part of medical propaedeutics in addition to its existing components and building blocks.

Modern medical reasoning and decision making in medicine are, as is the case for any similar endeavor outside the health sciences, based on principles, rules, and an increasing number of structured and pragmatic methods and techniques. In clinical practice and research, reasoning, decision making, and communication also rely and depend on methodology, experience, and previous secular accomplishments in biostatistics, fundamental, "shoe leather" (field, community) epidemiology and "clinical epidemiology," rational production, evaluation and uses of medical evidence in the framework of more recent "evidence-based medicine." Let us add to the scientific method-based and evidence-based medicine, testimony-based (scientific method and cause–effect free), case-based, overall evidence-based, patient-centered, and patient-specific medicines. More recently, evidence-grounded/critical thinking–based medicine[23,24] has come into play, as discussed in Chapter 2. All this must be integrated into our ways of caring for individual patients and communities as well. It cannot be otherwise. Sooner or later, you will acquire a fuller understanding of the principles, methods, techniques, and applications of all these disciplines. For now, just the essence of their message is worthy of attention.

Many foundations and principles of medical reasoning and decision making are built and somehow hidden behind various names used by several, now traditional, disciplines. They have made many remarkable, essential, crucial, and necessary contributions to medical understanding and decision making, and they include biostatistics, epidemiology, ethics, behavioral sciences, philosophy (informal and formal logic), and sociology to name just a few. Even token examples abound often assigned more or less related names such as clinical judgment,[10–11] "clinical decision making,"[25,26] "clinical decision analysis."[27–30] They are also sometimes presented as "clinical biostatistics,"[31] clinical epidemiology,[32–36] evidence-based medicine,[20,37] "evidence-based health care,"[38] "evidence-based clinical practice,"[39] "evidence-based public health,"[40] and others,[41] which were made more or less fully explicit and explicated during the past decade. It was just a question of time before it was discovered that logic and critical thinking are the main themes of the literature covering this topic in clinical and community medicine practice and research.[14,21,22]

Most often taught in distinct disciplinary courses of biostatistics or epidemiology, such information reaches medical students sooner or later and most often when they are in the middle of their first clinical experience and learning. Being related more traditionally to public health and community and preventive medicines, this information was originally presented in the second part of the medical undergraduate curriculum. However, it should be introduced as early as possible allowing clinical clerks to make the most of their patient care experience.

Are there other domains that support this new kind of medical propaedeutics? Is there a way to integrate the aforementioned disciplines and develop new ones?

Beyond medicine, cognitive sciences, and operational research, development and evaluation of new technologies are bringing to the health sciences an additional important methodology and its applications.

Mastering clinical sensorimotor skills, learning how to function within the hospital culture, and knowing when to call a nurse or an attending do not constitute sufficient preparation for what is coming in your more specific training. As we learn clinical procedures, we must also learn their logic and how to think about them; how to understand health problems and their related health care; as well as how to select, share, and exchange experience and evidence with other providers of clinical and community care and with all their intended and real recipients of cure and prevention. For most of our readers, more complete and formal courses and programs in basic and applied sciences and discipline follow at the undergraduate and graduate levels. This book is intended as a joining point between them.

With a few exceptions, bibliographical references are mostly of an introductory and illustrative nature only.

What This Book Is Not

This book is not

- A clinical epidemiology textbook
- A biostatistics textbook
- An introduction to behavioral sciences
- A primer on hospital management and administration
- A compulsory reading before your licensure examinations (at least, not yet)

Accused of oversimplification by specialists of a "multiaxial orthogonal rotation of endogenous and exogenous variables in a multidimensional fuzzy space of push-pull interactive multientropic tangential coefficients of rectal bleeding" (just kidding!), we have a choice: Make this book as methodologically sophisticated as possible or make it as simple as possible. We have chosen the latter.

Besides our intentional oversimplifications (which may be perceived as such by some), certain topics including probabilities and risk are also briefly repeated in various chapters and explained within the context of different messages. Some readers choosing to focus only on specific parts of the book might miss the nuances stemming from these different contexts.

Keeping in mind readers just starting out in this area, our clinical examples, statements, and exchanges of ideas as they might occur between health professionals have been kept as simple as possible. Dialogs are not recorded transcripts from daily practice because actual conversations might carry more information than needed, are not always to the point, and do not always contribute to the clarity of the essential message and its reason. Many dialogs presented in this book have been construed somewhat artificially to clearly illustrate a specific point in critical thinking and decision making. Views, facts, and decisions are not necessarily prescriptive for daily life because some additional considerations were omitted for the sake of brevity and simplicity.

Detailed courses and programs in morphology, function, laboratory and experimental sciences, clinical specialties, biostatistics, epidemiology, evidence-based medicine principles and methods, behavioral sciences, and health economics and management will follow, sooner or later. They occur in most undergraduate curricula.

What This Book Is

This book is

- A primer on how physicians and other health professionals reason, make decisions, and share their views by communicating with others (or how they should do so).
- A primer on how all health professionals, dentists, nurses, physiotherapists, dieticians, or social workers in health care should reason the common way, make decisions, and communicate; the rules of the game are same for all. We all share the same ways of thinking.

This reading should facilitate a common understanding of the most fundamental principles of understanding and decision making and their uses by the reader. It does not replace any of the above.

What Follows in This Book

In the spirit of the aforementioned philosophy and strategies, let us discuss, not necessarily in the exact order given here, some worthy topics:

- General and medical ways of thinking, reasoning, argumentation, fact finding, and using evidence: Thinking alone and with others

- Evaluating and using evidence about risks, causes, diagnosis, treatment, and prognosis separating facts from *factoids* (i.e., apparent facts that are not facts)
- Components of medical decision making in clinical and community settings
- Evaluating successes (effectiveness and cure) and failures (error and harm) of clinical and community actions
- Communication with patients and its strategies, successes, failures, and possible remedies (offices, bedside, intervention, and care settings)
- Communication with peers, and its strategies, successes, failures, and possible remedies (interpersonal communication, morning and other reports, rounds, research gatherings)
- Beyond practice: Implications for research, management, planning, and evaluation

In these areas, dear reader, your teachers and any other more experienced colleague with whom you will be working should understand you and you should understand them. This mutual understanding is definitely a two-way challenge and is impossible without some kind of common language and similar ways of thinking, values, and goals. Some of the "elders," too, may find these pages interesting, new, and useful for this purpose. This book is for unprepared clinical novices. However, if you want to become an academic clinician, you also need to read these pages. Otherwise, how can you communicate meaningfully with those you are training? How can you be on the same wave length with them?

If you as a newcomer to the hospital do not understand your clinical teacher, ask him or her: What do you mean by that? How does it help? Why is it so? Who will benefit from it? Your clinical teacher should be able to answer these questions, but beware. There are some absolutely brilliant clinicians who are not equally brilliant teachers. Find a common language. Ask, share, approve, or disprove to find a better way.

Let us reiterate: All who are interested in patient care including physicians, nurses, and other health professionals and health administration and management experts must speak and understand the same language. This book is for all of them.

Certain readers might be interested in key books on critical thinking. These books are indicated in the References section of this Introductory Comments. To complete this section, readers are encouraged to refer to a selection of definitions and their sources given in the Glossary and also mentioned at the end of some of our own other titles.[13,14,22] A few of them may be quite new in the domain of health sciences.

Why Are We Doing All This?

We need to teach, learn, master, and practice problem solving within the context of practical and concrete questions, for example,

- "Is this finding worthy of further consideration and a basis for clinical care decisions?" rather than "Is it 'significant'?"
- "Is this sufficient proof of a causal link (strong and specific enough) between alcohol abuse and liver cirrhosis? Is it good enough to justify some prevention program?" rather than musing about relative risks, odds ratios, etiological fractions, or attributable risk percentage between drinking or not drinking and being healthy or suffering from a life-threatening liver disease.
- "Is this diagnostic test worth using in my practice and is it beneficial for my patients?" rather than "What are its sensitivity, specificity, or predictive values?"

All these and other important tools can be found just behind a simpler language once we leave the printed page and talk about such matters with our colleagues and patients. Let us try to convey the message of this book in this spirit.

Conclusion

Do you not understand what the person talking to you is saying or why he or she is saying it? Before you rush to the most recent issues of medical journals or to your nearest health sciences library and its specialized volumes of family or internal medicine, surgery, psychiatry, gynecology and obstetrics, pediatrics, or pathology for more facts or factoids, you might like to read some of the pages that follow in this book.

First clinical experiences are transdisciplinary, from an across-disciplines approach. First-year students are not looking at patients and hospital environments and considering them as a medical, sociological, epidemiological, biostatistical, epistemological, logical experience. Clinical experience from its beginning is an amalgam of such and other paradigms of patient–doctor interactions, and it should be learned and mastered, if possible, in a transdisciplinary manner.

If such a first experience leads us to further reading, learning, and mastering of underlying basic and applied clinical sciences and specialties, as well as realizing more effectively their relevance for practice and research, then it is even better.

Learning and teaching in a clinical environment have many advantages, but there are also problems and challenges[42] such as a lack of clear objectives, a focus on factual recall rather than the development of problem-solving skills and attitudes, teaching not geared to the learners' level of knowledge, a lack of participation of learners, little time for reflection and discussion, teaching by humiliation (pimping as we call it in North America; more about this in Chapter 5), time pressures, competing demands, unfriendly teaching environments like hospital wards, and poor rewards and recognition for teachers. A constructive, mutually understood argumentation and critical thinking process shared by clinical teachers and their students is definitely the way to make the best of any clinical experience. In 2003, in its ABC of Learning and Teaching in Medicine,[43] the *British Medical Journal* was correct to raise such questions, challenges, and rewards in developing and improving further the medical (and other health sciences) curriculum.

Make the most of your clinical experience. In order to do so, there must be mutual understanding between the teacher and the learner. If you as a student do not understand your clinical teacher, you and/or your teacher may be at fault. If you as a clinical teacher are not sure that your students are getting the message, it may be the fault of any party involved in the clinical experience. Solving such misunderstandings makes better students and teachers.

First clinical experiences are always stressful, time consuming, and otherwise overwhelming. Let us not complicate them further by not making our message as short and sweet as possible.

In many parts of the world, the third year of undergraduate programs in medicine is a critical moment of transition from the acquisition of basic knowledge to the reality of people of varying ages entering the hospital in crisis; injured; bleeding; with compromised vital functions; not responding to emergency maneuvers; or otherwise unresponsive, dying, or left to the mercy of their close ones and their community (if any). Can we afford to respond to their needs counting on only our best knowledge, intentions, and skills? We must do this, but as rationally as possible.

To be good critical thinkers, decision makers, and communicators, we have much to learn from experiences outside health sciences and not only from fundamental domains in philosophy or psychology. For example, our introductory reflection about the hospital as a battlefield is not just a parable. Understandably military brass is trained now in critical thinking[44–50] more than we may think. A similar trend can be perceived in the business world.[51] All of us in the health sciences field must master the reasoning behind understanding and knowledge as well as the reasoning behind decision making. Both are supported by effective and purposeful communication. Reading this book should help.

Two valuable books bearing the same title are already available: *How Doctors Think*.[8,18] This book, under a different title, focuses on how to *really think* in the daily reality of medicine and all other health professions. Is this book too ambitious? Perhaps it is. But as a Canadian hockey saying goes, "Someone must throw another puck on the ice rink."

In another line of thought, protagonists of evidence-based medicine correctly stress the need for integrating within the practice of medicine the best research evidence, our clinical expertise, and our patient's unique values and circumstances[52] and ethics. Some proponents do not say much about how to do so. This book proposes one possible way.

Our last book[13] was not dedicated to all those who (think they) do not make errors. It was dedicated to the rest of us and it is precisely the rest of us who write medical textbooks, determined to avoid any errors that might occur despite our best intentions and attentions. Writing a medical textbook is a profoundly humbling experience. The author takes responsibility for any errors within these pages and is ready to do his best to correct them at the nearest opportunity.

Acknowledgments

There are so many highly qualified and supportive colleagues and coworkers without whom these pages would never have been presented to the reader:

Pat Croskerry, professor of emergency medicine at Dalhousie University, embedder of critical thinking and decision making into the overall objectives, strategies, and orientation of the undergraduate curriculum at the Dalhousie

Faculty of Medicine; my colleague and friend who has written the Foreword to this book. In fact, this Foreword is more than the often customary and polite words about the author and the book. It sets the tone for everything that follows and reflects all Pat Croskerry's expertise and engagement in the advance of teaching and learning in the health sciences and health professions.

Nicole Kinney, chief executive officer of Linguamax Services, Ltd., Mississauga, Ontario, Canada, for her relentless review of language and style.

Rand MacIvor, creative design supervisor, and Steve Janzen, designer at Media Production Services at McMaster University, for their masterful touch in developing and producing reader-friendly artwork.

Noel Fraser, manager of the Department of Clinical Epidemiology and Biostatistics, McMaster University, and his administrative team for all necessary human and material resources support and almost daily assistance in this project.

Kristine Mednansky, senior editor of business improvement, Health Care Management organization at CRC Press, a division of the Taylor & Francis Group, who was an invaluable guide in the orientation of this book in view of the potential readership. Her reasoning was more than welcome, especially when putting the finishing touches on this project, which must have served for a long time as her bedside reading. We owe her also the strategic orientation of the book. Moreover, Kristine was an essential and sensible liaison between the author and his team and her colleagues at CRC Press at various stages in the realization of this endeavor.

Last but not least, I thank my wife Jana for her enduring tolerance of my seclusion, and protracted and almost never-ending isolation in my home office and various libraries, where I was constantly typing at the keyboard instead of smelling the roses of daily communication, life's duties, and other pleasures.

A Note about the References in This Book

Throughout this book, in addition to standard scientific sources, the reader will find several references, definitions, and other referrals to less traditional scientific sources. These are mainly electronic in nature, such as Wikipedia or various independent websites, which may evolve and change with time. These are not always peer reviewed, but are quoted here for many reasons:

■ We believe that the sites we have chosen are correct, independent of the reputation of the source.

- We believe that the information from these sites is not available elsewhere, especially not in other entry-level books intended for the health professions and sciences.
- The author was the peer reviewer of all references proposed in this reading.
- At times, we did not find any better and more easily understood sources for this purpose elsewhere.
- Beginners may use Google or other broadly accessible search engines before using more specialized ones such as PubMed, OvidSP, and Embase to find more complete and advanced information.
- Some selected sites and topics contain additional references not to be missed and allow the reader to expand his or her initial understanding of the subject.

The reader is free to adopt, compare, and use them at his or her discretion.

References

1. Wikipedia, the free encyclopedia. *Propaedeutics*. 1 page at http://en.wikipedia.org/wiki/Propaedeutics, retrieved April 8, 2010.
2. Wikipedia, the free encyclopedia. *Threshold knowledge.* 2 pages with essential bibliography at http://en.wikipedia.org/wiki/Threshold knowledge, retrieved April 8, 2010.
3. Medizinische Universität Wien. *Medical propedeutics—Syllabus Themes.* 4 pages at http://www.medunivwien.ac.at/studienabteilung/content/studium-lehre/studienangebot/n09, retrieved September 15, 2010.
4. Wikilectures. *Portal: Questions for final examination in Clinical propedeutics of Surgery.* (From the First Faculty of Medicine, Charles University, Prague.) 3 pages from http://www.wikilectures.eu/index.php/Portal:Questions_for_final_examination_in_Clinic..., retrieved September 16, 2010.
5. Third Faculty of Medicine, Charles University, Prague. *Module IIB: Questions from clinical propedeutics—3rd year.* 6 pages at http://oldlf3.cuni.cz/english/students/questions_2B.htm, retrieved April 8, 2010.
6. First Faculty of Medicine, Charles University, Prague. *Examination Questions in Propedeutics in Internal Medicine.* 2 pages at http://www.lf1.cuni.cz/en/examination-questions-in-propedeutics-in-internal-medicine, retrieved April 8, 2010.
7. Wikipedia, the free encyclopedia. *Propedeuse.* 2 pages at http://en.wikipedia.org/wiki/Propedeuse, retrieved April 8, 2010.
8. Groopman J. *How Doctors Think.* New York: Houghton Mifflin Company, 2007.

9. Slotnick HB. How doctors learn: Education and learning across the medical school-to-practice trajectory. *Acad Med,* 2001;**76**(10):1013–26.

10. Feinstein AR. *Clinical Judgment.* Baltimore: The Williams & Wilkins Company, 1967.

11. White S, Stancombe J. *Clinical Judgment in the Health and Welfare Professions. Extending the Evidence Base.* Maidenhead/Philadelphia: Open University Press/McGraw-Hill Education, 2003.

12. Ruscio J. The clinician as subject. Practitioners are prone to the same judgment errors as everyone else, pp. 29–47, in: *The Great Ideas of Clinical Science. 17 Principles That Every Mental Health Professional Should Understand.* Edited by SO Lilienfeld and WT O'Donohue. New York/London: Routledge/Taylor & Francis, 2007.

13. Jenicek M. *Medical Error and Harm. Understanding, Prevention, and Control.* Boca Raton/London/New York: CRC Press/Taylor & Francis/Productivity Press, 2011.

14. Jenicek M, Hitchcock DL. *Evidence-Based Practice. Logic and Critical Thinking in Medicine.* Chicago: American Medical Association (AMA Press), 2005, p. 270.

15. Thorne FC. Clinical Judgment: A Study of Clinical Errors. Brandson, VT: *Journal of Clinical Psychology,* 1961.

16. *Mosby's Medical Dictionary.* Eighth Edition. St. Louis, MO: Mosby, Inc., 2009.

17. Weed LL. Clinical judgment revisited. *Meth Inf Med,* 199;**38**:279–86.

18. Montgomery K. *How Doctors Think. Clinical Judgment and the Practice of Medicine.* Oxford/New York: Oxford University Press, 2006.

19. Facione NC, Facione PA. Critical thinking and clinical judgment, pp. 1–13, in: *Critical Thinking and Clinical Reasoning in the Health Sciences. A Teaching Anthology.* Milbrae, CA: California Academic Press, 2008.

20. Jenicek M. *Foundations of Evidence-Based Medicine.* Boca Raton/London/New York/Washington: Parthenon Publishing/CRC Press, 2003.

21. Jenicek M. *A Physician's Self-Paced Guide to Critical Thinking.* Chicago: American Medical Association (AMA Press), 2006.

22. Jenicek M. *Fallacy-Free Reasoning in Medicine. Improving Communication and Decision Making in Research and Practice.* Chicago: American Medical Association (AMA Press), 2009.

23. Jenicek M. Towards evidence-based critical thinking medicine? Uses of best evidence in flawless argumentations. *Med Sci Monit,* 2006;**12**(8):RA149–53.

24. Jenicek M, Croskerry P, Hitchcock DL. Evidence and its uses in health care and research: The role of critical thinking. *Med Sci Monit,* 2011;**17**(1):RA12–7.

25. Patrick EA. *Decision Analysis in Medicine. Methods and Applications.* Boca Raton, FL: CRC Press, 1979.

26. Weinstein MC, Fineberg HV, Elstein AS et al. *Clinical Decision Analysis.* Philadelphia: WB Saunders, 1980.

27. *Teaching Clinical Decision Making.* Edited by ED Cebul and LH Beck. New York: Praeger, 1985.

28. Sox JC Jr., Blatt MA, Higgins MC, Morton KI. *Medical Decision Making.* Boston: Butterworths, 1988.

29. Eddy DM. *Clinical Decision Making. From Theory to Practice. A Collection of Essays from the* Journal of the American Medical Association. Boston/London/Singapore: Jones and Bartlett Publishers, 1996.

30. Gross R. *Decisions and Evidence in Medical Practice. Applying Evidence-Based Medicine to Clinical Decision Making.* St. Louis/London/Philadelphia: Mosby, 2001.

31. Feinstein AR. *Clinical Biostatistics.* St. Louis: The C.V. Mosby Company, 1977.

32. Fletcher RH, Fletcher SW, Wagner EH. *Clinical Epidemiology. The Essentials.* Baltimore/Philadelphia/London: Williams & Wilkins, 1982.

33. Sackett DL, Haynes BR, Tugwell P. *Clinical Epidemiology. A Basic Science for Clinical Medicine.* Boston/Toronto/London: Little, Brown & Company, 1985.

34. Feinstein AR. *Clinical Epidemiology. The Architecture of Clinical Research.* Philadelphia: WB Saunders, 1985.

35. Jenicek M, Cléroux R. *Épidémiologie clinique. Clinimétrie.* (Clinical Epidemiology. Clinimetrics.) St. Hyacinthe et Paris: EDISEM et Maloine Éditeurs, 1985.

36. Kramer MS. *Clinical Epidemiology and Biostatistics. A Primer for Clinical Investigators and Decision-Makers.* Berlin/Heidelberg/New York/London: Springer-Verlag, 1988.

37. Sackett DL, Richardson WS, Rosenberg W, Haynes RB. *Evidence-Based Medicine. How to Practice and Teach EBM.* New York: Churchill Livingstone, 1997.

38. Muir Gray JA. *Evidence-Based Healthcare. How to Make Health Policy and Management Decisions.* New York/Edinburgh/London: Churchill Livingstone, 1997.

39. *Users' Guide to the Medical Literature. A Manual for Evidence-Based Clinical Practice.* Edited by G Guyatt and D Rennie. Chicago: AMA Press (American Medical Association/JAMA & Archives Journals), 2002. Second Edition: 2008.

40. Brownson RC, Baker EA, Leet TL, Gillespie KN. *Evidence-Based Public Health.* Oxford/New York: Oxford University Press, 2003.

41. Jenicek M. *Epidemiology. The Logic of Modern Medicine.* Montréal: EPIMED International, 1995.

42. Spencer J. Learning and teaching in the clinical environment. *BMJ,* 2003;**326**(7389):591–4.

43. The *British Medical Journal (BMJ)* series ABC of Learning and Teaching Medicine from *BMJ,* **326**(73383): 268–70 to *BMJ* 2003;**326**(7394):870–3.

44. Cohen MS, Thompson BB, Adelman L, Bresnick TA, Shastri L, Riedel SL. *Training Critical Thinking for the Battlefield. Volume I: Basis in Cognitive Theory and Research.* 69 p. at www.au.af/mil/auawc/awcgate/army/critical/vol_1_research.pdf, retrieved December 27, 2010.

45. Cohen MS, Thompson BB, Adelman L, Bresnick TA, Shastri L, Riedel SL. *Volume II. Training System and Evaluation.* Arlington, VA/Ft. Leavenworth, KS: Cognitive Technologies, Inc./U.S. Army Research Institute, Field Unit-Leavenworth, 2000. xiii +118 pages at http://www.cog-tech.com/papers/mentalmodels/VolIITraining.pdf, retrieved December 27, 2010.

46. Air War College, Gateway to the Internet. *Creativity & Thinking Skills.* 37 pages at http://www.au.af.mil/au/awc/awcgate/awc-thkg.htm, retrieved April 18, 2010.

47. Air War College. Gateway to the Internet. *Communication Skills.* 27 pages at http://www.au.af.mil/au/awc/awcgate/awc-comm.htm, retrieved April 18, 2010.

48. *Training Critical Thinking Skills for Battle Command. ARI Workshop Proceedings, 5–6 December 2000, Fort Leavenworth, Kansas.* Conducted by U.S. Army Research Institute for the Behavioral and Social Sciences. Edited by SL Riedel, RA Morath, and TP McGonigle. v+130 pages at http://www.au.af.mil/u/awc/awcgate/army/critical/criticalthinkig1777.pdf., retrieved December 27, 2010.

49. Allen CD, Gerras SJ. Developing creative and critical thinkers. *Military Review,* Nov–Dec 2009, 77–83.

50. Cognitive Technologies, Inc. Publications on Critical Thinking Training. A 2 p. list at http://www.cog-tech.com/Publications/PubsCT_Training.htm, retrieved December 27, 2010.

51. Smith GF. Beyond critical thinking and decision making: Teaching business students how to think. *J Manag Educ,* 2003;**27**(1):24–51.

52. Straus SE, Richardson WS, Glasziou P, Haynes RB. *Evidence-Based Medicine. How to Practice and Teach EBM.* Edinburgh/London/New York: Elsevier/Churchill Livingstone, 2005.

Chapter 1

Ways We See, Learn, and Practice Medicine Today: Paradigms of What We Are Doing

Executive Summary

Medicine today includes health protection (actions to eliminate possible risks to health), disease prevention (policies to eliminate a disease and minimize its effects), and health promotion as actions to improve and strengthen health of individuals and communities.

To reach such goals, medicine is practiced as art, science (relying heavily on the scientific method), and craft, that is, actions based on sensory–motor skills and dexterities relying on both art and science.

Results produced by causes of disease and health or by medical actions are less often deterministic, rather more often subject to probabilities, uncertainty, fuzziness, and even chaos. The science of medicine means a structured and organized way of using probability, uncertainty, and facts for the benefit of the patient.

Medicine means both theory and practice. The theory of medicine includes conceptions, views, and propositions to explain phenomena of interest. Philosophy and its branches (logic, ethics, **epistemology**) are behind the theory of medicine. The practice of medicine means actions and processes as exercise of physician's knowledge of both facts and theory and includes both reasoning and actions and their evaluation.

Practice of clinical and community medicine becomes not only evidence based but also value based and patient and his or her narratives based, which are all grounded in critical thinking, informal logic argumentation, and increasingly structured decision making.

All chapters that follow reflect and develop further such multiple views and approaches to medicine as we understand them today. Views as proposed in this introduction should help us to understand why and what we should learn from the experience of elders. Reciprocally, elders should know what learners expect from them and in what spirit. Both learning and teaching of medicine and other health sciences and professions are a beautiful challenge today, as they always have been.

Not-So-Random Leading Thoughts

Starting third year is like going to a foreign country.
You don't speak the language,
you don't understand the customs,
and the natives are not necessarily friendly.

Ana Eva Ricks, 1982

The person who knows "how"
will always have a job.
The person who knows "why"
will always be his boss.

Diane Ravitch, 1985

Be assured that no man can know
his own profession perfectly, who
knows nothing else; and he who
aspires to eminence in any particular
science, must first acquire the habit
of philosophizing on matters in general.

Abraham Colles, 1773–1843

Knowledge makes the physician,
not the name or the school.

Paracelsus, 1493–1541

Learning without thinking is useless.
Thinking without learning is dangerous.

Confucius, 551–478 BC

Facts are not science—as
the dictionary is not literature.

Martin H. Fischer, 1879–1962

Don't so many views, approaches, and paradigms of medicine make it challenging to learn medicine in that context and to put it into practice? Just imagine how even more challenging it is for your clinical teachers, elders, and role models.

How should we see and understand medicine before starting to learn it? Let us define it first. So many ways to see medicine! In this introductory chapter, let us try to understand them beyond pure theory and realize their relevance for our understanding and practice.

Introductory Comments

Do we really need to define medicine itself? We believe so. Its definition specifies not only its content but also its extent and, then, also the expectations from our work.

Definitions of medicine abound. Medicine is currently defined as "the art and science of diagnosis, treatment, and prevention of disease, and the maintenance of good health."[1] In 2006, largely in the conformity with prevailing trends, we have stressed that "... This definition applies both to the care of individual patients and to the care of the community."[2] Another more recent (and much broader) definition identifies medicine as "the profession and calling concerned with the care of the sick, including care by skilled professional staff, lay healers, and family members. 'Medicine' is a wideranging field of human activity, not confined to the profession that requires a university education."[3] The latter implies a much broader focus, content and methods and techniques, more actors, less reliance on the scientific method, and often different target populations. This book focuses at the former (ours).

In the spirit of the above, medicine includes the following:

- **Health protection:** The activity that focuses mainly at the actions "that can be taken to eliminate as far as possible the risk of adverse consequences for health attributable (most often) to environmental hazards."[3]
- Disease prevention: "Policies and actions to eliminate a disease or minimize its effect."[3]
  - **Primordial prevention** "consists of conditions, actions, and measures to minimize hazards to health and that hence inhibit the emergence and establishment of processes and factors (environmental, economic, social, behavioral, cultural) known to

increase the risk of disease."[4] Defined as such, it largely overlaps the definition of health protection.

- – **Primary prevention** "aims to reduce the incidence of disease by personal and communal factors."[4,5]
- – **Secondary prevention** aims to reduce the prevalence of disease by shortening its duration.[4,5] If this is so, the most of clinical medicine falls in this domain. Are all physicians then practitioners of some kind of prevention? To a large extent, they are. (N.B. Screening for disease and early treatment is a good example of this level of prevention.)
- – **Tertiary prevention** "consists of measures aimed at softening the impact of long term disease and disability, and handicap; minimizing suffering, and maximizing potential years of useful life."[4] Hence, even the duration of disease is not in focus but rather the severity, spectrum, and gradient of the disease.[5]
- – **Quaternary prevention** "consists of actions that identify patients at risk of overdiagnosis or overmedication and that protect them from excessive medical intervention."[4,6]
- ■ **Health promotion** as "the policies and processes that enable people to increase control over and improve their health."[3] Communities, their behavior, and their environment are largely in focus.

Medicine, as a multifaceted domain may be seen from several angles as the

- ■ Art and science
- ■ Theory and practice
- ■ Knowledge, attitudes, and skills
- ■ Finding and using in the most rational way the best evidence
- ■ Critical thinking, argumentation, and decision making in our practice of medicine
- ■ Execution of sensory and motor skills
- ■ Evaluation of how well we have done what we have done

Understanding and keeping on one's mind such angles warrant two ways of doing medicine:

1. As a rational and purposeful professional exercise and activity
2. As an act of belief, good will, and best intention (however, sincere they might be)

Both ways are needed, but without the first one, the second risks to become just an act of faith, however sincere and well intentioned it might be. Patient's physical, mental, social, and spiritual health maintenance or improvement and his, her, and our satisfaction as of health professionals all depend on them.

In this chapter, let us see first how the above mentioned facets should be understood and how our teaching and learning of clinical care and community health activities should be performed in their spirit. Hence, what are those facets?

The expectations from physicians are challenging in their extent and scope, which include the following:

- Assimilation of a considerable volume of facts such as elements of anatomy, hundreds of syndromes for further pattern recognition, dosages of drugs, and pieces of legislation or administrative rules governing medical practice
- Acquisition of automatisms necessary for the execution of many clinical maneuvers such as those required to perform a physical examination or to practice emergency medicine
- Ability to effectively communicate (listening and talking) with the patient, the patient's family, as well as members of the health team
- Assessment of patient risks
- Making of diagnosis and prognosis
- Listing of problems and creation of a hierarchical classification
- Making of decisions (choices)
- Mastery of exploratory medical and surgical procedures (performance)
- Management of patients after intervention (follow-up and care, control of disease course)
- Evaluation of the effectiveness and efficiency of cure and care
- Respect of medical, cultural, spiritual, and social ethics, as well as of patient values, preferences, and expectations
- Empathy

Practicing medicine means not only applying our humanism, compassion, knowledge, or skills but also basing our actions on the fundamentals of philosophy, science, art, and logic in their universal sense. Medicine is an integral part of such a universe, and often, we do not realize the extent to which we follow its general rules.

This book is about reasoning and making decisions when dealing with patients in a clinical setting or with groups of individuals in communities under our care. It also covers what we should know and the application of this knowledge.

1.1 Art, Science, and Craft of Medicine

The art and science of medicine, what they are, how they differ, and how they complement each other remains the subject of a still open and ongoing discussion.

> The **art of medicine** may be defined as a mastery of dealing with human interactions, feelings and sensations, ideas, making meaningful lateral and holistic connections, and contributing thusly to the body of medical knowledge, attitudes, and skills.[7]

Is there a better way to define art of medicine? Some possible answers are in Section 1.1.1 of this chapter.

Both quantitative (based on counting and measurement) and qualitative (based on understanding and interpretation) research methodologies are necessary to understand the workings of medicine today. In fact, there is no other way to evaluate and understand the expectations of both Canadian and American physicians and health professionals,[8,9] namely

- Placing patients' needs ahead of self-interest; commitment to scholarship; responsiveness to societal needs; working optimally with other health professionals
- Integrity, respect, compassion, responsibility, courtesy, and sensitivity to patients' needs and to colleagues and other health care personnel
- High standards of moral and ethical behavior
- Recognition and management of physician impairment in peers and self
- Concern for psychosocial aspects of care
- Recognition of the importance of self-assessment, and willingness to teach
- Understanding of the requirements for involvement of patients in research

- ■ Awareness of the effects of differences in gender, age, cultural, and social background
- ■ Honesty and dependability

Many of these virtues reflect expectations for physicians already proposed at the time of Paracelsus (1493–1541), with some notable exceptions such as: "… not to be married to the bigot, … not to be a runaway monk, … not practice a self-abuse, … and … not to have a red beard.…"[10]

Hence, health professionals require more than a discrete body of knowledge and skills. They are expected to value performance above reward and are held to higher standards of behavior than are nonprofessionals.[11]

To better understand the justification, uses and purposes of various methods and techniques of study, understanding, decision making, and evaluation in medicine, we must first define the context of medicine. This is because everything we do is based on the way we see things around us and on the values given to our actions and endeavors. For instance, the consideration and practice of euthanasia is heavily influenced by our understanding and interpretation of the commandment "Thou shall not kill" in a given setting of faith, culture, and societal values. The order *primum non nocere* ("first, do not harm") in the Hippocratic oath can be challenged in situations when some harm is necessary to heal and prevent the worse. Health promotion, screening for disease, or treatment of complex health problems will depend not only on medical considerations of relevance or effectiveness but also on economics, politics, administration, and management in health sciences and society as a whole.

Similarly, the value and justification of our reasoning, decisions, methods, and techniques in medicine depend on the context of our practice. A lecturer who enters a classroom and tells his or her unprepared students that today, they will learn about case-control studies in etiological research should expect a "what for?" question.

Therefore, let us first define major paradigms in medicine, that is, the ways we perceive major issues and characteristics of health, disease, and care.

To be a good physician, it is necessary to develop the art of medicine and to master medicine as a science in two areas. In clinical medicine, these art and science relate to a clinic or to the bedside in the actual observation and treatment of patients. In **community medicine,** preventive medicine, and **public health**, they pertain to a body of individuals living in a defined area and having a common interest or organization[6] or characteristics, or all three of them. The sections that follow apply to both.

1.1.1 Medicine as Art

Historically, medicine was learned mostly as an art.

Art, in general, has several pragmatic definitions and components. Some of them, like skills, might fall today in the category of *medical craft* (*vide infra*):

- The employment of means to accomplish some desired end
- A system of rules serving to facilitate the performance of certain actions
- A system of principles and rules for attaining a desired end
- A method of doing some special work well
- The systematic application of knowledge or skill in effecting a desired result
- An occupation or business requiring such a knowledge and skill[12]
- Skill as the result of knowledge and practice
- A practical application of any science
- A pursuit of occupation in which skill is directed toward the work of imagination, imitation, or design or toward the gratification of the aesthetic senses[13] (N.B. 'Élégance' or senses gratification are subjective and hard to define pleasing practices of medical interviewing and communication, aesthetic or reconstructive surgery, or physical examination)
- Skill of expression in language, speech, and reasoning[14]
- A system of principles and methods employed in the performance of a set of activities
- A trade or craft that applies such a system of principles and methods, for example, the art of plastic surgery
- Skill that is attained by study, practice, or observation: The art of the physician
- Skill arising from the exercise of intuitive faculties (N.B. This being important in differential diagnosis or emergency medicine[15])
- Both skill and creative imagination[16]

These definitions all focus on art as a *way of doing things*. Other definitions, however, highlight the *product of such endeavors*, that is, not only oil paintings but also a successful rhinoplasty or facelift. Such an extensive list of even the most general definitions of art illustrates not only how differently we can approach things around us but also that art, evidence, science, philosophy, or logic are not purely abstract terms. In fact, they have important practical meanings and implications, as will be shown throughout this reading.

The art of medicine requires the following:

■ A clinician with an open mind and flexibility of reasoning
■ The ability to establish a good relationship with the patient
■ Bedside manners
■ Tutoring or guidance of peers in reasoning, decision making, and acting
■ Compassion
■ Empathy
■ Clinician's attitude toward nature and patient
■ Aptitude to individualize interpretations, decisions, and care to a particular patient
■ Manual and sensory skills
■ Clinical flair and intuition; that is, an aptitude to infer from previous experience, without active and concrete recall, in order to make appropriate decisions
■ Clinical imagination
■ The capacity to persuade the patient to take responsibility for his or her own health and to convince the patient that the clinician will also share that responsibility
■ The aptitude to convert serendipity into insight of patient problems
■ The preservation and maintenance of human dignity (this is one difference between medicine and the advanced technical manipulation of human beings)
■ The aestheticism, elegance, and style in the conceptualization, execution, evaluation, and communication of a clinical experience lived

All these components of the art of medicine are of a highly subjective nature and are therefore hard to define and measure and often even harder to teach.

In all instances, let us correctly define in operational, mutually understood, nonoverlapping, and reproducible terms everything we observe, do, and study (including subjects and individuals involved as well as medical and nonmedical circumstances important to the problem). Otherwise, speaking beautifully and "scientifically" does not warrant meaningful, purposeful work. The study, development, use, and evaluation of definitions, which we might call **orismology** (from Greek *orisomos* = definition and *logos* = study), is explained in more detail in Section 2.1.3.3 of Chapter 2 and in the subsequent chapters.

Hence, art of medicine is what is based on emotions, sensations, and feelings[17] and mental operations behind physician's behavior toward the patient.

The *art of medicine* may be then defined as the systematic application of sensory and motor skills, creative imagination, faithful imitation, innovation, intuition and knowledge in speech, reasoning, or motion in the care of the health of patients and communities.[2]

1.1.2 Medicine as Science

But we also call medicine a science. Is it?

Science, in general, is *the study of the material universe or physical reality in order to understand it*.[12]

The **science of medicine**, on the contrary, is *organized reasoning*. Also, *science in medicine means discovery, implementation, uses, and evaluation of evidence in understanding human health, disease, and care decisions, implementation and evaluation, which are based on the scientific method*.[2]

The science of medicine is complementary to the art of medicine since when they are combined, we obtain a better understanding of what good medicine, in the fullest sense of the term, should be.

1.1.2.1 Scientific Theory

Scientific theory is a plausible and consistent explanation for observable phenomena.[18] In the sciences, it comprises a collection of concepts, including abstractions of observable phenomena expressed as quantifiable properties, together with rules, called scientific laws, that express relationships between observations of such concepts.[19] Theories are mostly constructed to explain, predict, and master phenomena such as health and disease in the world of medicine.

Theories are generated from an original idea, which is subjected to experimentation. If the evidence from the experiment supports the idea, a theory is formulated. If the theory is used to better understand the universe concerned and new evidence is discovered in the process and can be modified to explain the new evidence, the theory is modified in a circular way from the original idea reviewed.[19] In medicine, the path from the first diagnostic impression to the final diagnosis follows a very similar logic and steps.

In modern science, "a scientific theory is a tested and expanded hypothesis that explains many experiments and fits ideas together in a framework.... To be a scientific theory, a theory must be tested a large number of times, by many different scientists in many different places, and must pass the test every time."[20] This is like generating the best evidence in the world of diagnosis or effectiveness of treatment in medicine.

1.1.2.2 Scientific Method

What is "scientific" in medicine? Whatever was obtained, analyzed, and used by a general scientific method. This method follows four objectives:

1. *Creating research on the basis of currently available experience and evidence.* Such creation is based on various observations, formulations of the problem, defining the problem of interest, and obtaining relevant background evidence providing elements to solve the problem.
2. *Formulation of hypotheses and research questions to explain the problem (most often a cause–effect relationship).* Their formulation and development is followed by their conceptual evaluation, establishing testable consequences allowing the acceptance or rejection of hypotheses and questions, and using hypotheses and questions-based experience to make testable quantitative and qualitative predictions on the basis of new observations and experience.
3. *Conducting either observational and/or experimental studies to test hypotheses and predictions.* Empirical tests are built and performed and include a search for both favorable and unfavorable evidences that include examples and counterexamples.
4. *Analyzing results, drawing conclusions, and reporting the experience.* These steps include first the critical examination and biostatistical processing of data in search of error, anomalous events (outliers), making inferences, and evaluation of hypothesis(es) in the light of the background knowledge and newly acquired evidence and experience by the study. Formulations of meaningful conclusions in the light of the new experience and proposals of future directions for research and/or practice on the basis of the newly acquired experience follow.

Science then is anything based on scientific method, which requires several steps[21]:

- Defining and characterizing the domain of interest
- Formulating the research question(s) once the problem is defined
- Formulating a **hypothesis** as a testable proposition to be accepted or rejected, which is built on operational definitions of phenomena as dependent and independent variables to observe
- Making predictions as a formal way to test a hypothesis (hypotheses)
- Detection and control of **errors, biases**, and **fallacies** to improve study claims (conclusions)
- Identifying conditions and circumstances in which findings and conclusions stemming from them do not apply (called also falsifiability of results)
- Replicating the study to confirm the consistency of findings
- Making decisions, recommendations, and directions for future research on the basis of the study and the previously acquired experience and knowledge
- Taking action to rectify or further improve the situation
- Evaluating the effectiveness of corrective measures

1.1.3 Medicine as Craft

As in other fields, both art and science in medicine require technical skills. Both focus on the creation of order from seemingly random and diverse experiences, on an understanding of the world, and on conveying experience to others. The scientist, however, tends to use observations to discover laws or concepts that may be invalidated later. By contrast, the artist creates rather some kind of more permanent and/or valid statement. The clinical craftsman makes realities through actions, which are based on both art and science, unique in their quality, adequacy, impact and value for the patient, his or her human, social, and physical environment.

Craft is defined as a practical art, trade, or occupation requiring especially manual skill and dexterity. It is a skill, especially involving practical arts. Crafts are defined either by their relationship to functional or utilitarian products or by the use of particular media such as wood, clay, glass, textiles, and metal.[22,23] Studio crafts are those which are practiced by independent artists working alone in small groups. (N.B. Isn't is what most surgery-based specialties are doing while acting?)

The world of engineering is recognized as a "craft," which is more scientific and systematic than an "art" but not quite a "science." It applies science in ways that leave a lot of room for individual expression. It produces "things" that seem to be a requirement for "craftsmanship."[24] It may be then considered as a "grey" third zone after arts and science of medicine. Sensorimotor skills are a dominant feature of medical craft. (N.B. A pejorative sense given sometimes in colloquial communication to craft(s) does not apply here.)

In these terms and sense, do skills in history taking, physical examination, case presentations, communication, learning skills, nonverbal communication, or specialty evaluations (mental status, bodily systems, etc.) contain a high dose of craftsmanship?

Practically all surgery-based specialties (all surgical subspecialties, gynecology and obstetrics, otorhinolaryngology, ophthalmology, etc.) depend on a high degree of craftsmanship and art as defined earlier.

As the debate on whether medicine is art or science continues,[7,17,25–31] we may agree that it is an interface of both. A medical student or clerk must look for the elements of both and master them as much as possible.

Therefore, medicine means the application of the fundamentals of art, science, and craft as defined earlier to the treatment and prevention of disease, health protection, and promotion of health.

1.2 Deterministic vs. Probabilistic Paradigm of Medicine: Uncertainty, Fuzziness, and Chaos

Historically, the science of medicine was focused on rigorous observation, measurement, and interpretation. With the development of microbiology, biochemistry, histology, pathology, genetics, and other basic sciences, the goal of medicine became a search for the true picture of a disease, the identification of real causes, and a search for the best treatment. Such an approach was clearly deterministic: the absolute truth (as much as possible) was rigorously sought. Today, experimental medicine is often based on such an approach. Models are built, undesirable factors are controlled or excluded, and rigorous experimental conditions are sought in the search for an unequivocal result. Exact information, reality without error, is the ideal and the basis for the *deterministic paradigm of medicine.*

However, the *deterministic paradigm of science and life is now progressively being replaced by a probabilistic approach.*

Survival after surgery is probable but not certain. It is probable that susceptible individuals in the midst of an epidemic of new strain of influenza will get it but it is not certain. Such probabilities and chances can be quantified in terms of rates or decimal fractions (more about it later). Rates may be compared in terms of ratios and some causal relationships can be derived to some degree from such comparisons.

1.2.1 Probability and Clinical Uncertainty

From the latter point of view, any endeavor in the health sciences is subject to random and systematic error, even in the most controlled conditions. Moreover, information for decision making is *almost never complete*, and decision makers always work with a considerable measure of *uncertainty*.

Let us define **uncertainty in medicine** as "any situation where probabilities of different possible phenomena or outcomes are not known due to our poor knowledge of them whatever reason of such imperfect knowledge might be." Uncertainty may be caused by

- Purely psychological reasons
- The quality and quantity of data (probabilistic assessment and quantification of events and information)
- The way we handle them in our reasoning and decision making

Probability means *quantification of uncertainty.*

As in economics and finance, research and practice in medicine become probabilistic when faced with uncertainty and missing information as a ubiquitous reality. All subjects who smoke will not develop lung cancer, and all subjects who abstain from drinking will not be absolutely free of the risk of hepatic cirrhosis. Just a few generations ago, a middle-aged man with a productive cough of abundant sputum and a loss of weight was supposed to have tuberculosis, especially if there was confirmation based on Koch's mycobacterium isolation at the laboratory. With our current knowledge of competing problems, such as bronchiectasies, silicosis, silicotuberculosis, or neoplasms of the lung and bronchial tree, this diagnosis becomes probable, but not entirely certain (without the exclusion of other competing health problems).

Clinical uncertainty is a reality today. It is caused by

- Incomplete knowledge of the clinical problem (entity, etiology, controllability, prognosis, natural and clinical course of the disease)
- Incomplete information given by the patient
- Incomplete informatio n obtained by the physician
- Erroneous information given by the patient (shame, lack of memory, lie)
- Erroneous recording of information by the physician
- Erroneous interpretation of information by the physician
- Missing observations (not sought)
- Information not recorded
- Erratic reasoning and intellectual handling of information by health professionals

All clinical decisions are and will be made with a variable degree of uncertainty depending on a variable probability of events and outcomes. Neglecting those leads often to **medical error** and **medical harm**.[32,33]

For example, using various rates of morbidity or mortality or other health events in the assessment of risk in the patient is a quantification of our certainty (or uncertainty) about problems of health or care. Calculating and presenting their confidence intervals is one of the ways to quantify our uncertainty about disease frequency. However, uses of confidence intervals in today biostatistics are much broader.[34,35]

For Timmermans and Angell, managing uncertainty develops along with evidence-based clinical judgment that has some important characteristics: It mixes together evidence and experience, exhibits an awareness of all the factors necessary to reach a satisfactory medical decision, includes both epidemiological and social skills, and is grounded firmly in a Western allopathic and professionalized approach to medicine.[36] Should not all medicines reflect also such characteristics?

Another contributor to our uncertainties is a fuzzy theory.

1.2.2 Fuzzy Theory

Fuzzy theory[37-40] holds the view that that the physiological, pathological, and other clinical phenomena of interest are not necessarily dichotomous (healthy or sick, handicapped or not, etc.), but that many health phenomena are a matter of degree and should be analyzed and understood as such. Being obese or in pain is a matter of degree, and there is no "excluded middle." Grading and categorizing clinical phenomena defined in operational terms makes them manageable for decision making and care (Figure 1.1).

Uncertainties and imprecision are ubiquitous in medicine. Fuzzy logic in medicine is developing to do the best to make right decisions in such situations. It is now increasingly used in various specialties, neurology,

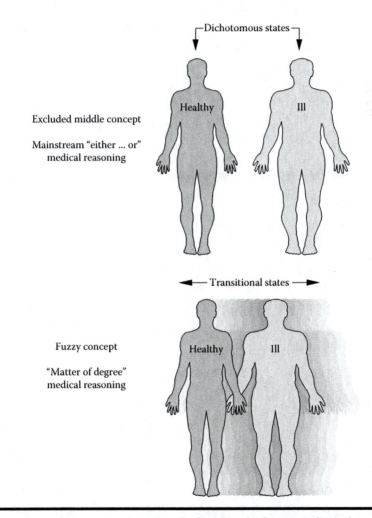

Figure 1.1   Fuzzy theory concept. (Partly from Jenicek, M. and Hitchcock, D. L., *Evidence-Based Practice. Logic and Critical Thinking in Medicine,* **American Medical Association (AMA Press), Chicago, IL, 2006; Jenicek, M.,** *Foundations of Evidence-Based Medicine,* **The Parthenon Publishing Group/CRC Press, Boca Raton/London/New York/Washington, 2003.)**

psychiatry, anesthesia, dermatology, epidemiology, and elsewhere. Domains of its uses and applications are increasing.[41]

Moreover, Burton[42] is questioning our own brain management of certainty, proposing that it is neither conscientious choice nor even a thought process. His central premise is that certainty and similar states of "knowing what we know" are sensations that feel like thoughts, but arise out of involuntary brain mechanisms that function independently of reason. Biostatistical and epidemiological management of probabilities to quantify uncertainty remains so far the most meaningful and operational tool available to health professional layman and laywoman.

Subias[43] believes that in the case of biorhythms, a chaotic/nonchaotic ratio that underlies them provides, in case of being quantifiable, a more exact evaluation of the state of health and illness and a diagnosis and prognosis that would not be possible by other means of the traditional medicine.

Medical phenomena may be not only fuzzy but also "chaotic."

1.2.3 Chaos Theory in Medicine

In the framework of this theory, human functions are not seen as stable (homeostasis), but they are also subject to chaotic behavior defined as "an aperiodic, seemingly random behaviour in a deterministic system that exhibits sensitive dependence on initial conditions"[44] or "apparently random or unpredictable behaviour in systems governed by deterministic laws."[45] Phenomena subject to chaos are unpredictable, and their cause–effect relationships are unpredictable. If true, correct diagnosis, treatment decisions, and prognosis in such circumstances may be a challenge.[46]

Chaos theory points out the limitations of a linear, reductionist approach to our understanding and management of natural phenomena, the medical ones included. The chaos theory has evolved from descriptions to the discovery of laws that describe the behavior of these systems. One of the names of these activities is "complexity theory."[47]

All those various concepts leading to our uncertainties lead to a view that health care delivery consists of numerous "simple" and "complex" systems ranging from those that are deterministic to those with features of randomness. Deterministic systems feature predictable outcomes, others do not. Deterministic and other systems are considered complex systems, and they are subject to complexity theory.[48–50]

We are only at the beginning of our understanding of this theory and systems.

> In this context, rather than synonymous to rigorous laboratory work only, the **science of medicine** becomes also a structured and organized way of using probability, uncertainty, and facts in preventive medicine and clinical care to best benefit the patient and the community. It is a logical and systematic approach to the exploration, organization, and interpretation of data from initial observations to clinical decisions and final conclusions concerning problems of interest. The latter are defined, measured, categorized, classified, analyzed, and interpreted with a satisfactory degree of reproducibility.

Such a scientific approach to medicine should be applied to the entire scope of medical activities. The debate about this approach, however, continues.[51]

1.3 Medicine as Philosophy: Philosophy in Medicine and Philosophy of Medicine

As in any other domain of human endeavor, **philosophy** means "systematic analysis and critical examination of fundamental problems and the nature of being, reality and thinking, perception, values, causes and choices underlying principles of physical and ethical phenomena. Its fundamental branches are metaphysics, epistemology, logic and ethics."[2] Until today, attention was paid to medical ethics, and rightly so. However, all of branches of philosophy have their equal place in medicine.

We may think about two complementary facets of philosophy: **Philosophy in medicine** and **philosophy of medicine**.

1.3.1 Philosophy in Medicine

Often, philosophy is still considered by some as a domain far away from reality, and of speculative nature. Today, modern philosophy is closely related to the practice and of primary importance for medical reasoning and decision making. From its fourth main branches, that is metaphysics and ontology (being and reality), epistemology (knowledge), logic (inference), and ethics (values), ethics is perhaps a branch that is widely established, valued, and practiced. Logic in particular is historically now interspersed between clinical and fundamental epidemiology, biostatistics, health economics and administration, and etiological research, and more rooted there than in clinical disciplines.

> For us, philosophy *in* medicine means "the uses and application of philosophy to health, disease and medical care."[2] It examines the methods used by medicine to formulate hypotheses (like questions about diagnosis and treatment) and directions on the basis of evidence (what to do), as well as the grounds on which claims (diagnoses, treatment decisions and effects, prognoses made) about patients and health problems may be justified. Hence, it is about uses and applications of philosophy regarding various problems in medicine.

1.3.2 Philosophy of Medicine

> Philosophy *of* medicine encompasses rather *philosophical considerations of the nature of medicine's own additional contributions to philosophy in general* such as the experience from clinical trials or other studies of cause–effect relationships; *the focus is on the advancement of the theory of medicine.*[2]

Both "in" and "of" directions as well as more than one branch of philosophy (including often ethics) are explored in a more or less balanced way in several key monographs.[52–57]

Several periodicals are now devoted to philosophy in medicine and of medicine, such as *The Journal of Medicine and Philosophy* (mostly ethics) or *Theoretical Medicine.*

> From all branches of philosophy, we will be the most concerned here about logic and its ways of critical thinking, argumentation, and decision making in clinical and community care and research. All these branches are behind all our understanding of the nature and origins (causes) of patient's problems, clinical care of them, daily decisions about them, forecasting their outcomes, and future care. The patient safety and survival as well as the quality of care rely on it.

1.4 Practice and Theory of Medicine: Which One Will You Learn?

Medicine must be mastered from both a theoretical and a practical standpoint. We must know what is behind our actions, and we must practice it in the light of its theoretical foundations.

1.4.1 Practice of Medicine

Practice in general means "the action or process of performing or doing something."[58]

Practice of medicine means in lexical terms "the utilization of knowledge in a particular profession, the practice of medicine being the exercise of one's knowledge in the practical recognition and treatment of disease."[59] We may see also this kind of practice as *reasoning* about patient and/or community health and disease followed by and coupled with *corrective action(s)* and *evaluation* of what was done." Hence, practice of medicine does not mean action only but also what preceded and triggered it (reasoning) and what followed it (evaluation).

Practice of medicine is then "an action, sensorimotor, or other, in the domain of health and disease resulting from critical thinking about the problems and decisions for what to do. Physician's mental activity in this role is then an integral part of the practice of medicine as it also underlies the theory of medicine." "Just thinking" must evolve into action or "justified doing nothing." Hence, a proper learning of medicine must include how to think before one acts, how to act and understand what has been done and how.

The practice of clinical medicine is about problem solving and solutions.

"Rational medicine"[59] may be seen as a precursor of evidence-based medicine, being defined in the sixties as "practice of medicine based upon actual knowledge." Distinctions between "actual knowledge" and "evidence" (without specifying which evidence is the best) remain blurred.

1.4.2 Theory of Medicine

Since Murphy's renewed call for theory of medicine,[60] both theory and practice of medicine have their place in how we see medicine today.

In general, theory means "a coherent group of general propositions used as principles of explanation for a class of phenomena. … a particular conception or view of something to be done or of the method of doing it; a system of rules or principles"[58] and "… the doctrine or the principles underlying an art as distinguished from the practice of that particular art."[59]

Theory of medicine is "the body of principles of the science and art of medicine as distinguished from the 'practice of medicine', or the application of those principles in actual practice."[59] Colloquially speaking, it is anything that happens in the head of the physician, researcher, or practitioner of medicine before orders by word or stroke of the pen are given and an action by hand or other technological tools are taken.

Wikipedia specifies that "scientific" theory refers to "a proposed explanation of empiric phenomena, made in a way consistent with the scientific method. Such theories are preferably described in such a way that any scientist in the field is in a position to understand, verify, and challenge (or 'falsify') it. In this modern scientific context, the distinction between theory and practice corresponds roughly to the distinction between theoretical science and technology or applied science."[61]

Modern reflections about both theoretical medicine[62] and theoretical surgery[63,64] link intimately reasoning as a part of theory to actions together with the whole nonsurgical support system such as basic sciences, clinical epidemiology, social sciences, even patient, and so on.[63,64] Theoretical surgery was hence proposed as "a nonoperative decision analysis and clinical basic research supporting system for surgery. It consists of an essential, predominant integration concept completed by a supplementary cooperation concept."[63,64]

Several journals were created to cover the domain of the theory of medicine in English such as the *Journal of Theoretical Medicine, Theoretical Medicine*, or *Theoretical Medicine and Bioethics.*

1.5 Evidence-Based Medicine and Other Evidence-Based Health Sciences

Rightly so, contemporary medicine relies not only on the best available evidence about and proofs of the origins, nature, and manageability of health and disease but also on additional considerations such as clinical settings and circumstances, patient values and preferences, and best available knowledge and experience of its assessors, evaluators, users, and all decision makers in clinical and community care. This reality is responsible in part for the evidence-based domain of medicine.

Evidence itself in medicine is a broad entity encompassing "any data or information, whether solid or weak, obtained through experience, observational research or experimental work (trials). This data or information must be relevant and convincing to some (best possible) degree either to the understanding of the problem (case) or the diagnostic, therapeutic, or otherwise care oriented clinical decisions made about the case. 'Evidence' is not automatically correct, complete, satisfactory and useful. It must be first evaluated, graded and used based on its own merit."[5] Which one is the best and for what purpose remains a great challenge for its user and decision maker.

Evidence-based clinical medicine (EBM)[65] may be seen, then, through its current numerous definitions

- The process of systematically finding, appraising, and using contemporaneous research findings as the basis for clinical decisions.[66] (*Too little today.*)
- The conscientious, explicit, and judicious use of current best evidence in making decisions about the care of individual patients.[67] (*Limited for uses as operational definition.*)
- Practice of medicine based on the integration of the best research evidence with clinical experience and patient unique values and circumstances.[68] (*But how?*)
- Consistent use of the best available evidence, preferably from current peer-reviewed sources in electronic and print media, to inform decisions about optimum patient management; decisions should consider the needs and preferences of individual patients.[3] (*Much better.*)
- The practice of medicine in which the physician finds, assesses, and implements methods of diagnosis and treatment on the basis of the best available current research, their expertise, and the needs of the patient.[69,70] The expertise here means special skills or knowledge acquired by a person through education, training, or experience. (*Expertise also includes the respect and practice of medical ethics.*)

Wherever so many definitions appear, the defined entity still requires further refinements and clarifications. (*How does all this connect and what are ethical considerations?*)

Evidence-based community medicine and public health (EBPH)[71-73] means similarly

- "The application of best available evidence in setting public health policies and priorities. ... Evidence-based public health is an approach that makes informed, explicit use of validated studies to arrive to judicious decisions on public health policies and best practices."[5]
- "The process of systematically finding, appraising and using contemporaneous clinical and community research findings as the basis for decisions in public health."[72]
- "The conscientious, explicit and judicious use of current best evidence in making decisions about the care of communities and populations in the domain of health protection, disease prevention, and health maintenance and improvement (health promotion)."[72]

Evidence-based healthcare[74] as formulated by Muir Gray integrates in its concept both clinical and community medicine, care, and public health.

The EBM-driven initial steps of both clinical and community medicines are the following:

1. Formulation of a clear clinical or community medicine question from a patient or community problem which has to be answered.
2. Searching the literature for relevant sources of information (i.e., **evidence**).
3. Critical appraisal (analysis, evaluation, and grading) of the original and integrated evidence. Its main points include most often the relevance of the evidence to user's issue and setting, objectivity of evidence presented, clarity of a bias-free methodology, justification of conclusion about evidence presented, confidence about findings (evidence) presented, and applicability to particular individuals, site, setting, practice, rules, and culture.

    For example, critical appraisal of a cause–effect study brings answers to several questions such as
    - Are we dealing with a questionable and uncertain problem?
    - How well is the problem defined?
    - Was the question to be answered properly formulated?
    - Was the search for evidence (other studies) adequate and complete?
    - What is the design of an etiological study? How valid is it?
    - Are biostatistical considerations such as sampling or analysis and epidemiological considerations such as exposure to possible multiple causes adequately handled and answered?

- Were clinical aspects of the disease considered (subjects' characteristics, comorbidity, outcomes, follow-up, and others)?
- How was the effect (impact) of a presumed cause (validity of results) evaluated?
- Which criteria of causality are fulfilled by the study results?
- Was the broader balance between harm, benefits, costs, and controllability assessed and is it adequate?
- Is it the best evidence available?
- Are the results usable in the user's setting (caring for a specific patient, groups of patients, community groups) and in which settings are they not?
- If relevant, how much could and should such findings be generalized?
- Were possible competing causes considered and evaluated?
- If this problem was also a subject of other studies, should a systematic review and research synthesis of all these available experiences be attempted and would such expanded research bring additional relevant information?

4. *Selection* of the best evidence for clinical or community decision.
5. *Linking evidence* with clinical and community medicine (public health) experience, knowledge, and practice and with patient and/or community values and preferences.
6. *Implementation* of useful findings in clinical (clinical care) and community (public health policies and programs) medicines' decisions and practice.
7. *Evaluation* of the implementations and the overall performance of the EBM/EBPH practitioner.
8. *Teaching* others how to practice EBM/EBPH.

Physicians in their clinical practice should answer several questions before choosing and using available evidence from the literature or from their own experience and work for their decisions in clinical and community care:

1. What is the problem to be solved and is there a clearly formulated question to be answered?
2. What kind of study or demonstration can we refer to in order to obtain such an answer?
3. What are the results?
4. Are those results valid?

5. Are such results relevant for understanding and/or decision making about the problem at hand?
6. Are the results applicable to a particular group of patients we are dealing with?
7. Are those results applicable to a specific ("my") patient?

The current edition of the *User's Guides to the Medical Literature*[65] lists most of these questions and offers many answers. Evidence, supported by clinical and fundamental epidemiology, biostatistical methods and grading of evidence (mostly for cause–effect relationships) applied to clinical activities, and problem solving, is at the core of this EBM strategy.

In addition to the above mentioned seven question points, other more specific problem-solving practical questions will determine the type of research, clinical topic to be elucidated, and its inherent methodology. Table 1.1 provides examples of such links between research, clinical domain applications, and problems to be solved

Table 1.1   Questions in Medical Research, Clinical Domains of Application, and Examples of Practical Problems to Be Solved

Examples of Questions in Medical Research	Clinical Domain and Type of Research to Answer the Questions: Examples	Fields of Application: Examples of Practical Problems to Be Solved
Diagnosis and New Exploratory Technologies		
What is the subject of the diagnosis? How serious is it? How do we arrive at the diagnosis?	Forming clinical entities Measuring disease severity Understanding the diagnostic process	Evaluation of internal and external validity of diagnostic and screening tests Establishment of diagnostic criteria for daily practice and disease surveillance
Health Event Occurrence		
When, where, and in whom do problems (health events) appear?	Descriptive longitudinal or cross-sectional studies in the hospital and the community Studies of natural or clinical course of cases	Epidemiological portrait of disease Disease spread Epidemiological surveillance Disease clustering

Table 1.1 Questions in Medical Research, Clinical Domains of Application, and Examples of Practical Problems to Be Solved (*Continued*)

Examples of Questions in Medical Research	Clinical Domain and Type of Research to Answer the Questions: Examples	Fields of Application: Examples of Practical Problems to Be Solved
Causal Research		
Why did it happen? What or who is responsible?	Etiological research by observational analytical studies; disease etiology research by comparative studies of exposure to various factors and disease occurrence using cohort and case-control studies	Identification of causes of desirable and undesirable health events Risk factors explanation Hypotheses generation about health events based on probabilities of events derived from case studies (disease course)
Intervention (Prevention and/or Treatment)		
Can we control case(s) or disease? Did we control case(s) or disease? Will it control or solve the problem?	Efficacy, effectiveness, and efficiency evaluation Systematic reviews and meta-analyses of interventions and their effect	Phase 1–4 clinical trials Field trials Pharmacoepidemiological studies Impact of secondary and tertiary prevention (mainly) Decision analysis
Prognosis		
What might or will happen later on?	Study of disease outcomes Survival studies Descriptive and analytical studies of probabilities of events derived from case studies (disease course)	Epidemiological and clinical forecasting of exposures to beneficial or noxious factors, disease occurrence and spread based on clinical follow-up and epidemiological surveillance

Look for the definitions of some new terms in Chapters 2 and 3 and in the Glossary.

In the domain of cause–effect relationships (noxious agent → disease, treatment → cure, etc.), the hierarchy of evidence goes from the weakest (clinical anecdotes, single or multiple clinical cases descriptions) to observational analytical (case-control or **cohort**) studies and their systematic reviews and research synthesis. Hierarchies of evidence beyond etiology remain still subject of our better understanding.

Both EBM and EBPH are not even two decades old, and they are still developing and remain widely discussed domains and paradigms in many health sciences and professions.

1.6 Beyond the Original Concept of Evidence-Based Medicine: Evidence-Based Critical Thinking Medicine and Reflective Uses of Evidence

Producing or finding and evaluating the best evidence is not enough for good clinical and community medicine practice. Using it in the framework of critical thinking is. Let us conclude then that medicine is taught and learned through all those multiple angles and eyes as defined earlier in this chapter. We will see all those paradigms reflected in all of medical reasoning, communication, and decision making as discussed in the following chapters.

1.6.1 Critical Thinking

But what exactly is critical thinking today? Its concept, content, methodology, and applications are more close to practical and pragmatic medicine that we might initially think. Thank you, philosophers!

Its definitions that follow are complementary, and they reflect well the scientific method in medicine and what we are doing in our daily reasoning about health problems and our patients.

■ *Critical thinking* is the intellectually disciplined process of actively and skillfully conceptualizing, applying, synthesizing, and/or evaluating information gathered from, or generated by observation, experience, reflection, reasoning, or communication as a guide to belief and action.

In its exemplary form, it is based on universal intellectual values that transcend subject matter divisions: clarity, accuracy, precision, consistency, relevance, sound evidence, good reasons, depth, breadth, and fairness. It entails the examination of those structures or elements of thought implicit in all reasoning: purpose, problem, or question-at-issue, assumptions, concepts, empirical grounding; reasoning leading to conclusions, implications and consequences, objections from alternative viewpoints, and frame of reference. Critical thinking—in being responsive to variable subject matter, issues, and purposes—is thinking, mathematical thinking, and philosophical thinking.[76]

Let us add medicine and all other sciences to these modes!

■ *Critical thinking is a* "purposeful, self-regulatory judgment which results in interpretation, analysis and evaluation and inference, as well as explanation of the evidential, conceptual, methodological, criteriological, or contextual considerations, upon which that judgment is based…."[77]

All our clinical practice, medical research, and public health are a perpetual exercise of critical thinking about health problems, how we understand them, making and choosing decisions of what to do, and evaluating results of what we have done.

1.6.2 Reflective Uses of Evidence

Producing the best evidence is not enough. The best evidence must also be applied through the critical thinking process as defined and outlined earlier. Let us discuss this more in Chapter 2.

Conclusions: What Exactly Should We Teach and Learn Then?

Our recent position paper summarizes the following:

Obtaining and critically appraising evidence is clearly not enough to make better decisions in clinical care. The evidence should be linked to the clinician's expertise, the patient's individual circumstances (including values and preferences), and clinical context and settings. We propose critical thinking and decision making as the tools for making that link.

Critical thinking is also called for in medical research and medical writing, especially where pre-canned methodologies are not enough. It is also involved in our exchanges of ideas at floor rounds, grand rounds and case discussions; our communications with patients and lay stakeholders in health care; and our writing of research papers, grant applications and grant reviews.

Critical thinking is a learned process, which benefits from teaching and guided practice like any discipline in health sciences. Training in critical thinking should be a part or a pre-requisite of the medical curriculum.[78]

An **evidence- and critical thinking-based medicine** then? Teaching it should provide the student essential desirable knowledge, attitudes, and skills to put it in practice for the full benefit of all parties involved in care and research.

Medicine today embraces both the experience from natural sciences, strong in scientific method and quantitative methodologies. It embraces and integrates together with the above and also the experience from humanities: academic disciplines that study the human condition primarily by methods of analytical, critical, or speculative nature,[79] including informal logic, argumentation, or critical thinking from philosophy.

Learning and practicing medicine today is based on a blend of two ways of health problem solving:

1. On one side is scientific, quantitative, probabilistic, and managed uncertainty inquiry. The science of medicine is practiced this way.
2. On the other side lies an interconnected web of medical humanities, which blend together uses not only of arts, literature, ethics, religion, history, sociology, and law but also of cognitive sciences and philosophy. Within the latter, logic, structured reasoning, and argumentation are taking an increasingly prominent place.

Medical humanities are defined as "... an interdisciplinary field which includes humanities (literature, philosophy, ethics, history and religion), social science (anthropology, cultural studies, psychology, sociology) and the arts (literature, theatre, film and visual arts) and their application to medical education and practice."[80]

Their purpose is to improve the delivery of effective health care through a better understanding of disease in the society and in the individual. Rather than occupational and professional skills based on scientific principles and their applications, medical humanities contribute to provide more general knowledge and intellectual skills behind the former.

At least two titles[81,82] and the *Medical Humanities* journal currently cover this domain.

The debate about medical humanities continues.[83]

Quo vadis medicina ex testimoniis? What further directions will evidence-based medicine and other health sciences and professions take?[84–86] We will certainly see in the near future.

Medicine today should be seen through all those multiple eyes and views, as summarized earlier. It is less relevant where this or that element of teaching belongs: Theory or practice of medicine, evidence- or something else-based medicine (narrative-based, patient-centered), scientific method- and theory-based (allopathic) medicine or alternative medicine, and philosophy- and beliefs-based medicine? Newcomers in the clinical in-house or extra hospital environment will all face the challenge of how to integrate multiple views into some meaningful reasoning and decision making behind any element of our practice or research. Let us turn some pages to learn how.

References

1. *Mosby's Medical Dictionary.* Revised Second Edition. St. Louis: The C. V. Mosby Co., 1987.
2. Jenicek M, Hitchcock DL. *Evidence-Based Practice. Logic and Critical Thinking in Medicine.* Chicago, IL: American Medical Association (AMA Press), 2006.
3. Last JM. *A Dictionary of Public Health.* Oxford and New York: Oxford University Press, 2007.
4. *A Dictionary of Epidemiology.* Fifth Edition. Edited by M. Porta, S. Greenland and J.M. Last Associate Editors. A Handbook Sponsored by the I.E.A. Oxford and New York: Oxford University Press, 2008.
5. Jenicek M. *Foundations of Evidence-Based Medicine.* Boca Raton/London/New York/Washington: The Parthenon Publishing Group/CRC Press, 2003.
6. *WONCA Dictionary of General/Family Practice.* Copenhagen: Laegeforeningens Forlag, 2003.
7. Morrell P. *Medicine: Art or Science?* http://www.homeoint.org/morrell/ other-articles/artsci.htm, retrieved June 28, 2010 (7 pages).
8. American Board of Medicine. *Project Professionalism.* Philadelphia, PA: American Board of Medicine, 1998.

9. Sugar LM, Catton PA, Tallet SE, Rothman AI. Assessment of residents' professional attitudes and behaviours. *Annals RCPSC*, 2000;**33**:305–9.

10. Jacobi J (ed.), Guterman N (trans.). *Paracelsus. Selected Writings*. Princeton: Princeton University Press, Bollingen Series XXVIII, 1979.

11. Cruess SR, Cruess RL. Professionalism must be taught. *BMJ*, 1997;**315**:1674–7.

12. Art. On-line Medical Dictionary. www.graylab.ac.uk.

13. *The New Shorter Oxford English Dictionary on Historical Principles*. Edited by I. Brown. Volume 1, Fourth Edition. Oxford: Clarendon Press, 1993.

14. *The New Encyclopaedia Britannica*. Volume 1. Micropedia. Chicago, IL: Encyclopaedia Britannica, 1992.

15. *The American Heritage Dictionary of English Language*. Fourth Edition, 2000. Electronic Edition: www.bartleby.com.

16. Entries "Art" and "Philosophy, Western." *Encarta*® *Encyclopedia.* 1993–1997, Microsoft Corporation, electronic edition. See also: www.encarta.msn.com.

17. Gregg D. The art and the science of medicine. *Boston Med Surg J*, 1923;**189**:438–40.

18. Conservapedia. *Scientific theory.* http://www.coservapedia.com/Scientific_theory, retrieved June 27, 2010 (4 pages).

19. Wikipedia, the free encyclopedia. *Scientific theory.* http://en.wikipedia.org/wiki/Scientific_theory, retrieved June 27, 2010 (8 pages).

20. Simple Wikipedia, the free encyclopedia. *Scientific theory.* (Another entry with an identical title.) http://simple.wikipedia.org/wiki/Scientific_theory, retrieved June 27, 2010 (2 pages).

21. Jenicek M. *Fallacy-Free Reasoning in Medicine. Improving Communication and Decision Making in Research and Practice*. Chicago, IL: American Medical Association (AMA Press), 2009.

22. Entry "Craft." *Random House Webster's Unabridged Dictionary*. Antwerpen: Random House Inc., 1998 and 2003.

23. Wikipedia, the free encyclopedia. *Outline of crafts.* http://en.wikipedia.org/wiki/Outline_of_crafts, retrieved October 6, 2010 (2 pages).

24. Harriet H. The "art" of clinical decision-making. *Science-Based Med*, 2008 (May 13). http://www.sciencebasedmedicine.org/?p=106, retrieved June 28, 2010 [12 pages (with responses)]. Comment 1 (Science or art?), by #oveshooton, from engineering (p. 2).

25. Guttentag OE. The phrase, "art and science of medicine." *Calif Western Med*, 1939;**50**:86–7.

26. Fillers. Endpiece Medicine: Art or science? *BMJ*, 2000;**320**:1322.

27. Herman J. Medicine: The science and the art. *Med Humanities*, 2001;**27**:42–6.

28. Harrington JA. Art or science? Understanding medicine and the common law. *Health Law J*, 2001;**9**:129–48.

29. Panda SC. Medicine: Science or art? *Mens Sana Monogr*, 2006;**4**:127–38.

30. Kirkpatrick JN, Groninger H. Putting it all together: The art and science of medicine. *Virtual Mentor*, 2006 (July);**8**:452–8.

31. Tucker NH. President's message—Medicine: Art versus science. *Jacksonville Med* (Dec 1999). http://www.dcmsonline.org/jax-medicine/1999journals/december99/presmess.htm, retrieved June 28, 2010 (2 pages).

32. White S, Stancombe J. *Clinical Judgment in the Health and Welfare Professions. Extending the Evidence Base.* Maidenhead and Philadelphia: Open University Press/McGraw-Hill, 2003.

33. Jenicek M. *Medical Error and Harm. Understanding, Prevention, and Control.* Boca Raton/London/New York: CRC Press/Taylor & Francis/Productivity Press, 2011.

34. Gardner MJ, Altman DG. *Statistics with Confidence—Confidence Intervals and Statistical Guidelines.* London: British Medical Journal, 1989.

35. Jenicek M. 'Classical' theory of probability, section 3.3.1.1, pp. 53–55, in: *Foundations of Evidence-Based Medicine.* Boca Raton/London/New York/Washington: The Parthenon Publishing Group/CRC Press, 2003.

36. Timmermans S, Angell A. Evidence-based medicine, clinical uncertainty, and learning to doctor. *J Health Soc Beh*, 2001;**42**(4):342–59.

37. Jenicek M. Fuzzy logic and fuzzy sets theory, section 3.3.1.3, pp. 58–62, in: *Foundations of Evidence-Based Medicine.* Boca Raton/London/New York/Washington: The Parthenon Publishing Group/CRC Press, 2003.

38. Gleick J. *Chaos. Making a New Science.* New York and London: Penguin Books, 1987.

39. Zadeh LA. Knowledge representation in fuzzy logic, pp. 1–26, in: *An Introduction to Fuzzy Logic. Application in Intelligent Systems.* Dordrecht, NL: Kluwer Academic Publishers, 1992.

40. Jenicek M, Hitchcock DL. Fuzzy sets and fuzzy logic, section 3.7, pp. 83–89, in: *Evidence-Based Practice. Logic and Critical Thinking in Medicine.* Chicago, IL: American Medical Association (AMA Press), 2005.

41. Torres A, Nieto JJ. Fuzzy logic in medicine and bioinformatics. *J Biomed Biotech*, 2006; article ID 9108: 1–7.

42. Burton RA. *On Being Certain. Believing You Are Right Even When You're Not.* New York, NY: St. Martin's Press, 2008.

43. Subias JL. *Applications of chaos theory in medicine.* http://www.didyf.unizar.es/info/jlsubias/Cor_tv04.eng.htm, retrieved April 1, 2010 (6 pages).

44. Denton TA, Diamond GA, Gelfand RH, Khan S, Karaguezian H. Fascinating rhythm: A primer on chaos theory and its application to cardiology. *Am Heart J*, 1990;**120**:1419–40.

45. *The New Encyclopaedia Britannica. Micropaedia.* Volume 7. Chicago, IL: Encyclopaedia Britannica Inc., 1992.

46. Jenicek M. Chaos theory vs. probability theory. Beyond classical logic and probability, section 3.3.1.2, pp. 55–58, in: *Foundations of Evidence-Based Medicine.* Boca Raton/London/New York/Washington: The Parthenon Publishing Group/CRC Press, 2003.

47. Goodwin JS. Chaos and the limits of modern medicine. *JAMA*, 1997;**278**(17): 1399–40.

48. Litaker D, Tomolo A, Liberatore V, Stange KC, Aron D. Using complexity theory to build interventions that improve health care delivery in primary care. *J Gen Intern Med*, 2006;**21**:S30–S34.

49. Sturmberg JP, Martin CM. Complexity and health—Yesterday's traditions, tomorrow's future. *J Eval Clin Pract*, 2009;**15**:543–8.

50. Martin C, Sturmberg JP. Perturbing ongoing conversations about systems and complexity of health services and systems. *J Eval Clin Pract*, 2009;**15**:549–52.

51. Waymack MH. Yearning for certainty and the critique of medicine as "science." *Theor Med Bioeth*, 2009;**30**:215–29.

52. Lederman EK. *Philosophy and Medicine*. Revised Edition. Hants/Aldershot and Brookfield, VT: Gower Publishing Company, 1986.

53. Wulff HR, Gotzche PC. *Rational Diagnosis and Treatment. Evidence-Based Clinical Decision Making*. Third Edition. Oxford and Malden, MA: Blackwell Science, 2000.

54. Pellegrino ED, Thomasma DC. *A Philosophical Basis of Medical Practice. Toward a Philosophy and Ethic of the Healing Professions*. New York and Oxford: Oxford University Press, 1981.

55. Wulff HR, Pedersen SA, Rosenberg R, Introduction by A Storr. *Philosophy of Medicine. An Introduction*. Second Edition. Oxford and Boston, MA: Blackwell Scientific Publications, 1990.

56. Engelhardt Jr. HT (ed.). *The Philosophy of Medicine. Framing the Field*. Dordrecht/Boston/London: Kluwer Academic Publishers, 2000.

57. Engelhardt Jr. HT, Jotterand F (eds.). *The Philosophy of Medicine Reborn: A Pellegrino Reader*. Notre Dame, IN: University of Notre Dame Press, 2008.

58. *Random House Webster's Unabridged Dictionary*. Antwerpen: Random House Inc., 1998 and 2003.

59. *Dorland's Illustrated Medical Dictionary*. Twenty fourth Edition. Philadelphia and London: W.B. Saunders Company, 1965.

60. Murphy EA. *The Logic of Medicine*. Second edition. Baltimore and London: The Johns Hopkins University Press, 1997.

61. Wikipedia, the free encyclopedia. *Theory*. http://en.wikipedia.org/wiki/ Theory, retrieved June 27, 2010 (8 pages).

62. Lolas F. Theoretical medicine: A proposal for reconceptualising medicine as a science of actions. *J Med Phil*, 1996;**21**(6):659–70.

63. Lorenz W, Rothmund M. Theoretical surgery: A new specialty in operative medicine. *World J Surg*, 1989;**13**:292–9.

64. Koller M, Barth H, Celik I, Rothmund M. A short history of theoretical surgery. *Inflamm Res*, 2004;**53**(Suppl 2):S99–S104.

65. The Evidence-Based Medicine Working Group. *Users' Guides to the Medical Literature. A Manual for Evidence-Based Clinical Practice*. Chicago, IL: American Medical Association (AMA Press)/JAMA & Archives Journals, 2002. Second Edition edited by G. Guyatt, D. Rennie, M. O. Meade and D. J. Cook. New York and Chicago: McGraw-Hill Medical and JAMA & Archives Journals (AMA), 2008.

66. Evidence-Based Medicine Working Group (G. Guyatt et al.). A new approach to teaching the practice of medicine. *JAMA*, 1992;**268**:2420–5.

67. Sackett DL, Rosenberg WMC, Muir Gray JA, Haynes RB, Richardson WB. Evidence-based medicine: what it is and what it isn't. *BMJ*, 1996;**312**:71–2.

68. Straus SE, Scott Richardson W, Glasziou P, Haynes RB. *Evidence-Based Medicine. How to Practice and Teach EBM*. Third Edition. Edinburgh/London/ New York: Elsevier/Churchill Livingstone, 2005.

69. *Mosby's Dictionary of Medicine, Nursing & Health Professions.* Eighth Edition. St. Louis, MO: Mosby/Elsevier, 2009.
70. *Definitions of Evidence-Based Medicine on the Web.* http://www.google.ca/search?hl=en&biw=1339&bih=562&defl=en&q=define:Evidence-..., retrieved October 12, 2010 (1 page).
71. Jenicek M. Epidemiology, evidence-based medicine, and evidence-based public health. *J Epidemiol* (Japan Epidemiological Association), 1997;**7**(4):187–97.
72. Jenicek M, Stachenko S. Evidence-based public health, community medicine, preventive care. *Med Sci Monit*, 2003;**9**(2):SR1–SR7.
73. Brownson RC, Baker EA, Leet TL, Gillespie KN. *Evidence-Based Public Health.* Oxford and New York: Oxford University Press, 2003.
74. Muir Gray JA. *Evidence-based Healthcare. How to Make Health Policy and Management Decisions.* New York and Edinburgh: Churchill Livingstone, 1997.
75. Ennis RH. *Critical Thinking.* Upper Saddle River, NJ: Prentice Hall, 1996.
76. Scriven M, Paul R. *Critical Thinking Community. A Working Definition of Critical Thinking.* http://lonestar.texas.net/~mseifert/crit2.html, retrieved June 2005.
77. Facione PA. *Critical Thinking: A Statement of Expert Consensus for Purposes of Educational Assessment and Instruction.* Research findings and recommendations prepared for the Committee on Pre-College Philosophy of the American Philosophical Association. Newark, DE: American Philosophical Association, ERIC Document, no. ED 315–423, 1990.
78. Jenicek M, Croskerry P, Hitchcock DL. Evidence and its uses in health care and research: The role of critical thinking. *Med Sci Monit*, 2011;**17**(1):RA12–RA17.
79. Wikipedia, the free encyclopedia. *Humanities.* http://en.wikipedia.org/wiki/humanities, retrieved February 16, 2011 (13 pages).
80. Aull F. *Mission Statement.* Medical Humanities, New York University School of Medicine. http://medhum.med.nyu.edu/, retrieved March 18, 2011 (1 page).
81. Evans M, Finlay L (eds.). *Medical Humanities.* London: BMJ Books, 2001.
82. Kirklin D, Richardson R (eds.). *Medical Humanities: A Practical Introduction.* London: Royal College of Physicians, 2001.
83. Shapiro J, Coulehan J, Wear D. Medical humanities and their discontents: Definitions, critiques and implications. *Acad Med*, 2009;**84**(2):192–8.
84. Jenicek M. Towards evidence-based critical thinking medicine? Uses of best evidence in flawless argumentations. *Med Sci Monit*, 2006;**12**(1):RA149–RA153.
85. Jenicek M. Evidence-based medicine: Fifteen years later. Golem the good, the bad, and the ugly in need of a review? *Med Sci Monit*, 2006;**12**(11): RA241–RA251.
86. Jenicek M. The hard art of soft science: Evidence-based medicine, reasoned medicine or both? *J Eval Clin Pract*, 2006;**12**(4):410–9.

Chapter 2

How Physicians and Other Health Professionals Really (or Should) Think

Executive Summary

Critical thinking and decision making (CTDM) in medicine (and in other health sciences and professions) is now a well-organized and structured process to be mastered, used, and evaluated in practice and in research. From a methodological perspective, it is steadily developing as are epidemiology, biostatistics, and other domains applied to risk, diagnosis, treatment, or prognosis.

CTDM must have as an objective better understanding, rational decision making, or both. It relies on argumentation as a dialog to improve the views and conclusions stemming from the exchanges between interested individuals or bodies. The simplest two-element arguments (reason → conclusion), categorical syllogisms as classical forms of reasoning or Toulmin's modern argumentation model, might, are, and should be used in **Socratic dialogue** and problem solving, development and discussion of research findings, or various clinical rounds discussions. All these ways of clinical problem solving and its components and building blocks must be supported by the best available evidence.

A cause → effect link demonstration is the most frequent and important (but not only) form of CTDM. It is widely used and applied to noxious factors → disease occurrence and beneficial factors → improvement in health links. Etiological considerations are based on both quantitative (disease and exposure frequencies) and qualitative methodologies and on the criteria of causation. Single causes, sets, chains, and webs of causes, and wider concepts (concept mapping) may all be of interest in teaching and learning. Inductive and deductive research, inferential statistics, and epidemiological analytical methods and techniques are available for cause–effect problem solving and its uses. Health intervention, patient care priority setting, and the evaluation of their effect and impact depend on the causal reasoning, the magnitude of the problem and its controllability, and the associated human and social price.

The current state and uses of CTDM benefit and rely not only on experiences in health research and practice development and evaluation methodologies, but also on wider experiences from the business world, military arts, law, health, economics, **evidence-based medicine (EBM)** developments, and uses. They are all supported by informal logic, argumentation, and critical thinking, as built by modern philosophers.

Medicine remains a domain of probabilities and uncertainties. Its successes and failures depend widely on all the above CTDM components and on their contributors and considerations, as summarized above and in this chapter.

Not-So-Random Leading Thoughts

We are too much accustomed to attribute
to a single cause that which is the product
of several, and the majority of our
controversies come from that.

Attributed to Baron Justus von Liebig, 1803–1873
German chemist

The essential characteristic of philosophy,
which makes it a study distinct from
science, is criticism. It examines
critically principles employed in science
and in daily life; it searches out any
inconsistencies there may be in
these principles, and it only accepts
them when, as the result of critical
inquiry, there is no reason
for rejecting them.

Bertrand Arthur William Russell, 1912

The ability to reason is the fundamental characteristic
of human beings…. Virtually every conscious human
activity involves reasoning: we reason whenever
we solve problems, make decisions, assess character,
explain events, write poems, balance chequebooks,
predict elections, make discoveries, interpret works of art,
or repair carburetors. We reason about everything from
the meaning of life to what to have for dinner.[1]

William Hughes and Jonathan Lavery, 2008

We also reason at every step
of clinical care, making diagnoses,
prescribing drugs, performing surgery
or caring for bedridden patients
and their friends and family.
With understanding, there is
no such thing as inevitability.

Marshall (Herbert) McLuhan, 1911–1980

Toulmin's method of practical reasoning
permits the clinician to test a claim
about the management of patients and
the meaning of findings reported in a
research paper.... The process of
questioning our claims and assumptions
in clinical decision making is part
of a recent interpretive turn in medicine.
... The argument is the fundamental
unit of medical thought....[2]

Richard Horton, 1998
Former editor of The Lancet

Should we not learn this like anything else?
"... Scientific papers are not just baskets
carrying unconnected facts like a telephone
directory: They are instruments of persuasion.
Scientific papers must argue you into believing
what they conclude; they must be built on the
principles of critical arguments...."[3]

Edward J. Huth, 1999
Former Editor-in-Chief, Annals of Internal Medicine

Introductory Comments

Structured reasoning and critical thinking also underlie exchanges of thoughts, opinions, and ideas between clinicians in their daily practice, teaching, and learning. Finding and grading the best evidence in today's world of evidence-based medicine is just fine. The rest depends on how you'll use it in your reasoning and decision making.

If I understand how my teachers reason and why they are doing what they are doing, I will obtain optimal benefits from my medical training. Additionally, the teachers will be happy that their efforts and messages have found a receptive audience and readership.

2.1 General Medical Thinking and Reasoning

Thinking and reasoning in medicine, regardless of their form, are materialized in series of statements about the following:

- Original ideas triggering the reasoning process
- The premises that cover triggering ideas
- Conclusion(s) that follow from premises analysis and integration

In the analysis of our reasoning processes, all types of statements may be identified by idea indicators, premise indicators and conclusion indicators. Figure 2.1 illustrates such a structure in different types of argumentation as summarized in this section.

2.1.1 Basic Considerations Related to Clinical Care and Caregivers' Reasoning

Physicians follow several steps and considerations when taking care of their patients:

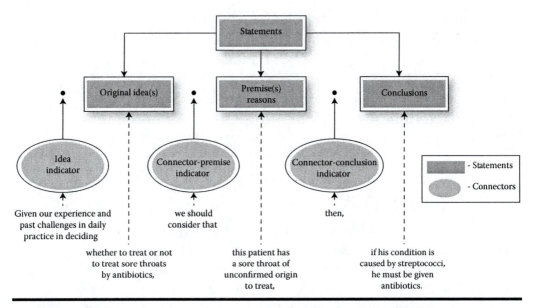

Figure 2.1   Three major types of statements in medical communication: Ideas, premises, and conclusions.

■ Learning about the patient's past and present through medical history; gathering written and oral information about their past and present (chief complaint ant other complaints)

■ Conducting physical examination and/or mental status assessment and paraclinical exploration (laboratory and other technology-dependent procedures) leading to and making diagnosis

■ Taking into account the risks (future health problems) and health problems already present (diagnosis)

■ Considering the treatment choices, decisions, plan, and orders

■ Assessing the prognosis

■ Evaluating the effectiveness, efficiency, and efficacy of the collection of the above-mentioned steps in health care

■ Considering the future steps in care

At each of the above-mentioned steps in clinical work, conclusions, which are a sort of claim (the endpoint in argumentation, as described below), are based on what we have done with all the positive or negative aspects and the impact of our care:

■ Those data and information are relevant for further assessment of the patient.

■ The patient has this disease, syndrome, and other health problem.

■ Considering what I have heard, read, and seen in this patient, he or she may develop health problems that he or she does not have yet.

■ The patient should receive the following medical, surgical, psychiatric, or other treatment and care (social care and support included).

■ The outlook for the patient (prognosis) with or without treatment is good or bad.

■ Our treatment plan and its execution were effective (did some good in habitual conditions), efficient (in line with money, resources, and time invested), and efficacious (consistent, specious, and beneficial under ideal conditions).

At any step of clinical care, decisions are made and recommendations and orders are given through various channels (admission notes, consults, discharge summaries, etc.). Ideas, propositions, and conclusions are also communicated to peers, other health professionals, managers and administrators, and last but not least, to the patient and their friends and family and other society members. Such **communication** is a bilateral activity that must "make sense." Chapter 5 is devoted to this important topic.

In this chapter, let us see first how we should approach (and practice) general medical reasoning about what we should understand and what we should decide to do.

2.1.2 Our Thinking and Reasoning: Essential Definitions and Meanings

Should we learn how to reason? By all means! Correct reasoning is necessary to achieve the objectives of any teaching and learning process such as acquiring desirable, necessary, and useful knowledge, attitudes, and skills.

Our thinking and reasoning have two distinct and different purposes and a common vehicle and tool that define their ways and content:

1. The first purpose is **understanding**, engendering a mental process to understand the nature of the problem of interest such as what causes cancer or what is effective in its treatment.
2. The second purpose is **decision making**. We reason about the best ways to solve a health problem, such as deciding if surgery or conservative treatment is the best way to treat an advanced cancer and what to do in a particular clinical case or which available surgical procedures and techniques are the best for this patient.
3. Sharing our thoughts about both understanding and decisions requires communication, that is, moving ideas, thoughts, proposals, recommendation directions, rules, or orders between individuals (health professionals and their patients and community) and organizations (hospitals, other health services, community groups).

This chapter is about understanding, Chapter 4 is about decision making, and Chapter 5 is devoted to the communication problem and rules. But let us look at understanding first.

In the spirit of Bloom's taxonomy of learning and teaching processes, in general,[4] we must master several abilities:

■ *Knowledge* (observation and recall of information)
■ *Comprehension* (understanding information, translation into the specific context, interpretation, and prediction of consequences)
■ *Application* (uses of information or evidence and solving the problem)
■ *Analysis* (identification of patterns, meaning of the whole and its components)

- *Synthesis* (generalizations, new idea generation, merging knowledge from several areas, and making conclusions and predictions)
- *Evaluation of our mental processes* (comparisons of and making discriminations between ideas, assessing the value of claims, making choices based on reasoned argument, verifying the value of evidence, and making distinctions between subjectivity and objectivity)

Let us add the following to this set:

- *Decision making* (what to do given the above; communicating with all the involved parties such as patients and other health and social professionals; and management as partners in the execution of decided actions)
- *Execution* of the decided actions
- *Evaluation of the impact of actions performed* (results as they appear to both providers and recipients of clinical and other health care)

None of this works without proper reasoning. Proper reasoning will help avoid a sizeable number of medical errors at any site and step of clinical work, while contributing to patient safety and quality of care. Our ways of thinking and decision making are now increasingly pragmatic, structured, and practice-oriented, often as much as our thinking as epidemiologists, biostatisticians, surgeons, or psychiatrists.

And so, what lies behind the most important terms we encounter and use in the world of medical reasoning today? The following definitions of some basic concepts in thinking apply perfectly to medicine.

Thinking is a *mental action that, if verbalized, is a matter of combining words in propositions.*[5,6] Needless to say, this general definition applies to and includes the mental processes dealing with health and disease. Its elements in general[7] and in clinical settings[8] are the following:

- Purposes (goals, objectives, functions)
- Relevant questions (problems to deal with and solve)
- Information (data, facts, evidence, observations, experiences, reasons)
- Interpretation and inference (conclusions, solutions)
- Concepts (theories, definitions, laws, principles, models)
- Assumptions (presuppositions, axioms, taking for granted)
- Implications and consequences (effects, that which follows logically)
- Points of view (frames of reference, perspectives, orientations, world views)

Reasoning is *thinking leading to a conclusion*. We think about signs and symptoms in a patient and come to a conclusion about the diagnosis of his or her health problem. We review our knowledge about a drug and conclude if it should be prescribed to a patient or not. Our patient asks us what will happen given his or her health problem and what this implies for his or her care and outcomes. We conclude that his or her prognosis is good or bad. Without good reasoning, there is no good medicine.

Formally and more generally, reasoning is the *process of forming conclusions, judgments, or inferences from facts, observations, and/or hypotheses.* Its elements are, as already mentioned above, purpose, question, information, inferences, assumptions, concepts, implications, and points of view.[6,7]

Types of reasoning include the following not mutually exclusive methods;[8,9] Abduction, analogic reasoning, cause–effect reasoning, comparative reasoning, conditional reasoning, criterial reasoning, decompositional reasoning, deductive reasoning, inductive reasoning, modal logic, traditional logic, pros versus cons reasoning, set-based reasoning, systemic reasoning, and syllogistic reasoning.

When reasoning, we look at various *propositions, statements*, or *proposals*, which lead to the current and new view of the problem under scrutiny to be solved. Ideally, all propositions and statements about risks, diagnosis, treatment, or prognosis should be based on the best evidence through which we identify, know, and understand a problem.

An **argument** is a vehicle of reasoning. It consists of various statements or propositions (logicians call them premises or reasons) from which we infer to another statement or conclusion. It is supported and/or justified by propositions that lead us to something new, another statement or conclusion stemming from our argumentation process. In other words, an argument is a connected series of statements or reasons intended to establish a position leading to another statement as a conclusion. An argument is a vehicle of our medical logic.

Argumentation itself is a discussion between two or more people in which at least one advances an argument,[4] a manner and vehicle for the presentation of arguments. It means putting forward propositions by one or more proponents and their integration to reach a mutually acceptable solution. In this light, a physician's discussion with his or her patient(s), exchanging ideas between physicians, researching and publishing results, and proposing decisions in medical care and prevention are part of the wider field of medical argumentation. To obtain the best outcomes and for the patients' utmost benefit, we want our argumentation to be as flawless as possible: Impeccable argument-based medicine. Argumentation falls into the domain of reasoning, that is, as a tool to form conclusions, judgments, or inferences from facts or premises. It is a methodological use or presentation of arguments. Correct argumentation with ourselves and with other interested parties is one of the important ways of dealing with a given health problem, disease, medical care, and medical error as well.

Figure 2.2 illustrates "how doctors think, reason, decide, and do." We will follow this path throughout this book.

Argumentation may also be seen as the study of the principles by which beliefs and actions are evaluated and related to one another. It enables us to discover what beliefs and actions are reasonable in any social (professional practice and research in a community functioning related framework) context and that are concerned with the selection and organization of ideas to justify particular positions.

In medicine, we argue all the time: About patient history, his or her risks, diagnosis, how to treat the conditions that were found, what will happen after prognosis, and what should be done next and long term.

It is a two-dimensional process: As *inquiry*, it leads to the finding of appropriate beliefs and actions. As **advocacy**, it is a tool for using language strategies to justify our beliefs and actions to others.

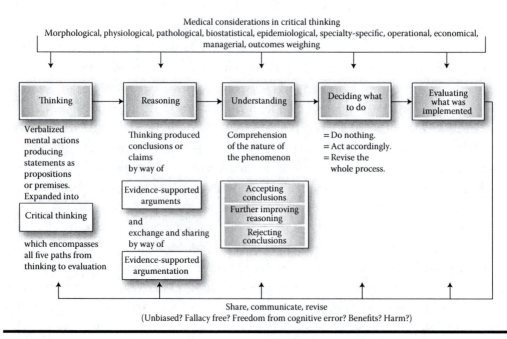

Figure 2.2 Components and sequence of mental processes and operations in medicine.

Premises or statements worded in argumentations are either *perceptual*, reflecting the nature of things, or *value judgments*, reflecting the worthiness of something, such as goodness, rightfulness, importance, or ethical acceptability.

Various premises and the ensuing conclusions of their use in the argumentative process represent descriptive, predictive, or evaluative statements, *propositions of facts or values* that assert the existence or worth of something: "This patient has a fever." As *propositions of policy*, they represent statements that assert actions to be taken and a desired change: "We must find out why and treat him accordingly." Those advocating change have to provide sufficient evidence and arguments to overcome the presumption (inherent advantage in opposing change) of existing beliefs and policies.

Again, conclusions must provide meaningful and usable information to improve our *understanding* of the health problem, *actions* to be taken, or both.

We have already covered argument and argumentation purposes, structure, and uses in this chapter. How should we understand them in the critical thinking and decision making context?

> Argumentation is the communicative process of advancing, supporting, criticizing, and modifying claims so that appropriate decision makers, defined by relevant spheres, may grant or deny adherence.[10]

In this framework, adherence means informed support by individuals involved in argumentation. They represent *spheres*, that is, collections of people in the process of interacting upon and making critical decisions. We may see medical or surgical multidisciplinary teams, medical research and its recipient groups, or graduate and undergraduate students as "spheres" in this context. Spheres may be personal or interpersonal, technical (specialty or profession related) or public, involving individuals and groups under the care and attention of decision makers.

Argumentation is a manner and vehicle for the presentation of arguments.

An *argument* is a unit encompassing various supports for some claim and must offer justifications to relevant decision makers, allowing them to adhere to the claim. Generalizations, analogies, authority, causes, signs may underlie all its ways.[10]

Various premises leading to its conclusion or ideas regarding what might be the conclusion of an argument before necessary information is gathered are also called **presumptions**, that is, positions or argumentative grounds available until some sufficient reason is adduced against them. Hypotheses at the beginning of medical research or working diagnoses before a more complete assessment of a patient to be admitted to hospital care and related reasons are presumptions in a critical thinking and decision making sense.

Our argumentation and its results are often subject to error and/or harm due in part to our fallacious reasoning biases and cognitive errors. Some definitions first might help to understand such challenges.

Medical logic (logic in medicine) is a system of thought and reasoning that governs understanding and decisions in clinical and community care, research, and communication.[5]

Informal logic helps us deal with health problems by looking at arguments as they occur in the context of natural language used in everyday life.

Error in general is an act of commission (doing something wrong) or omission (failing to do the right thing) that leads to an undesirable outcome or significant potential for such an outcome.[11,12]

Reasoning, deciding, or acting poorly can lead to medical errors and harm. **Medical error** may be defined then as an individual and/or system failure resulting from human behavior made by a health professional who, in a health establishment or community setting, provides direct clinical or community care, acts, or services (e.g., operating surgeon, prescribing internist, consulting psychiatrist, nurse at floors or in a surgical or office setting). It may be knowledge-based, rule-based, or skill (execution)-based[5] and often (but not always) produces medical harm. These two entities, however, must not be confounded.[13]

Medical harm is a temporary or permanent physical impairment in body functions (including sensory functions, mental functioning, social and occupational functioning, pain, disease, injury, disability, death) and structures and suffering that disrupts a patient's physical, mental, and/or social well-being. Some errors result in medical harm, but many errors do not. Conversely, many incidents of medical harm are not the results of any errors.[13]

Medical error, therefore, is a reasoning- and decision making–based inaccurate or incomplete assessment and management of patient risks and diagnosis, choosing and executing radical or conservative treatment, making prognosis, and extending and widening patient and community care. Such faults fall into the category of fallacies, biases, and cognitive errors.[14] Absence of errors and harm in medical practice is an important warrant of patient safety and quality of clinical and community health care.

Fallacy, in more general terms, is some mistake or flaw in reasoning or argument. It is a violation of the norms of good reasoning, rules of critical discussion, dispute resolution, and adequate communication.[14,15] **Fallacy in medicine** refers to any error of reasoning pertaining to a health problem and its supporting evidence(s) and pertaining to the handling of evidence in our reasoning and, throughout the process of argumentation, interfering with the best possible understanding and decision making in the task of health problem solving.[15,16] It may be a product of the physician's reasoning, communication, and decision making as well. For example, a *cum hoc ergo propter hoc* fallacy means drawing conclusions about cause–effect relationships on the basis of loosely defined "associations" or "correlations" instead of on the basis of a more formal cause–effect proof. Anything that precedes medical error and its potential consequences (harm) should not automatically be considered a "cause" of harm until it conforms to criteria of causality.

Often, fallacious reasoning occurs when a problem as a whole is reduced to one of its parts and generalizations from its solution are applied to the whole problem. For example, we may emphasize that an association between a toxic agent and cancer is strong given a high relative risk or odds ratio of exposure, nonexposure, developing or having the disease or not. However, the strength of the cause–effect association is just one criterion among many to confirm or reject a cause–effect relationship. Elsewhere, as shown above in the case of a *cum hoc ergo propter hoc* fallacy, a correct temporal sequence is not sufficient. Other criteria must be fulfilled too. Regardless, authors of medical articles about causality involving beneficial (trials) or noxious (etiological observations of uncontrolled individuals and events) factors frequently present high odds ratios or relative risks as a demonstration of causality. This is just a part of the picture and will be discussed further in this chapter and in Chapters 3 and 4.

The meaning of the word *bias* in medicine is most strongly influenced by its meaning in biostatistics: a deviation from some real or reference value. In a more general context, bias may be considered a nonrandom, systematic deviation from truth or a well-defined "reality." Often, bias is a term used in an undistinguished way from cognitive error or cognitive bias.

A **cognitive error** or **cognitive bias** (terms often used interchangeably across the literature) denote a pattern of deviation in judgment that occurs, in particular, within our area of interest, in medical and clinical situations or in medical research reasoning and conclusions.[12] For example, **Hindsight bias** (loosely synonymous with outcome bias) is a cognitive error as well. It is a tendency for people with outcome knowledge to exaggerate the extent to which they would have predicted the event beforehand. Bias as it is used currently across the medical literature has multiple meanings including almost any flaw in reasoning and decision making, especially in medical research (research design, execution, and evaluation). It is increasingly discussed because even "biased" research results and their uses may be detrimental to patient safety and health. In this context, bias is in a great part synonymous with fallacy.

Still, terms like bias, fallacy, or cognitive error are used interchangeably across the good portion of literature.

In light of current evidence in the medicine paradigm, *argument-based medicine*[15,16] refers to the research and practice of medicine in which understanding and decisions in patient and population care are supported by and based on flawless arguments using the best research and practice evidence and experience as argument and argumentation building blocks in a structured, fallacy-free manner.

2.1.3 Tools for Argumentation

There are several ways to explain and defend our views and positions, starting with a simple link between two statements and moving on to more complex and complete forms that better reflect the reality of the problem to be solved.

In essence, any kind of argumentation relies on varying the numbers of statements, connected and identified by linking words called "connectors." Figure 2.1 illustrates this concept and the basic organization of the statements and their connections in argumentation.

2.1.3.1 "Naked" Argument (Enthymeme) or Argument at Its Simplest: A "Two-Element" Reasoning

In daily reasoning and communication, however risky for conclusions it might be, we usually move from one *reason* (statement, proposition, and premise) to some *conclusion* (claim, recommendation, and orders) through the use of an *indicator*, which links the reason to the conclusion:

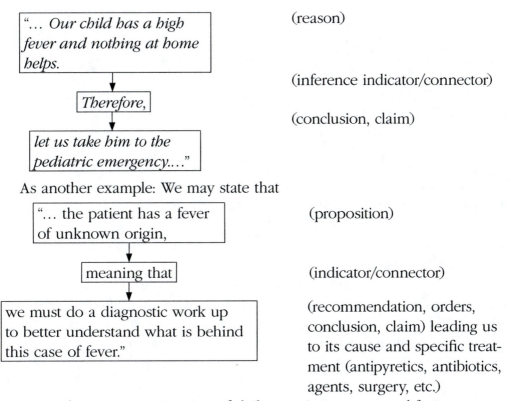

As another example: We may state that

we must do a diagnostic work up to better understand what is behind this case of fever."

(recommendation, orders, conclusion, claim) leading us to its cause and specific treatment (antipyretics, antibiotics, agents, surgery, etc.)

In another common situation of daily practice, we proceed from some reason to some conclusion:

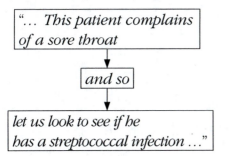

In some situations, we may also proceed in the reverse direction by stating (concluding, claiming) what we intend or want to do:

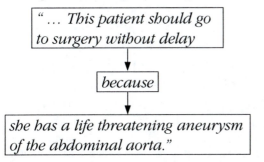

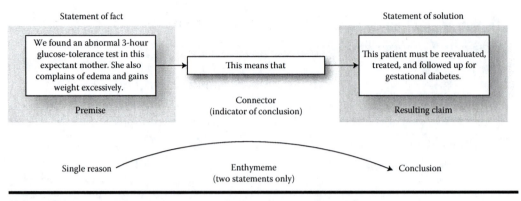

Figure 2.3   A "single reason → conclusion" argument: enthymeme.

Figure 2.3 is another illustration of an enthymeme used in clinical practice communication.

This "one-element" form of reasoning called *enthymeme* is, for Hitchcock, a kind of reasoning or argument that is not deductively valid, but which can be made deductively valid by adding one or more premises.[5] Enthymematic way of reasoning and argumentation is fairly ubiquitous in charged clinical practice.

As a vehicle of reasoning, enthymeme may be often behind the **abductive reasoning**, one of the three basic forms of inference besides induction and deduction. Its form is: "The surprising fact is observed. If a hypothesis were true, the fact would be commonplace. Therefore, hypothesis is possibly true." We reason from observed phenomena to a hypothesis. It shows that only the hypothesis is a possible explanation; more (further observation, experiment, reasoning) is needed to fully justify the hypothesis. In syllogistic reasoning as summarized in Section 2.1.3.2, the uncertainty in inference may be due to a weak connection between the major and middle terms or the middle and major terms in a categorical syllogism. But let us see first what a categorical syllogism is.

2.1.3.2   "Classical" Form of Reasoning: Categorical Syllogism or "Three-Element" Reasoning

In the most ancient and traditional form of reasoning, we base our understanding and decisions on classical Greek philosophy dating back more than two millennia and on Aristotle's proposal of a **categorical syllogism** as a model to move from various propositions (premises) to some conclusion.[16,17] Its three constituting elements are as follows:

1. A *general statement* (major premise) is made: All subjects with blond or red hair are more sensitive to sunlight (ultraviolet light) as a cause of skin cancer.
2. A *specific statement* (minor premise) is made about a specific case: This patient has blond or red hair and often vacations in tropical and sub-tropical countries or goes to sun tanning salons to look "healthy."
3. A *conclusion* resulting from the link between the general and specific statement (i.e., a statement about the specific case in light of the general statement) is made: This patient is at high risk of skin cancer, so this patient should limit his or her exposure to ultraviolet light (conclusion, recommendation), should be followed more closely by others for early signs of potentially malignant skin lesions, and should be treated for them if required (two additional recommendations if supported by other arguments specific to them).

From one element of a syllogism to another, we insert, most often in natural language, *connectors* between the statements or *indicators* of a statement that follows from the preceding in a meaningful way. (See Figures 2.1 and 2.3.)

For example, a premise indicator may be words such as since, because, assuming that, in view of, given that, and so on.

A conclusion indicator such as therefore, hence, for this reason, which means that, which proves that, which lead us to, indicating us to (do), showing a mandatory action as follows somehow justifies and prepares us for the rightness of the final conclusion of the argument.

A more complete list may be found elsewhere (in Ref. 5).

All supporting statements must be based on the best available evidence for the purpose leading to the evidence-based conclusion. Let us consider another example: "... All sore throats require attention even if they are not caused by a streptococcal infection (major premise) ... given that (connector, following premise indicator) ... my patient has a sore throat (minor premise) ... so (conclusion indicator), ... I must be sure that he does not have this kind of bacterial infection before reassuring him that he does not need antibiotics...." (conclusion). Good evidence must exist behind general considerations regarding how to treat bacterial or nonbacterial throat infections (major premise), the state of our particular patient (minor premise), and their connection leading to the conclusion. Figure 2.4 illustrates graphically this way of reasoning.

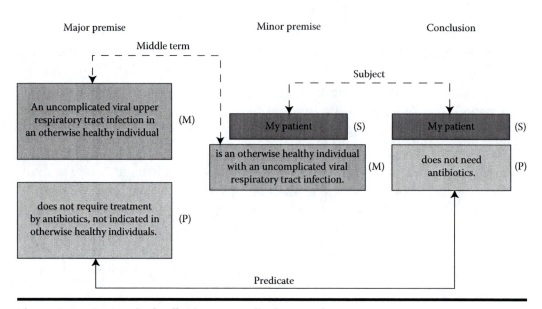

Figure 2.4   Categorical syllogism: a medical example.

In the context of argumentation and medicine, evidence *in medicine* means any piece of information and data needed and used either for *understanding* a health problem or *making decisions* about it.

In its broadest sense, *evidence* in argumentation means answering questions like "How do you know?" or "What do you have to go on?" by applying the following strategies:

1. Providing *examples* as materials from which a generalization will be built, something that is true about a problem as a whole.
2. *Statistics*: Quantitative (numerical) information in the form of frequencies, rates, ratios, odds, quantification of associations, and so on.
3. A *rate of change* based on repeated experience in terms of the outcomes of experiments or observational analytical studies.
4. *Tangible objects* as actual things or pictures of actual things, like those often used as evidence in criminal law, in *medical* textbooks, articles, pathology, or bedside teaching and experience.
5. A *testimony of factor of opinion* as a judgment of people who are in a position of knowing directly as a credible source.
6. A *social consensus* so widely believed that the individuals concerned consider it to be a fact. "Common knowledge" *is a type of social consensus* (partly from Ref. 18).

It does *not* mean solely a cause–effect relationship in observational or experimental analytical (trials) domains. It may concern risk, diagnosis, prognosis, or any other domain of health sciences and it may range from the worthless to the best available today. For practical decisions, it is graded according to the nature and purpose of the problem to be solved. Hence, the notion and meaning of the "best" evidence may vary from one case and problem to another.

2.1.3.3 "Modern" Form of Toulmin's Model of Argument: A "Multiple (Six-) Element" Way of Reasoning to Reach Valid Conclusions

In the 1950s, Stephen Toulmin, a British/American philosopher, proposed a new model of argument[19,20] in the hope that it would better fit our ways of reasoning today and the questions and problems of modern life. It does, and it is applied and used in an expanding number of domains in arts and sciences, including medicine. Compared to previous models, it often reflects reasoning backwards from the conclusion (claim) to all elements (argument building blocks) that contributed to its support and value. However, we anticipate the uses of this kind of argumentation when developing and executing a research project or when we admit or see a patient for the first time and develop "the case" from the initial "impression" to the planning and execution of clinical or community care with all decisions that such plans carry and imply.

Let us look at modern argumentation from a philosophical and a more formal standpoint first and then in terms of its applications to medicine.

Toulmin offered an original example of an argument[19] redrawn here in the form of Figure 2.5.

Philosophically speaking, Toulmin's model contains six elements or building blocks with connectors between them:

■ The *claim* is a conclusion to which we arrive through our reasoning supported by the present argument, such as "a high incidence of cancers in this rapidly developing industrial area is due to the high level of air pollution." Our clinical statements such as "this patient should be admitted," "this patient should be discharged," "this patient must get anti-rejection drugs," or "this patient has pneumonia" are all conclusions from various argumentative processes, leading us to such claims. The claim in this example is: "Harry is a British subject."

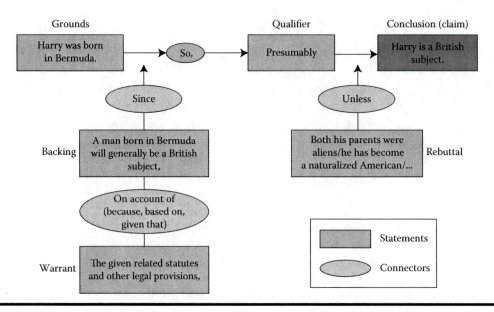

Figure 2.5 Toulmin's original example of a modern argument. (Redrawn with modifications from Toulmin, S. E., *The Uses of Argument*, Cambridge University Press, Cambridge, England, 1958 [Updated Edition, 2003].)

- The *grounds* are the basis from which we reason, the *fundamental data and information,* our own findings: A high incidence of cancers and high levels of industrial air pollution as we observed in the area of interest. In EBM, we may see this as "first-hand evidence." "Harry was born in Bermuda" in this example.

- The *backing* is the *body of experience and evidence* that supports the warrant: Our past studies and experience, literature review of similar and dissimilar findings. In EBM, we may see this as "second-hand evidence," critically appraised or not (… *the following other studies offer similar findings and conclusions.…*) In this example, "the following statutes and other legal provisions" are the backing.

- The *warrant* is a *general rule or experience, understanding of the nature of the problem under study,* allowing us to infer to the claim: Similar findings in the literature, methodological experience, and explanation of pathological and physiological mechanisms underlying the health problem, such as our general understanding of the carcinogenicity of specific air pollutants. In EBM, it is our understanding of the nature of first- and second-hand evidence. In this example, "… a man born in Bermuda will generally be a British subject" is the warrant.

- The *qualifier* is an expression, often a single word or number, somehow quantifying our certainty about our claim in light of the preceding argument blocks and connections between them: The high incidence of cancers is "definitely," "probably," and "more certainly than uncertainly" due to the air pollution, "80%" of cancer cases are due to the carcinogens in the air, "we are 90% sure that this health problem is an environmental problem," and so on. In this example, "presumably" is a qualifier.

■ *Rebuttals* are conditions or circumstances under which our claim does not apply. They undermine the force of supporting grounds and other building blocks of the argument. In the cancer-related example, they would be other undetected carcinogens of nonindustrial origin (naturally occurring in soil, waters, etc.), difficult differential diagnosis criteria with other competing health problems, individual endogenous factors in the population leading to the high probability of cancer incidence ("cancer families"), and others. In a broader framework, rebuttals may contain ethical considerations, contraindications, differential diagnoses, or patient preferences and values, which may differ from the health professional and/or scientific point of view. As exclusion criteria in a clinical sense, they must be based on the best evidence available and otherwise justified. In this example, "both his parents were Aliens/he has become a naturalized American/ …" is a rebuttal.

Let us add the following:

■ "Since," "on account of (because, based on, given that)," "so," "unless" are all *connectors* between various statements, building blocks of the argument.

Does all this have anything to do with medicine? It definitely does.

In another domain unrelated to medicine,[19] a demographer may reason: "Petersen is not a Roman Catholic" (claim to be evaluated and discussed) … why? … "Petersen is a Swede" (data, grounds) … and … *since a Swede can be taken to be almost certainly not a Roman Catholic* (warrant) … and given that … *the proportion of Roman Catholic Swedes is less than 2%* (backing) … *he almost certainly* (qualifier) … *is not a Roman Catholic* … (back to the claim as conclusion of an argument).

Similarly, in medicine, for example, we may reflect: *My young patient, immunized against measles has a rash which looks like measles* (data and impression).… Besides the clinical manifestations of his or her rash … since … *there is a very low probability that a well immunized child would get measles* (warrant) … and because … *he comes from a community in which almost all children are immunized against measles and the herd immunity there is then high enough to prevent measles spread and high occurrence of cases* (backing) … so, … *almost certainly* (qualifier) … *my young patient does not have measles and we must also look at another more probable diagnosis of his or her problem* (conclusion, claim stemming from this diagnostic argumentation and argument). N.B. The protective efficacy of the vaccine is not absolute!

"N.B. Pattern recognition plays an important role in this way of reasoning. More generally speaking in medicine, and in simpler terms, what do we need?

- We need some *grounds* for argumentation, be it spoken or written. Clinical and paraclinical data and information particular to the case serve this purpose.
- We look at grounds in light of a *warrant*, that is, some kind of general rule, accepted understanding and evidence. Plausibility is in focus.
- Whatever we conclude on the basis of grounds and warrant is evaluated in a confirmation, line or distinct pattern as seen through *backing*, that is, research findings, graded evidence, past practical clinical experience, "external evidence," "what literature tells us."
- Putting all this together, we try to somehow quantify the certainty or probability that our ensuing claims or conclusions of the argument are correct in terms of a *qualifier*, often the hardest challenge of an argument.
- Our *conclusions* or argument *claim* are then the result of synthesis of the above argument building blocks.
- Argument conclusions are valid provided only that there are existing exclusionary circumstances or criteria that Toulmin termed *rebuttals*. Besides qualifiers, rebuttals are often sorely missing (and they should not be) in our conclusions or claim statements.

Therefore, errors occur and mistakes happen if considering the following:

- Grounds are of poor quality, incomplete, or unrelated to the problem under study.
- Our understanding of the essence of the problem is not clear.
- The backing is of poor quality, incomplete, or unrelated again.
- We are unsure of our certainty regarding our conclusions and claims.
- We act as if exceptions would not apply to what we conclude about the problem.
- There is no meaningful link between each of the argument building blocks.

Let us consider again the sore throat/antibiotics example to illustrate Toulmin's way of argumentation: "I will prescribe you antibiotics for your bacterial throat infection (claim, conclusion of an argument) because looking at your red throat, patched tonsils, tender cervical nodes and fever, and positive results of our rapid laboratory test (grounds).... a treatment with penicillin may be the best choice in your case (warrant) ... All our past experience and clinical studies show that we must do this to spare you from serious complications of such an infection (backing) ... so, let us definitely proceed this way (qualifier), if you agree, and unless you are allergic to penicillin (rebuttals), in which case we should choose another kind of treatment ...," a new claim to be supported by alternative premises or statements applying to a different condition. Figure 2.6 represents a graphical structure of this kind of modern argument.

Table 2.1 illustrates this type of argument as it might be (and is) used in medicine and other health sciences. The flowchart was originally proposed for medical article understanding and writing, with particular attention given to the discussion section.[21,22] Its principles apply to any other argument and argumentation in health sciences research and practice, communication of both pinpoint and broader experience and research experience as well.

The claim (already appearing as building block 3) reappears now again and represents the result of the argument.

Figure 2.7 represents, then, Toulmin's model of argument with the addition of thesis and adducts entities.[23,24] It is redrawn from left → right orientation to the top ↓ bottom one, as flowcharts usually appear in health sciences.

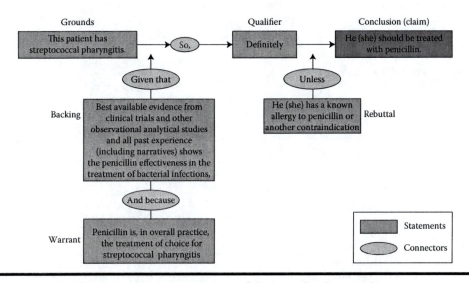

Figure 2.6   Toulmin's modern argument model. A medical example.

Table 2.1   The Medical Article as an Exercise in Argumentation

Definition	*What It Does*	*Comments*
1. Argument as a whole		
Structured path from an initial idea, across series of considerations (building blocks), leading to a conclusion (claim) confirming, rejecting, or modifying the triggering thought about the problem.	Defines the problem in context (structured question, hypothesis, setting), gathers and critically appraises each argument building block with attention to a proper connection between them, up to the final claim.	It is the article as a whole.
2. Problem in context or thesis		
An ensemble that includes to varying degrees hypothesis, research question(s), setting, study objectives, initial impression of the problem under study. A "what exactly is the question" statement.	Proposes an original operational and structured idea to be evaluated by an argument process.	To be meaningful and useful for interpretation, the original idea must be supported by a clear hypothesis, research question, setting of the objective(s) of the critical process of argument building, analysis, and evaluation. It is usually in the "Introduction" section.
3. Claim		
Conclusion drawn by the end of reasoning path (argument); thesis drawn from or evaluated by the study. A "what do we think about it" statement.	Confirms or modifies the thesis initiating the argument; generates a new thesis from findings.	**Factual:** Does it exist, what is, was, or will be?
		Definitional: What is it, how can it be classified?
		Causal: What caused it, what will it produce?
		Value asserting: Is it harmful or beneficial? Good or bad?
		Policy/direction giving: What we should do.
		It is in the "Title" and at the core of the "Conclusions" of the article.

Table 2.1   The Medical Article as an Exercise in Argumentation (*Continued*)

Definition	What It Does	Comments
4. Grounds: (syn. data, support)		
Data and/or information that support the claim. A "facts and evidence" statement.	Provide essential and direct basis for the claim.	They are in the "Material and Methods" and "Results" sections.
5. Backing		
Information that justifies and makes explicit the warrant. Experimental and theoretical foundations from other sources. A "given that" statement.	Provides additional information and clarification(s) for the warrant. Justifies the move from grounds (data) to the claim. Offers cultural assumptions, support, and the theoretical basis for the warrant.	It is usually in the "Literature Review" section.
6. Warrant		
Explanation of how grounds support the claim; general (other) statements, assumptions, propositions bridging claim, and data. Information about the arguer's reasoning. A "general wisdom about" statement.	Shows how grounds support the claim. Justifies the move from data and/or backing to the claim.	It may be located in several sections of an article, "Introduction" and "Discussion" sections included.
7. Rebuttals (syn. reservations)		
Circumstances invalidating the claim. An "unless" statement.	Defines limits of the claim. Offers counter-arguments. Specifies conditions under which the claim does not apply.	They should be in the "Discussion" section.
8. Qualifier (syn. modality)		
The arguer's degree of belief or certainty about the claim. A "conviction" statement.	Quantifies strengths and limitations given by the reasoning process and its building blocks to the claim.	Some, many, often, probably, certainly, quite, presumably, surely, definitely, almost certainly, may, with a 75% probability, and so on.
		It should be located in the "Conclusions" section of the article.

(*Continued*)

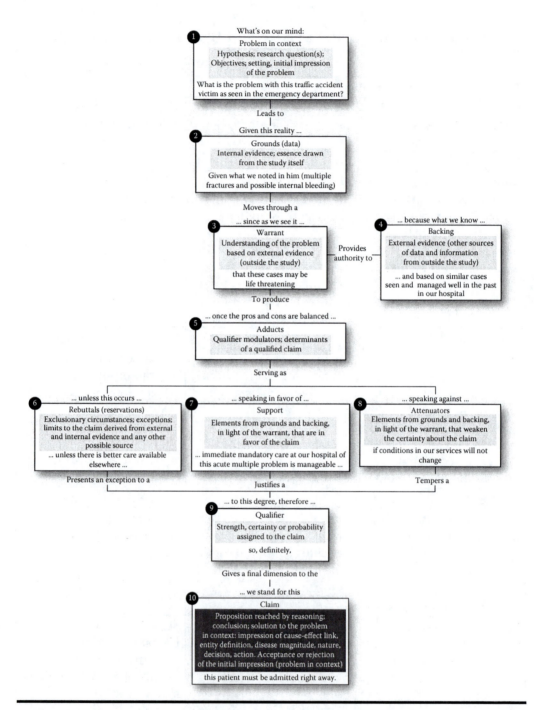

Figure 2.7 Expanded model of Toulmin's modern argument: A medical example. (Based on Jenicek, M., *A Physician's Self-Paced Guide to Critical Thinking*, American Medical Association [AMA Press], Chicago, IL, 2006; Jenicek, M., *Fallacy-Free Reasoning in Medicine. Improving Communication and Decision Making in Research and Practice*, American Medical Association [AMA Press], Chicago, IL, 2009.)

Toulmin's six classical building blocks, "organs within a living system of argument," as he calls them, may be completed conveniently by a *problem statement or thesis* into which argumentation is set. Pros (warrants stemming from grounds and backing speaking for conclusion) and cons (rebuttals) represent an ensemble of **adducts** within which we search for a balance of elements justifying or not our claim(s) or conclusion.

As we may see and feel from the above described argument concepts, in practice, an argument is either built from some original idea (thesis) up to its conclusion (claim) or is reconstructed retrospectively and evaluated for its validity and absence of fallacies.

Reasoning this way may be either valid or invalid. Deductively valid arguments are those whose conclusions follow necessarily from their premises. Given true premises and a valid argument, the conclusion is necessarily true. Given false premises and a valid argument, the conclusion may or may not be true. The quality of premises is given by the argumentation that led to them as new statements and by the quality of evidence (data or information necessary for the understanding of and/or decision making about a health problem), as we understand evidence and best evidence in EBM.

Argumentations based on any of the above-mentioned three models work if and only if they are based on solid evidence underlying each premise and if this evidence is correctly linked (inferring) to conclusions that are based on them. Any error in evidence and its handling through our reasoning (argumentation) is a fallacy to be prevented or corrected.

An argument makes sense only if it is exercised in view and in the framework of a well-defined problem in context or thesis. A *thesis* is *a proposition stated and put forward for consideration, especially one to be discussed and proved or to be maintained against objections.*[25] Ideally it should include the definition of the *problem in focus* (research or practice situation or event) itself, *objectives* to tackle the problem, *hypothesis(es)*, a research or practice *question*, as well as all necessary operational *definitions* of entities and variables of interest. In most cases, there is no meaningful discussion and argumentation without pre-specifying the thesis and its components (problem in focus, objectives, hypotheses, research questions, and definitions of variables of interest). *Context, setting, and framing* (vide infra) are also indispensable for any meaningful discussion.

The *problem (topic) in focus* is the health problem that you try to solve in practice or research.

From the domain of orismology as defined in Chapter 1, a word about *definitions*: **Definitions** are the formal statements of the meaning and significance of entities of interest (variables, tools, conditions, settings, etc.). To be practical in medicine, they should be as *operational* (usable as decision making tools) and precise and usable in practice and research as possible. Other definitions are *stipulative* (coining new phenomena), lexical or *reportive* (how the word is actually used), *precising* (eliminating vagueness), *theoretical* (formulating an adequate characterization), *motivational* and *persuasive* (influencing attitudes in a rather metaphysical manner) or *essentialist* (specifying the nature of the phenomenon to which the term refers).[26]

For a health professional, entities are defined in the context of and in comparison with other entities defined in a way to make them usable and useful if they

- Discriminate and are clearly separated from other possibly competing entities related to the problem
- Represent a distinct substrate, different from others
- Are, if possible and desired, measurable and otherwise subject to quantification (counting)
- Are subject to grading (degree, direction attributing)
- Are categorizable within a classification in a specific context
- Reflect and relate to a specific decision about an action to be taken
- Have operational inclusion and exclusion criteria which distinguish such an entity from others
- Are mutually understood, hence warranting reproduction, repetition, and reuse

Definitions themselves, regardless of how we deal with the problem of interest, establish if our understanding and approach are good, bad, usable, or meaningless.

For example, a definition of EBM as "the conscientious, explicit and judicious use of current best evidence in making decisions about the care of individual patients"[27] may be an excellent motivational definition, but if we do not define "evidence" in context, as well as conscientious, explicit, judicious use, and *best* evidence, can the reader say in operational terms who is a practitioner of EBM and who is not, and ultimately, what is EBM and what is not? We doubt it.[28]

Elsewhere, for example, saying that "... our medicine *is about* ..." rather than *"is"* may be read by some as avoiding its definition itself.

In the new domain of knowledge translation, there are so many definitions of it that they merit an online regroupment.[29]

Definitions are a strategic resource for the arguer, ideally clear enough to avoid common fallacies of meaning[18] like vagueness, equivocation (same word having different meanings in the same argument), and others.[16]

Persuasive definitions are a form of slanting in which a definition is used to gain an argumentative advantage. They often alter the meaning of a term by associating it with a term of clear positive or negative connotation. They may or may not be based on evidence. ("That is what they call it and how they do it at 'the other' hospital!") Stipulative and operational definitions are better.

Definitions are the first determinants if what we understand and do is good, bad, or meaningless.

Framing means *in social sciences* and psychology the social construction of a social phenomenon by mass media or specific political or social movements and organizations.[30] It is considered as an inevitable process of selective influence over the individual's perception of the meanings attributed to words and phrases. Health activities, care and programs, and medical information (journals, books, spoken word) are and may be subject to framing. Rhetoric is used to encourage certain interpretations and discourage others. Defining, structuring, and interpreting medical research is a necessary subject of framing which allows, preferably in an unbiased way, the "frame" within which a research finding applies (setting, human context, applicability, etc.). It may be then good or bad.

In medicine, defining health problems in the context of target population (patients, community, etc.), prevailing or specific practices of clinical and community care, or social, political, economical, spiritual (faith) environments means building and specifying a "frame" within which our views of health problems and events are valid.

In epidemiology, expressing specificity of a causal association in terms of risk differences (absolute risk difference, attributable risk), etiological fractions (attributable risk percent, relative risk reduction), and ensuing interpretation of the importance of findings may depend on how the meaning of each measure is "framed": An absolute measure may be interpreted and considered more important for ensuing practical and research interpretations and decisions than its relative equivalent and vice versa.

Our *hypotheses* are propositions to be evaluated, accepted, or refuted in light of clinical experience with the case or problem or by a research study.

Questions for clinical or research problem solving[31–34] offer (in various combinations and completeness from case to case) specifications about the *population* under consideration (in the study and/or beyond the study), *intervention* (treatment, care), *condition* of interest (disease stage, spectrum, gradient, etc.), *controls* when comparisons are made for the sake of interpretations, *outcomes* (possible results), *setting* (specifics about the clinical care human and physical environment), and *time frame* (interval within the course of disease, period over which patients will be followed and studied, etc.).[31] Initially proposed for systematic reviews of evidence, these models apply equally to questions raised in original research studies and to questions in practice.

Meaningful practical and research questions include several of the above-mentioned considerations in the form of acronyms and anagrams like PICO (population, intervention, controls, outcomes) and PCICOST (population, condition of interest, intervention, control(s), outcome(s), setting, time frame) questions. We may ask the following:

1. *Is this antithrombotic treatment good for you? Ask your doctor!* This is a kind of question used in television advertising to reach the largest audience. Let us leave it there and not use it.
2. *Does antithrombotic treatment do well for patients?* The least specific and most general question. A PI question.
3. *In patients surviving myocardial infarction (P), does antithrombotic therapy (I) decrease the risk of myocardial reinfarction and death (O)?* A PICO question.
4. *In patients discharged from our hospital (P) after myocardial infarction (C), does antithrombotic therapy (I) in comparison to similar patients who do not receive it (C) improve survival and prevent reinfarction and stroke (O) when such a program is implemented in our hospital and regional clinics (S) over a period of 1, 5, and 10 years (T)?* A PCICOST question.

Components of research questions vary with the nature of the problem and clinical considerations and circumstances. The third question is the most "scientific," specifying as much as possible to what and to whom it applies. Let us also note that this more concrete kind of question is most often used for the study of cause–effect relationships. Questions about the validity of diagnostic tests, about disease occurrence (descriptive) studies, and elsewhere should contain all relevant components (PICO or more) in various combinations of the above.

Objectives are points to be reached in practical clinical problem solving or in research, either *specific* to the problem or *general*, encompassing a broader context into which the problem belongs. For example, we wish to evaluate the effectiveness of vein stenting (or "liberation") to alleviate symptoms of patients suffering from multiple sclerosis (a specific objective of a defined activity) and contribute this way to the control of the severity of cases of multiple sclerosis (a general objective for the problem of multiple sclerosis as a whole).

Thesis or theses are essential to build and evaluate the extent to which an argument is grounded in evidence, the setting and the reality of the problem. An argument may be formally valid per se, but not necessarily solid, meaningful, and evidence-grounded.

Essential building blocks already exist, but are somehow "hidden" in various medical articles and in clinical reasoning in medical practice as well. As might be expected, the thesis may be found in the Introduction, grounds in Material, Methods, and Results sections, backing and warrant in the Review of the literature and Discussion, rebuttals in Discussion as well, and the claim often appears in the Title itself and in the Conclusions of the article.[21-23] Table 2.3 represents an overview of Toulmin's original argument building blocks ("organs within a living system of argument," as he calls them) and indicates a possible location of these building blocks in medical argumentation.[20] Currently, there is no formal rule regarding where they should be found. In the literature, they are usually scattered in bits and pieces across the IMRAD (Introduction, Material and Methods, Results, and Discussion) medical article sections and worded in natural language. Statements in natural language, in italics in the following 10-item list (Table 2.2), are and should be supported by argument building blocks. In any dialogue or written message, consider stating, explaining, and supporting them.

Table 2.3 shows how argumentation is "hidden" in the natural language of communication between clinicians in daily life on hospital floors.

Table 2.2   Connectors and Indicators of Argument Building Blocks behind Natural Language

Argument Building Block Indicator	*Building Block to Which You Refer*
1. ... What's on our mind: ...	Refer briefly to your "Problem in context."
2. ... Given this reality of ...	Present your "Grounds" represented by the internal evidence; data; essence drawn from the study itself.
3. ... since as we see it ...	A "Warrant" reflects your overall view of the problem under study, your understanding of the problem based on external evidence (outside the study).
4. ... because what we know ...	It's your "Backing"—you have tackled it already in part in your literature review.

(Continued)

Table 2.2 Connectors and Indicators of Argument Building Blocks behind Natural Language (*Continued*)

Argument Building Block Indicator	Building Block to Which You Refer
5. … once pros and cons are balanced …	Adducts, qualifier modulators; they are determinants of your qualified claim. You express here the degree of certainty (and uncertainty) in your claim (findings of the study).
6. … unless this occurs …	"Rebuttals": These are your reservations and the exclusionary conditions under which the conclusions of your study do not apply. For example, therapeutic contraindications may be set into this category.
7. … speaking in favor of …	You may emphasize again briefly "Support" for your findings like selected elements from grounds, and so on.
8. … speaking against …	You balance your pros and cons in terms of "Attenuators": Elements from grounds and backing, in light of the warrant, that weaken the certainty about the claim.
9. … to this degree, therefore …	In terms of your "Qualifier," your certainty about your claim, your conclusion.
10. … we stand for this.	These are the conclusions of your study and article, your "Claim": Proposition reached, impression of cause-effect link, effectiveness of intervention, entity definition, disease magnitude, nature of the problem, decision, recommended action.

Toulmin's argumentation is so attractive and appropriate in medicine because it follows a line of thought similar to the scientific method and reasoning in medical practice and research. As we will also see in forthcoming chapters, Toulmin's model of argumentation backed by the best specific and general evidence available applies not only to clinical and community medicine research, but also to various ways of reasoning and its communication, be it dialogs between colleagues, progress notes in patients' charts, discussing cases on morning reports, morbidity and mortality review meetings, consults or discharge notes. Let us keep it in mind.

Table 2.3 Daily Communication of an Argumentative Nature between Clinicians in Natural Language in a Hospital Setting

Question	Statement	Component of the Argument
Attending: "I was told that you had a busy morning here. Any new admissions at our floor?"	**Resident:** "Yes, we **admitted an elderly lady with chest pain.**"	**Original idea, problem in context:** Setting of the problem to be solved.
Attending: "What led you to admit her?"	**Resident:** "Well, the senior resident told me to do so! But more seriously, this patient was transferred to us from the emergency room with a **working diagnosis of myocardial infarction.**"	**Claim:** Proposition resulting from our reasoning.
Attending: "What brought you to this diagnosis and treatment and care orders?"	**Resident:** "In the past, this patient had some **unchecked chest pains,** but this time, her **pain radiated** to both arms, she had **low systolic blood pressure,** and we heard a **third heart sound** on auscultation. On the ECG, we saw a **new ST segment elevation, a new Q wave and a new conduction defect.**"	**Grounds:** Basis from which we reason and argue. Facts supporting the claim.
Resident: "I would like to know if there are any steps that I must follow in future similar cases."	**Attending:** "In such and similar cases of myocardial infarction, especially if confirmed by ECG, MRI, serum cardiac enzymes, we give aspirin and clopidogrel, start thrombolytic treatment and consider coronary angiography and stenting."	**Warrant:** General rule that permits us to infer a claim from grounds.

(Continued)

Table 2.3   Daily Communication of an Argumentative Nature between Clinicians in Natural Language in a Hospital Setting (*Continued*)

Question	Statement	Component of the Argument
Resident: "*How sure are we that this kind of treatment and care will work?*"	**Attending:** "*All our **past experience** in this hospital, and **several critically reviewed studies** and their **systematic reviews of outcomes** in patients treated this way make us sure, if not almost certain, that this kind of care works and it should in this patient.*"	***Backing:*** Body of experience and evidence which supports the warrant, and
		Qualifier: A word or phrase that indicates the strength conferred by the warrant and thus the strength of support for our conclusion.
Resident: "*Are there any additional or alternative problems and treatments which we should keep in mind?*"	**Attending:** "***Chest pain as originally seen in this patient may occur and be confounded with*** manifestations of pericarditis, pulmonary embolism, esophageal perforation, aortic dissection among several other problems to exclude. ***These other problems should be ruled out.***"	***Rebuttals:*** Differential diagnosis to consider as a possible exclusionary condition and criterion for other management of this kind of patient.
Resident: "*So, if we successfully rule out all those other problems, does it look like we did the right thing?*"	**Attending:** "*You definitely did! Yes, **this is a case of myocardial infarction which required the clinical management** you proposed and ordered.*"	***Conclusion of the argument. Claim:*** Proposition at which we arrive as a result of our reasoning and which we defend in the argument by citing all supporting elements and argument building blocks.

2.1.4 Reminder Regarding Some Additional and Fundamental Considerations

Is our correct reasoning and argumentation important to maintain and improve the quality of care, patient safety and understanding, prevention and control of medical error and harm? Yes, it is.

To understand this even better, let us start with a practical example: An internist examines a patient suffering from coronary heart disease. He or she is faced with the dilemma of pursuing the conservative (medical) treatment of coronary pathology and dysfunction or to refer the patient to invasive cardiologists for angioplasty or to surgeons for coronary bypass surgery. Where might errors occur and how should they be prevented?

In the example above, at a later date, a catheter for angioplasty malfunctions, the patient does not need angioplasty after all, and the patient's prognosis worsens: Why is this the case?

Two visions of the cognitive and decision making processes must be retained, namely that of an argument and argumentation process based on evidences and that of a step-by-step review of our diagnostic, therapeutic, or prognostic processes both for short- and long-term care:

1. A decision such as "this patient must be transferred to surgery" can be considered a conclusion or claim (as philosophers use to say) of the **argumentation process** using evidence of all kinds. Errors may occur not only due to the uses of poor evidence or failures to use good evidence from one step of argumentation to another, but also due to the linking together of various components on the way to conclusions and recommendations. The argumentation process and model applies practically at all steps and stages of clinical practice and health and community care.
2. The additional, more specific *cognition pathways in various clinical practices and components of care* from their original triggers to their final understanding and ensuing decisions to be considered must be recognized in the development of any necessary steps in risk assessment (as we will see in greater detail in Chapter 3), diagnostic process, treatment plan work-up, or prognosis with its ensuing short- and long-term actions in care. Errors in any of these steps may cause numerous incidents and their consequences.

Correct or incorrect argumentation, reasoning, critical thinking, and decision making underlie such processes.

We do not always realize that modern argumentation and argument are behind most of our evidence and critical thinking–based, clinical epidemiology grounded reasoning and decision making. Flawed argumentation and reasoning are sites and generators of error and harm. Correct argumentation and human error and harm analysis from a logical perspective contribute to the quality of medical care and patient safety.

A step-by-step evaluation of both argumentation and cognition processes must contribute to improvements in the medical error domain. And they do. These processes are used at each of the following steps in medical care: A step-by-step evaluation of both argumentation and cognition processes must contribute to improvements in the medical error domain. And they do.

These processes are used at each of the following steps in medical care:

- **Evidence build-up**, structured or unstructured (history, literature, physical and paraclinical examination, past experience)

  ↓

- **Reasoning** about the case, problem or situation, structured acquisition of **new knowledge** (differential diagnosis, final diagnosis, comorbidity assessment)

  ↓

- **Decision making** (medical, surgical, psychiatric, and other orders and plans for care)

  ↓

- **Sensorimotor execution of medical acts** (operation, invasive diagnostic procedures, physiotherapy, parenteral applications of drugs, new technologies devises implantation, etc.)

  ↓

- **Getting results** (positive and adverse)

  ↓

- **Evaluation** (of all the preceding steps, one-by-one and the entire process; successes, errors, failures)

  ↓

- **Prognosis and further risk assessment** (morbidity, comorbidity, further outcomes)

  ↓

- **Follow-up, surveillance, forecasting** (risk factors and markers, prognostic factors and markers, possible outcomes, errors and failures).

In **lathology** (the study and management of error and harm in medicine and other health sciences),[12] knowing, understanding, and avoiding fallacies, biases, and cognitive errors eliminate some potential sources of harm as a result of our reasoning and decision making. An exhaustive list of biases as flaws in research is well beyond the scope of this text and it must be sought in the above quoted literature and paired with more general lists of cognitive biases found elsewhere.[12]

2.2 Challenges of Causal Reasoning within the General Context of Medical Thinking and Reasoning

Usually, we have several questions about the health problems we encounter:

■ *What have we seen?* Diagnosis and counting cases help.
■ *How often do they occur?* Case series are the first source of information.
■ *What is their overall burden?* Prevalence rates reflect this.
■ *How fast and how much do they spread?* Incidence rates must be established.
■ *How serious are they?* Disease spectrum and gradient, mortality, and case fatality measure the gravity of the situation.
■ *What do they explain? What are their causes?* Causal reasoning based on comparisons of various sets of observations are essential to answer such questions.
■ *What are the causes of improvement or deterioration in health and disease if we do something about it?* Treatment in clinical trials or health programs in community medicine are analyzed as possible causes of improvement in patient and community health.

To establish and demonstrate the relationship of cause and effect between two or more variables in medicine remains a Rosetta Stone challenge and a subject for further interpretations, methodological developments, and improvements by both philosophers[35] and health professionals.[36–38] Philosophers like John Stuart Mill or biostatisticians like Sir Austin Bradford Hill and many others contributed to our view of causality in medicine today. Their contribution is reviewed elsewhere.[15,36–39]

Within the general framework of reasoning, as explained in Section 2.1, perhaps the most important problem-related reasoning focuses on the relationship between causes and consequences. What causes coronary heart disease? What are the consequences of cocaine abuse? Do daily low doses of aspirin prevent coronary heart disease? Does psychiatric support prevent suicide in patient with suicide ideations?

Hence, causal relationships apply both of the following:

■ Noxious causes → disease occurrence and/or course
■ Beneficial factors (drug, vaccine, surgery, psychiatric care) → prevention of disease and/or improvement of its severity, course, and outcomes

Ultimately, does a morphological and/or physiological anomaly produce a positive result for a diagnostic test, method, or technique? (N.B. Their evaluation occurs through other methods and criteria to answer practical and operational questions beyond causality as we will see when discussing diagnosis as a step in clinical care.)

Causal reasoning serves as a confirmation or a refutation of our impression that one phenomenon produces another.

2.2.1 Causal Reasoning in a Quantitative and Qualitative Way

Causal reasoning is a mental process whose objective is to establish on the basis of available data and information whether some phenomenon (a) under study causes leads to or produces another phenomenon (b) as a consequence of the former. In medicine, as already mentioned above, a *causal relationship* may be between a noxious factor and the deterioration of health (smoking causes cancer) or a beneficial factor and the improvement of health (drug treatment cures an infection, surgery alleviates coronary heart disease, psychotherapy improves an affective disorder).

For pragmatic reasons, we can make a distinction between *risk factors*, that is, causally related characteristics that can be modified (such as changing unhealthy dietary habits to control overweight) and *risk markers* that cannot be modified in their possible causal relationship such as age or gender. (N.B. Similar distinctions may be made between **prognostic factors** and **prognostic markers** as possible causes of disease and treatment outcomes.)

The process of causal reasoning is triggered by some *hypothesis about a cause–effect relationship*: A proposal to be accepted or rejected by ad hoc research. Three types of research are also related to hypothesis generation and testing:

More traditionally, medical research is a *quantitative research*: A study of multiple cases brought together provides an idea about a common problem and the question that they represent. Cases are counted, measured, and otherwise quantified and analyzed on the basis of numerical information. Hypotheses and findings are confirmed or rejected this way.

More recently, *qualitative research*[40–42] is increasingly strong methodologically, focused and applied beyond social sciences to medicine, nursing, and other health sciences.[43–46] It is based often on the study of single cases or single specific "cases" as situations or settings. Its emphasis on "in-depth understanding" generates hypotheses. It does not confirm them the way quantitative research does. Qualitative research seeks out the "why," not the "how" on the basis of more or less structured information; a better insight of the problem is in focus and it may and should generate new hypotheses studied later by quantitative methods of ad hoc further generated data.

Developed even more recently, *mixed methods research* combines and uses both quantitative and qualitative approaches.[47–50] Creswell summarized them well.[47,49] Their uses in medicine may expand rapidly.[50]

There are several models and ways to demonstrate a cause–effect relationship.

2.2.1.1 How We Look at Causes: Single or Multiple Sets, Chains, Webs, Concept Maps

There are at least five main approaches to looking at causes in medicine because health phenomena may have one or more causes and consequences, interrelated or not:

1. Looking at health problems and their causes often starts with the idea of a *single cause–single consequence relationship*:

   - Driving while impaired → Traffic accident and injury
   - Smoking → Lung cancer

   However, a traffic injury may be caused not only by drinking, but also by fatigue, stress, drug abuse, the driver's poorly controlled chronic or acute morbidity, experience, road and vehicle condition, and other factors.

   We are aware today that smoking is not the only cause of bronchogenic carcinoma: passive smoking, miners' exposure to radon gas, asbestos, metals like arsenic, chromium, nickel, or iron oxide, other industrial and environmental carcinogens, familial predisposition, predisposing diseases like pulmonary fibrosis, chronic obstructive lung disease, or sarcoidosis must also be taken into consideration as potentially causal or contributing agents.

2. In medicine, multiple causes as *sets of causes* are often at the origin of a health problem. Multiple consequences as *sets of consequences* may follow the action of the same beneficial factor. We will call them "sets" rather than "webs" as originally illustrated.[39] The real webs are explained in approach 4 below. (N.B. Sets and webs require different biostatistical and other methods and techniques of analysis like path analysis[51] and various multivariate independent variables and multivariable dependent variables techniques and analyses.)[52] Friedman offers a good introduction to them in the context of epidemiology.[53] Figure 2.8 illustrates this concept and paradigm applied to a set of causes of medical error and harm and a set of consequences of alcohol abuse.

There are numerous possible sets of causes of medical error and harm including combinations and even interactions, varying case by

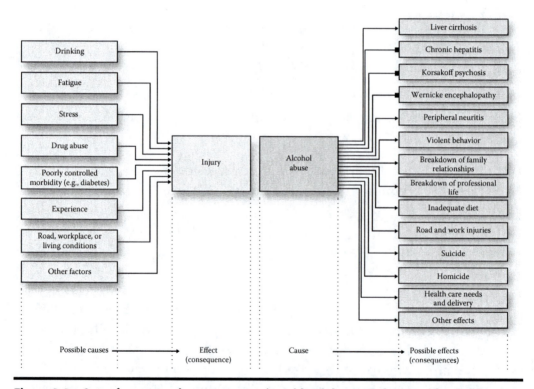

Figure 2.8   Sets of causes and consequences in epidemiology. (Redrawn with modifications from Jenicek, M., *Epidemiology. The Logic of Modern Medicine*, EPIMED International, Montréal, 1995; Jenicek, M., *Foundations of Evidence-Based Medicine*, The Parthenon Publishing Group/CRC Press, Boca Raton/London/New York/Washington, 2003.)

case, not only of the professional competencies of the healthcare providers (knowledge, attitudes, skills), but also of the dispositional states of all health professionals involved (outlook, mood, inclinations, ethics), their psychological and physiological condition (stress, fatigue), patient specifics, dispositional and interactive states (clinical, participation, communication), logistic failures (communication, information, management), professional setting (physical environment, tools, agents and technologies used), rules (protocols, guidelines to follow), critical thinking failures (argumentation, conditionals, rebuttals, lateral thinking, conditions sine qua non), logistic failures (ensuing decisions made and not made, their execution and evaluation) good or bad. Alcohol abuse leads to a set of consequences such as several medical, surgical, neurological, and psychiatric problems, violent behavior, breakdown of family and professional relationships, road and work injuries, suicide, and homicide.

In other situations, hereditary predisposition, physical inactivity, diabetes, high blood pressure, diet, stress, and other factors are an example of a set of causes of heart disease.

Aspirin produces multiple beneficial effects leading to the control of fever, having an analgesic effect, being a mild anticoagulant preventing coronary heart disease and perhaps still other unknown effects representing a set of consequences.

3. *Chains of causes or consequences* may apply to other cases. Figure 2.9 presents an example of a chain of causes.

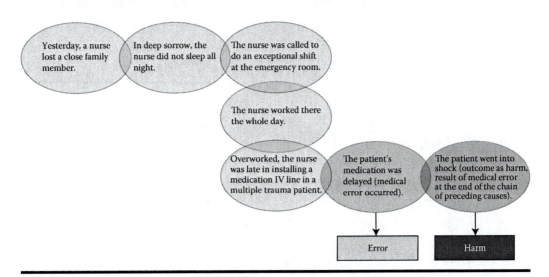

Figure 2.9   Chain of causes. A hospital setting example.

4. *Causes* and consequences may be also seen, studied, and understood as *webs*. Given possible multidirectional, causal, and other relationships between multiple causes and consequences, *webs of causes* and *webs of consequences* are studied not only for better understanding of cause → effect relationships, but also to find the best ways to intervene. Figure 2.10 represents the modified Friedman's web of causes of myocardial infarction.[53]

5. For a better understanding of the problems, for both learning and teaching and research purposes, *concept maps* are developed and used. Originally, they were developed mostly for the nonmedical world.[54] Causal factors are part of them, but in an even broader concept that visualizes overall thinking about a health problem, its components, and interactions between them. Webs of causes and consequences, views about the underlying biological, pathological, and other mechanisms underlying health problems and clinical considerations (diagnostic, therapeutic, prognostic, and others), decisions and actions about them may be part of the concept maps. The resulting picture, therefore, goes well beyond any kind of cause–effect relationship only. Figure 2.11 is a good example of a concept map. Causal factors are highlighted as parts of this wider health problem context.

    N.B. Usually, concept maps are developed and presented in sequence, ramification, and direction from top to bottom. Arrows indicate such a sequence and direction. How can this figure be read and understood? In this presentation, we propose a sequence, ramification, and direction from left to right. Arrows indicating cause–effect relationships show the direction from cause to effect rather than the direction of the development and reading of the concept map. The sequence and direction are preserved in the spatial distribution of the concept map elements from left to right.

    In this example, we can identify several areas and paths indicated by their *connectors*.

    For example, epidemiologically speaking,

- By "can be," "caused by," "causes," "due to," we may follow a chain or web of causes and their consequences developing into a cause of the next or another consequence.
- By "as in" or "type of," we may consider location, body systemic site, and some aspects of diagnosis.
- "Can result in" indicates outcomes or consequences.
- "Requires," "prevention of," "treated with," "prevented by" suggests interventions at various levels of prevention (primary or secondary in this case).

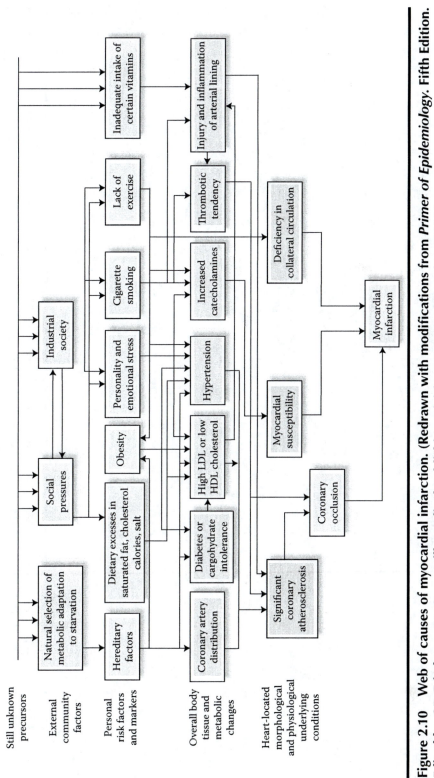

Figure 2.10 Web of causes of myocardial infarction. (Redrawn with modifications from *Primer of Epidemiology.* **Fifth Edition. Edited by GD Friedman. McGraw-Hill, Medical Publishing Division, New York/London, 2004.)**

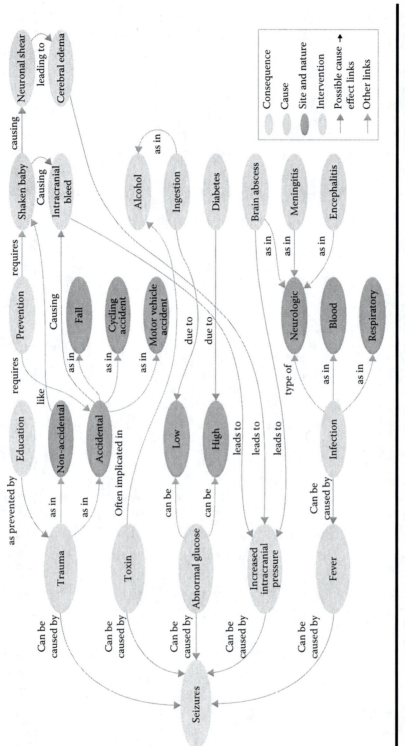

Figure 2.11 A concept map of understanding and management of seizures used in a clinical learning process. (Redrawn with modifications from West, D. C. et al., *JAMA*, 284(9):1105–10, 2000.)

In this light, the upper and central portion of the concept map covers a good part of cause–effect relationships. Peripheral areas reflect more sites, mechanisms, interventions, and outcomes.

Visually, concept maps might be confused with webs of causes or consequences maps by uninitiated persons. However, as we can see, concept maps go well beyond a simple cause–effect path or web. Concept maps are now finding development and uses in teaching clinical medicine[56,57] in various clinical specialties, in community medicine (disease prevention),[58,59] and elsewhere in health sciences and other domains.[60–62]

6. *Additive* effect and *potentiation* of effect.

A particular challenge in the study of multiple etiological factors in their webs or sets is their possible additive effect or an effect of potentiation in a synergy of their action. An **additive effect** occurs when the combined effect of multiple factors is a sum of their isolated effects. **Potentiation of effect** occurs when the combined effect of multiple causal factors is more than the sum of the effects of each. Clinical pharmacologists know perhaps more than other specialists about the study and the effect of this phenomenon in the domain of disease treatment by multiple drugs and their effects.

Our views of causality are important well beyond the scientific search for causality. In daily practice, they affect our anamnestic inquiry, review of systems, methods and extent of treatment, outcomes assessment and follow up, and extension of care.

2.2.1.2 Ways of Searching for Causes

In epidemiology, the search for causes may now be carried out in two ways.[15,39] **Inductive research** means using existing information and data (whatever the purpose of their collection might be) to generate and/or confirm a hypothesis. In another words, a hypothesis is generated by preestablished facts, data, and information. Sometimes, the derogatory expression "milking and dredging" of the data is used as qualification of this, often only available approach.

Inductive research can often lead to what philosophers call **inductive reasoning:** premises bring only *some degree of support* to conclusions (findings from the study).

Deductive research works in an opposite direction: A general principle or hypothesis is used as a starting point for data collection, analysis, and interpretation in order to confirm or refute this principle. The hypothesis is formulated first on the basis of past experience, independent of the planned research. The study (data collection, analysis, and interpretation) is planned to confirm or refute the hypothesis.

Deductive research should lead more often (at least theoretically) to **deductive reasoning** in which a conclusion (findings) is *definitely true if premises are true*. A study as a deductive argument provides (at least theoretically) the *absolute support* for study findings (conclusions). The study as a logical argument is deductively valid.

Some aspects of argumentation, reasoning, or scientific method in general are also considered by many as **inference in general:** The process of logical reasoning combines observed phenomena with accepted truths or axioms in order to formulate generalizable statements.[63] *Statistical inference* applies such a process to series of observations and calculates degrees of uncertainty in comparisons of various data sets. *Causal inference* is the thought process and methods that assess or test whether a relation of cause to effect does or does not exist.[64]

In medicine, we infer in two directions:

1. Either from observing individuals individually and applying experience from these observations to the whole problem that those individuals represent. "Classical" or field epidemiologists often do so looking at the characteristics of patients one by one to establish the clinical picture of disease they represent or studying disease outbreaks or cancer occurrence in the community.
2. Or as in clinical medicine, the "clinical epidemiology way," solving individual patients' problems individually by inferring (seeing how they fit) from what we already know about groups of similar patients, medical care, and the disease they represent.

Figure 2.12 illustrates these two strategies and ways of reasoning. Both are necessary for good understanding and decision making.

2.2.1.3 Criteria of Causality

The still-evolving criteria of causality in health sciences are largely based on those of the British philosopher, John Stuart Mill, expanded and adapted for health sciences much later by Sir Austin Bradford Hill,[65] and applied for example to smoking and health by the U.S. Surgeon General's Advisory Committee on Smoking and Health.[66] Their chronological journey was reviewed by Evans.[67]

As Table 2.4 shows, there are multiple criteria of causation to be discussed and confirmed from one case to another. Most of them are subjects of reflection, others are subjects of calculation, quantification, and interpretation.

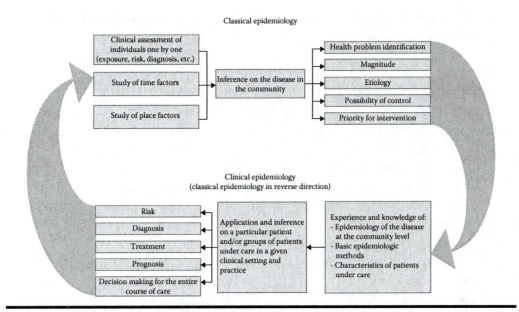

Figure 2.12 Directions of reasoning in fundamental and clinical epidemiology. (Redrawn with modifications from Jenicek, M., *Foundations of Evidence-Based Medicine,* **The Parthenon Publishing Group/CRC Press, Boca Raton/London/ New York/Washington, 2003; Jenicek, M.,** *Epidemiology. The Logic of Modern Medicine* **EPIMED International, Montréal, 1995.)**

Table 2.4 Fundamental Prerequisites and Assessment Criteria of the Cause–Effect Relationship

Individual cause–effect criteria under scrutiny
Assumptions or prerequisites (what should be confirmed before any causal criteria apply)
Possible roles in argumentation: grounds, rebuttals.
<ul><li>Exclusion of *randomness*</li><li>Consistency of results with *prediction* (conditional)</li><li>Even observational studies respect as much as possible the same logic and similar precautions as used in *experimental research*</li><li>Studies are based on *clinimetrically valid data*</li><li>Data are subject to *unbiased observations, comparisons, and analysis*</li><li>*Uncontrollable and uninterpretable factors* are ideally absent from the study</li></ul>
Criteria of causation (for a study already performed)
Possible roles in argumentation: Backing, warrant, claim.
Argumentation for causality is based on the high quality evidence-backed building blocks of an argument and a proper connection between them.

(Continued)

Table 2.4   Fundamental Prerequisites and Assessment Criteria of the Cause–Effect Relationship (*Continued*)

Major (to be evaluated individually)

- *Temporality* ("cart behind the horse")
- *Strength* (relative risk, odds ratio, hazard ratio)
- *Specificity* (exclusivity or predominance of an observation and its effect)
  - *Manifestational* ("unique" pattern of clinical spectrum and gradient as a presumed consequence of exposure)
  - *Causal* (etiological fraction, preventable fraction, protective or curative effect, attributable risk, risk difference, attributable risk percent, attributable hazard, proportional hazard)
- *Biological gradient* (more exposure = stronger association)
- *Consistency* (assessment of homogeneity of findings across studies, settings, time, place, and people)
- *Biological plausibility* (explanation of underlying mechanisms or nature of association)

Conditional (not always necessary for new discoveries)

- *Coherence with prevalent knowledge*
- *Analogy*

Reference (within the framework of the scientific method)

- *Experimental proof* (preventability, curability): Clinical trials, other kinds of controlled experiments, or "cessation studies"
- *Confirmation* (providing a clear problem definition, research question, relevant dependent and independent variables, and target population)
- *Systematic review* and *meta-analysis* of evidence

Criteria for the causal reasoning process and demonstration of causality as a whole:

Interpretation of the brought up causal proof

Possible role in argumentation: Conclusions, claim stemming for an argument, claim, rebuttals

1. A single criterion is not used as a sole proof of causality

2. Each and every criterion of causality was a subject of evaluation and interpretation by a fallacy-free confirmation or refutation

3. Completeness and validity of the criteria fulfilled were assessed

---

Source: Modified and redrawn from Jenicek, M., *Epidemiology. The Logic of Modern Medicine*, EPIMED International, Montréal, 1995; Jenicek, M., *Foundations of Evidence-Based Medicine*, The Parthenon Publishing Group/CRC Press, Boca Raton/London/New York/Washington, 2003.

Case by case, and in a selective manner, all such considerations and criteria as indicated may be used in various building blocks of an argument.

From such a list of criteria, causation may be evaluated by listing their applicability individually, as was done in the historical example of the Surgeon General's evaluation of smoking and health[66]:

Criteria of Causality	Surgeon General's Report on Smoking and Health (Especially Lung Cancer)[65,66]
Temporality	Yes
Strength	Yes
Specificity	
Manifestational	Poorly known
Causal	Yes
Biological gradient	Yes
Consistency	Yes
Biological plausibility	Yes
Coherence with prevalent knowledge	To be followed
Analogy	Hard to assess
Experimental proof	Yes

Other similar evaluations were done in an increasing number of domains including social support and various aspects of health[68] and medicine as well.[69]

Hence from all these causal criteria and considerations, especially strength, specificity of a cause–effect relationship and biological gradient are subject to quantification. For this purpose, disease frequency is used in absolute and relative terms.

2.2.1.4 Disease or Event Frequencies and Fractions in Causal Reasoning

To see and compare, we need number of events (disease, exposure to causal factors, their results): either *absolute numbers* (*frequencies*) or **fractions (relative frequencies)** such as rates, ratios, or odds. An idea of causality requires comparisons of events (disease cases, exposure to noxious factors, being treated by drugs, having surgery, having complications, suffering from adverse effects of treatment and care, etc.) in various groups of individuals.

Events are presented and studied in two forms: frequencies or fractions.

Frequencies are simple numbers of events happening. Example: 250 cases of chronic obstructive pulmonary disease (COPD) exist in our community. It is a total of events as they were observed. *Frequencies* such as 1000 cases of cancer or their *rates* (1,000 cases per 100,000 subjects in the community; i.e., a rate of 1/100 or 10/1,000, etc.) represent *absolute values* of what we observed, usually a total of events as they were observed in a given category, set, or group.

Fractions are two related frequencies as expressions of relationship between them. Frequencies of events are numerators presented as parts of some whole. The whole is presented as the denominator. Example: 25 cases of COPD occur in a community of 35,000 inhabitants (25 diseased + 34,775 nondiseased). In epidemiology, they are usually presented as *rates* or *ratios*. *Fractions* are expressions of the relationship between two entities. In our case, these expressions are most often rates (proportions) or ratios.

Rates are couplings of a set of observations in the numerator like disease cases (a) with a set in the denominator including those same observations (a) and some additional ones such as noncases (b) such as two sets creating a community: $a/a + b$. A rate in our example is then $25/(25 + 34,775)$. It can be presented as such or multiplied by some coefficient like 100,000 for comparability: $25/35,000 \times 100,000$, that is, $7142.85/100,000$. For less frequent phenomena like cancer, rates per 100,000 may be presented. For frequent phenomena like diarrhea cases during a food born disease outbreak per 100, adverse drug effects may be reported per 1,000,000, and so on. As in our COPD case, rates may also be presented as a percentage (07.14%) or as decimal fractions (0,00714) for various computational purposes.

Ratios are relationships between different entities in the numerator (a) and the denominator (b): a/b. In our case: 25/34,775. The entity in the numerator is not reproduced in the denominator. For example, comparing rates of events (incidence of events in one community) to other rates of events (incidence of events in another community) yields *ratios* such as cancer incidence rate in smokers/cancer incidence rate in nonsmokers (risk ratio in this case). **Odds** (cross product ratio, relative odds) are ratios of the probability of occurrence of an event to that of nonoccurrence of that same event in another set of observations. In other words, it is the ratio of the probability that something is one way to the probability that it is other way.[64] *Odds*, in fact, are fractions having an event in the nominator and nonevents in the denominator: There are 100 cases of cancer and 900 healthy subjects in a community of 1,000. Odds of having cancer are 100/900. Odds in one group of subjects/odds in another group yield an **odds ratio.**

Ratios and odds give us an idea about *relative values* of what we see and compare.

Odds ratio (syn. cross-product ratio, relative odds) is the ratio of two odds.[64]

Likelihood means the general state of being likely or probable that an event has already occurred would yield a specific outcome. Formally, it differs from *probability*, which refers to the occurrence of future events.

Statistically speaking, a **likelihood ratio** is the ratio of the values of the likelihood function at two different parameter values or under two different data models.[64] In the domain of diagnostic methods and tests evaluation, it is the probability that a given test result would occur in a person with the target disorder divided by the probability that the same result would occur in a person without that disorder.[64]

Figure 2.13 represents a basic model of comparison of two groups of events from which an event frequency is derived. It serves with other considerations to assess causality, what it represents, and to what it applies (target population or patients as individuals). A subset (sample) of individuals representing a larger (target) population to which the results of the study should apply and be representative of is selected. Groups exposed and nonexposed to the event (noxious factor, treatment, or other beneficial intervention) are formed. They are compared for their "initial state" or state before the event of interest. Then, the "intervention," "event," "maneuvre," "exposures" as they are called across the literature are compared to their alternatives: nonevent, alternative event. Additional events (like co-morbidity or co-treatments) may be considered. "Subsequent states," event outcomes, in groups are then compared for their differences and distinctions. Causality and the role of the actions under study are clarified. Findings are then evaluated based on what they actually apply to: The original target population, individuals beyond the original target population (further generalizations), particular and specific patients or individuals in the community, and so on.

To study and explain the cases, we need *disease frequency*, a total of events as they were observed, and its expression in *fractions* explaining relationships between two entities (series of observations). Fractions appear in two forms, either as *rates* (disease or event frequency in the numerator, population in which they occur, cases and noncases, events and nonevents included in the denominator) or *ratios* (events in the numerator, nonevents or other events in the denominator).

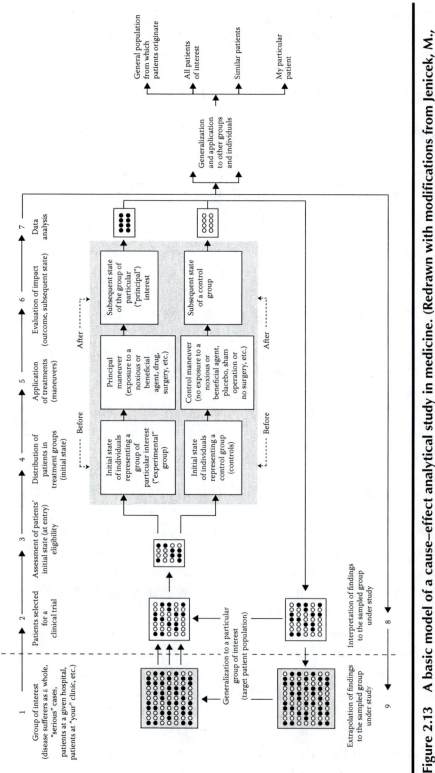

Figure 2.13 A basic model of a cause–effect analytical study in medicine. (Redrawn with modifications from Jenicek, M., *Epidemiology. The Logic of Modern Medicine*, EPIMED International, Montréal, 1995; Jenicek, M., *Foundations of Evidence-Based Medicine*, The Parthenon Publishing Group/CRC Press, Boca Raton/London/New York/Washington, 2003; Jenicek, M., *Medical Error and Harm. Understanding, Prevention, and Control*, CRC Press/Taylor & Francis/Productivity Press, Boca Raton/London/New York, 2011.)

Disease and exposure frequencies as well as studies of beneficial effects of care (outcomes) such as improvement or cure are obtained either from *cohort studies* (follow ups of disease occurrence in time in exposed and unexposed groups) or *case–control studies* in which the exposure is compared in cases and noncases of the health event of interest.

Here is an oversimplified example of noxious factors and following cases of disease events studied both by cohort and case control studies. This example should help us understand how disease cases, death, or favorable or unfavorable outcomes and exposures to various beneficial or noxious factors frequencies and their comparisons are applied to various uses and interpretations.

Cohort (longitudinal) study				Case control (transversal) study		
	New cases	Non-cases	Total		Cases	Non-cases
Exposed	A (80)	B (99,920)	100,000	Exposed	a (80)	b (50)
Nonexposed	C (20)	D (99,980)	100,000	Nonexposed	c (20)	d (50)
				Total	100	100

Frequencies of disease, death, or change in health status are numerous. Morbidity (disease prevalence and incidence), mortality, case fatality, and their relationships in the form of rates, ratios, or odds are the most important ones. Figure 2.14 represents a simplified example of some such

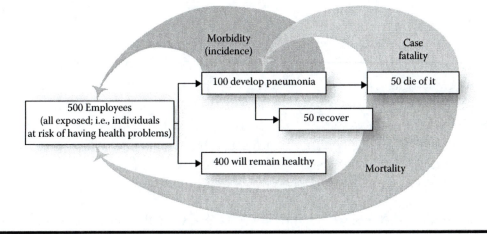

Figure 2.14 Morbidity, mortality, and case fatality in a health event. Periods of exposure and event occurrence are defined.

frequencies. It describes the situation in a group of workers exposed over a period of time to an industrial carcinogenic substance from which some workers develop cancer and some die. Quantification in this example is self-explanatory.

Morbidity rates are rates of disease cases in a community defined in time and space. The two most important are as follows:

1. *Prevalence rates*, disease frequency (cases, spells, manifestations, individuals treated, etc.) at a given point in time (point prevalence) or over a period of time (period prevalence), independent of the moment of its occurrence as it appears in a population of interest (cases and noncases confounded) give us an idea of the *overall magnitude* of the health problem either at a given moment or over a defined period of time. Very often, chronic disease, handicaps, and other health problems of long duration are in focus.
2. In *incidence rates*, frequencies of *new* cases of disease or another event in a defined period of time (hours, days, years) are related to a population in which they occur (preferably subjects susceptible to get it). In our case, $A/A+B$ and $C/C+D$. From one period of time to another, the speed of disease spread can be measured. New cases, incidence spells, incidence of various manifestations, or incidence of newly diagnosed cases may be of interest from one problem to another. Infectious disease, injury, cancer, or cardiovascular diseases are often followed this way.

Deaths in communities or any other group of interest are studied through mortality and case fatality rates:

■ *Mortality rates* are rates of death in such a community for *all individuals,* healthy, diseased, or suffering from other health problems confounded (in the denominator of a rate). They may encompass general mortality rates or specific rates, which may be specific to disease, age, sex, and other demographic or social-specific elements.
■ *Case fatality rates* are deaths occurring in a given number of cases of disease toward a given moment (cumulative events) or over a certain period of time. They are therefore an occurrence of deaths by a disease between *cases only (those who suffer from it already).*

Rates reflect the *absolute* magnitude of a given health problem. To get an idea of the *relative* magnitude, we need health event ratios, event odds, and other ways to compare rates, risks, or deaths. The most important ones for medical understanding and decision making are relative risks, attributable risks, and etiological fractions (attributable risk percent).

In analytical studies, *ratios*, as already mentioned above, are fractions relating two entities (two different health events or their related characteristics) in which the entity in the numerator is not reproduced (with something else added) in the denominator. *Odds* (cross product ratios, relative odds) are ratios of the probability of occurrence of an event to that of nonoccurrence, or the ratio of the probability that something is one way to the probability than it is another way: In our case of a case control study, ad/cb.

Relative risk (relative benefit increase or reduction) is a fraction relating incidence of events in one group of subjects, such as those exposed to some factor, to another group or groups nonexposed to it. Relative risks are quantifications of the *strength of the causal relationship*. In the case of a study of noxious factors, the higher the relative risk, the stronger the causal association. If the relative risk of a presumably noxious factor is lower than 1.0, the factor (agent) has a protective effect, not a noxious one. Cohort studies (observations of new events over a certain period of time) of groups (cohorts) to be compared serve this purpose.

In our example:

$$\frac{80/100,000}{20/100,000} = 4.0$$

Hence, relative risk may be called also a ratio of rates or rate ratio.

Odds ratios most often exposures/non-exposure frequencies in cases to exposures/non-exposures frequencies in non-cases are another kind of estimation of the *strength of a causal association* derived from case–control studies.

In our example:

$$\frac{a/d}{b/c} = \frac{80 \times 50}{20 \times 50} = \frac{4,000}{1,000} = 4.0$$

N.B. If case–control studies are based on incident cases and if the proportion of subjects exposed is similar as in the cohort study, both cohort and case–control studies yield comparable estimations of the strength of causal association.

Attributable risk (risk difference, absolute risk reduction) is the difference between the rate of events in a group of interest (exposed to a noxious or beneficial factor) and the rate of events in a nonexposed group. The rationale behind an attributable risk is that in the case of a multifactorial cause (web of causes) of the disease or health event shared both by the exposed or nonexposed group, the difference is due to the factor in question, the rest of the web of causes, and their consequences being the same for both groups compared. In our cohort study: $80/100,000 - 20/100,000 = 60/100,000$.

For example, in searching for cause(s) of a foodborne infectious disease, we want to detect the most probable contaminated dish from among many, eaten in various combinations, by a group of people. By establishing an attributable risk (risk difference) for each meal as consumed or not (attack rate of disease in this dish's eaters compared to such an attack rate in non-eaters), we may consider as the most probable vehicle of infection the dish showing the greatest attributable risk among them all. Specificity of causal association from one meal to another is shown by the biggest risk difference; relative risks show its strength and etiological fractions (see below) show the role and predominance of each dish in a given web of causes (all dishes under consideration as potential sources/causes of infection in the entire study).[15,39] Nosocomial (hospital) infections or other outbreaks of events with underlying sets or webs of causes may also be analyzed this way.

Etiological fraction (attributable benefit fraction) is a proportion of events in exposed subjects, which is due to the factor of interest from the web of causes of the health problem under study. It is estimated either from the proportion of the attributable risk from the total of the risk in the exposed group (in the cohort or longitudinal studies) yielding an *attributable risk percent* or as an odds ratio minus one (in case–control studies), *attributable odds*. These computations provide some insight into the *specificity of one causal factor* and its prevalent role in the web of causes. We presume that other causes form the web of causes are similarly present and manifested in the exposed and unexposed groups of interest. The closer the etiological fraction is to 100%, the more specific (exclusive, prevalent, dominant) the role of this factor is among all other causal factors under consideration.

In our cohort study,

$$\frac{80/100,000 - 20/100,000}{80/100,000} \times 100 = 75\%$$

That is, three quarters of cases in the exposed are due to the exposure under study; this factor is predominant among others being part of the web of causes.

Hence, strength and specificity (exclusivity) criteria of causality may be estimated quantitatively by using ratios and other quantifications. Dose–effect relationships (biological gradient) and concomitant variations may be studied by biostatistical methods, experimental studies like clinical trials or field trials of vaccine protective effect (protective efficacy ratios are one of the epidemiological tools used) require both epidemiological and biostatistical methods. The rest relies mostly on qualitative judgment. The magnitude and spread of health problems are quantified by rates.

As the frequency of bad events following exposure to a bad factor may be quantified and compared, so beneficial interventions (medicines, surgeries, care) can be related to their beneficial effects. In both cases, groups with a higher frequency of results are in the numerator, those with a lower frequency represent the denominator of such ratios in such comparative expressions. Only the name changes in some instances:

Bad Events (Factors and Outcomes)	Good Events (Factors and Outcomes)
Individual risk (frequency, rate)	Individual risk (frequency, rate)
Relative risk	Relative risk of good events
Attributable risk	Attributable benefit increase
Etiological (attributable) fraction	Attributable benefit fraction
Relative risk increase (difference in rates in exposed and unexposed)	Relative benefit increase (difference in rates of outcomes in treated and untreated groups)
Number needed to harm: Number of individuals exposed to the factor that would lead to one additional person being harmed compared with individuals who are not exposed to this factor, that is, 1/attributable risk difference, hence the reciprocal of the attributable risk difference	Number needed to treat: Number of patients who must receive the treatment (beneficial factor) to create one additional improved outcome in comparison with the control treatment group, that is, 1/absolute risk reduction, hence the reciprocal of the attributable risk reduction

The American College of Medicine's *ACP Journal Club* periodically updates the glossary of these epidemiological and biostatistical terms.

Such various risks, rates, proportions, and ratios are presented across the medical literature as point estimates (as seen in the study). The uncertainty of these measurements is quantified by computing the confidence intervals (CI), usually reported as ranges within those true values for the whole population (community or patients) most probably are, that is, 95% CI or 99% CI.

2.2.1.5 Beyond Causality: Combining Frequencies, Fractions, Risks, and Proportions

As we have seen, various rates and ratios may be treated separately, each reflecting a particular problem such as relative risks measuring the strength of causal associations or etiological (attributable) fractions (proportional hazards in the domain of prognosis) or the attributable benefit increase to quantify the specificity (one cause among other) of a particular factor as a presumed cause.

Also, as an example, various frequencies and fractions are combined to evaluate the diagnostic considerations (see Section 3.2 of Chapter 3 regarding the validity of diagnostic tests).

How can various frequencies, rates, and ratios help us in our health programs and medical care priorities determinations?

At various levels of prevention, choices must often be made between various health programs. As Table 2.5 shows, incidence or prevalence frequencies

Table 2.5   Uses of Frequencies, Rates, Ratios or Proportions at Various Levels of Prevention and Choices in Health Program Considerations

Priority=	Occurrence	×Clinical Importance	×Controllability (in proportional terms)	×Operational Considerations of Health Programs (target population)
Level of prevention				
Primordial and primary (control of disease incidence)	Incidence	Disease severity (case fatality rate, severity score, etc.)	Etiological (attributable) fraction of risk	General population proportion reached by the disease prevention program

Table 2.5   Uses of Frequencies, Rates, Ratios or Proportions at Various Levels of Prevention and Choices in Health Program Considerations (*Continued*)

Priority=	Occurrence	×Clinical Importance	×Controllability (in proportional terms)	×Operational Considerations of Health Programs (target population)
Secondary (control of disease prevalence by controlling the duration of cases)	Prevalence	Disease severity (case fatality rate, severity score, etc.)	Etiological (attributable) fraction of prognosis (survival or duration of disease)[a]	Group of patients reached by the health care program
Tertiary and quarternary (control of disease spectrum and/or gradient without affecting its duration)	Clinical events	Disease severity (case fatality rate, severity score, etc.)	Etiological (attributable) fraction of prognosis (outcomes' occurrence timing and duration in terms of disease spectrum and/or gradient)[b]	Group of patients reached by the health care program

Source: Modified, expanded, and redrawn from Jenicek, M., *Epidemiology. The Logic of Modern Medicine*, EPIMED International, Montréal, 1995; Jenicek, M., *Foundations of Evidence-Based Medicine*, The Parthenon Publishing Group/CRC Press, Boca Raton/London/New York/Washington, 2003.

All components may be considered in terms of absolute frequencies, rates, or proportional rates, depending on the view of importance.

For more about levels of prevention, see Chapter 3, Section 3.3.1.

[a] From observational analytical studies, more desirable from clinical and community trials.

[b] Mainly from clinical trials.

and fractions, etiological and prognostic fractions, and other considerations are combined in our choice of possible most successful interventions.

N.B. For detailed definitions of levels of prevention, see Section 3.3.1 of this book.

All frequencies and fractions used have a specific meaning from the point of view of causality (importance of the event and its controllability and success of intervention). Some, like risks, are important for primary prevention. Others are important for different levels of health intervention such as prevalence for secondary prevention or prognostic frequencies and fractions beyond primary prevention.

2.2.1.6 Quantifying Our Uncertainties

An absolute certainty in medicine is rare. Our experience, understanding, and decision making vary due to our previous experience and doings, different patients, and settings in which health phenomena happen. Such uncertainties are worth measuring, interpreting, and using for practical decisions.

We are well aware that all our observations, analyses, and studies are subject to various random and systematic errors. Repeating studies of herd immunity (what proportion of the population, "herd," is immune after an immunization program) or integrating results from clinical trials yield ranges of results. Errors, samplings, detection, counting, health professionals' activities, and clinical practices may all contribute to the variety of findings from one study and population to another. So, can we be certain that a finding of 70% of herd immunity is appropriate to guide us to implementing an immunization program or not?

For all these and other reasons, we make decisions on the basis of point and interval estimates.

Point estimates provide an idea of "exact" frequencies, proportions, rates, incidence, and so on, such as 70% in the case of our herd immunity study (the term "herd immunity" is used in infectious disease epidemiology for the proportion of subjects in a given community who are resistant to the disease of interest).

Interval estimates, for example, 65%–75%, offer ranges within which a "true" value lies. More precisely, they are intervals within which the true estimates would fall given the variations of such estimates that might be seen in multiple studies of the same problem in the same group of patients or community. 95% or 99% CI specify our certainty regarding where our observations might be found.

The *range of observations* also counts. If multiple studies indicate a herd immunity range of 50%–90% (too wide in this example for the sake of explicitness), a true value within such an interval may have practical implications. If we know in the case of a particular infectious disease that a herd immunity of 80% is enough to make immunization unnecessary, in the case of a true value of 60%, immunization would be necessary and in the case of 85%, it would not.

Additional information about the diversity of individuals and their states is given then by the analysis of the ranges of observations within and between various sets. *Beginners must be aware that confidence intervals and ranges of observation are different subjects and that they have different meanings.* Both are relevant and useful and provide complementary information.

Our uncertainty about most quantitative parameters found, physiological and pathological parameters like averages or quantiles, rates, ratios, proportions, relative risks, etiological fractions, or protective efficacy rates are then expressed by interval estimates of what we have seen with all possible implications for our decision making to solve the problem under study. Overlapping confidence intervals of effectiveness of treatment in various clinical trials make us think whether such results are similar or dissimilar.

British biostatisticians have presented an overall fundamental and detailed overview of obtaining, interpreting, and using confidence intervals in describing health phenomena and using them.[70]

2.3 Fallacies in Medical Reasoning and Scientific Thinking in General

Perhaps the most important source of fallacies in medical and scientific thinking in general is to derive conclusions and make proposals about causal relationships based on one fulfilled criterion of a cause–effect link only. For example, if some relative risks or odds ratio are found to be unusually high, we can conclude that the causal link may be strong but we know nothing else. A different situation may occur in a field trial of a new vaccine's effectiveness, indicating a high protective efficacy ratio (proportion of the whole of cases prevented by intervention), let us say 80%. This is a good indicator of causality provided that other causal criteria are fulfilled. A controlled clinical trial is closer to this ideal than other observational analytical or other type of research.

Covering the entire main body of fallacies in medicine might be overwhelming for uninitiated readers and it goes well beyond the scope of this introductory reading. We have devoted a book to the topic, titled *Fallacy Free Reasoning in Medicine*[16] that may be welcomed by some readers as an extension of this chapter and section.

Some of them are also of common importance in the risk and cause assessment domains as covered in this chapter and in Section 3.1.6 of Chapter 3 that follows.

2.4 Role of Causal Reasoning in Medical Thinking

Causal reasoning is not the only reasoning in medicine, however, important and primordial it is. We reason also about other problems to solve, such as ethical considerations in medical care, assessing patient attitudes and values among others.

In the framework of a broader concept of argumentation and critical thinking, causal reasoning proves useful at most of the steps and in assessing the building blocks of the argument, grounds, backing, and warrant (perhaps being the most prominent of them all).

If we want to reach a conclusion about the cause of some consequence, there is no other way than to do so by a cause–effect review, as outlined in this chapter.

2.5 Critical Thinking, Communication, and Decision Making and Their Connection to Medical Ethics

Is there a connection between medical ethics and reasoning, communication, and decision making in health sciences? Yes. They are not only vehicles governed by the rules of ethics, but also part of medical ethics themselves. Correct rules and ways of reasoning, communication, and decision making lie behind good ethics in the health domain. In the opposite direction, good ethics are needed as a framework for reasoning, communication, and decision making in all health professions.

Medical ethics may be virtue-based, principle-based, or duty-based. Six values apply: *autonomy* (the patient has the last word), *beneficence* (acting in the best interest of the patient), *non-maleficence (primum non nocere)*, *justice* (fairness and equality in the distribution of resources and care), *dignity*, and *truthfulness and honesty* (informed consent).

> We may *define medical ethics* as "… rules of conduct for a health professional to distinguish between right and wrong. They serve as a moral basis in medical, nursing, and other care, research, and administration." Medical ethics falls into the broader framework of bioethics and ethics in its largest sense.[71]

Many professional institutions such as the American Medical Association (*AMA Code of Ethics*), British Medical Association (*BMA Code of Ethics*), Canadian Medical Association (*CMA Code of Ethics*), and others have their own codes. Medical ethics are also covered in general bioethics and in all major religions such as Christianity, Judaism, Islam, Buddhism, and Hinduism.

Mutual understanding, participatory decision making, and meaningful multilateral and multidirectional communication all depend on structured and problem solving–directed argumentation and shared critical thinking and its content. We may then consider argumentation, critical thinking, decision making, and communication not only as having to be ethical themselves, but also as an integral part of the medical ethics itself.

Any routine patient–physician encounter and its issues and outcomes, nursing care, clinical pharmacology decisions, adoption and uses of new medical technologies, surgical interventions, medical genetics, gene therapy, assisted suicide, euthanasia, stem cell research and its applications, procreative techniques, organ and tissue transplantations, or uses and abuses of psychiatry beyond its own domain are just a few examples of modern medical ethics challenges. Argumentation and communication and uses of their results largely define our success.

Conclusion

All in all, our thinking processes in medicine, be it in clinical practice or research, have two purposes: understanding the nature of the health problem and/or deciding what to do to solve it. Philosophers' principles, methods, and ways of critical thinking in general are extremely well adapted to what we are doing in health sciences. Epidemiologists, biostatisticians, health economists, and clinical specialists have developed many original contributions, which are crucial for all pragmatic purposes. Our reasoning is geared to concrete decision making and actions whose course and results we are responsible for as health professionals.

Logicians may be interested primarily in the purity of argumentation and thinking processes themselves. In medicine, even the best argumentative process must be based on the best evidence for the stated purpose first. That is where EBM joins critical thinking about the uses of the best evidence and evolves into a kind of *evidence-based critical thinking (argumentation) grounded medicine.*

Beyond health sciences, we are enriching our experience and practice through the experience and practice of others. Military arts or business experience as mentioned in our *Author's Welcome and Introduction* are just two of the many helpful areas. We must be open to them and adapt them in a well-structured way to manage health problems. In fact, medicine is also a health business battle-field where beyond health economics, our care and its outcomes must take into account the money that passes between the health producer, supplier, and pro-vider (health professionals, hospitals, medical offices or community medicine and public health units, etc.) and the consumer, patients, and our community.

For lawyers, judges, and expert witnesses in courts of law, pleading for a health cause is (and should be) an exercise in argumentation (inquiry and advo-cacy)[72,73] and critical thinking as it has been outlined here for health sciences.

In this diversity of experience, we cannot insist enough on clear, usable, and operational definitions of what we see and do. Again, orismology helps. For example,

- An *EBM practitioner* may define evidence as "any data or information, whether solid or weak, obtained through experience, observational research, or experimental work (clinical or field trials), relevant to some degree (more is better) either to the understanding of the problem (case) or to the clinical and community medicine decisions made about the case (meaning clinical case or the community health problem to solve)."[15]
- For a *philosopher/critical thinker,* **evidence** is "the data on which a judgment or conclusion might be based or by which proof or probabil-ity might be established … something to prove."[6]
- For *lawyers,* as might be expected, evidence is "information and things pertaining to the events that are the subject of an investigation or a case: especially, the testimony or objects (but not the questions or com-ments of the lawyers) offered at a trial or hearing for the judge or the jury to consider in deciding the issue in a case."[72]

Grading evidence in EBM is based most often on the validity of different types of studies as cause–effect proofs, from the least convincing to the most convinc-ing: Narratives, single case observations, case series (no denominators, no control groups) → observational analytical studies (cohort studies, case control studies) → experimental studies (clinical trials, etc.) → systematic reviews, meta-analyses, and otherwise synthesized experimental and clinical experience and research of observational analytical or experimental experience from multiple studies.

Grading evidence remains an unfinished topic and the subject of further development, refinement, and expansion.

In various versions, the following "pyramid of evidence" can be found across the current literature:

Synopses
Meta-analyses
and systematic reviews
Experimental studies (clinical trials)
Observational analytical cohort studies
Observational analytical case–control studies
Observational descriptive studies of occurrence
Single clinical case reports and case series reports
Hearsays, anecdotes, narratives, plain ideas, opinions

This hierarchy of evidence may be valid for cause–effect relationships and their ways of proof, but other domains requiring evidence may call for another kind of "pyramid" or "hierarchy" of proof. For example, what might a hierarchy of evidence be for physical examination or diagnosis whenever the presence and absence of disease causing a positive or negative test result is not of primary interest?

Grading evidence for types of research other than causal relationships between noxious or beneficial factors in relation to health or disease such as in the domain of validation of diagnostic tests requires a different approach. Besides etiological considerations, any grading must have some sense and practical purpose for decision making. Ideally, any stage or grade in a grading system must differ from the other by expanding the understanding, changing the understanding (different meanings such as different prognosis or differential diagnosis), or modifying clinical decisions (treatment indications). Staging cancer in these terms is well done; staging evidence is still more challenging in these practical terms.

From one situation to another, we must always find some mutually acceptable language or specify differences between the participating professions and domains. The same holds true, for example, for a "case" and, in

Besides the evidence used in argumentation, the value and relevance of the entire argumentative process depends on its *conceptual framework* or *framing*. Within such a framework, we are always defining the problem and its biological and physical setting, raising hypotheses about what is going on, specifying objectives regarding what we intend to do or how we intend to intervene, and at what we wish to arrive in general and specific terms and dimensions. *Our reasoning, understanding, decisions and actions only have meaning and value if such a framework is determined and known, preferably beforehand.*

clinical medicine, for any noxious or beneficial factor and their outcomes, disease signs or symptoms, or the disease itself, its diagnosis, or remedial clinical actions (treatments) and their outcomes.

Last but not least, our reasoning and decision making must remain fallacy-free, which is also a learned experience.

Let us see now, in the chapter that follows, how our ways of reasoning and decision making apply to various steps and stages of clinical practice and care such as assessing risk in patients (communities), making diagnosis, choosing and administering treatment, assessing patient outcomes (prognosis), and establishing follow-up and long-term care for individuals under our responsibility.

References

1. Hughes W, Lavery J. *Critical Thinking. An Introduction to the Basic Skills*. Fifth Edition. Peterborough, ON/Buffalo, NY: Broadview Press, 2008.
2. Horton R. The grammar of interpretive medicine. *Can Med Ass J*, 1998;**159**:245–9.
3. Huth EJ. *Writing and Publishing in Medicine*. Third Edition. Baltimore, MD: Williams & Wilkins, 1999.
4. Bloom BS. *Taxonomy of Educational Objectives*. Boston, MA: Allyn & Bacon, 1956.
5. Jenicek M, Hitchcock DL. *Evidence-Based Practice. Logic and Critical Thinking in Medicine*. Chicago, IL: American Medical Association (AMA Press), 2005.
6. Elder L, Paul R. *A Glossary of Critical Thinking Terms and Concepts. The Critical Analytic Vocabulary of the English Language*. Dillon Beach, CA: The Foundation for Critical Thinking, 2009.
7. Paul R, Elder L. *The Miniature Guide to Critical Thinking. Concepts and Tools*. Dillon Beach, CA: Foundation for Critical Thinking Press, 2009.
8. Hawkins D, Elder L, Paul R. *The Thinkers Guide to Clinical Reasoning*. Based on *Critical Thinking Concepts and Tools*. Dillon Beach, CA: The Foundation for Critical Thinking Press, 2010.
9. Changing Minds.org. *Types of reasoning*. Variable number of pages at http://changingminds.org/disciplines/argument/types_reasoning/types_reasoning.htm, retrieved November 4, 2009.
10. Rieke RD, Sillars MO, Peterson TR. *Argumentation and Critical Decision Making*. Sixth Edition. Boston/New York/San Francisco: Pearson Education Inc., 2005.
11. Agency for Healthcare Research and Quality (AHRQ), US Department of Health & Human Services. *Glossary*. 31 pages at http://www.wbmm.ahrq.gov/popup_gov/glossary.aspx, retrieved January 3, 2009, and 30 pages at http://www.wbmm.ahrq.gov/glossary.aspx, retrieved July 7, 2009.
12. Jenicek M. *Medical Error and Harm. Understanding, Prevention, and Control*. Boca Raton/London/New York: CRC Press/Taylor & Francis/Productivity Press, 2011.

13. Institute of Medicine, Committee on Quality of Health Care in America. *To Err Is Human. Building a Safer Health System*. Edited by LT Kohn, JM Corrigan, and MS Donaldson. Washington, DC: National Academy Press, 2000.
14. Dowden B. *The Internet Encyclopedia of Philosophy. Fallacies*. 44 pages at http://www.iep.utm.edu/f/fallacy.htm, retrieved October 31, 2006.
15. Jenicek M. *Foundations of Evidence-Based Medicine*. Boca Raton/London/New York/Washington: The Parthenon Publishing Group/CRC Press, 2003.
16. Jenicek M. *Fallacy-Free Reasoning in Medicine. Improving Communication and Decision Making in Research and Practice*. Chicago, IL: American Medical Association (AMA Press), 2009.
17. Smith R. Aristotle's logic, in: *Stanford Encyclopedia of Philosophy, Fall 2004 Edition*. Edited by EN Zalta. http://plato.stanford.edu/entries/Aristotle-logic, accessed December 2004.
18. Zarefsky D. *Argumentation: The Study of Effective Reasoning*. The Transcript Book, Second Edition. Chantilly, VA: The Great Courses/The Teaching Company, 2005.
19. Toulmin SE. *The Uses of Argument*. Cambridge, England: Cambridge University Press, 1958 (Updated Edition, 2003).
20. Toulmin S, Rieke R, Janik A. *An Introduction to Reasoning*. Second Edition. New York, NY: Collier Macmillan Publishers, 1984.
21. Jenicek M. How to read, understand, and write 'Discussion' sections in medical articles. An exercise in critical thinking. *Med Sci Monit*, 2006;**12**(6): SR28–36.
22. Jenicek M. Writing a 'Discussion' section in a medical article: An exercise in critical thinking and argumentation, chapter 27, pp. 457–65, in: *Biomedical Research. From Ideation to Publication*. Edited by G. Jagadeesh, S Murthy, YK Gupta, and A Prakash. New Delhi/Philadelphia/London: Wolters Kluwer Health (India)/Lippincott/Williams & Wilkins, 2010.
23. Jenicek M. *A Physician's Self-Paced Guide to Critical Thinking*. Chicago, IL: American Medical Association (AMA Press), 2006.
24. Jenicek M. *Fallacy-Free Reasoning in Medicine. Improving Communication and Decision Making in Research and Practice*. Chicago, IL: American Medical Association (AMA Press), 2009.
25. *Random House Webster's Unabridged Dictionary 3.0*. Electronic edition on CD. Antwerpen: Random House Inc., 1998 and 2003.
26. Hughes W, Lavery J. Meaning and definition, pp. 33–60, in: *Critical Thinking: An Introduction to Basic Skills*. Fourth Edition. Peterborough, ON/Orchard Park, NY: Broadview Press, 2004.
27. Sackett DL, Rosenberg WMC, Muir Gray JA, Haynes RB, Richardson WS. Evidence based medicine: What it is and what it isn't. *BMJ*, 1996;**312**(Jan 13): 71–2. doi:10.1136bmj.312.7023.71 (Published 13 January 1996.)
28. Jenicek M. Evidence-based medicine: Fifteen years later. Golem the good, the bad and the ugly in the need of a review? *Med Sci Monit*, 2006;**12**(11):RA241–51.
29. WhatisKT. *KT Terms*. Variable number of pages at http://whatiskt.wikispaces.com/KT+terms, retrieved January 10, 2011.

30. Wikipedia, the free encyclopedia. *Framing (social sciences)*. 10 pages at http://en.wikipedia.org.wiki/Framing_(social_sciences), retrieved September 19, 2011.

31. Jenicek M. The four cornerstones of a research project: health problem in focus, objectives, hypothesis, research question, chapter 3, pp. 28–35, in: Jagadeesh, G, Murthy, S, Gupta, YK, and Prakash A (eds). *Biomedical Research: From Ideation to Publication*. New Delhi: Wolters Kluwer Health (India)/Williams & Wilkins, 2010.

32. Mulrow CM, Oxman A, editors. *How to Conduct a Cochrane Systematic Review*. Third Edition. San Antonio, YX: San Antonio Cochrane Center, 1996.

33. Counsell C. Formulating questions and locating primary studies for inclusion in systematic reviews. *Ann Intern Med*, 1997;**127**:380–7.

34. Eng J. Getting started in cardiology research: Asking the right question and identifying an appropriate study population. Critical Thinking Skills Symposium. *Acad Radiol*, 2004;**11**:149–54.

35. Deleskamp-Hayes C, Gardell Cutter MA (eds). *Science, Technology, and the Art of Medicine. European-American Dialogues*. Dordrecht/Boston/London: Kluwer Academic Publishers, 1993.

36. Rothman KJ, editor. *Causal Inference*. Chestnut Hill, MA: Epidemiology Resources Inc., 1988.

37. *Fundamental philosophy and criteria of cause-effect relationship*, Section 6.3, pp. 162–8 in Jenicek, M. *Epidemiology: The Logic of Modern Medicine*. Montréal: EPIMED International, 1995.

38. *Search for causes of disease occurrence. Why does disease occur?* Chapter 8, pp. 183–228 in Ref 15.

39. Jenicek M. *Epidemiology. The Logic of Modern Medicine*. Montréal: EPIMED International. 1995.

40. Denzin NK, Lincoln YS, editors. *The Sage Handbook of Qualitative Research. Third Edition*. Thousand Oaks/London/New Delhi: SAGE Publications, 2005.

41. Creswell JW. *Qualitative Inquiry & Research Design. Choosing Among Five Approaches*. Thousand Oaks, CA: SAGE Publications, 2007.

42. Corbin J, Strauss A. *Basics of Qualitative Research*. Third Edition. Thousand Oaks, CA/London, UK: SAGE Publications Inc., 2008.

43. Greenhalgh T, Taylor R. How to read a paper: Papers that go beyond numbers (qualitative research). *BMJ*, 1997;**315** 7110(Sep 20):740(4). Online.

44. Poses RM, Isen AM. Qualitative research in medicine and health care. *J Gen Intern Med*, 1998;**13**(1):32–8.

45. Green J, Britten N. Qualitative research and evidence based medicine. *BMJ*, 1998;**316**(April 18):1230–40.

46. Pope C, Mays N, editors. *Qualitative Research in Health Care*. Third Edition. Oxford/London: Blackwell Publishing/BMJ Publishing Group Ltd., 2006.

47. Creswell JW. *Research Design. Qualitative, Quantitative, and Mixed Methods Approaches*. Thousand Oaks, CA/London/New Delhi: SAGE Publications, 2008.

48. Tashakkor A, Teddhie C, editors. *Handbook of Mixed Methods in Social and Behavioral Research*. Thousand Oaks/London/New Delhi: SAGE Publications, 2003.

49. Creswell JW, Fetters MD, Ivankova NV. Designing a mixed methods study in primary care. *Ann Fam Med*, 2004;**2**(1):7–12.
50. Morgan DL. Practical strategies for combining qualitative and quantitative methods: Applications for health research. *Qual Health Res*, 1998;**8**:362–76.
51. Li CC. *Path Analysis—A Primer*. Pacific Grove, CA: The Boxwood Press, 1975.
52. Introduction to multivariate analysis, Chapter 12, pp. 225–245, in: *Primer of Epidemiology*. Fifth Edition. Edited by GD Friedman. New York and London: McGraw-Hill, Medical Publishing Division, 2004.
53. Figure 1-1, p. 4, in: *Primer of Epidemiology*. Fifth Edition. Edited by GD Friedman. New York and London: McGraw-Hill, Medical Publishing Division, 2004.
54. Moon BM, Hoffman RR, Novak JD, Canas AJ. *Applied Concept Mapping. Capturing, Analyzing, and Organizing Knowledge*. Boca Raton/London/ New York: CRC Press (Taylor & Francis), 2011.
55. West DC, Pomeroy JR, Park JK, Gerstenberger EA, Sandoval J. Critical thinking in graduate medical education. A role model concept mapping assessment? *JAMA*, 2000;**284**(9):1105–10.
56. Pinto AJ, Zeitz HJ. Concept mapping: a strategy for promoting meaning-ful learning in medical education. Pelley JW. *Concept Mapping—A Tool for Teaching Integrative Thinking*. A 30 ppt presentation at www.iamse.org/ development/2005/webcast_050305.pdf, retrieved February 3, 2011.
57. Pelley JW. *Effective Learning through Concept Mapping*. 4 pages at www.ttuhsc.edu/.../Concept%20Mapping%20in%20Med%20School.pdf - Similar, retrieved February 3, 2011.
58. Anderson LA, Gwaltney MK, Sundra DL, Brownson RC, Kane M, Cross AW, Mack Jr. R, Schwartz R, Sims T, White R. Using concept mapping to develop a logic model for the prevention research centers program. *Prev Chron Dis Pub Health Res Pract Pol*, 2006;**3**(1):1–8. (http://www.cdc.gov/pcd/issues/2006/ jan/05_0153.htm).
59. Cinnamon J, Rinner C, Cusimano MD, Marshall S, Bekele T, Hernandez T, Glazier RH, Chipman ML. Evaluating web-based static, animated and integra-tive maps for injury prevention. *Geospatial Health*, 2009;**4**(1):3–16.
60. Baldwin CM, Kroesen K, Trochim WM, Bell IR. Complementary and conven-tional medicine: a concept map. *BMC Compl Alt Med*, 2004, **4**(Feb 3) online <doi: 10.1186/1472-6882-4-2>, PMCID: PMC356920.
61. Concepts Systems Inc. *Concept Mapping Methodology. Bibliography and Recent Publications*. 4 pages at www.*concepts*systems.com/.../bibliography_ examples_of_cm_projects_4.pdf, retrieved February 3, 2011.
62. BMC Complementary and Alternative Medicine. *Concept Mapping. Published Literature*. 7 pages at www.socialresearch methods.net/research/cm.htm, retrieved February 3, 2011.
63. *A Dictionary of Public Health*. Edited by JM Last. Oxford/New York: Oxford University Press, 2007.
64. A Dictionary of Epidemiology. Fifth Edition. Edited by M Porta. Oxford/ New York: Oxford University Press, 2008.

65. Hill AB. The environment and disease: Association or causation? *Proc Roy Soc Med*, 1965;**58**:41–6.
66. Surgeon General's Advisory Committee on Smoking and Health. *Smoking and Health*. Washington, DC: Public Health Service Publ. No 1103, 1973.
67. Evans AS. Causation and disease. A chronological journey. *Am J Epidemiol*, 1978;**108**:249–57.
68. Broadhead WE, Kaplan BH, James SA et al. The epidemiologic evidence for a relationship between social support and health. *Am J Epidemiol*, 1983;**117**:521–37.
69. Guyatt GH, Weber CE, Mewa AA, Sackett DL. Determining causation–a case study: adrenocorticosteroids and osteoporosis. Should the fear of inducing clinically important osteoporosis influence the decision to prescribe adreno-corticosteroids? *J Chron Dis*, 1984;**37**:343–52.
70. *Statistics with Confidence. Confidence intervals and statistical guidelines.* Edited by MJ Gardner and DG Altman. London: British Medical Journal, 1989.
71. Wikipedia, the free encyclopedia. *Bioethics.* 8 pages at http://en.wikipedia.org/wiki/Bioethics, retrieved Oct. 25, 2011.
72. Clapp JE. *Random House Webster's Dictionary of the Law*. New York: Random House, 2000.
73. Ziegelmueller G., Kay J, Dause C. *Argumentation: Inquiry and Advocacy.* Second Edition. Englewood Cliffs, NJ: Prentice Hall, 1990.

Chapter 3

Reasoning in Step-by-Step Clinical Work and Care: Risk, Diagnosis, Treatment, and Prognosis

Executive Summary

In clinical practice and community medicine, and in public health as well, we reason and make decisions in four particular domains: (1) assessing risk (probability of new phenomena) in the individual patient and in the community; (2) detection and diagnosis of disease and other phenomena in individuals and their groups (sporadicity, epidemicity, endemicity, and pandemicity); (3) choosing, implementing, and evaluating success and failures of clinical treatment, prevention, and other active interventions; and (4) forecasting and evaluating potential and real outcomes of health phenomena of interest.

In the assessment of risk, risk factors (events that may be modified) are often of greater interest for pragmatic reasons than risk markers as uncontrollable predictors of disease and its cure. Results may be seen as significant not only from a biostatistical or epidemiological point of view but also from values attributed to them by patients and their communities. *Post hoc ergo propter hoc* or *cum hoc ergo propter hoc* and other fallacies in causal reasoning should be avoided.

Diagnosis is made by various reasoning methods such as pattern recognition, hypothetico-deductive, probability-based, or deterministic approaches.

The evaluation of the internal validity (how does it detect disease as such) or the external validity (how does it work from one individual to another) of diagnostic methods must be considered both for screening and for reference diagnostic tests. Anchoring (premature closure of the diagnostic workup), ordering and triage-related fallacies, ignoring Bayesian diagnostic prior/ posterior/revised probabilities or rhetorical manipulations are some examples of diagnostic reasoning to avoid and correct.

Treatment must be seen as a matter of intervention at various levels of prevention, health protection, and health promotion. Controlled clinical trials and their alternatives focus on the demonstration of a causal relationship between some beneficial factor and improvement in health and disease based on the rules outlined in Chapter 2. The best evidence according to evidence-based medicine rules is sought here. Ignoring webs of causes and consequences, appeals to authorities or tradition, or actions at any price are just some of the fallacies to know, prevent, and rectify.

Prognosis refers to a rather longitudinal (over time) study of multiple beneficial or noxious factors having both good and bad multiple consequences on what happened or will happen once the disease is acquired. Prognostic factors and markers often differ from risk factors and markers. They are the subjects of "survival"-type studies, proportional hazard (the impact of multiple prognostic factors) evaluations, and other methods. Case fatality, response to treatment rates, remissions, relapses, disease gradient, and spectrum may be in focus. Types of reasoning and argumentation are common to some of the other above-mentioned domains of clinical activity. Oversimplifications, divisions (whole entities and their parts), or misleading uses of statistics are additional fallacies to avoid.

General rules of reasoning, critical thinking, and decision making apply to all steps and stages of clinical work and care with individual patients as well as to the management, prevention, and control of the disease and health at community level.

Not-So-Random Leading Thoughts

There are four questions which in some form
or other every patient asks of his doctor:
(a) What is the matter with me? This is
diagnosis. Can you put me right?
(b) What will be my treatment and **prognosis**?
(c) How did I get it? This is causation.
(d) How can I avoid it in the future?
This is **prevention**. He may not be
called upon to attempt a full answer
to his patient, but he must give
a fair working answer to himself.

George Newman, 1931
in The Lancet

What can we say 80 years later? The same perhaps, but with some new perspectives, approaches, and answers.

He is the best prophet who guesses well,
and he is not the wisest man whose
guess turns out well in the event, but
he who, whatever the event be, takes
reason and probability for his guide.

Euripides, 489–406 BC

Forecasting is very difficult,
especially if it is about future.

Edgar B. Fiedler, 1977

Hindsight is always twenty-twenty.

Billy Wilder, 1979

When you have mastered the numbers,
you will in fact no longer be reading
numbers, any more that you read
words when reading a book.
You will be reading meanings.

Harold Geneen, 1984

Isn't this similar to what we do whencounting and measuring what we see at the bedside and when looking at lab results?

> The end cannot justify the means,
> for the simple and obvious reason
> that the means employed determine
> the nature of the end produced.

Aldous Huxley, 1937

> What we should do, I suggest, is to give up
> the idea of ultimate sources of knowledge,
> and admit that all knowledge is human; that
> it is mixed with our errors, our prejudices,
> our dreams, and our hopes; that all
> we can do is to grope for truth even
> though it be beyond our reach.

Sir Karl Raimund Popper, 1960

> The conclusion of your syllogism,
> I said lightly, is fallacious, being
> based upon licensed premises.

Flann O'Brien (Brian O'Nolan), 1911–1966
(*Chapter 1 in* At Swim-Two-Birds)

> Our clinical conclusions are as well!
> That's the beauty of the argument –
> if you argue correctly, you're never wrong.

Aaron Eckhart (Nick Taylor), 2005
in the Jason Reitman satirical film, Thank You for Smoking

Introductory Comments

For philosophers, reasoning means "thinking leading to the conclusion." Isn't this what physicians do all the time?

Once we know the patient's chief and other complaints or reasons bringing him or her under our care, we usually try to solve several problems when taking his or her medical, occupational, social, and other history, performing a physical examination and evaluating his or her mental state:

- We assess the patient's *risks*. Given the above information, what *might* be the patient's future health problems? *This is a health problem to deal with:* …
- We make *diagnoses*, often for the main problem of interest and other associated problems **(comorbidity)**. *This is my diagnosis:* …
- We choose and administer medical, surgical, and/or psychiatric *treatment* for the main problem of interest and for associated health problems (cotreatment for comorbidity). *His or her treatment should be then* …
- We make *prognosis* of outcomes and other future issues that result once the treatment and care of all the patient's health problems are implemented, during the care, and once it is completed. This is *what we can expect and should expect:* …
- We establish *plans* of possible long-term medical, social, and other care beyond current health problem resolution. This is *how we should care for this patient beyond the current problem and care:* ….

In all such cases, while reasoning well, we must arrive at meaningful conclusions, understand a clinical case or cases better, and derive the best possible decisions about what to do.

Let us see in this chapter how we reason in the domains of patient risk assessment, diagnosis, treatment, and prognosis, the most frequently encountered activities at the beginning of the learning process of clinical medicine.

Clinical steps practice, evaluation, and understanding depend heavily on crucial contributions from fundamental and clinical epidemiology and biostatistics. From a wider and more in-depth scope of clinical epidemiological, biostatistical, and other considerations, methods, and techniques applied here, let us highlight now some particular perspectives regarding our reasoning about them. This is crucial for the understanding shared by learners and their teachers. However, the points that follow do not replace the more formal training from which they are drawn.

HEALTH EVENTS

All steps in clinical care rely on and are subjects of argumentation, decision making, and communication. Cause–effect considerations are not limited only to disease and suffering and their causes (etiological factors of disease) but also encompass medical (clinical pharmacology, psychotherapy, behavior modification, etc.), surgical (including invasive exploratory methods and techniques), psychiatric, and social support interventions benefiting the patient, their successes and failures, adverse effects of treatment and care, medical error and harm, and the impact of all this on health professionals and services, economic and administrative functioning on health community and society beyond. Let us give them in this book the common name of **event(s)** or health event(s) since any of them (not only disease and its causes) may be and actually are subjects of argumentation, decision making, and communication.

CLINICAL REASONING ABOUT HEALTH EVENTS

In the broadest of terms, **clinical reasoning** is "… a context-dependent way of thinking and decision making in professional practice to guide practice actions. It involves the construction of narratives to make sense of multiple factors and interests pertaining to the current reasoning task. It occurs within a set of problem spaces informed by the practitioner's unique frames of reference, workplace context, and practice models, as well as by the patient or client contexts. It utilizes core dimensions of practice knowledge, reasoning, and metacognition and draws on these capacities of others."[1]

As already mentioned in the "Author's Welcome and Introduction," **clinical judgment** is "the capacity to make and choose data and information to produce useful (true or false) claims in clinical practice and research. It also means critical thinking in the practice of medicine based on the 'patient/evidence/setting' fit. Together with elements of knowledge and experience, it relies on the process of integrating meanings and values of clinical and paraclinical observation and data into the making of conclusions and decisions derived from such an integration."

3.1 "You Are at Risk." What Does This Mean and How Can It Be Mutually Understood by Us, Our Patients, and the Community?

When we speak of risk, we mean "bad" factors, causes of health problems, complications, and undesirable outcomes of medical care. "Beneficial" factors, that is, those that improve health and cure disease, relate to treatment. Being "at risk" is perhaps one of the terms and notions most used and misused in daily practice and communication and can signify many things. For laypersons, in particular, it sounds "scientific," technical, and knowledgeable. Such "risk of the risk" should be minimized through some basic clarifications. Otherwise, even flawless argumentation is useless in the context.

In the domain of risk, as elsewhere in medicine, we often think in terms of probabilities, answers to "what are my, our, or their chances." **Probability** is *a measure that ranges from zero to 1 of the likelihood that a random event will occur or the degree to which a statement or assumption is true.*[2] In other words, closer to the epidemiological notion of rate or risk, the probability (*P*) is *a quantitative expression of the chance that an event (A) will occur. ... then, ...*[3]

$$P(A) = \frac{\text{number of times A occurs}}{\text{number of times A } could \text{ occur}}$$

(N.B. Probabilities were already discussed at length in Chapter 2.)

Quantifications of the realities or predictions of the presence, occurrence, frequency, or prognosis of disease are made in terms of probabilities. Their comparisons are used in statistical inference, in comparing theory and practice, or to better understand the cause–effect relationships. For example, **rates** of disease such as 20/1000 or 0.020 (20/1000 in decimal form) are probabilistic expressions. Holland provides further explanations of probabilities (without equations) to clinicians.[4]

3.1.1 What Is "Risk" in Health Sciences?

Risk is the probability that a *new* good or bad event will happen over a defined period of time or moment. Both the patient and his or her physician should speak about and understand the same event and its person/time/place context. It should be specified often on a case-per-case basis, especially if laypersons are involved.

The risk of disease and other events is a probability derived from observations and comparisons of two or more sets of **incidence rates**, that is, the frequencies of new events over a defined period of time often related to some denominators of various size (%, per 1,000, 100,000, etc.). Such denominators include both events and nonevents, sick and healthy individuals, and so on, in some target population of interest (to which observations apply). Incidence rates are particularly useful to follow the spread of the disease over time.

N.B. *Prevalence rates* as frequencies of events at a given moment or over a defined period of time, independently of when they occurred, are useful as a diagnostic a priori predictor of a possible health problem. They are particularly useful in understanding the overall burden of the disease at a given moment (point prevalence) or over a certain period of time (period prevalence). They may sometimes be used as estimators of risk from the relationship between prevalence, incidence, and duration of the disease provided that the duration of cases is comparable and stable over time. This is rather exceptional, however. Consider with caution!

3.1.2 Are Risk Characteristics All the Same? Risk Factors and Risk Markers

For practical and research purposes, they are not. Any patient may experience exposure to risk factors and risk markers.

Risk factors can be modified and consequently so can the risks of disease itself, such as smoking and health, physical activity, drug abuse, dietary patterns, occupational and environmental physical and chemical agents, or exposure to infectious agents, resistance, and so on.

Risk markers are those characteristics that may also be useful predictors of desirable or undesirable events but which cannot be modified: age, gender, some immutable cultural, societal, or faith values, and so on.

Risk markers prove useful in the domain of diagnosis and prognosis. Risk factors are of primary importance in advising the patient of the chances of successful treatment or prevention.

3.1.3 Why Are Some Risk Factors "Significant" and Others Not?

We always want to establish some hierarchy of importance of risk factors in deciding what we should control first and what might be done later. The notion of importance is most often derived from comparisons of two or more groups exposed to the factor of interest and its consequence(s) in cohort studies or from comparisons of past or present exposure in already diseased and nondiseased individuals, case–control studies. Both observational only and experimental studies yield various estimations of cause–effect relationships as already outlined in Chapter 2.

Having said this, which factors (causes or consequences) are more important than others? Which are most useful for decisions in practice and research?

The theoretical concept of cause–effect relationships presented in Chapter 2 also applies to any kind of intervention in medicine at any level of prevention: the control of exposure to noxious factors, immunization in primary prevention, treatment in secondary prevention, avoiding metastases, or ensuring the comfort of a terminal patient in tertiary prevention. The same criteria of cause–effect relationships apply to various risk measurements (absolute, relative, attributable, fraction of the web of causes). Any evaluation of the role of noxious causal factors or treatment impact, such as effectiveness or adverse effects and their evaluation by additional methods, is derived from this basic consideration and approach.

Once comparisons of outcomes in groups are made, interpreters bring their experiences to the attention of readers and listeners. Results are interpreted as being "significant," "highly significant," or "statistically significant." ***p* values** from the statistical analysis of data are used to show the strength of evidence in analytical studies, be they observational or experimental. *p* values are also used to evaluate the degree of dissimilarity between two or more series of observations. Once again, let us remember that as a measure of the impact of treatment in clinical or epidemiological terms, *p* values can only "clear the way" (if they are small) for the epidemiological and clinical assessment of results of clinical trials.[5] The *p* value is "usually the probability of obtaining a result as extreme as, or more extreme than, the one observed if the dissimilarity is entirely due to variation in measurement or in subject response, that is, if it is the result of chance alone."[6]

In research, some funding agencies or institutions may still be happy with "small *p* values," indicating that a drug leading to different outcomes shows a very low probability of not working (null hypothesis would be true). This, however, does not indicate the magnitude of the effect. Hence, *p* values and significance of findings in terms of inferential statistics should be carefully interpreted and given their proper meaning.

If authors are happy stating that differences in disease outcomes between groups are statistically significant, they must keep the following in mind:

1. *What is statistically significant is not necessarily significant from an epidemiological point of view.* Statistically significant studies may still show low relative risks (a poor strength of association) or etiological fractions (specificity of improvements due to the treatment under study). Findings are not good enough to confirm a strong cause–effect association.
2. *All epidemiologically important results are not necessarily of equal clinical importance: what is epidemiologically important is not always equally clinically important.* For rare phenomena and outcomes that are not severe or life-threatening, strong associations may exist, but they are of lesser clinical importance in comparison to more frequent and serious health problems, where even less epidemiologically important findings might be of more clinical interest. These findings are not good enough for decision making.

In other words, if one needs to know some *p* value beyond its customary clearing power in the chain of quantitative analysis of clinical trial results, findings are probably not relevant ("significant") from the point of view of clinical reasoning and decision making. For example, smoking is epidemiologically more important in relation to lung cancer than in relation to cardiovascular problems. However, given the frequency of cardiovascular problems, control of smoking may be in some instances more clinically important for this area than for lung cancer.

Always specify exactly what you mean when saying that something is "highly significant," "significant," or "nonsignificant"! Funny enough, authors of some medical articles find that the results of their own studies are often "highly significant," whereas results of competing studies are not. Moreover, what is significant for clinicians may not always corroborate with the views of field epidemiologists. "Significance" then does not travel well from one specialty to another.

In the domain of treatment evaluation (vide infra), the fundamental epidemiological measures of treatment (or prevention modality) efficacy and effectiveness are the relative risk (strength of association), the risk difference, and the etiological fraction (specificity of association).

These risks are calculated traditionally on the basis of the occurrence of undesirable events (complications of disease, disease cases, deaths), using tradition and experience from field studies in community medicine.

The same can be done for expected improvements, provided they are well defined in clinimetrically acceptable terms.

3.1.4 Where Does Our Knowledge of Risk Factors and Markers Come From?

Most such knowledge comes from observational analytical studies of disease etiology. These studies are either of a cohort (sometimes called prospective) and/or case–control (sometimes understood as "retrospective") nature. They have been outlined in part in Chapter 2, and practically all textbooks on epidemiology, including our current one,[7] cover in more satisfactory detail these challenges.

Experimental studies are rather exceptional given the ethical unacceptability of controlled trials of a noxious factor and its consequences. What is left are observations and analyses of "natural experiments," that is, situations which allow comparisons of sets of observations reflecting the nature of a trial as they occur without being determined by the observer and the analyst.

3.1.5 Risk as a Subject of Argumentation

The quality of our knowledge, understanding, and use of risk is, like any other step of clinical work, a subject of argumentation, in which

- The best evidence is used in grounds, backing, warrants, rebuttals, and qualifiers leading to our conclusion about the causality problem and its value and relevance for practice and research.
- Meaningful links are established between component building blocks of our argument.
- The cause–effect criteria are fulfilled.
- Everything falls into a clear and well-defined conceptual frame.

3.1.6 Illustrative Fallacies

Fallacies as errors in reasoning are too numerous to list here. We have summarized them elsewhere.[8] However, many fallacies are also related to the formulations of questions about risk factors and other causes, study design, interpretation, or applications.

In considerations of possible risk factors or markers in the etiology of disease, let us mention the following:

a. The *post hoc ergo propter hoc* fallacy. We assume that because a health problem (or its improvement) occurs after exposure to a suspected noxious or beneficial factor, a change in health status occurred as a result.

b. The *cum hoc ergo propter hoc* fallacy has several self-explanatory synonyms: association/causation fallacy, correlation not cause fallacy, correlation for cause fallacy, *non causa pro causa*, and others. The culprit here is the ambiguous term "association," meaning either causality or something else when there is none. In an example from the non-medical world, when two show business stars are said to be "romantically linked," this means that the two stars have fallen in love or are engaged, married, involved with someone else, associated for pragmatic business and/or publicity reasons, whether romance is involved or not. The same should not happen in matters of health and disease and their causes and consequences. Also, as already mentioned in Chapter 2, a temporary sequence of events is not a sufficient proof of a cause–effect relationship.

c. *It speaks for itself fallacies, appeal for common practice fallacies, appeal to antiquity/tradition (ad antiquitatem) or false conservatism fallacies or newness (originality) fallacies* still occur as substitutes for the real causality.[8]

d. *Bias*: Other fallacies appear under the name of "bias" in the clinical epidemiological literature. They are related to design flaws in etiological studies, definition of variables, organization, and recording in studies, misrepresentation and misinterpretation of clinical course of the disease, individuals ending and not ending in research studies, their compliance, and losses. For example, consider the following:

 – *Berkson bias* means errors due to the study of individuals suffering or not from multiple morbidities, affecting their chances of hospitalization and being enrolled in studies in which they should be for the sake of the representativeness of the problem under study.

 – *Neyman bias* is related to the attrition of cases in etiological studies due to the fact that most serious, deceased "too early," as well as not serious cases escape attention in analytical studies covering longer periods of time. Such biases (fallacies) are more extensively covered in the epidemiological literature to quote just a few.[8–11]

– *Hindsight bias*: This kind of bias refers to a tendency to judge events, their causes or consequences (outcomes) as well as our interpretations and decisions about them on the basis of what we know now, after such events, rather than on the basis of what we knew before we faced those events and made our decisions. In retrospect, we did not have the same (and often richer) information that we have now. Everyone is wiser after an experience than before it: "after the war, everyone is a general" or "I knew it all along" as popular sayings go. Our judgment of patient risks, rightness of diagnosis, therapeutic decisions, or making prognosis may all be affected by this kind of directional reasoning.

N.B. The lists of fallacies and biases in this chapter are not exhaustive and are presented in this book only for illustrative purposes.

3.1.7 How Do We Think about Risk? Our Ways of Reasoning about Risk

There are several ways, paradigms, mental processes, types of reasoning, and pathways of thinking underlying risk assessment in the patient, which reflect the characteristics and content already partially outlined in Chapter 2:

■ Occurrence considerations
■ Cause–effect considerations
■ Inductive and deductive paths of reasoning
■ Considerations and analysis of webs of causes, temporal sequence, and interaction between multiple risk factors
■ Consideration and analysis of webs of consequences, temporal sequence, and interaction between multiple consequences
■ Validity assessment for understanding the "scientific value" of information about risk
■ Uses of both vertical thinking (within a specific argument) and lateral thinking (several topics, options, arguments, and choices about them)
■ Validity assessment for practical decision making in general and in a particular individual: "this patient" (patient's fit into grounds and backing)

They are all necessary for our reasoning, understanding, and decision making about a patient's risks.

3.2 "We Have a Problem Here": Properties of Meaningful Diagnosis

Diagnosis relies on two elements:

1. *Quality and completeness of data and findings* from patient history, physical and paraclinical examinations
2. *What we do with all this information* on our reasoning path to diagnose patient problem(s) or, in other words, *how diagnosis is made*

Clinicians arrive at their opinions on the basis of *soft data*, which is harder to define, measure, quantify, and classify such as pain, nausea, injected eyes, feeling sad, and many other observations, particularly in psychiatry. *Hard data* is the opposite: blood cell count, body temperature, skinfold thickness, cholesterol levels, and radiological findings of bone fractures. *Hardening of soft data* is a procedure to make soft data more meaningful for understanding and decision making: pain is quantified on a scale from 0 to 10 or a pictogram, overnight sputum is estimated as a spoonful, half-cup, or small cup. Both entities are useful, although hard data are easier to work with in **clinimetrics** or quantification, qualification, categorization, and other identifications of what we saw, heard, felt (and sometimes smelled and tasted) as clinicians working with the patient.

3.2.1 Quality and Completeness of the Diagnostic Material

Once the patient specifies his or her complaint or reason for consultation, his or her physician completes the idea about the complaint through a series of *open* ("How do you feel today?," "What else worries you?") and *closed* ("Is your chest pain still there?," "Can you move your right knee better today than yesterday?") *questions*. Most often, interviews start with open questions, and closed questions usually follow to specify the problem.

Patient history and physical findings are enriched by *paraclinical explorations and findings*: diagnostic imagery, biochemistry of body liquids and tissues, clinical microbiology, biopsy and other diagnostic methods in pathology.

All this information enters our reasoning process, leading to diagnosis.

3.2.2 How Is a Diagnosis Made?

Several steps are involved in making a diagnosis, ranging from simple recognitions to organized and structured pathways from initial observations to conclusions about them.[12]

- First, the patient is *observed globally*, then

  ↓

- Manifestations of interest are *isolated* from the global observation.

  ↓

- Following this, the manifestations of interest are properly *described* in reproducible terms.

  ↓

- And a *dimension* (making sense of what was seen and described) is given to them.

  ↓

- This allows their *interpretation* by an associative process linking previously observed elements with additional perceptions and clinical observations. This step leads to

  ↓

- A final inference on the patient's state by classifying it in a diagnostic category as the end of this clinimetric process, that is, path from observations to the final *diagnosis itself*.

There are several ways to make a diagnosis:

1. Diagnosis by *pattern recognition* is based on fitting what we saw in previously learned patterns. If we see a patient in shock, with a sharp retrosternal pain irradiating into the left arm, we may think about a myocardial infarction and order further testing and workup to accept or reject our working diagnosis and initial impression.
2. Diagnosis by *arborisation or multiple branching* is a procedure followed by going from one point of observation to another, each step depending on what was found beforehand. Clinical *algorithms and guidelines* may be based on this method. For example, we may consider a stab wound in the abdomen of a patient in the emergency room. If the anterior fascia is penetrated, we proceed to a peritoneal lavage and/or diagnostic imaging (if available), suggesting liquid accumulation in the abdominal cavity. If the red blood cell count exceeds

a certain amount and/or liquid accumulation is confirmed, we might consider exploratory laparotomy. If not, 24 h hospital observation might be a preferred alternative. The movement from one step to another on the procedure path depends unequivocally on the result of the previous step. More about algorithms and guidelines will follow in Chapter 4.

3. Diagnosis by *exclusive exploration of data* is an inductive procedure. Multiple data are gathered first and then dredged to obtain hypotheses, which can be formulated on the basis of the sequence and combination of clinical data available. This leads to a variable degree of certainty.

4. A *hypothetico-deductive diagnosis* path proceeds from one or several working ideas or hypotheses to an ad hoc evaluation, allowing the acceptance or rejection of original ideas (differential diagnosis). A young person complaining of nausea, vomiting, and abdominal pain will elicit differential diagnoses of appendicitis, mesenterial lymphadenitis, nephrolithiasis, gastroenteritis, or extrauterine pregnancy. A judicious set of hypotheses will be linked to patient characteristics, information obtained, and clinical setting of the case. Proceeding from one highest probability to another, Murphy's *steepest ascent method* is considered as characteristic of an experienced physician.[13] Therapeutic and other decisions using *decision trees* (also *vide infra*) are based on an approach similar to Murphy's steepest ascent method.[14]

5. A *probability-based diagnosis* is based on linking the meaning of clinical information in terms of its sensitivity, specificity, and predictive value of the diagnostic method. From the prevalence of the disease in the patient community combined with such "conditional probabilities" as the occurrence of positive or negative results and the sensitivity and specificity of the diagnostic procedure, a "revised" or "posterior" probability is obtained through this kind of Bayesian procedure (*vide infra*).

6. In a *deterministic diagnostic pathway*, unambiguous rules are followed on the basis of compiled knowledge: "If *a throat culture is positive for a bacterial infection*, then *treatment by antibiotics is mandatory.*" This kind of diagnostic reasoning is an extension or sequence of deterministic and/or categorical diagnostic reasoning.

7. *Computer-assisted* diagnosis is based on "if ... then" categorical and deterministic reasoning.

3.2.3 How Good Are Our Diagnostic Methods and Techniques?

Most often, we are interested in the internal and external validity of the diagnostic procedures we perform. We want to know how good they are on their own and how good they are if used repeatedly, in different patients, communities, and settings.

By *diagnostic method,* we do not only mean laboratory tests in clinical biochemistry, hematology, or microbiology. The same logic and criteria apply to manual and sensory diagnostic maneuvers in physical examination, mental state evaluation, and even screening tests.

Screening tests are presumptive diagnostic techniques whose purpose is not to establish a definitive diagnosis and prescribe treatment but to lead patients with positive results to a more complete diagnostic workup and evaluation and treatment if needed.

In essence, each diagnostic method is another kind of proof of a cause–effect relationship: a given morphological or physiological state leads to a positive test result. In practice, we already take such relationships for granted and look at how positive or negative test results corroborate with having or not an anomalous pathological state. Most often, two tests are performed on each patient, the reference test (biopsy, imagery, surgery) and a test to be evaluated if it confirms or rejects correctly the results of the reference test.

We may reason that a family physician's diagnosis of a possible colorectal cancer is a screening procedure (rectal bleeding and other considerations) leading the patient to histopathologic confirmation and surgery, as required. Table 3.1 shows the four most important criteria of a good test[4] and an example.[15]

Sensitivity tells us how many cases may be detected from all cases in a group of patients of interest. In our example, every one case in four would be missed. If the disease is treatable and fatal, if not treated, we want to have a test as sensitive as possible. By using sensitive tests, *we want to detect as many cases as possible and treat them accordingly.*

Specificity tells us how many healthy individuals are confirmed as such by a negative result of the test. This information is useful in cases that are drawn to an in-depth diagnostic workup and treatment. In our example,

Table 3.1   Basic Contingency Table to Evaluate the Internal Validity of a Diagnostic Test

		Result of a Reference Diagnostic Method or a True State of Health		
		Diseased persons (patient **has** cancer)	Persons without disease (patient **does not have** cancer)	
	Positive: patient **may have** cancer	**True positive** results or TP (disease confirmed): **12**	**False positive** or FP (health not confirmed) absence of disease: **46**	Total of positive results for a test (TP + FP): 58
Result of a diagnostic clinical procedure or of a laboratory test: Family physician's working diagnosis	Negative: Patient **may not have** cancer	**False negative** or FN (cases of disease missed): **4**	**True negative** or TN (absence of disease confirmed): **83**	Total of negative results for a test (TN + FN): 87
		Total of diseased persons targeted by the test (TP + FN): 16	Total of healthy subjects who are candidates for a diagnostic procedure (TN + FP): 129	

Source: Reworked and redrawn from data in Goulston, K. J. et al., *The Lancet*, 2, 261–5, 1986.

Sensitivity: TP/TP + FN = 12/12 + 4 × 100 = 75%.

Specificity: TN/TN + FP = 83/83 + 46 × 100 = 64.3%.

Predictive value of a positive test result (syn. Positive predictive value)*:* TP/TP + FN = 12/12 + 46 × 100 = 20.7%.

Predictive value of a negative test result (syn. Negative predictive value)*:* TN/TN + FN = 83/83 + 4 × 100 = 95.4%.

Other clinical reasoning underlying computations using rates, ratios, likelihoods, and odds for future more in-depth (beyond this text) uses.

Likelihood ratio (LR): Ratio of the probability of the test result among individuals with the target disorder (diseased) to the probability of that same test result among individuals who are free of that target disorder (nondiseased, healthy).

Likelihood ratio for a positive test result: LR = sensitivity/(1 − specificity).

Likelihood ratio for a negative test result: LR = (1 − sensitivity)/specificity.

Odds: The ratio of the probability of the occurrence of an event to that of its nonoccurrence. The ratio of the probability that something is one way to the probability that it is another way.

Pretest odds: prevalence/(1 − prevalence).

Posttest odds: pretest odds × likelihood ratio.

Posttest probability: posttest odds/posttest odds + 1.

about one-third of patients fall into this undesirable category. By using highly specific tests, *we want to exclude from further care individuals who do not have the disease and who would be treated then for something that they do not have, that is, we try to avoid "treatment for nothing."*

When a test is highly specific, its positive result rules *in* the diagnosis. (The mnemonic *SpPin* reflects this property of a diagnostic test.)[16] A highly specific test will rule out by its negative result patients who do not deserve further care. Positive test results, whatever their sensitivity might be, make us more certain that the patient has the disease. If the patient did not have the disorder, a negative test result would confirm it.

A highly sensitive test would find by its positive result most of those individuals who do have the disease of interest. This is a highly desirable property in screening programs for disease; community medicine and public health specialists aim for the maximum of cases to be detected to control the problem. On the other hand, a clinician facing an individual patient may be sure that, when using a highly sensitive test yielding a negative result in a particular patient, the patient in question does not have the disease. In other terms, when using a highly sensitive test, its negative result rules *out* the diagnosis. (The mnemonic *SnNout* reflects this property of a highly sensitive test.)[16]

Predictive value of a positive test result tells the clinician what is the probability that the patient really has the disease. We want to be certain *before* the action, before doing something (treatment) that would follow diagnosis. *We want to be sure that the patient really has the disease if tested positive for it.* We are concerned by possible adverse effects and cost, time, and other requirements for needless procedures in patients who do not need these procedures or for whom they are eventually contraindicated. In our example, more than one-half of positively tested patients would fall into this situation.

Predictive value of a negative test result indicates the probability that the patient really does not have the disease if the patient is tested negative. The clinician wants to have certainty before deciding *not* to take action (to treat). In our example, the physician may be almost certain that *doing nothing was a good decision* (95.4% in our case).

In clinical epidemiology terms, the Bayesian reassessment of the predictive values of diagnostic and screening tests is based on linking the prevalence of the problem of interest (i.e., before testing) to the sensitivity and specificity of the test in order to yield revised probabilities of the positive and negative test results' predictive values.

In the eighteenth century, Reverend Thomas Bayes, studying betting, probabilities, and chances, proposed a theorem connecting the conditional and marginal probabilities of events, such as in the case of the so-called a priori probability (before the test is performed) related to posttest probabilities (given the test performed) including sensitivity and specificity, yielding a revised probability for a predictive value of the text taking into account both of the above.[17] (N.B. We have indicated appropriate formulas and equations elsewhere.[18]) It is a way of understanding, in our case, how probability (like the predictive value of a diagnostic or screening test) is updated or revised in light of a new piece of evidence or prevalence (disease frequency or occurrence in the community) in our case.[19]

The Bayesian approach to biostatistics in the health sciences domain is one of the paradigms to draw inferences from observed data. Gustafson specifies correctly that the Bayesian approach distinguishes itself from other approaches and paradigms as opposed to probabilistic statements about mechanistically random processes by the use of probabilistic statements about fixed but unknown quantities of interest. "… At the heart of Bayesian analysis is Bayes's theorem, which describes how knowledge is updated on observing data."[20]

Bayesian analysis has been used in a variety of contexts ranging from marine biology to medicine (diagnostic and screening testing), philosophy of science (relationships between evidence and theory), and even in the development of "Bayesian" spam blockers for e-mail systems.[20]

For example, Bayesian reasoning is worthy of consideration in situations when prevalence of disease in the target or patient's community is too high or low. Even without using appropriate nomograms like Fagan's[21] or other formulae,[12] we can realize what would happen if we tested extensively or otherwise systematically for AIDS in a community in which the prevalence of AIDS is extremely high. We might and would obtain more false negative results than in a very low prevalence community. Predictive value of a negative test result in a high-risk community would be lower; we might lose from prevention and care a good number of patients who would be left unattended in the community with all negative consequences for them and their contacts. Clinical epidemiology offers us more information about the Bayesian management of diagnosis and subsequent clinical remedial decisions.

Diagnostic tests are not only used individually, but also in series and in parallel known as *serial* (i.e., *sequential*) or *parallel testing*. In the case of *sequential testing*, we perform one test (preferably the most sensitive one) first, and, if positive, we add another test, and so on. Each added test depends on the result of the test that preceded it. This way, the entire sequential testing procedure is more specific at its end than a single test. In the case of *parallel testing*, we perform several tests at once and independently of the result of another test. What one test does not detect, the other will. The sensitivity of this type of testing is better than the sensitivity of using a single test.

3.2.4 Diagnosis as a Subject of Argumentation

Making a diagnosis is a process of reasoning aimed at finding the *cause(s)* of a *particular* configuration of signs, symptoms, and test results in a particular patient. In other words, in making a diagnosis, we seek to establish a causal link between some unusual morphology, function, and biological, physical, chemical, or social agent and some particular manifestations of disease, illness, or sickness. As such, the process of making a diagnosis shares many features with the *general* causal reasoning that is required to establish the cause(s) of diseases and the effectiveness of treatments.

3.2.5 Illustrative Fallacies

Fallacious reasoning and decision making may occur anywhere.[8] Some of them are related to the structure of our diagnostic argumentation or to its building blocks and components. They are more extensively reviewed in another title.[8] Only a few of them will be quoted here. (N.B. Some of them may also affect decision making, as reviewed in Chapter 4.)

 a. In *anchoring or premature closure*, we tend to overly relate to early observed features of disease presentation in the diagnostic process and to jump prematurely to conclusions. This happens when everything stops at the "working diagnosis" or "impression" at patient admission without proceeding to a more definitive diagnosis.
 b. Making an *ascertainment bias (fallacy)*, our thinking is preshaped by our expectations or by what we specifically hope to find. We do not detach ourselves enough from preformed notions, expectations, or beliefs that may impact the subsequent interpretation of data.
 c. *Diagnostic creep (diagnosis momentum) fallacy* is committed if the lack of more relevant evidence and information is replaced by an accumulation of opinions creeping in from the patient via paramedics, nurses, and others before they reach, "prediagnosed," the physician—diagnostician. An *order effect fallacy* may be considered a subcategory of the diagnostic momentum: The first information obtained is better

remembered and treated than subsequent information. *Triage cueing* in emergency medicine may also serve as another example of where this fallacy can occur.

d. We commit a *representativeness restraint* fallacy if we ignore a possible diagnosis because patient features and manifestations of the health problem are atypical. Pattern recognition is one of the cornerstones of heuristic practice but should not exclude alternative options.

e. *Calling off* or *search satisficing* fallacy means calling off procedures from preestablished diagnostic or therapeutic planning and workup once some important problem is found. The identification of one serious injury does not exclude a still undetected multiple trauma, other comorbidity, and cotreatments. Sutton's (bank robber's) slip (robbing a bank because that is where the money is), that is, *going for the obvious* or the *hindsight bias*, is other reductionist practice that may also be placed in this category of right or wrong reasoning errors.

f. *Vertical line failure* fallacy is due to exclusively following only the vertical line of thinking and ignoring De Bono's lateral thinking. We reason about one problem when there are in fact many and often interconnected problems. Delayed or missed diagnoses may be minimized by coupling both vertical and lateral thinking.

g. *Ignoring Bayes fallacy* is committed by ignoring and/or misrepresenting any element of Bayesian diagnostic making, such as prior or posterior probabilities, internal validity of diagnostic methods, and their improper linking. *Base rate neglect fallacy* and *availability/nonavailability fallacy* both belong to this category of erroneous reasoning.

h. *Availability and nonavailability* fallacy takes place when we judge a disease from events or experiences that readily come to the physician's mind. As epidemiologists used to say, "looking for horses rather than zebras on hearing the sound of hoofs" should be avoided. Faulty Bayesian reasoning may result from "diagnostic impressionism" based on disproportionate estimates of the frequency of a particular diagnosis or condition. "Zebras" should not be excluded from differential diagnosis. On the other hand, ignoring "zebras" is an omission of lateral thinking in favor of vertical thinking only. This fallacy should be carefully pondered as an error or omission.

i. *Base rate neglect* fallacy happens when we fail to take into account the prevalence of the health condition in a Bayesian approach to diagnosis and replace it with the typical presentation of the health condition in a "natural" setting at the clinical practice site (emergency room). This failure may result in the overestimation of the disease. Elsewhere, a heuristic approach may be the only possible (and maybe successful) approach.

j. *Diagnostic oversimplification* fallacy *(false dilemma)* occurs in reasoning and arguments that are based on exclusive and exhaustive "yes or no" considerations when other alternatives and options exist. This fallacy may take place in differential diagnosis. For example, a patient after receiving a kidney transplant develops a fever. Is the fever due to an infection related to the surgery itself or is it a sign of organ rejection? Are these two options the only possible ones or are there any others? What about another concurrent, new, additional infectious disease? A drug reaction? Some other comorbidity? Infection or rejection may be the most prevalent considerations but are not the only ones. If the diagnosis would be oversimplified (therapeutic decision made only on the basis of fever), a patient suffering from organ rejection would not benefit from treatment by anti-infective agents; a patient suffering from infection might be harmed by receiving immunosuppressive treatment. Needless to say, a differential diagnostic process should be based on all clinically important possibilities and options.

k. The *argumentum ad verecundiam* fallacy ("argument from bashfulness") is almost ubiquitous in daily hospital practice in the advancing and/or accepting of claims based solely on the prestige, status, or respect of its protagonists and proponents. For example, two clinical clerks discuss the relevance of a lumbar puncture in a multiple trauma sufferer. "Why should we perform this procedure on this patient? ... Because the staff-man said so!" This is an unquestioning appeal to the prestige of someone whose dictum is unsupported by evidence, reasoning, or argument. Such appeals should be distinguished from appeals to the legitimate authority of peer-reviewed scientific publications, where data are reported and arguments are given. Of course, a clinical clerk or intern must do what the attending physician orders. But the order is not in itself a justification for doing the procedure. If one wants to know why it is the right thing to do in the circumstances, substantive reasons should be given. The *ad verecundiam* fallacy occurs not only in the diagnostic domain but also in treatment decisions and prognosis.

l. Applied to diagnosis, *ignoring Ockham's razor fallacy* means the following: If you can explain all the observations, reported symptoms, and test results by a condition that you know the patient has, do not bother ruling out another condition that might explain some or all of the same data. The razor is a useful rule of thumb but not an infallible guideline. Sometimes a patient who has suffered a fall has two broken bones, not just the one visible on the x-ray. Sometimes a patient has two infections, not just the one identified by laboratory testing. It is a fallacy to think that knowing a patient has a condition that explains all the data *proves conclusively* that the patient does not have some other condition as well, which would explain some or all of the data. To think this way is to take something that follows inductively (probabilistically) from the data as following deductively (necessarily). Ockham's razor is a warrant that can be defeated by further information. It is therefore a defeasible and not a necessary warrant.

m. The *is-ought* fallacy is based on an assumption that if something *is* now in practice, it *ought* to be so. This assumption, or warrant, is not justified! You need some reason to think that what you are doing now has a good basis other than the fact that you are doing it. "In our practice, the periodical examination for male patients over fifty includes doing a chest x-ray. A chest x-ray ought to be an integral part of the periodical examination of healthy senior adults." (This, of course, is not the case.)

n. The *criterion/criteria* fallacy also exists. As in etiological research, substituting one criterion of validity for the validity of a diagnostic tool as a whole (provided that other criteria are fulfilled too) may not be satisfactory. For example, we may conclude that a diagnostic test's low sensitivity shows that the test is not good. However, although the test is not good for screening, if the same test is highly specific (as it occurs), it may be valuable in clinical practice to confirm the diagnosis and that the patient should be evaluated further and treated for his or her problem.

3.2.6 How Do We Think and Reason in the Diagnosis Domain?

There is not a unique and uniform way to make and use diagnosis in clinical care. Mental processes, types of reasoning, and pathways of thinking underlying diagnosis making and subsequent decision making include the following:

1. Common sense
2. Intuition
3. Pattern recognition
4. Dealing with diagnosis as a logical argument and its outcome (result, claim) in terms of vertical thinking
5. Probabilistic considerations
6. Deterministic building of diagnosis
7. Inductive path and exhaustive approach
8. Hypothetico-deductive path
9. Direction-driven algorithmic path
10. Decision analysis if diagnosis is a part of a multiple-component decision consideration
11. Differential approach between multiple options; differential diagnosis; uses of lateral thinking
12. Building-up and assessing diagnosis through critical thinking imbedded in a modern argument
13. Causal assessment (this anomaly leads to this test result)
14. Validity assessment for practical uses; in general and in a particular individual (compatibility with subjects in grounds and backing)
15. Fallacy watch and corrections

Any of the above-mentioned ways and their combination will vary from one diagnostic problem-solving approach to another.

The challenge of diagnosis making is further amplified by the reality of medical practice, especially in emergency medicine, and anywhere else where information is missing and vague, where there are not enough health professionals to deal with serious patient problems, and where there are constraints of time, facilities, space, and equipment. Discursive, mostly deductive, and analytical thinking as described briefly above must and is often replaced by nondiscursive, mostly inductive, and intuitive thinking proposed by Croskerry as a *dual process model of reasoning in medicine.*[22]

Stolper et al.[23] also recognize that complex tasks often require both analytical and nonanalytical processes under uncertainty to which gut feelings are added as another element to consider. Because these concepts related to situations of uncertainty, incomplete knowledge and other constraints apply not only to diagnosis but also to other steps of clinical work and related decision making. We will discuss these in detail in the next chapter, which covers decision making.

3.3 "That's What We'll Do about It": Reasoning and Deciding How to Treat and if the Treatment Works

Once the diagnosis is made, we want to treat the patient in the best way possible and by the best treatment possible. Our ways of deciding on the appropriate treatment are the same, be it a conservative treatment by drugs, a radical and reconstituting treatment by surgery, or psychotherapy in psychiatry, nursing care, or social support. Also, there is nothing that would exclude from the general rules of reasoning and decision making alternative medicines such as homeopathy, osteopathy, chiropractic, herbalism, aroma therapy, or therapeutic touch in nursing, or any restoring procedures like physiotherapy or beauty enhancers such as sun tanning. Mainstream medicine (also called "allopathic" medicine by naturopaths) and its alternatives are all subject to the same logic, reasoning, and decision making. Once again, cause–effect relationships are at the core of our concerns and considerations.

In the risk domain, we deal with noxious factors and undesirable events such as disease case occurrence. In the treatment domain, we most often pay attention to positive phenomena such as beneficial factors (treatment and care) and improvements in health: cure, lessening the severity of disease, and prevention. Adverse effects of care may be an exception. Both categories of phenomena are an ensemble of *health events that are subject to conceptually similar reasoning*, dealing with probabilities, uncertainties, their quantification, comparisons, interpretation, and use in our decision making. Methodologically, they are subject to similar logic and reasoning. Let us keep this in mind throughout this chapter.

3.3.1 Types and Levels of Medical Therapeutic and Preventive Interventions

Five types of preventive or therapeutic interventions can be considered:[24]

1. *Modification of the factor* or cause of disease. For example, sodium chloride intake in relation to hypertension may be partly replaced by the consumption of other salts.
2. *Modification of exposure*, in terms of avoidance, lesser doses, or its spread in time: abstention from some foods or alcohol, a gluten-free diet in phenylketonuria, and so on.

3. *Modification of the response* or *modification of the function,* such as augmenting subject resistance through vaccines, better nutrition, drugs, operations, and so on.
4. *Avoidance of response,* such as in personal hygiene.
5. *Suppression of the target organ (modification of the morphology),* such as performing an appendectomy or hernia repair. A woman whose mother and sister died of breast cancer may ask her surgeon to perform a bilateral mastectomy, eliminating the biological terrain for a high-probability cancer, given that various endogenous and exogenous factors or causes remain unknown.

We want to know if treatment works at any level of prevention:[25]

■ *Primordial prevention,* a more recent entity, means the control of conditions, actions, and measures that minimize hazards to health and hence inhibit the emergence and establishment of processes and factors (environmental, economic, social, behavioral, and cultural) known to increase the risk of disease. Primordial prevention is accomplished through many public and private health policies and intersectorial action. Focusing on the exposure to potential causes, it may be considered a part of primary prevention (no disease involved yet). By definition, it falls into the domain of *health protection.*

■ *Primary prevention of medical error and medical error produced harm* means *controlling the incidence* (occurrence of *new* cases over a certain period of time). It is generally a task of primary care, family medicine, and public health.

■ *Secondary prevention of medical error and medical error-produced harm* means *controlling the prevalence* (occurrence of all cases at one moment or over a certain period of time) of an error event. Given that prevalence is a function of its average duration and incidence, secondary prevention includes both the control of incidence and disease duration.[7] The control of disease duration is more closely connected to clinical medicine; in preventive medicine sector, "screening for disease (or for medical error and harm)" remains an important tool in secondary prevention.

■ *Tertiary prevention of medical error and error-produced harm* means *controlling the gradient and severity of disease cases,* its long-term impact with regards to disability, impairment, and handicap. Minimizing suffering and maximizing potential years of useful life (partly from Ref. 24) is also its objective. Tertiary prevention focuses exclusively on the consequences of a health problem, not its causes.

■ *Quaternary prevention* consists of actions that identify patients at risk of overdiagnosis or overmedication and that protect them from excessive medical intervention: *actions that prevent iatrogenesis.*[25] Quaternary prevention may prove to be of interest for operational research, especially if supported by further evidence.

Given this multiple sense of prevention, isn't then clinical and community medicine as a whole "preventive"?

Specific epidemiological methods and techniques used in disease prevention in general are described in the epidemiological, public health, and evidence-based medicine literature.[7,26–28]

The concept of cause–effect relationships as discussed earlier (and in Chapter 2) also applies to any kind of intervention in medicine at any level of prevention: control of exposure to noxious factors; immunization in primary prevention; treatment in secondary prevention; avoiding metastases; or ensuring the comfort of a terminal patient in tertiary prevention. The same criteria of cause–effect relationships apply as well as various risk measurements (absolute, relative, attributable). Any evaluation of treatment impact such as effectiveness or adverse effects and their evaluation by additional methods are derived from this basic consideration and approach.

Paradigms, mental processes, and types of reasoning underlying treatment evaluation and decisions regarding a patient represent the same considerations as those of reasoning regarding the risk, plus

■ Equal chances for patients, treatments under comparison, evaluators of effect (randomization and blinding)
■ Equipoise when faced with the research question and the search for the answer
■ Considering the clinical trial as an argument leading to the acceptance or rejection of the treatment under evaluation (vertical thinking)
■ Weighing other options in terms of lateral thinking
■ Weighing benefits and risks (adverse effects)
■ Making distinctions in outcome evaluation: Efficacy, effectiveness, efficiency of treatment, constancy and consistency of its effect and outcomes
■ Considering clinical trials as an evaluation of another cause–effect relationship

■ Choosing the treatment for a particular patient with his or her eligibility to trials serving as grounds and backing for treatment recommendation (claim)

3.3.2 Which Treatment Works Best? How Is It Measured?

Treatment evaluation consists of various procedures, methods, and techniques needed to determine as objectively as possible the relevance, effect, and the impact of various therapeutic activities relative to their preestablished objectives.

Does a new analgesic control arthritis pain? Does a coronary bypass improve cardiac function? Does psychotherapy relieve anxiety in a patient under stress? All these interactions as cause–effect relationships must be examined with the same logic as that used for the assessment of criteria of causality, as explained above (see Table 2.1 in Chapter 2). In interventional or experimental studies, however, it is not the subject who chooses to be exposed (or not) to the factor under study but rather the health professional, be it the researcher or the practicing clinician, who decides who will be exposed to the active treatment or its inactive alternative (placebo), by statistically valid random assignments or otherwise. Since the factor under study (treatment, nursing care, rehabilitation, etc.) is expected to bring about a cure, healing, functional improvement, alleviation of pain, or comfort to the patient, there are fewer ethical obstacles to "voluntarily and deliberately" exposing the patient to such factors.

The major tools of evaluation of medical interventions are clinical and field trials. New interventions, that is, all those that have not yet been more objectively evaluated, go through five distinct phases:[7]

1. A *Phase I* clinical trial is performed on healthy subjects in a descriptive manner only to see *how healthy individuals will respond* to the drug physiologically, morphologically, and otherwise.
2. A *Phase II* clinical trial has as its purpose to find out *how patients (disease sufferers) will respond to the treatment* (drug, etc.). There may be a small control group for basic comparison.
3. A *Phase III* clinical trial shows *if the treatment can and does really work.* The classical randomized double-blind controlled clinical trial belongs to this category. Limited spectrum and gradient of disease is studied first and further expanded later on.
4. A *Phase IV* clinical trial is expected to show how the treatment will work *once it is put to general use.* A nonselective *group of "clean" cases*

(no comorbidity and no treatment for comorbidity) of "whoever comes through the door" is studied.

5. A *Phase V* clinical trial may be considered as a late phase IV, *post-marketing study in which "dirty" cases are involved; those with comorbidities* (multiple additional health problems besides the problem of main interest) *and cotreatment for such additional health problems in all their interaction of indication and response.*

Are all these phases "scientific"? They are. They only increase in their power of causal proof of treatment and cure and in their reproduction of the reality of targeted populations, patients, and setting of care.

Three areas and levels of intervention have their own specificities, requirements, and resulting methodologies requiring special comments: disease treatment and cure, disease prevention, and health maintenance or health promotion.

Any treatment is an intervention, and it represents a cause in relation to its expected impact (result and effect, such as cure or improvement in health and disease). Four questions are usually explored:

1. Is the proposed action *sound* ("does it make sense")?
2. Is the *structure* of the intervention adequate ("how is it organized")?
3. Is its *process* acceptable ("does it happen as desired")?
4. What is the *result* or *impact* of the treatment ("what does it do")?

Any result may be evaluated on four different levels:

1. Does the treatment work in *ideal conditions* (uniform, laboratory, or hospital)? This represents the *efficacy* of the treatment ("Can the treatment work?" In other words, "Are treatment or prevention specious and consistent?").
2. Does the treatment work in *habitual conditions* ("everyday life")? The *effectiveness* of the treatment is then understood ("Does the treatment work?").
3. Does the treatment work *adequately* in relation to the amount of money, time, and resources spent? The *efficiency* of the treatment is examined this way. ("What is the prize of such gains?")
4. "Does the treatment continue to work *once put into action?*" The *constancy* of the performance is highly desirable.
5. Is the current treatment experience *consistent* with the past and other experience?

Health economics, operational research, and health-care organizations focus on the efficiency of interventions. In clinical practice, we particularly want to know the treatment efficacy and effectiveness.

Evaluating effectiveness or efficacy is just a matter of comparison either with the *current* situation (rates without intervention of interest) yielding *effectiveness* or to some reference point, likely the *best* situation. The latter offers an idea regarding the *efficacy* of the proposed intervention.

Any evaluation of treatment impact is an analytical study either by observation or experimentation. Clinical trials are the embodiment of the experimental method across sciences reflected in Figure 2.8 (in Chapter 2): Subjects are partitioned based on the will of the experimenter, preferably at random into two or more groups, that is, a treated group and another group, untreated or treated by some alternative procedure or drug. Data are collected in a "controlled" manner: Experimenters are "blinded" in their readings by ignoring to which group the subjects (patients in the trial) belong and patients ignore to which group they belong. A "randomized double-blind controlled clinical trial" is born. It allows more objective conclusions to be drawn about the cause (treatment of interest or something else) of the outcomes in the trial.

Not only can patients be randomized but also treatment modalities in the case of an episodic disease with multiple spells like migraine or asthma. An *N-of-1 trial* is believed to improve patient management.[29]

Wherever trials are not feasible or available, the impact of treatment may be and is evaluated as a cause–effect relationship by observational studies (case–control studies, studies with historical controls, analysis of time trends, etc.).

Given the heterogeneity of trial designs, comparisons, target groups, and selected patients, findings from multiple trials are brought together by the way of *research integration*, which is essentially an epidemiological study of a set of studies[30–32] of the homogeneity and heterogeneity of their design and results to obtain a more comprehensive idea about a health problem, such as the beneficial impact of treatment or an adverse effect of a noxious factor. Some methodologists emphasize that there are two approaches to research integration:

1. The more quantitative approach, *meta-analysis*, is today seen as a mostly *biostatistical integration* of various fractions, odds or ratios found in original studies, subject to integration. Point and interval estimates of "typical odds ratios" are an example of this type of research integration.

2. *Systematic reviews* represents a more qualitative approach in which the person/place/time characteristics of the trial (or other study) are systematically identified and retrieved one by one, from one study to another. The picture of homogeneity and heterogeneity across studies is thus obtained, analyzed, and interpreted. A kind of *epidemiology of original studies* is done this way.

Both approaches are necessary. The meaning of quantitative integration would only otherwise be more than limited.

For other methodologists, meta-analysis covers both quantitative and qualitative studies (trials), which can be compared in terms of their subject, nature, and design. Systematic reviews analyze heterogeneous and less comparable studies.

The most often used indexes (mathematical relationships) both in original and integrated studies are absolute risk differences or attributable risks in the case of noxious factors or absolute benefit differences or relative benefit (attributable benefit) fraction increases. N.B. Methodologically speaking, a relative benefit notion here is the equivalent of the etiological fraction notion in fundamental epidemiology.

■ *An example of the case of a beneficial factor (treatment) and cases cured or prevented:*
  Rate of recovery in the case of treatment: 80%
  Rate of recovery in the case of not being subjected to this treatment: 20%
  Absolute rate due to the treatment: 80% − 20% = 60%
  Relative benefit fraction (equivalent to "etiological fraction"): 80% − 20%/80% = 75%, meaning that 75% of recoveries are due to the therapeutic intervention of interest.

In the case of the study of a preventive factor such as immunization (vaccination), where newly occurring disease cases (over a defined period of time) rather than recoveries are counted, it would mean a vaccine effectiveness (vaccine protective rate) of 75%, that is, 75% of all expected cases would be avoided (prevented) by (or are due to) immunization. Some may say simply that "... this vaccine is 75% effective."

■ *An example of the case of exposure to a noxious agent and new cases of disease:*

Incidence rate in the exposed group: 80%

Incidence rate in the nonexposed group: 20%

Absolute rate attributable to the factors of interest (from a web of causes shared by both groups under comparison): 80% − 20% = 60%

Attributable risk percent (syn. attributable fraction, attributable proportion, etiological fraction) is: 80% − 20%/80% = 75% of the total of cases (rate) due to the exposure to the factor of interest from the entire web of causal factors. Almost two-thirds of all cases occurring are due to the factor of interest, among others.

Some may say simply that "… this factor represents here three-quarters of the entire web of causes."

If a preventive program to avoid exposure and its consequences were to be implemented, such as smoking cessation to avoid lung cancer, 75% of all cancers occurring in a smoking and nonsmoking community under study (smokers and nonsmokers all together) would be prevented (would not occur) if smokers stopped smoking.

The closer the role of the etiological factor of interest is to 100% of all cases due to all factors forming the web of causes, the more prevalent, dominant, exclusive, or specific is the role of the etiological factor under study.

3.3.3 Which Treatment Modality Applies to a Particular Patient?

Ideally, your patient's characteristics should be similar to the characteristics of patients selected and participating in clinical trials assessing the treatment of interest and confirming the effectiveness of treatment. In other words, you should be asking yourself, "Would my patient be eligible to participate in a clinical trial from which information about treatment effectiveness is coming?" Even more ideally, your patient's characteristics should be compatible with the characteristics of patients participating in the trial and, ultimately, who have responded favorably to treatment. They may differ in all those aspects. However, randomization aside, clinical trial reports do not routinely provide detailed information about the characteristics of patients who responded well and if they differ from those who don't.

3.3.4 *Treatment as a Subject of Argumentation*

We may look at the choice, use, and evaluation of treatment as a kind of pleading for it: an argument leading to some claim or conclusion. We may do so using an evidence-based medicine (critical appraisal) approach or an argumentation (critical thinking) approach. Therefore,[33]

1. We may adopt a more traditional approach by appraising the choice, execution, and effect as *an exercise in critical appraisal as proposed in evidence-based medicine*:
   - Are we dealing with a questionable and uncertain problem?
   - How well is the problem defined?
   - Was the question to be answered properly formulated?
   - Was the search for evidence (other studies) adequate and complete?
   - What is the design of an etiological study? How valid is it?
   - Are biostatistical considerations such as sampling or analysis, and epidemiological considerations such as exposure to possible multiple causes adequately handled and answered?
   - Were clinical aspects of the disease considered (subjects' characteristics, comorbidity, outcomes, follow-up, others)?
   - How was the effect (impact) of a presumed cause (validity of results) evaluated?
   - Which criteria of causality are fulfilled by the study results?
   - Was the broader balance between harm, benefits, costs, and controllability assessed and is it adequate?
   - Is it the best evidence available?
2. We may (and we should) look at statements about treatment as *an exercise in critical thinking and argumentation*:
   - What is the proponents' claim?
   - What was the original question?
   - How solid and complete are grounds needed for the solution of the problem?
   - Is there any good backing for the claim?
   - Does the overall existing information provide some usable understanding of the nature of the problem (warrant)?
   - Are there any conditions (considerations) that might invalidate (rebuttals) or weaken ("negative" adducts) the ensuing final claim?

- How well are such building blocks of an argument interconnected to support or limit the claim?
- In the case of a cause–effect problem: Does the overall evidence fulfill the criteria of causality? Which ones?
- How certain are we about our claim (qualifier specified)?
- Were possible competing claims considered and evaluated?
- Are the results usable in the user's setting (caring of a specific patient, groups of patients, community groups) and in which settings are they not?
- If relevant, how much could and should such findings be generalized?
- Were possible competing causes considered and evaluated?

Both approaches and related paradigms are complementary, not exclusive! Both are needed.

3.3.5 Illustrative Fallacies

Our reasoning and judgment in the domain of treatment, as anything else in our medical reflections, may be prone to errors. Some of these fallacies[8] are worth mentioning. They are related to data and information, to the design of the studies (trials) that produced them, to their interpretation, or to all three aspects.

The same faulty mental processes and types of reasoning underlying risk or diagnosis apply with additional considerations to treatment evaluation and decisions regarding a patient, as already discussed in Section 3.3.1.

a. *Boeotian's fallacy (ignoring webs of causes and webs of consequences fallacy)* means simplistic reasoning due to the ignorance of webs of causes, such as various treatments offered for a particular disease and webs of treatment consequences such as more than one desirable and/or undesirable outcome(s). Formulation of questions about the treatment, its trials, and interpretations may be affected by pretending that this is the only treatment of interest, that alternatives to the clinical trial design do not exist, or that the only chosen outcome is worthy of analysis and interpretation.

b. From a biostatistical point of view, *omitting multivariate* (more than one independent variable) analysis *and/or multivariable* (more than one dependent variable) *analysis* falls also into this category of fallacious approach to treatment understanding.

c. *Confirmation fallacy* or *confirmation bias* stems from looking only for evidence that confirms the hypothesis (such as effectiveness of a particular drug) and omitting the disconfirming evidence. Evidence for the hypothesis may be weaker than the broader evidence gathered later on.

d. *Fallacy of commission* or *action fallacy* is due to the tendency to change the course of events (patient's outcomes) by choosing the treatment because this creates some action as opposed to doing something. "It's better to do something than nothing!" "I would look incompetent and indecisive if I said let's leave it as it is."

e. *Omission fallacy (omission bias)* is the opposite of the above. "I prefer to do nothing, I will avoid errors this way and possible adverse and undesirable outcomes of whatever I choose and will occur."

f. *Overconfidence fallacy* is the omission of critically appraised evidence that the treatment works or not, and its replacing by hunches, absent or incomplete evidence, and exaggerated faith in our own opinion. "It has always worked for me!" "It has always worked in this hospital!"

g. *Appeal to authority fallacy* is misjudging the problem and reasons for decisions because of the position of the decision maker or someone who is an authority in a different domain. "As chairman of this Committee, I must tell you that these clinical treatment guidelines are correct!" "As manager of this hospital I must say that this protocol of care is not the best from among all available alternatives." "I am a resident, I run this floor! Since you are a clinical clerk, do what I tell you." Anonymous authorities, associations with past or present disrepute persons, bodies, or literature are called as references to solve problems and challenges in the domain of treatment.

Let us avoid the above-mentioned fallacies as well as many others.[8]

3.3.6 How Do We Reason in the Domain of Treatment and Preventive Intervention?

In essence, in the domain of treatment and preventive intervention, as in any other domain of clinical reasoning and decision making, we argue for something: "… This drug treatment is best for you …. surgery is not an option for you … this vaccine is 80% effective …" Even in such an informal language, our recommendations are "claims" or conclusions of an argument in favor or disfavor of such a treatment. We look at data, studies, and other references as "grounds" to see if they are good and complete enough for our recommendation. We check other available information from our experience, from colleagues, literature, or electronic sources to see if such "backing" may be linked and useful with "grounds." We examine the explanatory value of such links as a "warrant" of our conclusions. Can we say (and why?) how sure we are about our claim? Such a "qualifier" expresses our certainty that our recommendation is good. A patient may effectively ask: "… Doctor, are you sure that your recommendation of surgery is correct?" If the patient asks "Isn't my problem exceptional and not applicable to your generally recommended strategy?," we must weigh our answer in terms of all positive elements and exclusionary elements, "rebuttals" as both positive and negative adducts, which lead us to our conclusions and recommendations. The patient may ask for such an explanation.

All elements of our reasoning are based on what we have seen in the patient and on the epidemiological and biostatistical information we have: our certainty and uncertainty, probabilities of events such as disease prevalence, incidence, case fatality, duration, causal association quantifications and criteria (rates, ratios odds), our knowledge of chances of cure (effectiveness of treatment), and long-term outcomes as part of prognosis.

Our best treatment recommendation will depend then on the quality and completeness of clinical and epidemiological evidences underlying the information that is at our disposal and on our correct ways of using such evidences in a fallacy-free argumentation path.

> Our professional and scientific information and argumentation as well will often be hidden in the natural language of all parties involved. We should be able to retrieve it anytime.

3.4 Reasoning about Prognosis: "You'll Be Doing Well" … Making Prognosis Meaningful

From the very beginning of a clinical experience, the health professionals involved will be asked: "What will happen to me?" Patients expect not only a favorable prognosis but also that such a prognosis will be as realistic as possible. As an example, it is discovered that a middle-aged multiparous mother has endometrial cancer and her attending physicians suggest a hysterectomy and other treatments as needed. She may ask: "… Is what you propose necessary? … What will happen if I choose not to have this operation? … What other possible problems should I expect and when? … What is my remaining life expectancy with or without my problem and its treatment? …" What will you tell her? In other words, what is your prognosis in this case? Again, our answers are not only a product of our knowledge of prognostic facts and experience but also of our reasoning about them translated into the argumentation and exchange of ideas with the patient and with other colleagues who are caring for her in the context of this and other health problems.

Prognosis is more than the art of foretelling the course of disease or "the prospect of survival and recovery from a disease as anticipated from the usual course of that disease or as indicated by the special features of the case in question."[34]

Contemporary prognosis is not a guess or a product of clinical flair. It is an estimation of probabilities, as is the evaluation of risk. The basic clinical epidemiological approach is governed by a similar spirit. In risk assessment, probabilities of developing disease are estimated according to the characteristics of the individual and his general environment. In prognostic assessment, the probabilities of various good *and* bad events as well as outcomes in the already diseased individual are assessed. While risk is usually related to one event (falling ill), prognostic studies are multidimensional in that they deal with several outcomes, not just death.

Although risk depends mostly on nonmedical factors, prognosis is largely determined by clinical factors, human biology, and pathology.

With these considerations in mind, let us understand *prognosis* then as "an assessment of the patient's future (based on probabilistic considerations of various beneficial and detrimental clinical outcomes as causally or otherwise determined by various clinical factors, biological and social characteristics of the patient) and of the pathology under study (disease course) itself. Its main purpose is to prevent undesirable events and to intervene precociously to modify disease course and drive it to its best possible outcome(s). Hence, prognosis is an important element of medical decision making that goes well beyond reassurance of the patient as part of good bedside manners. It is a professional act like any other, be it risk assessment, diagnosis, surgery or medication."[35]

Fries and Ehrlich[36] emphasize several characteristics of prognosis as we see it in some modified way today:

■ Prognosis is a prediction, a probabilistic consideration under uncertainty.
■ Prognosis may be dealt with in both qualitative and quantitative terms.
■ Prognosis is multidimensional, reflected by webs of causes and webs of consequences (outcomes).
■ Prognosis covers in meaningful terms a specific time period.

- Prognosis varies often from one subgroup of the health problem to another and must be dealt with as such and as a composite phenomenon.
- Prognosis does not rely exclusively on treatment. Other prognostic factors may be involved, including patient characteristics, comorbidity, type and setting of general care, and so on.
- The above considerations apply to a variable degree and combination from one health problem to another. The discussion of each prognosis should then be modified accordingly.

With regards to prognosis, a contemporary clinician must proceed with the same rigor when evaluating what will happen to an individual patient as others do when dealing with disease at the community level. The clinician must know, and use, all relevant information from community and clinical epidemiology findings to assess the probability of the worst possible events in order to prevent or alleviate them.

As patients or health professionals, we need to know and share prognosis for three major reasons:

1. For the patient, the *best possible estimation of the disease's future course and outcome* gives him or her either reassurance and improvement of mental well-being or (if the prognosis is poor) allows for timely considerations for the best possible quality of life remaining.
2. For physicians and nurses, good prognostic information allows for the *best therapies and care* to be planned for the patient.
3. For social services, good prognostic information allows for a *timely and optimal reintegration of the patient* into the family, occupation, and environment to an extent and degree corresponding to the foreseeable health status.

Given the considerable human and material resources involved, prognostic studies must arrive at conclusions that are as close to the future reality as possible.

3.4.1 Differences between the Prognosis Domain and the Risk Domain

Making a prognosis is more complicated than assessing risk. As in the risk domain where various risk markers and factors must be evaluated separately, *prognostic characteristics* fall into two categories: (1) *prognostic markers* (which cannot be modified and upon which disease course is dependent), and (2) *prognostic factors* (which can be modified; consequently, disease course can also be modified). Knowledge of both is necessary to make a good prognosis. In addition, methodological aspects of prognosis depend on different individuals under study, the duration of events, different causal factors, and the main topics under study, all differing from risk assessment. Table 3.2 summarizes these differences.

Traditionally, the knowledge of risk factors in medicine was automatically extrapolated to the field of prognostic factors. Doing so, however, is often quite misleading. For example, smoking is a powerful risk factor for lung cancer, but is it justified for a clinician to suggest that a lung cancer patient stop smoking at an advanced stage of disease? Is it wise to suggest that an octogenarian with a small facial basocellular lesion minimize exposure to the sun in order to avoid skin cancer, even if the patient is carefully followed, screened, and surgically treated in time?

Some risk factors lose their power as prognostic factors and some are important at both levels. For example, alcohol abuse is a powerful risk factor for chronic hepatitis and liver cirrhosis. Patients with chronic hepatitis and liver cirrhosis will further deteriorate if they continue to drink. Thus, alcohol is a powerful prognostic factor as well. An alcoholic, cirrhotic patient should stop drinking, but a lung cancer patient whose life expectancy is 2 years at best might possibly continue smoking without greatly altering the disease's course, even though smoking caused the fatal neoplasia in the first place.

In this context, the ethicist should be asked: Is such a recommendation acceptable from an ethical point of view?

Operationally, risk remains the focus of primary prevention, whereas prognosis and ensuing clinical decisions fall into the field of secondary and tertiary prevention. Consequently, effective secondary and tertiary prevention will depend on the knowledge of prognostic markers and factors in their best qualitative and quantitative terms. Certain states, already being consequences of other prognostic factors, lead to the diversification and aggravation of the disease spectrum and ultimately of its gradient:

- By **disease spectrum** we mean here the range of different systemic manifestations of the disease like the glandular, oculoglandular, oropahryngeal, pleuropulmonary, or typhoid forms of tularemia.
- **Disease gradient** is, however, an expression of different grades of disease according to the severity of cases. Subclinical, flu-like, benign, chronic, and fatally necrotic cases encompass the gradient of viral hepatitis.

Table 3.2   Basic Characteristics of Prognosis as Opposed to Risk

Topic of Interest	Risk	Prognosis
Individual	What will happen to healthy subjects	What will happen to subjects who already have disease under study
Occurrence of expected effects	Less frequent or rare	Frequent
Controllability of independent variable	Risk characteristics • Uncontrollable: risk markers • Controllable: risk factors	Prognostic characteristics • Uncontrollable: prognostic markers • Controllable: prognostic factors
Aim of study	• Primary prevention • Better assessment of individuals	• Secondary and tertiary prevention • Better clinical decisions
Population size	Many subjects are often studied (large size of studies)	Few patients are often available for the study (small size of studies)
Major focus of interest	Often • Causes • Nonmedical factors • Risk factors	Often • Consequences • Medical factors • Prognostic markers
Time factor	Occurrence of events toward a given moment (incidence, mortality, etc.)	Occurrence of events evolving in time ("survival" curves)
Target population	Mainly community at large	Hospital-bound individuals (bedridden patients, clinics, etc.)
Accessibility and compliance of participants	Poor or variable	Usually good
Interest and motivation of investigators	Variable	Usually high
Cost of study	Usually higher	Usually lower
Competence of investigators to do study	Usually better	Variable

Source: Partially from Jenicek, M. and Cléroux, R., *Épidémiologie Clinique. Clinimétrie (Clinical Epidemiology. Clinimetrics.)*, EDISEM/Maloine, St. Hyacinthe, QC/Paris, 1985.

Finally, prognostic factors arise not only from the web of causes of principal disease outcomes but also from concurrent diseases or newly appearing comorbid states (such as cross-infections, metabolic imbalances, etc.). Indeed, all may act upon the outcome of the disease of main interest and/or on any other comorbidity or additional new disease or health problem.

Nonetheless, probabilistic estimations and analyses of exposure to risk or to prognostic factors and their outcomes are still often merged and confounded in current literature.[36,38] Let us always read with care.

3.4.2 What Do We Need to Know about Prognostic Events and Outcomes?

A good or bad (qualitative) prognosis also requires quantification in terms of probabilities. A probabilistic prognosis can be expressed in many different ways, such as

- By establishing a *survival rate* after 5 years of observation, as is usually done in studies of cancer patients
- By determining a *case fatality rate* at any moment (N.B. Mortality may also be a measure of risk and prognosis since it is the product of incidence density and case fatality rate)[7]
- By detecting a *response rate to treatment* at any moment of a follow-up period (such as an improvement rate after the treatment of leukemia patients)
  - As a *remission rate* following a defined treatment (provided that a remission period and its criteria are well defined)
  - As a *relapse rate* (with the same conditions as above)
  - By establishing a *longitudinal picture of events during the natural or clinical course of disease*, known as a **survival curve.**

A *survival curve* is essentially a sequence of rates (proportions) of events of interest in time. Originally, a proportion of patients (usually cancer sufferers) surviving or dying at a given moment were the subject of study. Today, the terms "survival" or "survival studies" are rather awkward or misleading because, in addition to deaths, any event appearing during the natural or clinical course of disease may be the subject of a "survival" analysis: disease spells, recurrence, comorbid events, adverse reactions, and so on.

Figure 3.1 is an example of survival curves of an event with or without treatment. Such curves, as indicated by arrows in the figure, show that survival curves may be used to study *trends*. From such descriptions, hypotheses about the evolution of prognosis can be made. As the shadowed sections illustrate, comparisons of survival curves are used in etiological research to analyze and demonstrate the *role of prognostic factors*, noxious or beneficial, in good or bad prognosis.

Methodological note: Beginners may find two methods of graphical representation in the literature. If a larger number of events are available, an *actuarial method or life table method* yields rather "smooth"-looking curves based on comparable intervals of observations. If a limited number of events are available, durations or intervals resulting from case-by-case observations from one event to another yield "jagged" (irregular step pattern) curves based on the *Kaplan–Meier survival study method*.

The methodology of studying survival also applies to outcomes of disease other than death: the development of complications; another spell of disease such as a migraine attack or an epilepsy "mal"; surgical complications after an operation; adverse effects of treatment; and others. During the past two decades, a new term "time-to-event analysis" has been applied to

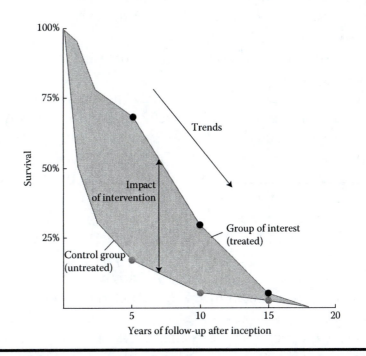

Figure 3.1 **Survival curves comparing clinical course in treated and untreated groups of patients. A fictitious example.**

these studies of morbid events. In studies of treatment effectiveness, time-to-event analysis may be even more specific. For example, in such studies of migraine treatment, time-to-event analysis becomes "time-to-relief analysis"; or, elsewhere, it may become "time-to-effect analysis."

3.4.3 What Do We Expect from Prognostic Studies in Order to Reason More Effectively about the Future of Our Patients? What Treatment Modality Best Applies to a Particular Patient?

Like studies of risk, studies of prognosis may be either descriptive, observational, analytical, or experimental and most are longitudinal cohort studies by nature.

As in descriptive studies of risk, descriptive studies of prognosis serve several purposes:

- To generate hypotheses on probable causes of a good or bad prognosis in patients
- To identify patients at high probability of a bad prognosis
- To give argument components and support those necessary for clinical decision analysis and clinical decisions themselves

Analytical observational (cohort and case–control studies) research can take place through comparative studies of "survival" in time.

Analytical studies of prognosis can be either inductive or deductive. Many studies in this area are based on an inductive approach to data (information already exists in clinical charts).

In cohort studies of prognosis, where hypotheses are constructed deductively and study designs built ad hoc, conclusions can be more solid than those in retrospective studies.

Finally, intervention studies, such as clinical trials, may be based on the comparison of survival curves (or prognostic curves) in different groups of patients subjected to different treatment modalities.

A simple comparison of the frequency of outcomes in treatment groups usually represents the assessment of treatment impact in the short term. A comparison of prognostic (survival) curves is an important method of evaluation of a treatment's long-term impact. In these studies, the natural (placebo) and clinical course are compared or various clinical courses (under various treatment modalities) are assessed with regard to their best efficacy and effectiveness.

Comparative studies of disease course represent yet another type of study dealing with cause–effect relationships between various nonclinical and clinical events and disease outcomes. Besides special statistical techniques, the principles of any analytical study, observational or experimental in the prognosis domain, are subject to the same clinimetric rigor and causal reasoning as any other study in clinical epidemiology.

Making a prognosis based simply on knowing how many patients will survive a certain time period (e.g., 5 years following the detection of cancer or any other disease) might yield very poor information since the exact timing (moment of occurrence) of the events in *this 5-year period* would be ignored. As shown by Fletcher et al.,[39] several diseases may show a comparable survival rate at a given moment, 10%, for example. Such a prognosis can be made for a rapidly dissecting aortic aneurysm: subjects mainly die within the first 1 or 2 years following its discovery. A similar 5-year survival rate can be observed in chronic granulocytic leukemia, but more patients survive beyond the first year and years after within the same 5-year period.

To describe and properly analyze prognostic events, a life table (which is a kind of summary of moments and events of interest) must first be established and then a survival curve must be estimated from it. Once survival curves are established through an appropriate survivorship study, a survival analysis, that is, comparison of curves, can be carried out.

A *life table* is a summarizing technique used to describe the pattern of mortality (or of any other event of clinical interest) and survival (i.e., nonevent) in populations. A *clinical life table* "describes the outcome experience of a group or cohort of individuals classified according to their exposure or treatment history."[24,39] It is "… a summarizing technique used to describe the pattern of morbidity and survival in populations."[25]

Survival curves for groups of patients must often be established. Then, different groups of patients can be compared in terms of survival.

A *survival curve* is "a curve that starts with 100% of the study population and shows the percentage of the population surviving at successive times for as long a period as information is available."[25,40]

There are three major reasons to establish, analyze, and use survival curves:

1. Survival curves depict trends and the evolution of prognostic events in time.
2. Analyses of time trends represented by survival curves allow hypotheses generations about the possible causal factors behind differing trends depicting prognosis.

3. The comparison of survival curves contributes to the establishment of causal relationships between disease course and prognostic and other factors.

As already mentioned, "survival" is not merely "avoiding death," when death represents the disease outcome of interest. It is a state until the occurrence of some event or outcome of interest. *It can be any discrete event such as a relapse, recovery, disease spell (well defined), or any other change of disease course. The term "survival" is chosen here because of its persistent use, although it represents "time-to-event," "survival time," or any "prognostic" function of interest.*

If the endpoint in "true" survival studies is too difficult or expensive to detect, some other "surrogate" point, more readily measurable, but well correlated with the former, and biologically well justified for substitution, may be selected and analyzed.[41] In survival studies of cancer, surrogates for tumor response may be its progression, reappearance of the disease, or the predefined particular value change of carcinoembryonic antigen.[42]

In the statistical literature, establishing a survival curve is called a "survivorship study," which is currently defined as the "use of a cohort life table to provide the probability that an event, such as death, will occur in successive intervals of time after diagnosis (or other time point defined a priori), and conversely, the probability of surviving each interval. The multiplication of these probabilities of survival for each time interval for those alive at the beginning of that interval yields a cumulative probability of surviving for the total period under study."[40] In these studies, the estimation of "survival" is based on information available about *all* patients including cases of incomplete follow-up for reasons unrelated to the outcome of interest such as patients dropping out, moving away, dying from other causes, and so on.

Survival analysis is then a "class of statistical procedures for estimating the survival function and for making inferences about the effects of treatments, prognostic factors, exposures, and other covariates."[40] Only principles of survival analysis are outlined in this section. Numerical examples abound in the medical literature and quantitative methodology of survival analysis are described in the statistical literature. However, all clinicians should know what information they need to provide for such an analysis and how to understand its findings. They are the final users of prognostic findings and decision makers.

3.4.3.1 How Should We Apply What We Know to an Individual Patient?

As in the domain of individual application of treatment evidence, general applicability of research evidence to individual patients and its integration with care is equally valid in the domain of prognosis. The applicability of a prognostic study to an individual patient under a physician's care may be summarized here in just a few questions:

- *Would my patient be eligible for a study of prognosis whose results should apply to him or her?*
- *Would my patient finish such a study?*
- *Would my patient finish in the "winning group," that is, those ending with a good prognosis?*
- *Are his or her clinical and demographic characteristics similar to those of the patients involved in the research on prognosis on the basis of which we reason?*

Needless to say, the third question is more difficult to answer than the three others.

Neither sociodemographic comparability nor clinical and paraclinical characteristics of the disease in the patient are sufficient in the domain of prognosis. The clinician must also ensure that the clinical setting and care, its accessibility and coverage, as well as the human and material resources needed for such care, are compatible. In other terms, *does the patient evolve in a similar environment of care* (primary care, hospital, long-term care, social services, and living conditions)?

Often, our prognostication is not flawless and it may be subject to multiple fallacies to know, avoid, and correct.

3.4.4 Prognosis as a Subject of Argumentation

The argumentative approach supported by the best evidence embedded in all building blocks of an argument is the best approach to consider.

Paradigms, mental processes, and types of reasoning underlying prognosis making in a patient are subject to all other considerations and reasoning similar to those in the study and interpretation of risk, diagnosis, and treatment, *plus*

- Assessing possible disease outcomes, a problem of both description and cause–effect link evaluation.

- Distinctions are made between prognostic markers (uncontrollable) and prognostic factors (controllable).
- The understanding of temporal sequence and of interactions between prognostic factors and markers remains a considerable challenge.
- While single outcomes are often studied in the assessment of risk or treatment effectiveness, prognostic studies focus more often on the web of outcomes (the consequences of disease course and its treatment).
- Understanding prognosis in terms of vertical thinking (within the study) and lateral thinking (multiple studies, experiences, and pathways to solve the problem).
- Applying prognostic experience to an individual patient means assessing the compatibility between the specific patient under our care and other patients who served as study subjects in our past prognostic research and practice experience.

Prognosis is another process of reasoning leading to a conclusion. Premises may include patient characteristics, past therapeutic experience, exposure to various risk, and prognostic factors as well as experience with desired and adverse effects of preventive and therapeutic interventions. The conclusion is that the patient will fare well or poorly within a defined time span.

As is the case for any other argument in the risk, diagnosis or treatment domains, concluding (or claiming, as philosophers/logicians/critical thinkers say) is an endpoint of some kind of reasoning process based on direct information (grounds, data), available past experience (backing), and an explanatory link between them (warrant) giving some probability of the righteousness of the claim (qualifier) provided that some exclusionary information (rebuttals) invalidates our claims, such as our prognosis is good or bad. There is no learning and understanding of prognosis without discussing such building blocks of modern argument and argumentation.

3.4.5 Illustrative Fallacies

The prognosis domain of clinical considerations also has its own flaws and fallacies like risk assessment, diagnosis, or treatment.[8] A few examples will introduce us to this area of errors in reasoning and decision making:

a. *Division and composition.* Taking the truth about some whole as applying to each one of its parts or vice versa is a fallacy that occurs both
in research, practice, and the outside world. "The prognosis of cancer
is bad!" Often yes, but is it true for all of its stages, all sites, all types
of medical facilities and care available? Not necessarily. Prostate cancer
has a better prognosis than pancreatic cancer. Similarly, angioplasty can
do marvels for single artery coronary disease, but not necessarily in
advanced atherosclerosis involving several coronary arteries.

b. *Fallacy of division* means concluding that the properties of an entity
as a whole apply to each of its part. A systematic review of the effectiveness of an anticancer drug improving prognosis across the entire
cancer domain does not mean that it applies to each type of cancer
under consideration, all of its (their) stages and coincidence with other
treatments.

c. *Fallacy of composition* is the opposite of the above: Reasoning that
since some part (and other parts) of a whole has a given property, the
entire entity that these parts constitute should also have that property.
Finding adverse effects of a new antibiotic in treating bacterial skin
infections does not mean that this drug will necessarily produce the
same adverse effects in other systemic infections.

d. *Oversimplification.* This fallacy occurs if we look at prognosis too globally, without "atomization," a term used by logicians for breaking down
a huge problem into manageable pieces. For example, a good or bad
prognosis may simply mean a principal outcome of the disease of interest like death and some of its determining clinical and other factors.
Another prognosis may concern the prediction of the occurrence of
additional other diseases, treatment for such a comorbidity, or outcomes
of the latter. To say that "a prognosis is good" or "bad" does not necessarily refer only to survival or indicate that the patient will walk out
alive from the hospital.

   *Saying that the prognosis in this patient is good or bad does not always
   mean a good or poor survival or life expectancy.* For example, exposure
   to some prognostic beneficial factor like treatment may lead to a better
   prognosis in terms of a better course of the major health problem under
   treatment, it may improve the course of other comorbid states (other
   diseases of interest), or it may be a good prognostic factor in relation
   to other health problems occurring with the index health problem, like
   cross-infection, new degenerative processes, or injuries without necessarily affecting overall survival.

e. *Misleading use of statistics.* Prognoses are often stated in terms of probabilities or in terms of measures of a central tendency. "Abdominal mesothelioma is incurable, with a median mortality of only 8 months after discovery." Does this mean that a patient diagnosed with abdominal mesothelioma will be dead within 8 months? Among other considerations, cases are *not always uniformly distributed* around a median (middle-ranking) value. In this instance, the 50% of recorded patients with abdominal mesothelioma who died in 8 months or less were clustered in this short period, but the 50% who lived for 8 months or more were spread out over a period that ranged up to several years. Statistical distributions *apply only to a prescribed set of circumstances.* In this instance, the reported median applied to patients given conventional treatment; it would be different in the case of some alternative, better treatment protocol.

3.4.6 *How Do We Think in the Domain of Prognosis? Considerations for Further Work and Understanding in the Area of Prognosis*

Intuition is even less important in prognostication than in treatment decisions and is more an attitude of faith than logic fueled by evidence. The best available evidence should be at hand to support building blocks of our argumentation. Fallacy-free connections between argument blocks (grounds, backing, warrant, adducts for the conclusion and rebuttals, ensuing conclusion and claim) is what makes medicine critical thinking-based and evidence-grounded.

In a more traditional approach and basis for understanding of prognosis, *outcomes of disease* may be studied by observational longitudinal studies to establish a particular probability of outcome (event) in time, like other disease spells, occurrence of new complications, new comorbidity, cure, or death.

Prognostic studies are derived from a time-extended follow-up of outcomes in clinical trials or observational analytical studies. More than one group of patients are then involved and compared. Absolute and relative probabilities of outcomes are formulated as a *hazard*, absolute for a given group or relative to some other control group.

Risk as the probability of new cases of disease in the community in previously healthy subjects has already been discussed. Let us stress again that risk as assessment of disease occurrence is essentially an evaluation of the cause–effect relationship between some *factors and disease before it occurs in individuals who do not have it and who might get it. Prognosis is the probability* of some events (outcomes) *occurring in individuals who already have the disease.* For some, prognosis also includes other predictions of outcomes in individuals who still either do not have the disease or have not been treated for it or anything else. This distinction between risk and prognostic characteristics (factors and markers) is often confounded in the current literature.

Despite the considerable development of a conceptual and methodological basis of prognosis, this field remains "young." Thousands of survival and other prognostic studies have taken place, but once published, their results are still used less often in practice than information obtained from the areas of diagnosis and treatment. However, prognostic information that goes beyond educated guesswork is necessary for patient counseling. Moreover, it is crucial when deciding what problem is worthy of prevention (secondary and tertiary prevention in particular).

Also, prognostic scoring systems are now increasingly the subject of pragmatic evaluations. As already mentioned, Hussain et al.'s study[42] of such systems in the field of gastrointestinal bleeding is an excellent example of such initiatives.

It is still necessary to know if the structured approach to prognosis (called "actuarial judgment"[43]) or the clinical approach supports the preference of actuarial judgment based on experience in psychiatry and medicine.

The prognostic performance of physicians may vary considerably from one physician to another and adversely affect care in emergency situations and in critical care. In cardiology, interphysician variability may be substantial. In coronary artery disease, statistical predictions can provide better predictions than the "expert" clinical judgment of individual cardiologists.[44]

Any prognostician should expect that his or her patient may not be happy with a sole quantitative prognosis, but the patient may also ask "why?"

Returning to this section's introductory example, the attending physician advising a patient to have a hysterectomy should, on the basis of the above-mentioned considerations, give the patient the second half of the answer: "You will be fine, because...." In other words, the physician tells the patient that specific prognostic data from description, research of causes, and clinical trials or other types of outcome research speak in her favor (her situation being similar to other patients in these studies). The physician can conclude by telling her: "... but given your past and present specific characteristics, here is how sure you can be about the following...."

Conclusion

Our reasoning and decision making at any stage of the clinical management of patients require more than an often monumental volume of information from reading, teaching, listening, and watching during our present and past experience. We must know their general value as well as values specific to patients who differ to a varying degree from one to another. What should we keep in mind?

Our views of risk assessment in the patient, diagnosis, treatment, and prognosis have been and are shaped by various traditional and less traditional disciplines: fundamental epidemiology, clinical epidemiology, biostatistics, but also from emerging cognitive science, decision making, and philosophy (informal logic, critical thinking, and argumentation). Our ways of reasoning come from among all the above-mentioned fields is less important than integrating them into some common view and uses from which all, patients and medical professionals as well, would benefit for the sake of the best possible quality of care.

At any level and step of clinical work, we must consider the underlying cause–effect relationships, judge them, and use them in our interpretations and decisions. Our broader views go well beyond causality. For example, in the diagnostic domain, evaluating the internal validity (how the test detects disease itself) and the external validity (how the test performs in practice once its internal quality is determined) rationalize further our diagnostic processes.

Epidemiological, biostatistical, and other methodologies will proportionally vary from one clinical activity to another. However, logic and critical thinking are and increasingly will be essential at any level of what we are doing in daily practice and medical research. All our statements, such as "… you must stop smoking … alcohol ruined your liver … take this pill, it will ease your pain … if you don't do this, you will shorten the years you have left …" are claims and conclusions of our argumentation held either between us or with our patients about such problems. Let us understand what is required and apply it more successfully in practice.

Sooner or later, all medical activities, be they practice or research-related, are evaluated in terms of several basic characteristics:

- Soundness: *Does it make sense?*
- Structure: *Is it properly organized and interconnected from one statement to the next?*
- Process: *Does it run logically from one step to the next and is it properly interconnected?*
- Impact: *Does it have a desired effect?*
- Constancy: *Does it remain the same under all circumstances?*
- Consistency: *Is there conformity between the findings in different studies, samples, strata or populations, different times and circumstances, methods and investigators?*
- "Fit": *Does it belong to and is it valid in the context of patient characteristics, health care practices and environment, prevailing local ethics, values, preferences, choices, and other settings?*
- "Cui prodest?" or "Cui bono?": *Who will benefit from all this?*

Anyone who proposes and prefers a particular activity and decision should be able to explain and defend his or her standpoint based on all the above-mentioned criteria.

Once the health information is deemed to be sound, well organized and structured, running well, once it has a desired or even better impact, fits in the context of the health problem to be managed, and its benefits are known, it may enter the decision making process, as outlined in Chapter 4.

References

1. Higgs J, Jones MA, Loftus S, Christensen N. *Clinical Reasoning in the Health Professions*. Third Edition. Amsterdam/Boston/Heidelberg/London: Elsevier/Butterworth Heinemann, 2008.
2. *A Dictionary of Public Health*. Edited by JM Last. Oxford and New York: Oxford University Press, 2007.
3. Everitt BS. *The Cambridge Dictionary of Statistics in the Medical Sciences*. Cambridge/New York/Melbourne: Cambridge University Press, 1995.
4. Holland BK. *Probability without Equations. Concepts for Clinicians*. Baltimore, MD/London, UK: The Johns Hopkins University Press, 1998.
5. Goodman SN. Toward evidence-based medical statistics. 1: The *P* value fallacy. 2: The Bayes factor. *Ann Intern Med*, 1996;**130**:995–1004 (part 1) and 1005–1013 (Part 2).

6. Ware JC, Mosteller F, Ingelfinger JA. P values, pp. 49–69, in: *Medical Uses of Statistics*. Edited by JC Bailar III and F Mosteller. Waltham, MA: NEHM Books, 1986.

7. Jenicek M. *Foundations of Evidence-Based Medicine*. Boca Raton/London/New York/Washington: The Parthenon Publishing Group/CRC Press, 2003.

8. Jenicek M. *Fallacy-Free Reasoning in Medicine. Improving Communication and Decision Making in Research and Practice*. Chicago, IL: American Medical Association (AMA Press), 2009.

9. Feinstein AR. *Clinical Epidemiology. The Architecture of Clinical Research*. Philadelphia/London: W.B. Saunders Company, 1985.

10. Fletcher RH, Fletcher SW, Wagner EH. *Clinical Epidemiology. The Essentials*. Third Edition. Baltimore/Philadelphia/London: Williams & Wilkins, 1996.

11. Gordis L. *Epidemiology*. Second Edition. Philadelphia/London/New York: W.B. Saunders Company, 2000.

12. Jenicek M. Identifying cases of disease. Clinimetrics and diagnosis, chapter 6, pp. 107–46, in: Ref. 7.

13. Murphy EA. *The Logic of Medicine*. Baltimore/London: The Johns Hopkins University Press, 1976.

14. Jenicek M. Decision analysis and decision-making in medicine. Beyond intuition, guts, and flair, chapter 13, pp. 341–78, in: Ref. 7.

15. Goulston KJ, Cook I, Dent OF. How important is rectal bleeding in the diagnosis of bowel cancer and polyps? *The Lancet*, 1986;**2**:261–5.

16. Straus SE, Scott Richardson W, Glasziou P, Haynes RB. *Evidence-Based Medicine. How to Practice and Teach EBM*. Third Edition. Edinburgh/London/New York: Elsevier/Churchill Livingstone, 2005.

17. Bayes T. An essay towards solving a problem in the doctrine of chances (Read 23 December 1763). *Biometrika*, 1958;**45**:296–315.

18. Jenicek M. Variability of predictive values of diagnostic and screening tests, Section 6.4.1.7, pp. 122–4, in: Ref. 7.

19. Fu R. Bayes's theorem, pp. 73–75, in: *Encyclopedia of Epidemiology*. Edited by S Boslaugh and L-A McNutt. Los Angeles/London/New Delhi/Singapore: SAGE Publications, 2008.

20. Gustafson P. Bayesian approach to statistics, pp. 72–3, in: *Encyclopedia of Epidemiology*. Edited by S Boslaugh and L-A McNutt. Los Angeles/London/New Delhi/Singapore: SAGE Publications, 2008.

21. Fagan TJ. Nomogram for Bayes' formula. *N Engl J Med*, 1975;**293**:257.

22. Croskerry P. Clinical cognition and diagnostic error: Applications of a dual process model of reasoning. *Adv in Health Sci Educ*, 2009;**14**:27–35. DOI 10.1007/s10459-009-9182-2.

23. Stolper E, Van de Wiel M, Van Royen P, Van Bokhoven, Van der Weijden T, Dinant GJ. Gut feelings as a third track in general practioners' diagnostic reasoning. *J Gen Intern Med*, 2010;**26**(2):197–203. DOI:10.1007/s11606-010-15240-5.

24. Jenicek M. The impact of treatment and other clinical and community health interventions. A "Does it work?" evaluation, chapter 9, pp. 229–68, in: Ref. 7.

25. *A Dictionary of Epidemiology.* Edited by M Porta, S Greenland and JM Last, Associate Editors. An IEA Sponsored Handbook. Fifth Edition. Oxford/New York: Oxford University Press, 2008.
26. Rossi PH, Lipsey MW, Freeman HE (eds.). An overview of program evaluation, pp. 1–30, in: *Evaluation. A Systematic Approach.* Seventh Edition. Thousand Oaks, CA: Sage Publications, 2004.
27. Wallace RB, Kohatsu N, Last JM (eds.). *Wallace/Maxcy-Rosenau-Last Public Health and Preventive Medicine.* New York: McGraw-Hill Medical, 2008.
28. Detels R, Holland WW, McEwen J, Omenn GS (eds.). *Oxford Textbook of Public Health.* Third Edition. New York/Oxford: Oxford University Press, 1997.
29. Scuffham PA, Nikles J, Mitchell GK, Yealland MJ, Vine N, Poulos CJ, Pillans PI, Bashford G, del Mar C, Schluter PJ, Glasziou P. Using N-of-1 trials to improve patient management and save costs. *J Gen Intern Med*, 2010;**25**(9):906–13. DOI 10-1007/s11606-010-1352-7.
30. Jenicek M. *Méta-analyse en medicine. Évaluation et synthèse de l'information clinique et épidémiologique. (Meta-Analysis in Medicine. Evaluation and Synthesis of Clinical and Epidemiological Information.)* St.Hyacinthe, QC and Maloine, Paris, 1987. (The first textbook on meta-analysis in medicine.)
31. Petiti DB. *Meta-Analysis, Decision-Analysis and Cost-Effectiveness Analysis. Methods for Quantitative Synthesis in Medicine.* New York/Oxford: Oxford University Press, 1994.
32. Jenicek M. Analyzing and integrating a body of knowledge. Systematic reviews and meta-analysis of evidence, chapter 11, pp. 297–326, in: Ref. 7.
33. Jenicek M. *A Physician's Self-Paced Guide to Critical Thinking.* Chicago, IL: American Medical Association (AMA Press), 2006.
34. *Dorland's Illustrated Medical Dictionary.* 27th Edition. Philadelphia: WB Saunders, 1988.
35. Jenicek M. *Prognosis. Studies of Disease Course and Outcomes*, chapter 10, pp. 269–94, in: Ref. 7.
36. Fries JF, Ehrlich GE (eds.). *Prognosis. Contemporary Outcomes of Disease.* Bowie, MD: The Charles Press Publishers, 1981.
37. Jenicek M, Cléroux R. *Épidémiologie Clinique. Clinimétrie (Clinical Epidemiology. Clinimetrics.)* St. Hyacinthe, QC/Paris: EDISEM/Maloine, 1985.
38. Eiseman B. *What Are My Chances?* Philadelphia/London/Toronto: The Saunders Press, A W.B. Saunders Company, 1980.
39. Fletcher RH, Fletcher SW, Wagner EH. Prognosis, chapter 6, pp. 111–35, in: *Clinical Epidemiology. The Essentials.* Third Edition. Baltimore/Philadelphia/London: Williams & Wilkins, 1996.
40. *A Dictionary of Epidemiology.* Second Edition. Edited by JM Last for the International Epidemiological Association. New York/Oxford: Oxford University Press, 1988 (see also Ref. 17.).
41. Ellenberg SS, Hamilton JM. Surrogate endpoints in clinical trials: Cancer. *Stat Med*, 1989;**8**:403–13.

42. Hussain H, Lapin S, Cappell MS. Clinical scoring systems for determining the prognosis of gastrointestinal bleeding. *Gastroenterol Clin North Amer*, 2000;**29**(June, No 2):445–64.
43. Dawes RM, Faust D, Meehl PE. Clinical versus actuarial judgment. *Science*, 1989;**243**:1668–74.
44. Lee KL, Prior DB, Harrell FE Jr. et al. Predicting outcome in coronary disease. Statistical models versus expert clinicians. *Am J Med*, 1986;**80**:553–60.

Chapter 4

Clinical and Community Medicine Decision Making

Executive Summary

Reasoning to understand and reasoning to make decisions are two distinct, but complementary ways to manage health and disease problems. All decision making processes require reasoning and judgment, as well as choices within these stages: "recognition → formulation → generation of alternatives → information and evidence search → selection from among options of what to do → action."

Decisions in patient and community care (health programs) can be made either in unstructured or in structured ways. The structured ways include consensus, various mathematical models, and clinical decision analysis techniques. The unstructured ways rely on the clinician's information inserted within the decision process.

The decision making activities in medicine involve both direction-seeking and direction-giving techniques and tools.

Cost–benefit analysis may be used to assess efficacy, effectiveness, efficiency, or equity of decisions, actions, and their consequences. They are all useful to answer the various complementary questions they reflect.

The decision making process is also a kind of argumentative process. Modern argumentation uses in the decision making domain prove useful and necessary.

Direction-giving tools include both tactical tools such as clinical algorithm development, uses, and evaluation, and strategic tools such as clinical practice guidelines (CPGs).

Evidence-based clinical decision making focuses on generally available evidence for care, its importance, and its applicability to individual patients and their groups of special interest. Assessment of the workplace setting in which decisions are made is integrated within the evidence-based decision making process.

Strategic tools as a structured process are expected to limit variations, reduce costs, make decisions more "scientific," and have an educational value. They are not prescriptive, but clinical protocols; distinctions have to be made and respected.

Decision making-related fallacies are often of a heuristic nature given the reality of clinical practice, especially in emergency and surgery settings.

All newcomers in the environment and reality of clinical and community care must understand how decisions are made and their strengths and weaknesses in order to adopt the best medical care options.

Not-So-Random Leading Thoughts

Nothing is more difficult,
and therefore more precious,
than to be able to decide.

Napoléon Bonaparte, 1804–1815

Thought is behaviour in rehearsal.

Sigmund Freud, 1856–1939
in the early 1930s

A physician who is 90 per cent "certain"
about any decision will always seek additional
information in the hope that it will increase
the "confidence" with which he makes such a
decision. The decision … will be either correct
or incorrect, and the outcome is independent of
the confidence with which the decision is
reached. When additional information cannot
possibly alter the decision, but only gives
rise to a greater sense of comfort on the part
of the physician, such additional information is
of no benefit to the patient. Its only benefit is
in reducing the discomfort of the physician.

Harold M. Schoolman, 1977

Efficiency is concerned with doing things right.
Effectiveness is doing the right things.

Peter F. Drucker, 1977

A problem is defined and isolated;
information is gathered;
alternatives are set forth;
an end is established;
means are created to achieve
the end; a choice is made.

James McGregor Burns, 1978

1. The information we have is not what we want.
2. The information we want is not what we need.
3 The information we need is not available.

Finagle's New Laws of Information, 1979

People whose lives are affected by
a decision must be part of the process
of arriving at that decision.

John Nesbitt, 1984

Doctor, you are asking me what I think
about what should be done in my case?
But, I am paying you as an educated
person in medicine, which I am not, to decide for me. So, decide!

**As told by a patient to the Author
in his young years in a dynamic
and changing country whose values
he was learning and understanding.**

Introductory Comments

Good evidence is not necessarily a high priority for intervention. In fact, a high priority for intervention may often lack good evidence. Evidence of priority is not a priority of evidence. It is just additional evidence. Clinicians must learn not only how to auscultate the heart, count blood cells, or remove an appendix, but also how to arrive at the right decisions.

   Mastering proper reasoning is a vital step to master correct decision making in medicine. But what is decision making in medicine?

Decision making in medicine is a process of selecting what to do in preventive and curative care from among various options already understood while also taking into account the health problem as a whole.

Let us take some examples: A fetal–pelvic disproportion is found in an expectant mother: What should we do? Given our clinical findings, past experience, and medical literature, should we perform a forceps delivery, a normal delivery, or a cesarean section? An ambulatory patient complains of a sore throat: Should we prescribe antibiotics or not with or without further clinical and paraclinicial workup? An elderly retired steelworker after a recent multiple coronary bypass surgery is almost unable to walk due to advanced and general osteoarthritis. Should a knee replacement be considered for him? In community medicine, a new vaccine against a viral infection is available for a community with low herd immunity against it: Should we implement an early immunization program to prevent an outbreak and further disease spread? Even if we have enough good evidence about what works in the circumstances, how should we use it? How should we reason to arrive at the best solution for those patients' problems? This chapter should at least in part introduce us to the reasoning pathways of clinical problem solving.

Making correct decisions may be challenging not only when working with new, advanced, expensive, and sophisticated technologies, but also in daily clinical practice when dealing with everyday problems. The latter, due to their sheer number, also requires the best possible decisions to benefit as many patients as possible and to minimize the costs and risks of less appropriate decisions.

Decision theory understanding, decision analysis, and decision making help us find answers to our daily questions.

As we will see in this chapter, good clinical decision making and its success depend, as many other endeavors in medicine, on the correct knowledge, attitudes, skills, and disposition in the decision making domain.

Knowledge as part of the cognitive domain encompasses both retention of data and information about the subject and the capacity to apply them to specific tasks.[1] Errors occur if the operator's knowledge, especially evidence based, is deficient and insufficient.

Attitudes as part of the affective domain may be seen here as learned tendencies to act and decide in a consistent manner toward a particular object and situation. It means, in the decision making process, having the capacity to sense and recognize the situation, and act in a controlled, predictable, and consistent manner relevant to the problem at hand.[1] The decision maker's attitudes must be appropriate for the task to avoid errors in decision making.

Skills as part of the psychomotor domain are defined in general as *expertness, practical ability, facility in doing something, dexterity, and tact.*[1] In the decision making domain, they are considered to be the abilities to use a structured decision making methodology to solve problems in practice. Errors may occur if the decision maker's skills are inadequate for the successful execution of the task.

Disposition means the right state of mind and inclination regarding something, the natural or prevailing aspect of one's mind as manifested in the behavior and relationships with patients and peers. A disposition is a habit, a preparation, a state of readiness, or a tendency to act in a specific way.[2] Acquiring an appropriate disposition is also an objective of this chapter.

At the end of this chapter, the reader should ask himself or herself the following:

■ What do I know about how to make the right decisions? Is my knowledge actively or passively acquired?
■ What are my attitudes (values and judgment of them) toward decision making to solve my clinical problem? Do I consider them worthy of consideration and why? How do I foresee their role, success, or failure?
■ Am I equipped, trained, and experienced enough to mentally and physically make the right decisions in clinical and community care?
■ Are my evaluation skills pertaining to my decisions good enough to propose, implement, and assess them?

The following sections should help provide answers to these questions.

4.1 Decision Theory, Decision Analysis, and Decision Making in General and in Medicine

Until now, we have dealt with health problems by trying to better understand the meaning of what we perceive: the problem, the patient or patients, related evidence. What do we know about how to make decisions regarding what to do with them?

Decision theory is the theory of rational decisions, often called "rational choice theory."[3] Particularly since the seventeenth century, social sciences, political and business sciences, have developed and now view decision theory as a set of quantitative methods for reaching optimal decisions. Initial solvable decision proposals and conditions are linked to possible consequences, which are not known with certainty and are expressed as sets of probabilistic outcomes. Outcomes are assigned "utility" values based on the assessment and preference of the decision maker. An optimal decision is one that maximizes the expected utility.[4]

Decision theory in medicine has been the subject of developments, reviews, and critiques since the 1970s.[5] An even more recent view outlines that decision theory must[6]

- Be evidence-based
- Be explanatory and predictive
- Be broader than a hypothesis
- Ideally encompass relevant data and prior theory, rather than reinvent the wheel or ignore contrary evidence

Decision making requires not only reasoning and judgment, but also choices. Memory, reasoning, and concept formation lie behind the "recognition → formulation → generation of alternatives → information (evidence) search → selection → action" steps and stages of the decision making process.[7]

The most valuable experience, methodology, applications for clinical research, practice, and health management produced by many experts in the medical decision making domain are available now in an increasing number of ad hoc reader-friendly books.[8–11] This and other experience are also summarized in a chapter of our book *Foundations of Evidence-Based Medicine*, which provides additional background information and an expanded bibliography for this chapter.[12]

4.2 How Decisions Are Made in Daily Life

Any decisions including to treat or not, to further pursue a diagnostic workup, and to follow up and care for a patient over a prolonged period of time can be made either in an unstructured way or in a structured way as an organized step-by-step process.

The unstructured approach is most often emotionally motivated.

- Teachers and older colleagues are often *blindly idolized*: They are never wrong. We do what they do.

- We are often *emotionally attached* to what has been laboriously learned: Why adopt and practice laparoscopic surgery if our proven general surgery was always good enough?
- Sometimes, *clinical ritualism* is "de rigueur": This diagnostic maneuver is a part of the "complete examination." Let us do it then.
- Sometimes, decisions are dictated by the *defensive practice of medicine*. Physicians may wish to *avoid lawsuits* and so do not take the risk of performing surgery if it is not the preferred way. They may also "over-immunize" children or travelers.
- *Something must be done* often rules. There is the *art of doing nothing* and the *art of waiting*. An old surgical saying holds that "it takes two years to get into the abdomen and twenty years to learn to stay out."
- Sometimes decisions are made *without taking into account epidemiological information* and methods.
- *Politically motivated* decisions such as screening or immunization campaigns fortunately occur less and less frequently.
- Some decisions are dictated by an *extraneous power* and/or justified socially, historically, culturally, or by faith. The debate about abortions is not over.
- Simple *blind willingness to please* decisions are still made. Anything that pleases the patient, the physician, and/or the onlookers or any parties connected to the patient may take precedence over rational decision making.

Unstructured decisions in medicine are frequent and may work well or not. However, they are most often feasible in busy practices with their time, human, and material resources constraints.

4.2.1 Direction Searching Tools through Unstructured Ways of Decision Making

Some unstructured decision making ways are as follows:

1. Gut feeling exploration focusing on intuitive feelings such as "sudden awareness of a clinical problem through thoughts that come to one's mind without apparent effort as something potentially serious and worthy of solution."[13] It may be based on a considerable wealth of evidence, experience, and knowledge; it is not "blind."
2. Knowledge of facts, experience, intuition, common sense, and gut feeling are the components of what is called today **distilled clinical**

judgment.[14] It goes beyond gut feeling: Decisions are made on the basis of hypothetico-deductive thinking, from major a priori formulated clues to the most probable diagnosis and treatment of possible problems. If a patient develops a fever after a kidney transplant, it may be equally due to an infection or rejection of the organ. In the case of an erroneous diagnosis, antibiotics would not prevent organ rejection with its possible fatal consequences for the patient, but immunosuppression would not help in the case of an infection. In such situations, a "steepest ascent type of thinking"[15] is mandatory.

3. The *Gestalt* or **pattern recognition** method is useful in other situations and allows for appropriate "right" decision making. A patient with nocturnal distress and dyspnea, who sleeps on several pillows and holds the bed frame with both hands "to breathe better," exhibits a pattern suggesting cardiac insufficiency.

4. When competing health conditions are at stake, two decisions can be considered. In a "minimax" approach, a solution is sought, which would give a minimum probability of a maximum loss. In a situation of a possible streptococcal infection of the throat, without the possibility of laboratory testing, a clinician may decide to prescribe antibiotics to prevent any late systemic complications (maximum loss) of this infection. In a "maximin" or "Las Vegas approach," decisions are made to reach a maximum probability of a minimal loss. In cancer medicine, a chemotherapeutic or physical agent leading to fewer secondary effects in cases of competent efficacy is often chosen for treatment.

5. Decisions are made on the basis of the magic of numbers. Is something which is "statistically highly significant" always better? How much and in what practical terms?

6. **Heuristic** decision making happens in extremis of restraining and constricting conditions of emergency,[16] crisis, or threat whatever their cause and reason might be. It may often be a kind of black box decision making for which reasoning mechanisms must still be analyzed and better understood. This kind of "rule of thumb" decision making is well known to all clinicians. It may lead to both right and wrong decisions.

7. Other shortcut decisions, most often without detectable heuristics, occur:
   Reaction as an immediate response bypassing the cortical decision centers
   Conditioning as a preprogrammed reaction based on past experience and training

Habit as simple repetitions of what worked last time

Intuition as choices without thinking is the product of a subconscious mind searching through our experiences and finding a good match for what we are facing.

Scripts as prepared short or protracted steps for what to say or do that we keep for various situations: "How are we doing today?" in sales instead of "Hello" without expecting an answer. At the bedside, we expect an answer even to a script.

This kind of shortcut decision making does not necessarily result in long-term internal change.[17]

4.2.2 Direction Searching Tools through Structured Ways of Decision Making

Information in medicine is never complete, never entirely true, because of the human nature of patients and physicians. Decisions are always probabilistic, no matter how confident the attitude of senior colleagues may be, and so decisions are always made with a variable degree of uncertainty. This does not mean that decisions are inevitably made in a disorganized and chaotic way—they can be structured.

More objective decisions may be arrived at in different ways:

1. Some agreement may be reached between several specialists and experienced professionals in the field. A *consensus* of the group is produced, representing either a unanimous or a prevalent agreement by its members. This kind of decision may be made in an even more organized and structured manner. For example, in the so-called *Delphi method*, the least important (or frequent) opinions are progressively removed from the array of choices. Such a reduced set is re-evaluated, additional deletions are made, and the whole process is repeated until the group reaches the best possible option. Decisions can also be rated.

2. Decision analysis is based on several *mathematical models*, such as decision trees, Markov models, Monte Carlo simulation, survival analysis and the hazard function, fuzzy logic, and sensitivity analysis.[18] Only decision analysis in general will be discussed here.

3. *Computer-assisted decision making* facilitates the use of structured approaches in medical decision making, as explained in this chapter,

and allows decisions to be made on the basis of a wider body of information, data, and premises, which go well beyond the capacity of a single deciding individual or group.

Clinical thinking may be understood and organized in a structured manner representing the basis of decision analysis in medicine as we understand it today.

4.2.2.1 Decision Analysis

A structured approach to making the best possible medical decisions is accomplished through a process called **clinical decision analysis**. It is already used in finance, business, military affairs, industry, and economics. Why not in medicine taking into account that human nature is involved and that the patient's opinion and decision prevails? The patient must have the last word as to whether a leg is amputated, a breast removed, or a colostomy opened.

Accumulation of data and information and their handling on the basis of clinical decision analysis as an organized intellectual process may be effectively achieved provided that there is sufficient time, conditions, and need (right patient case) to do so.

> Conceptually, a **medical decision** represents the choice of the best option in assessing risk (explanatory decisions), in treating patients (managerial decisions), or in making prognosis (both explanatory and managerial, if treatment decisions are involved).

> **Medical decision making** is a process by which one arrives at a given medical decision, the latter being the result or endpoint of such a process.

> **Decision analysis** tackles precisely such situations. It is a systematic approach to decision making under conditions of uncertainty.[19]

It has also been defined as a "derivative of operations research and game theory to identify all available choices, and potential outcomes of each, in a series of decisions that have to be made (e.g., about aspects of patient care as diagnostic procedures, preventive and therapeutic regimens, prognosis). Epidemiological data play a large part in determining the probabilities of outcomes following each potential choice."[20]

Clinical decision analysis is an application of decision analysis in a clinical setting. It has three main components: (1) Choices available either to the patient, his or her physician, or both; (2) chances as probabilities of outcome for each choice; and (3) values of treatment options and their outcomes for all interested stakeholders: health professionals, patients, and the community. It represents any activity, systematizes (organizes) decision making, clarifies decision making, and leads to the "correctness" of decisions.

A **decision tree** is one of the most important graphical, analytical, and probability- and quantification-based structure of clinical decision analysis. Its objective is to lead us to the best decisions about diagnosis, treatment, prognosis, and other aspects of quality care, which are most beneficial for the patient and other involved parties.

Clinical decisions incorporated into the decision tree are not only decisions to treat or not to treat. They may also concern whether or not to add another (presumably more modern and better) diagnostic method in serial or parallel testing in the clinical process preceding treatment decisions, additional medical or nursing care following an operation, social support and home care to convalescent patients, and so on.

Figure 4.1 is an example of a decision tree to visualize a situation in emergency medicine. We want to decide the best way to treat a patient presenting an acute abdomen. How can this be done, analyzed, and interpreted? Only a shortened summary and principles of this decision making tool will be given here for our elementary understanding; more details, especially the computational aspects, may be found elsewhere[9,12,21] by interested readers who may also notice that decision trees can cover single-stage events such as the problem to operate or not with ensuing outcomes and their values. Many clinical

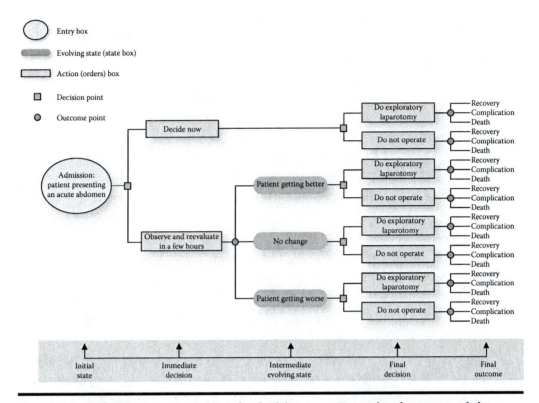

Figure 4.1   **Graphic representation of a decision tree. Example of an acute abdomen decision challenge.**

problems, especially chronic and episodic issues, in which events may occur repetitively at various moments in time, after multiple interventions have different values and utilities, such as in anticoagulant therapy and elsewhere. Such disease courses are analyzed by Markov models, which fraction them into multiple "Markov states" with their own events-decisions-outcomes-utilities sets that follow in time.[22] Our example is from the former simpler situation.

The obvious objective of this type of decision analysis using a decision tree approach is to find, among all options in a given clinical situation, the decision or the way that would be the most beneficial to the patient. As paradoxical as it may appear, the approach described here, which is full of probabilities, values, and computations, contributes much to the humanitarian aspect of medicine. It helps find by objective means a better clinical procedure or a choice of treatment for a given patient or for particular disease sufferers in general.

Decision tress are temporal and spatial representations, in a proper clinical sequence of options, offered to the clinician (to add a diagnostic method or not, to treat or not to treat, to choose different treatments, etc.) at moments of clinical work, represented as decision nodes of a decision tree (conventionally identified by squares) and its outcome nodes including probabilities of what will happen after each decision under consideration. They are structures containing three basic elements:

1. Choices of action, options offered to the clinician and his or her patient(s). Decision points or *decision nodes* (squares in Figure 4.1) indicate options: immediate or delayed decision, operate or not. More than one moment of choice in time may occur.

   Wherever possible, and without abandoning reality, preferably only two options should be attached to each decision node. However, more options do exist in the real world. For example, in the introductory example in this chapter, a physician must decide whether to treat a sore throat by antibiotics right away, not give antibiotics at all, or give antibiotics later depending on the result of a throat culture.

2. Chance or *probability nodes* (marked as circles) or probabilities of outcomes of each choice, such as recovery, complications, or death. They may follow each moment of choice.

3. *Values* given to each given outcome or *end utilities*. Case fatality, recovery or complications rates, related monetary, managerial or operational values, and the patient's own values may be considered and analyzed as endpoints of a decision tree. They represent final points from which analysis starts.

   Assigning utility to an outcome is a question of judgment and we already know that judgment means attributing a value to something. In fact, the assignment of utility is one of the greatest challenges of decision analysis. Should the outcome be some monetary value (such as the cost of subsequent cure and care), some measure of pain and/or suffering, the patient's quality of life, impact on a patient's surrounding, a physician's measure of therapeutic success or failure, or a score based on some or all of the above elements? There is no clear-cut answer to this problem. Decision analysis and its solution are valid only in the context of preestablished probabilities and utilities. These values are given to each outcome by the patient in the first place, by a physician in terms of a desired realistic result, or by an administrator or community health policy decision maker in terms of economic (monetary), social, or political gains.

4. Once the decision tree is built, the highest expected overall value ("utility") from the available pathways, "branches of the tree," is determined by a "folding back procedure" consisting of, starting retroactively at the final points, the "tips of the branches" of the decision tree, making from

there a progressive multiplication of end utilities by probabilities of outcomes following each decision point up to the initial question reflected
by the first decision point of the tree.

Having a better idea of what to do this way, we may consider a sensitivity
analysis ("robustness" analysis for some statisticians), which looks at how a
decision would change if probabilities, reference values, and/or probabilities
of outcomes and their value (utility) were to change.

Balancing various likelihoods of clinical risks and benefits through a
threshold analysis allows determining situations and ("toss up") moments
from which benefits for the patient outweigh risks of clinical procedures of
interest and preference.[23]

As we may see, this method systematically assesses essential treatment
available, possible outcomes, and desirability of each outcome of interest.

Even a well-performed clinical decision analysis has its own inherent
advantages and disadvantages.

The advantages are as follows:

1. It is much less costly than the search for the best decision through
   experimental research, which is often sophisticated in design and
   complex in execution and analysis.
2. It can be easily translated into clinical decisions and public health
   policies.
3. It is an important tool in medical education. It allows students to better
   structure their thinking and to navigate the maze of decision making.

The disadvantages are as follows:

1. It is less valuable if clinical data and information are of poor quality
   and/or uncertain.
2. It may take up precious time in emergency situations, especially if left
   in the hands of a less-experienced decision analyst.
3. Utilities may have different values and weights in different individuals,
   be they patients, doctors, or community decision makers (administrators, politicians, economists, etc.) or those of individual patients versus
   their community.

Obviously, all the above apply if (and only if) decision analysis is used to
solve real problems and not merely as an intellectual exercise.

4.2.2.2 Cost–Benefit/Effectiveness/Utility Analysis in Clinical Decision Making

Although classical clinical trials answer the main question about treatment effectiveness to solve a patient's problem, economic evaluation such as cost-effectiveness evaluation is a valuable "piggyback approach," yielding additional important information[24] for several purposes: Hospitalization, physician visits, and tests may all be used as outcomes and utilities. Decision analyses using decision trees, Markov models from the prognosis (survival) domain, and receiver operating characteristic curve analysis from the diagnosis domain are all also part of today's economic assessment of medical practice.

Many physicians still dislike taking costs into consideration. However, every clinical decision has its additional price, not only in monetary terms, but also in terms of complications, incapacity, handicaps, and so on. In this context, a cost-effectiveness analysis *seeks to determine the costs and effectiveness of an activity or to compare similar alternative activities to determine the relative degree to which they will obtain the desired objectives and outcomes.*[20]

On the other hand, a cost-utility analysis is an economic analysis in which outcomes are measured in terms of their social value. A widely used utility-based measure is quality-adjusted life years.[20]

The economic evaluation of medical care assesses four aspects of care:[20]

1. **Efficacy:** A beneficial result under ideal conditions. An answer to the "can it work?" question.
2. **Effectiveness:** Beneficial and other results under "ordinary," prevailing, or customary conditions and patients. An answer to the "does it work?" question.
3. **Efficiency:** Effects of end results in proportion to the effort (human and material resources, time) invested in the health care activity. An answer to "what does it cost for what it gives?" is sought.
4. **Equity:** Fairness and impartiality of health care activities such as access to health care as a possible cause or effect of a health care activity. An answer to "how well are costs and benefits distributed?" is sought under this term.

In clinical decision analysis, as covered in this chapter, the cost–benefit approach is a "scaled down and reoriented analysis" in accordance with the definition above. Monetary values are often replaced by clinically important "costs," such as operative case fatality, case fatality in treated and untreated individuals in the general population, occurrence of side effects of diagnosis and/or treatment, and occurrence of comorbidity and its impact. Survival or any other measure of "positive" impact is used as an indicator of "benefit." The subject of evaluation is efficiency from the four aspects of evaluation quoted above and based on the question "What does it cost, and of what value is it?" in clinical terms.

Monetary values can be taken into consideration, but they are not the principal focus of analysis. Rather, they are integrated into a larger frame of clinical considerations.

4.2.2.3 Decisions as Conclusions of an Argumentative Process

Welcome back to arguments and argumentation, this time in the decision making domain!

Just like medical understanding, medical decision making process may and should be considered an exercise in argumentation as already outlined in Chapter 2. Clinical decision analysis explained in Section 4.2.2 provides additional elements, specific to decision analysis and making, for the building blocks of an argumentative process, leading to clinical care and research decisions. It does not replace evidence-based decision making as originally suggested by Dickinson.[25] Let us view decision making in an integrative manner through Toulmin's already mentioned modern argumentation model and its adaptation by Rieke et al.[26] and adoption for the domain of decision making as follows:

Our decision to treat or not pursue a diagnostic workup or provide additional long-term care given the prognosis is a claim stemming from argumentation and the conclusion of its supportive process.

1. What we see in the patient is essentially **grounds** for argumentation. Grounds must be based on good evidence. **Grounds** for argumentation in the decision making context are statements made about persons (patients and/or health care professionals), conditions (care), events (clinical interventions, related outcomes), or things (methods and techniques used, etc.) representing the available support to provide a reason for a claim.
2. Clinical decision analysis should provide specific information and clues from a decisional process to understand and be part of a **warrant**.

Warrants, as they are in any other domain of argumentation, are broader, more general statements and understandings that justify using groups as a basis for the claim. Clinical and other related plausibility is in focus.

3. **Backing** in the decision making domain is any support (specific instances, statistics, testimony values, or credibility that provides more specific data for grounds or warrant).[26] Past experience from basic and clinical research and practice from other and similar related situations are used most often as warrants. Testimonies in medicine as evidence in support of a fact or statement are statements based on personal experience and/or knowledge. They may be good or bad if the claim is implausible or if it goes beyond reporting a person's professional and other personal qualifications, experiences, and competencies. It may be invaluable in some cases.

4. The **qualifier** as our degree of certainty about or claims and conclusions can be derived only from evidence based on past experience.

5. **Claim(s)** follow by suggesting what to do. *Claims* are statements that we want others to accept and act upon, gaining their *adherence*, that is, informed support of involved parties.

   For Rieke et al.,[26] claims may be as follows:

   – *Factual*, that is, affirming that certain conditions exist in the material world and could be observed; factual claims are confirmed by objective data from reliable sources.

      Research conclusions (smoking causes lung cancer), clinical care progress notes in patient charts (SOAPs), or orders (this surgical patient must also be seen by an internist or clinical pharmacologist) are factual claims.

   – *Value claims* assert the quality of a person, place, thing, or idea.

      The functioning of the emergency medicine services in our hospital *is the best* in our state or province.

   – *Policy claims* tell us how to behave.

      Smoking in designated areas ought to be permitted in this long-term care institution for the elderly. In this sense, clinical orders and guidelines are also policy claims.

6. **Rebuttals** should be considered as diverting our decisions in the light of the possible alternative clinical settings, practice, patients, and values, past or present. A *rebuttal* represents the basis on which the claim will be questioned by a decision maker.[26] It has a broader sense than Toulmin's modern argument, as defined in Chapter 2.

7. To a rebuttal, Rieke et al.[26] propose a *reservation*, that is, a qualification of the original claim that answers a rebuttal. Reservations are statements of the conditions under which a claim would not apply.

Contradictory clinical and paraclinical findings in a clinical workup of a patient's case that broaden and require differential diagnosis and subsequent dependent treatment decisions may be seen in this context as reservations.

The completeness of argument building blocks may vary from one case to be discussed with another.

In Figure 4.1, illustrating the management decision of an acute abdomen, operate or do not operate now or operate later are the possible decisions (claims, conclusions of an argumentative process). They are based on some grounds, that is, what we see in the patient (visceral pain, parietal pain, colic, vomiting, constipation, diarrhea, jaundice, hematemesis, hematuria). Gynecologic, family, travel and surgery histories, peristaltic "rushes" sounds, abdominal wall tenderness, abdominal masses and guarding on deep palpation, hip flexion or costo-vertebral tenderness, resistance and pain, urine and stool test, plain and contrast x-ray studies, angiography, ultrasonography, computerized tomography and radionuclide scans, endoscopy, and paracentesis may all be part of our grounds. Our past experience with decisions, probabilities, and utilities provides backing for our reasoning. We understand it better if we know the past decision analyses of this problem, their meaning, and their results (operate or not); they are our warrant in the present decision making process. How certain can we be about our claim? Our certainty as qualifier may be extrapolated from probabilities from the past experience and the present state of our actual patient. Differential diagnosis with considerations of volvolus, intussusceptions, mesenteric adenitis, malignant and vascular diseases in the elderly, cholecystitis, appendicitis, bowel obstruction, cancers, salpingitis, dysmenorrhea, ovarian lesions, urinary tract infections, atypical manifestations of any above, unexplained unrelenting diffuse abdominal pain without commensurate peritoneal signs or abnormalities in elderly or cardiac patients, pulmonary conditions such as pneumothorax or lower lobe pneumonia and other thoracic infections, acute rheumatic fever, polyarteritis nodosa or acute intermittent porphyria and others may all play the role of adducts, either in favor or as rebuttals of our final claim or solution.

Physical findings such as guarding, tenderness and rigidity, distension or deterioration after conservative treatment, radiologic findings of pneumoperitoneum, bowel distension, extravasation of contrast material, space-occupying lesions on scans (with fever), endoscopic findings of perforated or uncontrollable bleeding lesions or blood, bile, pus, urine, or bowel contents on paracentesis are indications for urgent operation in patients with an acute abdomen.[27]

Decision analyses based on decision trees may be a multistage process such as in our example: Our first claim may be either the immediate decision to operate or not or "observe, wait, make decision later" as another later claim. The next and final claim would be to operate or not as a second claim in our decision making process. Decision analyses and their conclusions may then be a multistage process and sequence of argumentation processes and their conclusions, even more than two, within the specific conceptual and methodological frame of decision analysis and making as described earlier.

Critical decisions are based on clearly articulated arguments that have been tested through refutations and disagreements. They "have survived" criticisms and remain open to potential future ones. Openness to uncertainty, internal and external dialogue, dialectic, rhetoric, and willingness to act are their necessary attributes.[26] For example, the acceptance of any new medical technology as a critical decision must carry such attributes.

Argumentation and critical decision making in the clinical decision making domain are then the process by which interested parties, physicians, nurses, their patients, and other stakeholders in health seek the best choices and decisions under uncertainty and ambiguity.[26]

4.2.3 Direction-Giving Tools in Decision Making

Once the best option (evidence) is obtained either through decision analysis, clinical trial, consensus, or other means, directions for decisions may be established. Such directions may have a tactical or strategic character.

Tactical tools (in military arts, "the tools needed to win the battle") focus on specific objects, solving an important part of the problem, for example, a diagnostic workup for breast cancer or diabetes. Clinical algorithms belong to this category.

Strategic tools (in military arts, "the tools needed to win the war") try to give the best directions (management skills) in a broader context. What should be done when caring for breast cancer patients from diagnosis and treatment to follow-up? How should patients suspected of having diabetes be cared for? CPGs are a good example of strategic tools in medicine.

As seen in Section 4.2.2, important progress has been made regarding the best way to navigate the mazes of possible decision options that appear in diagnosing and treating health problems. Once these best ways (and decisions) are found, they should be organized in an ensemble of optimal steps, leading to the best result and benefit for the patient or for the community if disease control is in question.

Such a "best kit" must be based on the best available evidence, from whatever source it may come: decision analysis as described earlier; original clinical and community research studies; meta-analysis of the best clinical and epidemiological experience of the deciding physician; or the physician's careful assessment of the specific situation relative to the patient or community.

4.2.3.1 Tactical Tools: Clinical Algorithms

Clinical **algorithms** and decision tables are offered in increasing numbers to the practicing community to fill a need for easy-to-use and practical guides to clinical decisions.

Experienced clinicians may be tempted to draw up graphical guides in a flow and chain of decisions. Others draw colored "quick fixes" for subsidized, mostly advertising-oriented periodicals for practitioners and call them "continuing education." There is a better way to develop and use clinical algorithms.

Clinical algorithms are step-by-step written protocols for health management.[28] They consist of an explicit description of steps to be taken in patient care in specified circumstances.[20] What diagnostic and therapeutic steps should be taken to properly treat a sore throat? How should a case of multiple trauma in (and en route to) an emergency room be managed? Clinical algorithms are a specific category of algorithms. An algorithm is defined as "a set of rules for approaching the solution to a complex problem by setting down individual steps and delineating how each step follows from the preceding one."[29] Its character as a "uniform procedure"[29] and as a "finite number of steps" for a solution to a given specific problem[30] is usually emphasized.

4.2.3.1.1 Algorithms as Flowcharts

Given its visual impact, the graphical form of algorithms is most widely used in medicine. An algorithm in its most well-known graphical form is a kind of flowchart. By definition, a **flowchart** is a *graphical representation of the progress of a system for the definition, analysis, or solution of a data processing (or manufacturing) problem in which symbols are used to represent operations and data (or material flow and equipment), and lines and arrows represent interrelationships among the components* (syn. control diagram; flow diagram; flow sheet).[30] A clinical algorithm is a flowchart.

Decision trees and algorithms are flowcharts as well. The fundamental difference between the two is that a decision tree portrays the choices available to those responsible for patient care and the probabilities and values of each possible outcome that will follow a particular strategy in patient or community care. It is an open system, like a menu in a restaurant. Algorithms are a closed system; they are orders reflecting what should be eaten, starting with an appetizer and working through the "pièce de résistance" to dessert.

Clinical algorithms have proven useful in almost all medical specialties and fields of practice. However, as a medical tool, like any diagnostic or therapeutic method, technique, or instrument, they must have a well-structured and understandable form, a reason for their creation and use, and they must be evaluated for their advantages and weaknesses in their use and impact. Consider these important aspects of algorithms.

Figure 4.2 illustrates an algorithm for the clinical workup and management of a stab wound of the abdomen[31] presented here in a standardized fashion.

It guides the practitioner from an initial evaluation of the patient by successive steps, represented alternatively by clinical findings and actions to be taken. An action may be either a final diagnosis or a surgical or medical procedure to correct the situation. This sequence progresses to the exit point from the algorithm, usually the resolution of the clinical problem, depending on the type of action points. Algorithms may be purely diagnostic (no treatment indicated), purely interventional, or a mixture of both.

Formally, clinical boxes (rounded rectangles), decision boxes (hexagons), action boxes (rectangles), and link boxes (small ovals) are put in a sequence flowing from top to bottom and from left to right. Arrows, never intersecting if possible, are unobstructed by writing except in decision boxes, "yes," arrows pointing right and "no," arrows pointing down. Sequential numbering of boxes in the above-mentioned directions is suitable, with the entire algorithm preferably covering a single page.

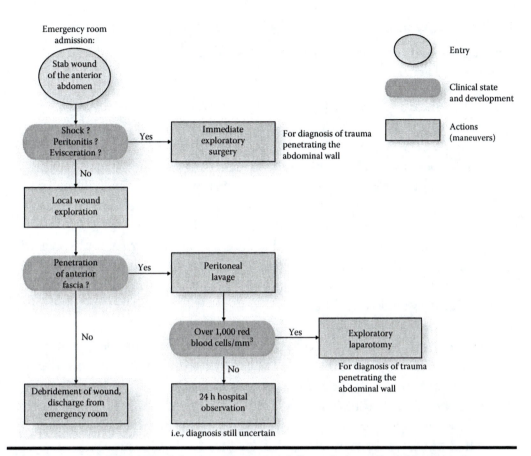

Figure 4.2   An algorithm of the management of the stab wound of the abdomen. (Redrawn with modifications from Oreskovich, M. R. and Carrico, C. J., *Ann Surg*, 198, 411–9, 1983.)*

The presentation of an algorithm in medicine is becoming increasingly standardized,[32,33] illustrating entry points as square rectangles, decision points as hexagonal frames or vertically standing squares, and end points (called also "terminators") as oval squares.[34]

An algorithm approach is indicated in specific clinical conditions, states of knowledge, or for particular users and working environments.

If CPGs are presented or viewed in an algorithmic form, the following applies equally to the domain of CPGs (see Section 4.2.3.3).

We have dealt with the algorithm challenge in the past. From those sources,[35,36] let us summarize what we might say today about the building and evaluation of algorithms in order to better understand them and their uses.

---

* N.B. Today, where available, modern imaging techniques might be preferred by some over peritoneal lavage to demonstrate fluid accumulation in the abdominal cavity.

4.2.3.1.2 How to Recognize Well-Constructed Algorithms

The construction of clinical algorithms should follow these clearly defined steps:

1. The clinical *problem* to be solved by the algorithm must be well formulated and defined[37] (diagnostic, occurrence, target population, users, expected results, etc.). Current practice must be described.

2. The expected *results* of algorithm use must be specified (gains for practice, economy, patient, physician workload, etc.). "Discriminators,"[38] that is, points in clinical workup leading to a suggested action, are well defined and described in explicit terms.

3. Clear *indications* are given as to when, where, and by whom the algorithm is supposed to be used and to what kind of patients should it be applied:
   - *Patients* eligible for the algorithmic approach must be well defined (target population for use of the algorithm).
   - *Situations* in which algorithms should be used must be defined.
   - *Sites and settings* are identified: emergency rooms, operating theaters, family practice offices, others?
   - *Users* of algorithms must be identified.

   These four specifications help in making pragmatic decisions (where, when, and in whom an algorithm might and should be used).

4. The *clinical situation* statement → diagnostic statement → therapeutic and/or diagnostic options must be clearly defined in a realistic time-and-space relationship.

5. Enough *data and information* must be retrieved from the literature, original studies, data analysis, clinical trials, consensus studies, medical audits, or personal and other clinical experience, or simple "gut feelings" or "flair" to justify each step of the algorithm. It must be clear, from the description of the proposed algorithm, which of the above-mentioned elements was used in its construction and justification; the *best available evidence* for the purpose must support the algorithms' constituting elements.

6. Each node indicating action to follow must be supported not only by the *best evidence*, but also by its justification through an *argumentative process* and its claims and conclusions in which the best evidence is used. We may reason poorly even when we have the best evidence at hand!

7. *Entry and exit* points of the algorithm need to be defined.

8. *Diagnostic steps* must be organized in order of their decreasing severity.
9. *Therapeutic steps* are organized either in order of their lifesaving importance (the worst first) or in order of their increasing cost and complexity (from the cheapest to the most expensive).
10. All indications in boxes (graphical components of the algorithm) are clear, explicit, and as complete as necessary.
11. The algorithm should be drawn in a conventional, consistent manner that is understandable to the user.

If an algorithm respecting the above-mentioned rules is put into practice, its performance and effect must be evaluated.

4.2.3.1.3 How to Evaluate Clinical Algorithms

An algorithm and its use is a type of clinical maneuver such as any other (diagnostic or therapeutic); its process (use) and impact must be evaluated, and its weaknesses and strengths should be known.

Evaluating the *process of algorithm use* means determining its security, appropriateness, economy, user-friendliness, recipient (patient) friendliness, accidents, errors, and potential harm.

Several topics are also of interest when *evaluating the impact* of algorithm use:

- Does it correctly evaluate the patient's state?
- Does it produce errors leading to undesirable effects, even if properly used?
- Does it cover an important proportion and spectrum of daily cases?
- Does it cover an important gradient of cases?
- Most importantly, does its use improve a patient's state more than any alternative approach in diagnosis and therapeutic decision making?

An algorithmic approach proves useful in the assessment of new technologies. Also, algorithms may be used to tell new technologies how to function. Controlled clinical trials, although the golden standard in treatment impact (effect) assessment, remain rarely used in the evaluation of the use of algorithms. They should become standard. Beyond the above-mentioned examples, the evaluation of algorithms across the literature focuses mainly on "process" evaluation. The "effect" evaluation is often more difficult.

What are algorithms worth? Komaroff will answer this question as a conclusion to this section: "… Algorithms are no substitute for experience, sensitivity, or compassion … algorithms can help us to articulate how we make decisions, to clarify our knowledge and to recognize our ignorance. They can help us to demystify the practice of medicine, and to demonstrate that much of what we call the 'art' of medicine is really a scientific process, a science which is waiting to be articulated…."[39]

There is a big difference between an "impressionist" and an "evidence-based" algorithm.

A medical algorithm today may be seen also as a graphic presentation of a clinical practice or community medicine activity guideline and be the subject of valid guideline rules.

4.2.3.2 Evidence-Based Clinical Decision Path

Entering the best evidence into the decision process creates a decision path in the form of a flowchart, as illustrated in Figure 4.3.

> The decision process starts by the best *evidence* in general for the appropriate problem, its *relevance*, and then *applicability* to a particular patient provided that the clinical *setting* in which the decision is made fits. *Patient* values, preferences, and choices and other *ethical considerations* serve as an ultimate condition and rebuttals before the final decision is made. Hence, clinical decisions must be made the ERASPEC (acronym) way.

4.2.3.3 Strategic Tools for Making the Right Decisions: Clinical Practice Guidelines and Clinical Protocols

Preoccupations with the best possible quality of care and cost containment lead health administration and professional institutions, at various local and international levels, to develop and implement CPGs. How should cancer patients be cared for after surgery? How should diabetic or hypertensive patients be cared for? What is the best long-term care for arthritis? **Clinical practice guidelines (CPGs)** should respond to such a need.

4.2.3.3.1 Clinical Practice Guidelines

But what are then CPGs?

The following characterizes well modern medical guidelines: "… they briefly identify, summarize and evaluate the highest quality evidence and most current data about prevention, diagnosis, prognosis, therapy including

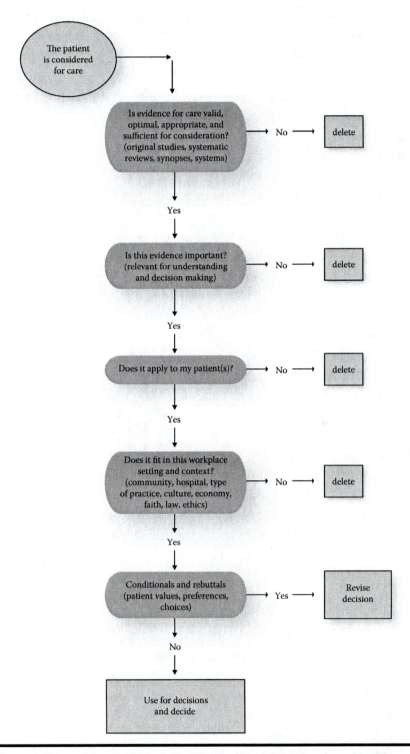

Figure 4.3 **Evidence-based clinical decision making flowchart or algorithm: necessary general considerations.**

dosage of medications, risk/benefit and cost-effectiveness. Then they define the most important questions related to clinical practice and identify all possible decision options and their outcomes. Some guidelines contain decision or computation algorithms to be followed...."[40]

CPGs have been defined as "systematically developed statements to assist practitioner and patient decisions about appropriate health care for specific clinical circumstances."[41]

In their overall mostly methodological review of chronic spinal pain management applied CPGs, Manchikanti et al.[42] state that CPGs as defined earlier[40] should lead to the best practice based on a thorough evaluation of the evidence from published studies on the outcome of the treatment. However, CPGs cover not only treatment, but also other steps in clinical care.

More precisely, *good CPGs* should consider the following:[43]

- Limit variations in practice
- Reduce necessary costs
- Give a scientific direction to care
- Provide useable summaries of the best evidence-based practices
- Have an educational value for risks and benefits of medical interventions and care

CPGs should be valid, reliable, reproducible, clear, flexible, and applicable in various settings of care.[43] The methodology of their development, content, and presentation should be clearly defined.[44]

There are several ways to develop CPGs. On the one hand, there is expert opinion and consensus; on the other hand, there are "evidence-based guidelines" as preferred today.[45,46]

There are several stages and steps in the evidence-based CPG development and use:

- A clinical problem is formulated.
- The best evidence is drawn from the literature and past experience.
- A systematic review of the evidence is done as a basis for draft practice guidelines.
- A draft practice is put to a test use in the practicing community.
- Feedback is integrated into the final version of CPGs.
- CPGs are approved and disseminated.

CPGs have to be *reported in a standard form*,[47] which includes (with some modifications) the following:

■ Definition of the *problem* and description of the *present practice* and situation
■ *Objective* of the proposed CPGs
■ *Options* (the maze through CPGs that guides the clinician)
■ *Outcomes* (health and economic)
■ *Evidence* about all major aspects of the problem and how it was obtained, synthetized, and graded
■ *Benefits*, *harms*, and *costs*
■ *Values* of potential outcomes (for clinicians and their patients as well)
■ Summary of *recommendations*
■ *Validation* of CPGs themselves
■ *Sponsors* (authors of CPGs, providers of funding, endorsers, and other important stakeholders). (N.B. CPG may be influenced by many interested parties such as the profession, business, the government, or insurance companies.)[42-45]

Examples of current guidelines abound. They have been developed for all major cancers (breast, colon, rectal, lung, ovarian, prostate, leukemia), ischemic heart disease, back pain, diabetes, pneumonia, schizophrenia, stroke, myocardial infarction, biliary tract disease, depression, preterm birth, acute pain, and many others. For example, *Canadian Clinical Practice Guidelines*[48] cover 30 key medical and therapeutic areas. Some CPGs may take the form of structured narrative directions to follow or an algorithm.[49,50]

Developing evidence-based guidelines is not a quick and easy task. Diagnostic and treatment options, as well as their validity, effectiveness, and desirable and adverse outcomes, must be ideally endorsed by the best available evidence, which should also be explained to CPG users.

Guidelines focusing on the process of care cannot always be founded on evidence. Such a consensus development may yield excellent results, such as guidelines for pre-hospital[51] and in-hospital[52] cardiopulmonary resuscitation, published by several leading medical journals and currently in field use.

Finally, CPGs have two additional challenges:

1. Implementation and evaluation of their use[53,54]
2. Evaluation of their effectiveness[55]

Good guidelines have to be used, but they must yield better results than unguided heterogeneous practices and care.

Several competing guidelines may be developed for the management of the same problem. Systematic reviews of such decision making tools may become more frequent in the near future if guidelines proliferate.

Fletecher[56] correctly stresses that CPGs are just recommendations for the evidence-based care of *average* patients, not rules for *all* patients. "… Although guidelines may point out the best research evidence to guide the care of average patients, they are not the substitute for clinical judgment, which should be applied to each individual patient."

Hence, *CPGs in the framework of evidence-based medicine* are an important part of a longer process. For Lilford and Braunholtz,[57] in the case of a novel treatment, a CPG proposal should be justified in several ways:

- Clinical trials show its effectiveness.
- *Meta-analyses* confirm it.
- *Decision analysis* weighs costs and benefits in favor of treatment.
- This preferred treatment option is made a part of *CPGs*.
- The impact of guidelines is evaluated by *clinical audit*.
- Implementation is handled by managerial action such as *clinical governance*.
- All of the above represent *evidence-based care*.

Most recently, the National Guideline Center[58] and Editors of the *Annals of Internal Medicine*[59] propose "guidelines to guidelines" together with examples of applications to delirium prevention[60] and cost-effectiveness assessment in the domain of health economics.[61]

4.2.3.3.2 Clinical Practice Guidelines versus Clinical Protocols

CPGs and clinical protocols offered to clinicians are different entities, especially from the point of view of their purpose and rules.

CPGs are *not* prescriptive. They are proposals to the clinician and/or his or her health institution to adopt or reject them, however well they are built, evidence based, and argumentatively justified and otherwise scientifically and clinically sound. Let us reiterate that they are not intended as a substitute for the judgment of the physician or other health professional. They are not the only approach to be considered for the best practice.

Clinical protocols originate in the domain of clinical trials and pharmacology. Clinical trial protocols are their embodiment. *Prescriptive*, they are structured and organized step-by-step activities prescribed to be followed in a given structure and setting. A practitioner in the domain of a clinical protocol *must* follow the protocol if he or she agrees to participate in a given activity.

A merging of both entities is currently under consideration in computerized settings.[62]

4.3 Illustrative Fallacies in the Decision Making Domain

Fallacies as errors in reasoning and decision making, often referred to as biases, cognitive errors, or decision errors, may be related either to the motivation to decide, to the decision-oriented thinking process, or to deciding itself.[63,64] Still, terms such as fallacies, biases, cognitive errors, or mistakes may be used interchangeably across the literature beyond fundamental philosophy and cognitive sciences basic domains. Let us quote here just a few examples applicable to the clinical problems. The world of medical fallacies is much wider and covered elsewhere by us.[65]

For Roberto,[66] poor decisions are not always due to incompetence, inexperience, or lack of intelligence, or bad intentions. They arise because of other factors such as faulty reasoning leading to erroneous decision making. Decisions are not just events. They are, in fact, processes to be analyzed and understood, and the causes of their failures should be identified and remedies drawn from such experiences.

From a much wider array of fallacies reviewed more extensively elsewhere,[65] there are several fallacies in reasoning leading to faulty decisions that are worth quoting as examples in this chapter devoted to decision making in health sciences.

4.3.1 Fallacies from an Individual Perspective: Individual-Related Fallacies

There are several fallacies in reasoning leading to faulty decisions. One group is related to individual reasoning and decision making, the other to collective team reasoning and interaction producing decisional failures. Sometimes, both groups are interwoven.

Individual-related fallacies may be reasoning based, from the motivation to decide domain, or related to decisions themselves.

Let us first have a look at some examples of individual-related fallacies.

4.3.1.1 Reasoning-Based Fallacies: Fallacies Related to the Thinking Process behind Decision Making

Satisficing means choosing an acceptable solution instead of looking for the optimal solution: Good enough may not be the best. Proven surgeries or medications may be subject to satisficing choices instead of choosing the best proven alternatives available today. Optimization of decisions is replaced by searching and opting for alternatives only to the point where an acceptable solution is found.

Overconfidence bias is due to what it says: Physicians or nurses who are overconfident in their judgment in general, overly optimistic in diagnosis and managing patient care.

Availability bias is generated by our tendency to place too much emphasis on the information which is readily available when decisions are to be made. Both diagnostic and therapeutic decisions may be at stake.

In a sunk cost trap, decision makers tend to escalate commitment to a course of action in which they have already made substantial investments of time, material, and human resources rather than making commitments based on marginal costs and benefits of their decisions and actions. Continuing to bet in a casino after multiple losses or continuing to practice surgical techniques into which we have already invested so much time, energy, or hospital and other technology resources may become sunk cost traps.

Recency effect or temporizing is due to too much emphasis being placed on recent events such as on the immediate experience preceding the impending decision.

We may commit a confirmation bias by our tendency to gather and base our decisions on the data and information that confirm our existing views and downplay information that is contrary to our preexisting hypotheses. For example, "do not resuscitate" orders may be subject to this kind of biased decision making.

Overreliance on pattern recognition and pattern matching is based on past experience, which may reduce considerations of a whole series of alternatives. Patterns are recognized in our past experience and the current situation is matched to such past patterns. It necessarily does not; decisions must be made in views of the current range of best options.

Pattern recognition and matching are not the same when experienced by health professionals and novices. In the latter, "feeling uncomfortable about," "something goes wrong," or "something is not right" is worth considering in decision making, but finding reasons or patterns leading to such perceptions should be the next step in a novice's performance.

In structured decision making, problems are defined, alternatives are generated, options are evaluated, actions are chosen and implemented, and their results are evaluated.

Intuition alone may lead to wrong decisions if a more formal analysis of a decisional process is available.

Reasoning by analogy is a double-edged decision making tool. On the one hand, analogical reasoning minimizes repetition of mistakes. On the other hand, it downplays or ignores differences and new phenomena and considerations that should necessarily refine or reorient decisions. Establishing lists of what is analogous and what is not and beyond helps.

The ambiguity effect fallacy means choosing an action or option that we know well in probabilistic terms before an action whose outcomes are unknown in probabilistic terms. Once the probabilities of the later actions are known, they may be better than the probabilities of the former. Choosing a treatment known for its effectiveness always follows a "playing for sure" route. Medical ethics are in favor of the "playing for sure" option even if some logicians might think the contrary.

Hyperbolic discounting means choosing actions yielding smaller benefits for a short term rather than a larger long-term benefit of another alternative action. "Making the patient comfortable" may be preferred by some to alternative decisions to treat the patient and significantly improve his or her survival.

A source credibility fallacy may occur if we prefer decisions of a person who is credible, an expert, and trustworthy. This fallacy may occur if we blindly follow the conclusions of consults by other experts from other specialties without assessing evidence from requesters as compared to the providers of a consult.

4.3.1.2 Fallacies from the Motivation to Decide Domain

A commitment fallacy occurs when we follow a social and/or professional commitment that we translate into our decisions. The Hippocratic Oath to act and help accordingly may be pursued, despite contrary evidence of the appropriateness of action. Our action derives from the fear of professional and/or social rejection while being blind to the evidence not to act in the circumstances.

A confirmation bias means actively seeking a posteriori elements of support, which will confirm the decision we already made. "… You see, you did better after taking this medication than others who didn't…."

A sunk cost effect fallacy occurs when once we have put effort into something, we are reluctant to pull out because of the loss we would incur, even if continued refusal would lead to an even more important loss. Choosing surgery before a conservative treatment may be an example of this fallacy.

4.3.1.3 Fallacies Related to Decisions Themselves

Our decision can be rational only within the limits of our knowledge, experience, and cognitive capability. This kind of *bounded rationality* is probably suitable for medicine. Best choices are not necessarily made due to the limitations of the human mind, the structure within which the mind operates, the best evidence available, and the ways we handle it. Our rationality will then always be bound and cannot be completely overcome.

Anchoring and adjustment heuristic means basic understanding and ensuing decisions regarding known "anchors" or familiar positions and preferred choices. By offering in advance a set of possible actions to choose from, we tend to adopt one of them without considering other actions based on a broader view of the problem to decide on. This may happen in the differential diagnosis domain and in the selection of actions that follow competing diagnoses.

Availability heuristic means making judgments based on what we can remember rather than on complete data and information. It affects our judgment of frequencies and likelihoods of events. Delayed decisions may compensate for incompatible information coming from vivid memory. However, delayed decisions are incompatible with the reality of emergency, surgery, or critical care medicines.

Fallacies, biases, and other judgment and decision errors are open ended, expanding, and ever-changing domains. They must be followed, understood, and corrected continuously. Hence, even our reference devoted specifically to fallacies[65] from which many of the above are drawn must not be seen as the final word about our understanding and decision making errors. Many others will decidedly follow, but we must always do our best with what we have at hand.

4.3.2 Collective-Related Fallacies: Groupthink

Thinking in groups and as a group creates another category of reasoning and decision making traps and leads to potential errors and fallacies.

On the basis of the experience from the world of politics in general and foreign policy,[67,68] Janis[67] concludes that erroneous decisions are sometimes made under stress and pressure by groups whose members think "collectively" and value, above all, the sense of belonging by "going along to get along." Mental efficiency, reality testing, and moral judgment may deteriorate as a result of in-group pressure. Pressure generates a strong need for affiliation, and stress generates group cohesiveness. Groups are committed to prior group decisions under pressure to conform and friendship is cherished even with incompetents. This attitude prevails over building rational individual and complementary contributions to decisions chosen by the group. Striving for unanimity overrides group members' motivation to realistically appraise alternative courses of action. Does such an attitude exist in health professions? The reader only needs to casually observe what happens in hospitals, in their services, or in academic departments in medicine and other health professions to be able to answer the question.

Roberto[66] recognizes three types of dysfunctional decision making cultures: A *culture of no*, a *culture of yes*, and a *culture of maybe*. The chronic inability to move from conflict to consensus and from deliberation to action results in such situations. Even if members of the group disagree, by being silent or otherwise, they opt for one of the three above-mentioned ways and cultures.

Do health care, academic, and research environments not often have similar characteristics? Groupthink may occur and be important in various domains: development of clinical guidelines, health administration, functioning and orientation of emergency medicine, strategies in surgical specialties or public health and preventive medicine programs, and policies development, implementation, and evaluation.

In the health domain–related administrative and scientific meetings, colloquiums, symposiums, consensus groups, specific topic-oriented working groups, and their recommendations, even clinical rounds at various levels, do not escape group-related decision making errors and fallacies.

Conclusion

Both patient- and management-centered decision making require a *sound a priori decision analysis,* as discussed in this chapter.

Another problem is that *decision analyses and their products, such as algorithms* (with their other components such as research, experience, or meta-analysis), *often do not travel well.* On the one hand, they are badly needed in certain environments given incomplete and imperfect data and information for straightforward matters and/or the proliferation of new medical technologies, such as diagnostic methods and treatments in medicine and surgery. On the other hand, according to Balla et al.,[69] biases exist between expert and novice users (expert decision analysis belongs to expert people). Diagnostic (base rate) errors abound. Variable meaning is attributed to findings as for their representativeness. Variable use of relevant findings exists. Unequal weight is given by different clinicians in their work and decisions to different findings (anchoring), and even wording of problems (framing) may affect the decision process and its result.

It appears from these and other authors' comments that reluctance to use decision analysis does not focus on its substance, intellectual quality, or scientific acceptability. Its greatest challenge is that it is somewhat inflexible and not adaptive enough for ever-changing daily life in different clinical environments and community health fields.

> These authors[69] conclude: "... We are not suggesting that it is neither feasible nor necessary to apply decision analytic methods to every clinical situation. Yet the insights into decision processes provided by the theory and the discrepancies between clinical intuition and formal theories should become part of the background and understanding of every clinician."

Decision analysis was also found to be preferable to second opinions for surgical decisions.[69]

We live in an action-oriented era and the domain of health endeavors is itself action oriented: Something must be done! Interestingly but not surprisingly enough, decision making and decision analysis rarely include "doing nothing" as decision points, choices, and options. Hippocrates might not be pleased.

Decision analysis, such as meta-analysis, may represent an alternative and/or complement to controlled clinical trials, whenever they are costly and/or ethically unacceptable or when additional information is sought.

Decision analysis is only as good as its data base.

In addition to further refinements in the quantitative methodology of decision analysis,[70–73] the evaluation of its results, considerations of human values, and the assessment of human weaknesses in clinical practice are the necessary ingredients for the improvement of decision making in clinical practice, community health, and medical research. This would probably explain why the results of clinical decision analyses may at times appear more counterintuitive than they really are.

Several additional readings might prove useful for the reader:

M. A. Roberto's *The Art of Critical Decision Making*[66] introduces us to the analysis and rules of decision making through case analyses of selected good or bad decisions in political and civic life.

The philosopher/nurse team of P. A. Facione and N. C. Facione brings us closer to health sciences while building on foundations of critical thinking and decision making, in general, in their *Thinking and Reasoning in Human Decision Making: The Method of Argument and Heuristic Analysis.*[74]

Wulf and Goetsche propose an additional approach via evidence-based clinical decision making.[75]

Medical errors are preventable. Understanding and improving medical decision making is one way to make the "epidemiology of medical errors"[76,77] easier.

References

1. Anon. *What are knowledge, skills and attitudes?* http://www.apaseq.com/docs/knowledge.doc, retrieved May 2, 2009.
2. Wikipedia, the free encyclopedia. *Disposition.* 1 page at http://en.wikipedia.org/wiki/Disposition, retrieved February 9, 2011.
3. Jeffrey R. Decision theory, pp. 207–9, in: *The Cambridge Dictionary of Philosophy.* Edited by R Audi, General Editor. Second Edition. Cambridge/New York: Cambridge University Press, 1999.
4. *Decision theory.* Encyclopaedia Britannica Article. 1 page at <ebcid:com.britannica.occ2.identifier.Articleidentifier?tockd=90297...>, retrieved from electronic edition June 27, 2010.
5. Albert DA. Decision theory in medicine. A review and critique. *Milbank Mem Fund Quart/Health Soc*, 1978;**56**(3, Summer):362–401.
6. Reyna VF. Theories of medical decision making and health: An evidence-based approach. *Med Dec Making*, 2008; Nov–Dec 2008:829–33. DOI: 10.1177/0272989X08327069.
7. TIP: Learning Domains. *Decision–making.* 1 page at http://tip.psychology.oreg/decision.html, retrieved January 16, 2010.
8. Patrick EA. *Decision Analysis in Medicine: Methods and Applications.* Boca Raton, FL: CRC Press, 1979.
9. Weinstein MC, Fineberg HV, Elstein AS, Frazier HS, Neutra RR, McNeil BJ. *Clinical Decision Analysis.* Philadelphia: WB Saunders, 1980.
10. Chapman GB, Sonnenberg FA (eds.). *Decision Making in Health Care. Theory, Psychology, and Applications.* Cambridge/New York: Cambridge University Press, 2000.
11. Alemi F, Gustafson DH. *Decision Analysis for Healthcare Managers.* Chicago/Washington: Health Administration Press/AUPHA Press, 2007.

12. Jenicek M. Decision analysis and decision-making in medicine. Beyond intuition, guts, and flair, chapter 13, pp. 341–78, in: *Foundations of Evidence-Based Medicine*. Boca Raton/London/New York/Washington: The Parthenon Publishing Group/CRC Press, 2003.

13. Stolper E, Van de Wiel M, Van Royen P, Van Bokhoven M, Van der Weiden T, Dinant GJ. Gut feelings as a third track in general practitioners' diagnostic reasoning. *J Gen Intern Med*, 2010;**26**(2):197–203. DOI: 10.1007/s1606-010-1524-5.

14. Kramer MS. *Clinical Epidemiology and Biostatistics. A Primer for Clinical Investigators and Decision-Makers*. Berlin/Heidelberg/New York/London: Springer-Verlag, 1988.

15. Murphy EA. *The Logic of Medicine*. Baltimore, MD: The Johns Hopkins University Press, 1976. (Second Edition, 1997.)

16. Tom E, Schulman KA. Mathematical models in decision analysis. *Infect Control Hosp Epidemiol*, 1997;**18**:65–73.

17. Changing Minds. *Short-cut decisions*. 2 pages at http://changingminds .org/explanations/decision/short-cut_decisions.htm, retrieved November 4, 2009.

18. Croskerry P. Clinical cognition and diagnostic error: Applications of dual process of reasoning. *Adv Health Sci Educ*, 2009;**14**:27–35.DOI 10.1007/s11606-010-15240-5.

19. Raiffa H. *Decision Analysis: Introductory Lectures on Choices under Uncertainty*. Reading: Addison Wesley, 1968.

20. *A Dictionary of Epidemiology*. Edited for the International Epidemiological Association by Miquel Porta. Fifth Edition. Oxford/New York: Oxford University Press, 2008.

21. Lee A, Joynt GM, Ho AMH, Keitz S, McGinn T, Wyer PC, and for the EBM Teaching Scripts Working Group. Tips for teachers of evidence-based medicine: Making sense of decision analysis using a decision tree. *J Gen Intern Med*, 2009;**24**(5):642–8.

22. Sonnenberg FA, Beck JR. Markov models in medical decision making: A practical guide. *Med Decis Making*, 1993;**13**:322–38.

23. Pauker SG, Kassirer JP. The threshold approach to clinical decision making. *N Engl J Med*, 1980;**320**:1109–17.

24. Tarride J-E, Blackhouse G, Bischof M, McCarron EC, Lim M, Ferrusi IL, Xie F, Goeree R. Approaches for economic evaluations of health care technologies. *J Am Coll Radiol*, 2009;**6**:307–16.

25. Dickinson HD. Evidence-based decision-making: An argumentative approach. *Int J Med Inform*, 1998;**51**:71-9-81.

26. Rieke RD, Sillars MO, Peterson TR. *Argumentation and Critical Decision Making*. Sixth Edition. Boston/New York/San Francisco: Pearson Education, 2005.

27. Doherty GM. The acute abdomen, chapter 21, pp. 451–63, in: *Current Diagnosis & Treatment Surgery*. Edited by GM Doherty. 13th Edition. New York/Chicago/London: McGraw-Hill Medical, 2010.

28. Stedman TL. *Stedman's Medical Dictionary*. Edited by WR Hensyl. 25th Edition. Baltimore: Williams & Wilkins, 1990.

29. *Encyclopaedia Britannica*. Chicago: William Benton Publisher, 1968.

30. *McGraw-Hill Dictionary of Scientific and Technical Terms*. Edited by SP Parker Editor-in-Chief. Fourth Edition. New York: McGraw-Hill, 1989.

31. Oreskovich MR, Carrico CJ. Stab wounds of the anterior abdomen. Analysis of a management plan using local wound exploration and quantitative peritoneal lavage. *Ann Surg*, 1983;**198**:411–9.

32. Society for Medical Decision Making Committee on Standardization of Clinical Algorithms. Proposal for clinical algorithm standards. *Med Decis Making*, 1992;**12**:149–54.

33. Pearson SD, Margolis CZ, Davis S, Schreier LK, Gottlieb LK. The clinical algorithm nosology: A method for comparing algorithmic guidelines. *Med Decis Making*, 1992;**12**:123–31.

34. Khalil PN, Kleespies A, Angele MK, Thasler WE, Siebeck M, Brunns CJ, Mutschler W, Kanz K-G. The formal requirements of algorithms and their implications in clinical medicine and quality management. *Langenbecks Arch Surg*, 2011;**396**(1):31–40.

35. Jenicek M. Direction giving tools in decision making, section 10.4, pp. 313–8, in: *Epidemiology. The Logic of Modern Medicine*. Montréal: EPIMED International, 1995.

36. Jenicek M. Tactical tools: Clinical algorithms and decision tables, section 13.4.1, pp. 360–6, in: *Foundations of Evidence-Based Medicine*. Boca Raton/London/New York/Washington: The Parthenon Publishing Group/CRC Press, 2003.

37. Hansen DT. Development and use of clinical algorithms in chiropractic. *J Manipul Physiol Ther*, 1991;**14**:478–82.

38. Green G, Defoe Jr EC. What is a clinical algorithm? *Clin Pediatr*, 1978;**17**:457–63.

39. Komaroff AL. Algorithms and the "art" of medicine. *Am J Public Health*, 1982;**72**:10–1.

40. Wikipedia, the free encyclopedia. *Medical guideline*. 3 pages at http://en,wikipedia.org/wiki/Medical_guideline, retrieved January 28, 2011.

41. Filed MJ, Lohr KN (eds.). *Guidelines for Clinical Practice: From Development to Use*. Washington: National Academy Press, 1992.

42. Manchikanti L, Singh V, Helm II S, Schultz DM, Datta S, Hirsch. An introduction to evidence-based approach to intervention techniques in the management of chronic spinal pain. *Pain Physician*, 2009;**12**:E1–E33.

43. Veale B, Weller D, Silagy C. Clinical practice guidelines and Australian general practice. *Aust Fam Physician*, 1999;**28**:744–9.

44. Jenicek M. Strategic tools for right decisions: Clinical practice guidelines, pp. 366–9, in Ref. 36.

45. Qasem A, Snow V, Owens DK, Shekelle P for the Clinical Guidelines Committee of the American College of Physicians. The development of clinical practice guidelines and guidance statements of the American College of Physicians: Summary of methods. *Ann Intern Med*, 2010;**153**:194–9.

46. Turner T, Misso M, Harris C, Green S. Development of evidence-based clinical practice guidelines (CPGs): Comparing approaches. *Implementation Science*, 2008;**3**:45. DOI: 10.1186/1748-5908-3-45. 8 pages published online at http://www.implementationscience.com/content/3/1/45, retrieved January 28, 2011.

47. Hayward RSA, Wilson MC, Tunis SR, Bass EB, Rubin HR, Haynes RB. More informative abstracts of articles describing clinical practice guidelines. *Ann Intern Med*, 1993;**118**:731–7.

48. Brook RH. Practice guidelines and practicing medicine. Are they compatible? *JAMA*, 1989;**262**(21):3027–30.

49. *Canadian Clinical Practice Guidelines*. Edited by DE Greenberg and M Muraca. 2008 Edition. Toronto: Elsevier Canada, 2008.

50. Pearson SD, Margolis CZ, Davis S, Schreier LK, Sokol HN, Gottlieb LK. Is consensus reproducible? A study of an algorithmic guidelines development process. *Med Care*, 1995;**33**:643–60.

51. Cummins RO, Chamberlain DA, Abramson NS, Allen M, Baskett P, Becker L, Bossaert L, Delooz H, Dick W, Eisenberg M, Evans T, Holmberg S, Kerber R, Mullie A, Ornato JP, Sandoe E, Skulberg A, Tunstall-Pedoe H, Swanson R, Theis WH. Recommended guidelines for uniform reporting of data from out-of-hospital cardiac arrest: The Utstein Style. *Ann Emerg Med*, 1991;**20**:861–74.

52. Cummins RO, Chamberlain DD, Hazinski MF, Nadkarni V, Kloeck W, Kramer E, Becker L, Robertson C, Koster R, Zaritski A, Bossaert L, Ornato JP, Callanan V, Allen M, Steen P, Connolly B, Sanders A, Idris A, Cobbe S. Recommended guidelines for reviewing, reporting, and conducting research on in-hospital resuscitation: The in-hospital "Utstein style." A statement for Healthcare Professionals from the American Heart Association, the European Resuscitation Council, the Heart and Stroke Foundation of Canada, the Australian Resuscitation Council, and the Resuscitation Councils of Southern Africa. *Resuscitation*, 1997;**34**:151–83.

53. Davis DA, Taylor-Vaisey A. Translating guidelines into practice. A systematic review of theoretic concepts, practical experience and research evidence in the adoption of clinical practice guidelines. *Can Med Assoc J*, 1997;**157**:408–16.

54. Hayward RSA, Guyatt GH, Moore K-A, McKibbon A, Carter AO. Canadian physicians' attitudes about preferences regarding clinical practice guidelines. *Can Med Assoc J*, 1997;**156**:1715–23.

55. Worrall G, Chaulk P, Freake D. The effects of clinical practice guidelines on patient outcomes in primary care: A systematic review. *Can Med Assoc J*, 1997;**156**:1705–12.

56. Fletcher RH. Practice guidelines and the practice of medicine: Is it the end of clinical judgment and expertise? *Schweiz Med Wochenschr*, 1998;**128**:1883–8.

57. Lilford RJ, Braunholtz D. Who's afraid of Thomas Bayes? *J Epidemiol Community Health*, 2000;**54**:731–9.

58. Hill J, Alderson P. A summary of methods that the National Guideline Centre uses to produce clinical guidelines for the National Institute for Health and Clinical Excellence. *Ann Intern Med*, 2011;**154**:752–7.

59. Laine C, Taichman DB, Mulrow C. Trustworthy clinical guidelines. (Editorial.) *Ann Intern Med*, 2011;**154**:774–5.

60. O'Mahony R, Murthy L, Akunne A, Young J for the Guideline Development Group. Synopsis of the National Institute for Health and Clinical Excellence guideline for prevention of delirium. *Ann Intern Med*, 2011;**154**:746–51.

61. Wonderling D, Sawyer L, Fenu E, Lovibond K, Laramée P. National Clinical Guideline Centre cost-effectiveness assessment for the National Institute for Health and Clinical Excellence. *Ann Intern Med*, 2011;**154**:758–65.

62. Raza Abidi S, Raza Abidi SS. Towards the merging of multiple clinical protocols and guidelines via ontology-driven modelling. 5 pdf pages at http://www.cs.dal.ca/~sraza/papers/aime09merging.pdf, retrieved February 7, 2011.

63. ChangingMinds.org. *Theories about decision-making*. Various number of pages at http://changingminds.org/explanations/theories/a_decision.htm, retrieved April 11, 2009.

64. ChangingMinds.org. *Theories about decision errors*. Various number of pages at http://changingminds.org/explanations/theories/a_decision_error.htm, retrieved February 14, 2009.

65. Jenicek M. *Fallacy-Free Reasoning in Medicine. Improving Communication and Decision Making in Research and Practice*. Chicago, IL: American Medical Association (AMA Press), 2009.

66. Roberto MA. *The Art of Critical Decision Making*. Transcript Book. Chantilly, VA: The Great Courses/The Teaching Company, 2009.

67. Janis IL. *Victims of Groupthink: A Psychological Study of Foreign Policy Decisions and Fiascoes*. Boston, MA: Houghton Mifflin Company, 1972 (Second Revised Edition, 1983).

68. Tetlock PE. Identifying victims of groupthink from public statements of decision makers. *J Pers Soc Psychol*, 1979;**37**(8):314–24.

69. Balla JI, Elstein AS, Christensen C. Obstacles to acceptance of clinical decision analysis. *Br Med J* 1989;**298**:579–82.

70. Clarke JR. A comparison of decision analysis and second opinions for surgical decisions. *Arch Surg*, 1985;**120**:844–7.

71. Fryback DG. Reflections on the beginnings and future of medical decision making. *MDM*, 2001;**21**:71–3.

72. Beck JR. Medical decision making: 20 years of advancing the field. *MDM*, 2001;**21**:73–5.

73. Habbema JDF, Bossuyt PMM, Dippel DWJ, Marshall S, Hilden J. Analyzing clinical decision analyses. *Stat Med*, 1990;**9**:1229–42.

74. Facione PA, Facione NC. *Thinking and Reasoning in Human Decision Making: The Method of Argument and Heuristic Analysis*. Millbrae, CA: The California Academic Press, 2007.

75. Wulff HR, Götzsche PC. *Rational Diagnosis and Treatment. Evidence-Based Clinical Decision-Making.* Third Edition. Oxford/London/Malden, MA: Blackwell Science, 2000. It's Fourth Edition under new title: Götzsche PC. *Rational Diagnosis and Treatment: Evidence-Based Clinical Decision-Making.* Chichester, WS/Hoboken, NJ: Wiley, 2007.
76. Meyer G, Lewin DI, Eisenberg J. To err is preventable: Medical errors and academic medicine. *Am J Med*, 2001;**110**:597–603.
77. Jenicek M. *Medical Error and Harm. Understanding, Prevention, and Control.* Boca Raton/London/New York: CRC Press/Taylor & Francis, 2011.

Chapter 5

How Physicians Communicate with Themselves, Their Patients, and Others: Clinical Communication and Its Vehicles

Executive Summary

Communication in medicine, a part of the emerging domain of communicology, represents a transactional process in which messages (evidence-based or not) are filtered through the perceptions, emotions, and experience of those involved. Interpersonal communication is not only the linchpin of medical practice but also an important element of health information usage and of the evaluation of its contribution to improve medical practice.

A communication environment includes the following as intellectual tools: **morning reports;** clinical, grand, and other rounds; less formal "hallway" discussions; **morbidity** and **mortality reports;** reading/writing/understanding/ use of medical articles; other types of clinical case(s) reporting; communication of an administrative nature; emergencies and error reporting; electronic communication device usage; scut work; unfocused quizzing ("pimping"); argumentation/critical thinking-based and evidence-grounded exchanges of data, information, and decision options; and preferably evidence-based and argumentation-supported Socratic dissent as teaching and training methods.

Greater benefits are derived from these ways of communication when the associated rules, strengths, weaknesses, and applications are understood.

Instrumental vehicles, opportunities, and environments for communication include admission notes, patient charts, consults, and other written or electronic documents and tools, as mentioned earlier.

All communication starts with interviewing the patient (usually at admissions), updating of such interviews (subsequent visits), other kinds of narratives, and clinical case reporting. Textual, creative, and affective skills are required.

The content of any case reporting must include specific objectives (from a large list of options) and a structure that eases the message transfer.

Fallacies in communication may be both of a rhetorical and nonrhetorical nature.

Knowledge translation as "an interactive process that includes the synthesis, dissemination, exchange, and ethically sound application of knowledge to improve health, to provide more effective health services and products, and to strengthen the health care system" relies heavily not only on communication methods but also on health structures, knowledge, information providers and recipients, and other specific settings. Effective communication is necessary for its success.

Not-So-Random Leading Thoughts

To think justly, we must understand
what others mean: to know the value
of our thoughts, we must try their
effect on other minds.

William Hazlitt, 1826

Precision of communication is more important than
ever, in our area of hair-trigger balances,
when a false, or misunderstood word
may create as much disaster as
a sudden thoughtless act.

James Thurber, 1961

The Medium is the Message.

Marshall (Herbert) McLuhan, 1964

Scientists estimate that medical student notes
account for more than 60% of a chart's weight.

Frederick L. Brancati, 1992

There are two rules that all medical students must learn:
Rule #1: The attending is always right.
Rule #2: Don't forget Rule #1.

Howard Bennett, 1994

At the end of a patient visit, review once more
(1) the working diagnosis and (2) the proposed
plan to deal with it. Then ask: "Is there
anything else?" You will be amazed (and patients
will be gratified) at how often a less
obvious reason for the visit is revealed.

Christopher D. Stanton, 1999

Whatever one sees, one must read,
and whatever one reads, one must see.
This is the only way to learn clinical medicine.

T. C. Goel, 1999

Any type of communication, oral or written
occurs more easily if you have something
meaningful to clearly say or put down on paper.

Paraphrasing Sholem Asch, 1955

The culmination of the research process
is the communication of results. This final
stage may be the most important part of
the process (in) that only shared information
can clarify, amplify and expand the professional
body of knowledge. ... The discussion section
is the heart of a research report.

Leslie G. Portney and Mary P. Watkins, 2009

Isn't this also the case for all clinical communication with peers and patients?

I told you I felt funny.

From the tombstone of one of your patients

Introductory Comments

For some, what isn't on Twitter or YouTube, or conveyed by cell phone or e-mail does not count. But does it? Yes, really, it does! In the health domain, it counts even more in an irreplaceable direct interaction and communication between warm-blooded human beings.

Communication is a vehicle of our reasoning, understanding, decision making, execution, results, evaluation, and improvements in our endless, often more or less perfect and realistic striving for perfection.

Is it enough to reason well, master and use the best evidence in our decision making, and execute skillful surgical and medical acts on patients? Obviously not. Quality health care is a matter of teamwork bringing together physicians, generalists and specialists, nurses, dieticians and nutritionists, respirologists, rehabilitation specialists, health administration and administrative staff, social services, and many others.

Communication is essential to succeed in medical care. Deficient communication, poor understandings, and breakdowns are responsible for medical error and harm. How can we communicate effectively in order to provide best care possible? This chapter offers several points to master and ponder starting with understanding the inner workings of the hospital, office, and community, as well as the failures and fallacies that may occur and must be avoided and/or corrected.

Any newcomer in the health care environment must thoroughly:

1. Understand what is essential, effective communication: *What is it all about?*
2. Know the vehicles and tools of effective communication: Encounters with patients, patient charts, reporting clinical cases, floor and other rounds, progress notes, referrals and consults, scientific oral communications, medical review articles, and original studies reports. *How can we get the message across to others? By what means?*
3. Be aware of potential failures in communication, how to avoid them, how to correct them. The most important fallacies in communication illustrate ways to prevent and correct medical error and harm. *How can we overcome our weaknesses?*
4. Realize that communication must not only have its own identity, methods, and techniques, but also a purpose. In medicine, communication contributes in an essential way to effective and efficient health care and its own and its users' improvement leading to the greatest benefit for and the well-being of the patient.

Let us examine professional communication in general and in medicine in particular since it almost always carries general elements of learning and teaching[1,2] for the parties involved, teachers and trainees, and ultimately the patient.

5.1 How to View Communication in General and in Its Medical Context

Making sense and sharing views and experience are based on two types of dialogue, both important for an effective communication and shared decision making:

1. Our own way of critical thinking is an internal dialogue: We think about something by ourselves, and we argue with ourselves. Did this patient improve enough to discharge him or her or stop his or her current treatment? Toulmin's modern argumentation may be used here as in an external dialogue.
2. The external dialogue is a process of *dialectic,* that is, seeking through social and professional dialogue (in our case) with others, a commonly acceptable solution to a given problem. Modern argumentation, as outlined in Chapter 2 and here, is at its core. It follows, expands, and brings together internal dialogues. We are opening ourselves to the reasoning of others to solutions, learning, and change.

In its broadest sense, *communication in general* is

■ *A process whereby information is enclosed in a package and is channeled and imparted by a sender to a receiver via some medium. The receiver then decodes the message and gives the sender feedback.*[3] All forms therefore require an information and evidence source, a sender (transmitter), a message, a channel of communication, and an intended recipient.
■ *... Communication takes place when one mind acts upon its environment and another mind is influenced, and in that other mind an experience occurs, which is like the experience in the first mind and is caused in part by that experience.*[4]
■ *Imparting or interchanging of thoughts, opinions, or information by speech, writing, or signs.*[5] *... a process by which information is exchanged between individuals through a common system of symbols, signs, or behavior.*[6]

Communication may take place through verbal, nonverbal, visual, or auditory means, conveyed directly or by various written, spoken, or electronic media. **Semiotics** is a study of such means, relying on semantics (study of meanings), syntactics (relationships among signs in formal structures of communication), and pragmatics (relationships between signs and their effects on the individuals or groups who use them).[7]

Not surprisingly, communication is essential in domains other than medicine, such as the military. Several useful general bibliographies covering communication skills across various fields are currently updated and available online.[8]

The new science of **communicology** was defined by Lanigan as *the study of human discourse in all of its semiotic and phenomenological manifestations*[9] or simply as *the science of human communication.*[10] It is introduced to us by at least one monograph[11] and covered also in its own *International Encyclopedia of Communication.*[12] It encompasses communication at the interpersonal, group, and intergroup level. Medical communication happens in all of the above.

In 1998, the Association of American Medical Colleges stressed among its objectives that even before graduation, students must acquire the ability to obtain an accurate medical history and to communicate effectively, both orally and in writing, with patients and their families, colleagues, and others with whom the physicians must exchange information.[13] It defines **communication in medicine** as a "transactional process in which messages are filtered through the perceptions, emotions, and experiences of those involved. ... Interpersonal communication remains the linchpin of medical practice." This linchpin is extremely well introduced and covered in Health Canada's resource booklet *Putting Communication Skills to Work.*[14]

As accurately reflected in Higgs et al.'s monograph,[15] clearly beyond physician–patient communication, effective practice and research in medicine requires equally valid oral, written, and electronic communication between peers and coworkers conveying essential information about how health problems and care are understood and what to do about them. This chapter is about the latter.

After reading the preceding chapters, we may feel that the meanings of evidence, argument, and argumentation may vary in their daily use within general and professional settings of communication. Rhetoric, sophisms, or sophistry are also subject to these variations when people communicate. Refutations also underlie the ways to right decisions. All those terms can be defined in the desirable or undesirable way. Table 5.1, as a reminder, illustrates and clarifies this point. We stand by the right side of this table.

Table 5.1 Medical and Nonmedical Meanings and Connotations of Some Elements of Reasoning and Communication

Frequent, but Not Exclusive Connotation in Daily Life	Meaning in General and in Medical Critical Thinking
Argument	
An oral disagreement; contention. Emotionally loaded and often tense exchange of words, statements harm and positions not always with a mutually acceptable solution in sight.	A vehicle of reasoning; a series of statements intended to establish a position in medical problem solving like diagnosis, treatment, or that occurred, or in other aspects of preventive and curative health care.
Argumentation	
Confrontational exchange of views or positions between two or more parties. An often emotionally tainted dispute about something.	The methodological use or presentation of medical arguments to solve a problem in medical practice and research through the exchange of ideas and statements between two or more health professionals, patients, and other stakeholders in health.
Refutation	
The destructive process of tearing down arguments of others in a game of anything goes; "whip shooting" counterproposals.	The constructive investigative process of exchange of arguments and counterarguments based on common understanding and cooperative will to reach a common goal; the best solution for the problem of interest by way of going from disagreement to agreement.
Rhetoric	
The undue use of exaggeration or display; bombast; using language to manipulate the listener by mere style or pretention. ("*It's only rhetoric!*")	The faculty or skill of discovering the available means of persuasion in a given case. A means of instruction involving not only invention, arrangement, style, memory, and what is correct, but also evidence and its delivery. The essence of communication today.

Sophism/sophistry	
A specious argument to display ingenuity in reasoning by subtle, tricky, superficially plausible, but generally fallacious ways of reasoning, sometimes for the purpose of deceiving someone. Empty appeals that do not really have any significant substance to them. Winning the case, not a search for truth, is the goal.	Argumentative skills to convince others on the basis of the appropriate evidence. Finding truth is the goal of such argumentation.
Evidence	
That which tends to prove or disprove something according to its proponent(s).	Any data or information, whether solid or weak, obtained through experience, observational research, or experimental work for understanding of a health problem, decisions about it, and related actions and their effect (our definition).

Communication in general now has a solid foundation in the literature, the journal *Communication & Medicine*, and in dedicated medicine textbooks listed elsewhere.[16]

5.2 Intellectual Vehicles of Communication: Some Less and Some More Interrogative Ways of Sharing Knowledge and Experience

If we define argumentation as a discussion between two or more people in which at least one advances an argument, that is, various statements or propositions allowing the inference from them to some conclusion (see Chapter 2), we can consider that various manners of communication carry various degrees of discussion. Some are more complete and satisfactory for a given purpose than others and at least five are of interest in the context of medicine.

5.2.1 Barking Orders

There is not much, if any, discussion here. The "transmitter," attending or any other person who is "running the show," tells the "receiver," clinical clerk, medical student, rotating intern, what to do and the latter executes.

This kind of communication is often dictated by the reality of practice, such as in emergency medicine or surgical or obstetrical operations where the speed of care is often lifesaving.

5.2.2 Just Watch Me!

Observation alone is supposed to lead to a passive acquisition of knowledge and fundamental ideas to develop further and later on by the "receiver's" repeated executions. There is no exchange of ideas at this stage.

5.2.3 Do It after Me!

Repeated executions are emphasized: "Please, finish the suturing of this wound!" … "Our next patient will also need a spinal tap. Please do it now the way we did in our last patient." Some degree of meaningful discussion may be reached by the way of argumentation between the senior and junior physician and student. Let us see now how a meaningful argumentation should be.

5.2.4 Pimping: A Refined Form of Bullying

This method of medical teaching and training[17–19] should not be confused with its more widely known nonmedical-related meaning; that is, the management of providers of carnal pleasures. In medicine, **pimping** is one of the ways of professional communication during various clinical encounters, such as morning reports, rounds, and less formal hallway discussions bringing together medical seniors and juniors. In medicine, pimping has three essential meanings:

1. It is a clinical practice where persons in power and entitled to make decisions (attending, seniors) ask questions (with blurred expectations) to their junior colleagues (medical students, residents) in order for the latter to correctly execute the assigned tasks.
2. It is the quizzing of juniors with objectives ranging from knowledge acquisition to embarrassment and humiliation; it may be positive or negative.
3. It is the barraging of juniors with seemingly random and topic/problem unrelated or unanswerable questions to which the juniors most often do not have answers, leading to humiliation regardless of the conscious intention of the attending or resident asking questions. It creates a feeling of "I do not know" in the face of peers and those who know better.

A "**pimper**" is an attending or resident quizzing subordinates on minutiae and medical trivia during rounds or in class ("… speaking of Mrs. Bowie's knee replacement, can you draw the Krebs cycle for me?….") as a questionable test of the junior's knowledge.

A "pimped" or "**pimpee**" is the unfortunate target and recipient of pimping by pimper(s). The pimpee is supposed to acquire a profound and abiding respect for the pimper and quickly learn who is the boss in the local pecking order. Having said this, pimping may be positive if it is done through a gentle, constructive, and purposeful approach showing the pimpee his or her incomplete knowledge, engaging a dialogue and creating a sense of inadequacy in the pimpee as a stimulus to further learning. Pimping has nothing to do with argumentation. It is a self-purposed endeavor, and any meaningful exchange of ideas is not intended by the pimper and expected by an experienced pimpee.

Student examinations are usually a private matter between the examiner and the examined. In pimping-flavored clinical encounters, student knowledge, attitudes, and skills are on public display,[19] however related or unrelated to the health problem discussed they might be. This does not always help communication between peers.

5.2.5 Uttering Wisdom

The senior physician vocally expresses his often apparently unrelated views regarding the topic of interest or some other topic. Juniors do not understand the mental associations underlying the senior's statements, whose relevance and meaning remain inexplicit. The reason for the message, however valuable it is, remains unknown. The junior is in a "take it or leave it" position. A word of wisdom may also be an attempt to hide the senior's ignorance of the topic.

Let us take an exaggerated example:

> This patient may be a good candidate for coronary bypass surgery.
> … As a matter of fact, I just read in the latest issue of *The Lancet*
> an interesting paper about the cost-effectiveness of immunization
> in some harder to reach communities in the Canadian North. …

The bypass statement may be correct or not. *The Lancet* statement may be correct too, but it is unrelated to the former and irrelevant for a cardiologist's conclusions and proposals.

The utterance of thoughts without explanation and expectation of exchanges in junior–senior communication and further justifications can often produce a *red herring fallacy*. This fallacy occurs when there is a diversion, usually tangential, from one topic to another. The diversion can be somewhat relevant, or even totally irrelevant, to the issue at hand. The "red herring" notion is derived from fox hunting when smoked red-colored herrings were used by hunters to distract dogs from the scent of the foxes they were hunting.

5.2.6 Argumentation and Critical Thinking–Based and Evidence-Grounded Exchange of Data and Information: A "What Do You Think?" Type of Medicine I

Yes, even successful communication relies on structured critical thinking and argumentation, as outlined in Chapter 2. If we define argumentation, in general, as a discussion between two or more people in which at least one person advances an argument, the same holds true in medicine. Physicians discuss among themselves and with other health professionals and patients their cases, the nature of the problem, how to understand it, and what to do about it. Our recommendations and proposals are in fact the *conclusions* (also called *claim*) of a modern argumentative process to which we arrive by some consensus linking our clinical and paraclinical findings about a particular case (*grounds*) to our past experiences and knowledge (*backing*) and that of others in order to make sense of such actual and past experiences (*warrant*) to some degree of certainty (*qualifier*) about our argument "claim," that is, what is our diagnosis then and how should we treat and care for our patient, provided that some contrary and opposite considerations ("rebuttals" in the argumentation sense) do not apply.

Even the best argumentation process makes sense and is useful if several prerequisite considerations are fulfilled:

- *Questions, objectives*, and *hypotheses* about the case (represented by an individual or a group) are appropriately formulated for analysis and interpretation.
- All dependent and independent *variables* that enter our hypotheses are well defined in operational and reproducible terms.
- The *quality* of the use of such variables is known.
- The *setting* of the problem and activities related to it are known, defined, and specified in sufficient details.
- We know who the *stakeholders* are for the health problems at hand, how they view it, how they understand it, and what their expectations are. Doctors, patients, their friends and families, other health and social

care professionals, and community actors and decision makers may differ in their views and expectations, but they are all to some degree involved in and responsible for what will happen to the patient in the future.

■ Both the "transmitter" in the communication (health professional) and the "receiver" (patients and others quoted above) know and have some essential common and *shared* degree of understanding about the subject of current reflections from an argumentative perspective.

Such prerequisites are often crucial for further understanding and solving health problems. Let us say, for example, that several medication errors occurred in a clinical service and several patients suffered from unexpected sensory problems, unstable blood pressure, nausea, and vomiting as a result of possible medical harm caused by overmedication and the suspected administering of medication to the wrong recipients.

To solve the problem, we must establish the following:

■ The exact nature of the problem and what we want to achieve by tackling it: Do we want to solve the problem of medical errors, of harm to the patient, or both? Do we want to solve this problem in patients for whom the drug is indicated, in patients who should not receive this drug, or both?

■ The drug (or drugs) involved, its (their) clinical pharmacological characteristics, and both desirable and undesirable (adverse) effects in qualitative and quantitative terms, indications, general patient (demographical) and clinical (principal disease of interest, comorbidity, treatments, and cotreatments for both) characteristics.

■ The working environment (wards, intensive care units, operating rooms, elsewhere), the health professionals working there, the type of patients under their care, the rules and clinical practice guidelines in use in such a setting.

■ Who is interested in such an enquiry and its results given his or her specific understanding of the health problem and its management and control of error and harm. Is it the patients, their doctors, nurses, pharmacists, pharmaceutical companies, others? What are their expectations in this problem solving?

■ Whether we understand each other, as mentioned above. Do we have the same understanding of the problem and expectations? "Are we on the same wavelength?"

All our analyses, interpretations, and corrective measures will depend on how such "rules of the game" will be determined beforehand. Cause–effect conclusions apply only if the setting in which they have been defined is known, specified, and shared.

The same applies to the ways in which such information is used in argumentations about the health problem at hand, whether it be practical or research oriented.

Views, proposals, or premises are communicated and exchanged, enabling us to understand all building blocks of a modern argument in order to solve a clinical problem and the relationships between them. As the example in Table 5.1 shows, even in (and specifically in) daily communication and exchanges about a clinical situation to be understood and solved, natural language is most often used to "hide" the more technical vocabulary of argumentation (Table 5.2).

Table 5.2 Clinical Rounds as Dialogue with Identification of Argument Components in Physician's Natural Language[20]

Question	Statement	Component of the Argument
Attending: "Kim (an intern who was on call tonight), anything new on our floor?"	**Intern:** "One of our diabetic and hypertensive patients showed a sudden sensory loss and became hemiplegic. Should he be further evaluated and treated for stroke?"	**Claim:** Proposition resulting from our reasoning
Attending: "Can you tell me what your impression (working assessment) is for this patient?"	**Intern:** "This patient most probably had *an ischemic stroke 2 hours ago.* His *computed tomography* is *normal.* Our consulting neurologist told me to *thrombolyse him right away.*" … By the way, … →	**Grounds:** Basis from which we reason and argue. Facts supporting the claim.
Intern: "→ … do we have some general rules regarding how to handle such cases?"	**Attending:** "Yes, as shown by our own review of evidence, *all patients who have an ischemic stroke within 3 hours should receive IV thrombolysis* to limit the ensuing neurologic deficit. Also, we should consider moving him to a stroke care unit."	**Warrant:** General rule that permits us to infer a claim from grounds.
Intern: "Is this treatment plan mandatory or do we have other choices? Is there anything else we should do?"	**Attending:** "It is mandatory. This patient *must* be thrombolysed and considered for endarferectomy or carotid angioplasty and stenting if carotid stenosis should prove to be an underlying problem."	**Qualifier:** A word or phrase that indicates the strength conferred by the warrant and thus the strength of support for our conclusion.

Intern: "Do we have any competing underlying diagnoses? What should we do to adjust treatment according to the pathology underlying this patient's state?"	Attending: "*Further diagnostic workup based among other things on CT scan, ultrasonography, and magnetic resonance angiography* should help us differentiate this case from intracranial venous thrombosis, aneurysm, arteriovenous aneurysms, or subarachnoidal hemorrhage."	Grounds: Basis from which we reason and argue. Facts supporting the claim. [Here the question is whether the ground is in fact correct.]
Intern: "What kind of evidence do you have available to you for your recommendations and orders?"	Attending: "Our *systematic review of the evidence* shows that emergency IV thrombolysis of stroke patients improves stroke outcomes like neurologic deficit... *Other treatments must also be considered depending on the underlying lesion:* obstruction by atherosclerosis and other types of stenosis, embolus, lacunar infarction, cerebral infarction, or intracerebral hemorrhage. Also, glucose and blood pressure control are important for all underlying diabetes and hypertension."	Backing: Body of experience and evidence that supports the warrant. *Confirmation of the claim and additional claims suggested:* Proposals for lateral thinking and argumentation for alternatives.
Attending: "Well done, Kim!"		

Source: Adapted from Jenicek M, Hitchcock DL. *Evidence-Based Practice. Logic and Critical Thinking in Medicine.* Chicago, IL: American Medical Association (AMA Press), 2005.

Meanings in clinical jargon: CT = computed tomography; IV = intravenous. To thrombolyse a patient = to give him or her thrombolytic therapy (e.g., by recombinant tissue plasminogen activator).

Our professional communication relies (or should rely) on proper argumentation. Translated into Toulmin's way of thinking, questions and answers in argumentation accurately reflect the kind of discussion outlined in the Socratic method question review:

- What is your claim?
- What was the original idea that led you to your problem solving?
- What are the data on which you base your claim?
- Do you have some backing for this problem solving?
- Is there any warrant (supporting understanding) stemming from backing in light of which the data interpretation might be viewed and understood?

■ How sure are you about your claim? What is your qualifier philosophically speaking?
■ What are the conditions and/or situations in which your conclusions (claim) do not apply? (These are the rebuttals.)

Argumentation in favor of a claim may focus either on building this kind of argument or on reconstructing the argument from already available information extracted for the purpose of its understanding. Fallacies here are based either on faulty evidence behind the argument building blocks or on how they are linked together. Additional challenges derive from the spoken word.

In practice, structured medical student debates must include weighing conflicting information from multiple sources, critically reviewing published research including the quality of evidence (accuracy and validity), relevance, and availability, and remaining skeptical about them, making evidence-based decisions, explaining risks and benefits of outcome/treatment options, being able to examine cost/benefit considerations, and using multiple sources for problem solving together with impromptu reasoning skills in a team approach to the problem to be solved.[21]

In a stepwise manner, several questions in decision making must be asked:[22]

1. Is the clinical situation familiar to the arguer(s)?
2. Is there a single answer or multiple answers to the problem to be considered?
3. Are there any important points to be ruled out or ruled in without additional explorations, questions, and answers (admission or not, additional clinical and paraclinical workup, etc.)?
4. Can I make all this work within the framework of a complete disease history, pattern, and course?
5. Does the condition require specific care in a hospital or in outpatient setting?
6. Does the patient understand and accept the proposed plan for further care as an active participant and co-decision maker in the dialogue?

Communication as a tool for exchanging ideas is usually most meaningful if it helps solve a clinical problem. Even if the best outcome occurs in a single health professional's mind, sharing the argumentative process with others produces even better results.

5.2.7 Socratic Dissent—A Refined Form of Pimping: A "What Do You Think?" Medicine II

The Socratic method has been qualified as "polite pimping." However, it is more than that. In essence, *it is a* negative *method of hypotheses elimination, in that better hypotheses are found by steadily identifying and eliminating those which lead to contradictions.*[23] Ideally, it is a method that gives everyone the opportunity to contribute to the discussion, to hear what others have to say, to share and improve understanding, and to experience through multidirectional communication. It should not be missed in dialogues between health professionals.

The Socratic method has a distinctive five-part form:

1. A question is stated.
2. An answer is proposed to the question.
3. Objectives and objections to the answer are explored.
4. The answer is revised in light of the objections.
5. If it evades those objections, objections to the revised answer are explored until the answer stands up to all known objections.

The Socratic method of questioning proceeds from one question to another, starting with a first question to clarify the issue. Each subsequent question is built on the information provided by the resolution of the preceding question until the solution to the problem is reached. It is a process in which the original question is responded to as though it were an answer. This in turn forces the thinker to reformulate a new question in light of the progress of the discourse.[23]

Dialogue is in some way the opposite of pimping. For example, rather than asking for a list of reasons or causes of low or high random blood sugar, the Socrates-minded attending may ask others to think about the factors affecting glycemia. The first way tests students' recollection, and the second tests students' capacity to think.[24,25]

Questions, whether open or closed, test subjective preference based on actual observations and past experience in search of the best alternative as a solution. Teachers are nonjudgmental and make learners feel safe to express their own ideas. Pimpers are often the opposite. They are directional, judgmental, and forcing. Learners must find their own way to the solution as much as possible. Errors in learners' logic are searched for and identified, and a common agreement is reached on how incorrect reasoning should be corrected and how such corrections should be reflected in the solution of the problem. Teachers' questions identify errors in students' reasoning and beliefs and subsequent questions are formulated in such a way that they cannot be answered except by a better (correct) argumentative process. Such a Socratic method helps make the best use of what learners already know and leads them not only to the solutions of a clinical health problem and question, but also to the ways of acquiring additional data and information to solve the particular problem at hand and similar ones in the future.

Hence, successful dialogue ends when the answer stands up to all known objections. Do we not do this when discussing differential diagnoses or choosing treatment options?

In its nature, it means the following:

- Shared exploration and examination by all dialoguing parties
- Steering student thinking and responses in a direction that is usually known ahead of time by the teacher who works backward to clarify with students the process of reaching a solution
- Learning reasoning skills (including handling fallacies) by talking out loud
- Maintaining a variable degree of dependency on authority figures or experts in problem solving
- Guiding answering learners to a self-awareness of their deficits and a recognition and correction of their errors
- Engaging learners by effective questioning in order to hone critical thinking skills, diagnose learning needs, offer immediate "teaching pearls of wisdom," seek knowledge, and the ability to learn in a self-directed manner

In medicine, it should lead not only to the sharpening of thought processes[26,27] (Socrates' own main objective), but also to an imparting of knowledge.

The focus of questions varies.[26,27] It may be as follows:

- *Clarifications* (Why do you say that? How does it relate to our discussion?)
- *Assumptions* (How could you verify or disprove that assumption? What could we assume instead?)

- *Reasons and evidence* (What would be an example? What do you think causes that to happen and why?)
- *Viewpoints and perspectives* (What is the best (diagnostic method, treatment, care)? What would be the alternatives? What are the strengths and weaknesses of your preferences and alternatives?)
- *Implications and consequences* (What generalization can be made? What are the consequences? What does it affect? What are the links with what we have learned before?)
- *Questions about questions* (What does it all mean? Why do you think that you asked the question? Was it out of scientific curiosity and/or to improve practice? How does all this apply to our practice?)

From these categories arise Socratic questions in the evaluation of an argument,[27-30] such as the following:

- What do you mean by … (your observation, diagnosis, treatment decision, or prognosis)?
- How did you come to that conclusion?
- Why do you believe that you are right?
- What is the source of your information?
- What assumption has led you to that conclusion?
- What happens if you are wrong?
- Can you give me at least two sources that disagree with you and explain why?
- Why is this significant?
- How do I know you are telling me the truth (based on how your clinical workup of the case or problem)?
- What is the alternate explanation for this phenomenon (case, problem)?

Beyond routine clinical work, a good example of Socratic questioning and dialogue is Grahame–Smith's debate about evidence-based medicine.[31]

Benefits of the Socratic method in teaching and learning medicine are numerous: Honing critical thinking skills in the context of patient care and challenging the learner's preconceived notions of medicine by asking questions in a stepwise manner, diagnosing the learner's level and further needs, understanding, engaging, and encouraging the learner toward focused self-directed learning, teaching, and learning relevant essentials.[26]

All questions, points, and counterpoints in Socratic dialogue are (and must be) supported by the best for-the-purpose evidence. In Socratic dialogue and dissent, it is up to the person answering a question to provide as answers the conclusions of a modern argument and be ready to specify all necessary building blocks and their connection in his or her proposals and counterproposals. The answers then must be viewed as claims and conclusions of some argumentative process that preceded each of them. Structured argumentation must work in both directions: Answers to students' questions should be brought up on the basis of the argumentative process. Students' replies to teachers' questions are conclusions (proposals) also supported by a modern argument and its building blocks. Hence, in some way, the Socratic method integrates multiple reasoning paths, as outlined in Section 5.2.6.

The ultimate benefit of Socratic thinking (critical thinking, argumentation, best evidence grounded) is our understanding, the decisions that we make in clinical and community care, the benefits for the patient, and the avoidance of errors and harming the patient.

5.3 Instrumental Vehicles, Opportunities, and Environments for Professional Communication: Oral and Written Exchanges of Experience in Clinical Practice

By instrumental vehicles of communication as environments, opportunities, and tools for communication between peers, we mean the following:

■ Putting down on paper for us and others what we are doing in daily practice. Running *patient charts* from *admission notes*, patient and disease histories, and other narratives to clinical and paraclinical workup, *progress reports* ("SOAPs," i.e., *s*ubjective and *o*bjective states and findings, *a*ssessments and *p*lans), *referrals*, and *discharge summaries*.

■ Sharing on request our particular expertise for the best benefit of the patient and the best direction of our always incomplete and imperfect decision making about care in *specialty consultations* and *consults*.[32-34]

■ Gathering *inpatient and outpatient*[35] *morning reports*[36-39] to review the management of the cases and the performance of the attending crew (faculty, house officers, students) and eventually the care provided by associate health professionals. Examples of topics abound.[40] Their formats are case-based sessions and skills sessions of a resident/medical student morning report, senior resident morning reports, combined morning reports, and outpatient morning reports.[39] In addition to the physician providing care, physician-scientists[41] and librarians[42] are also involved, especially if the evidence-based medicine orientation with[43] or without[44,45] mobile or handheld electronic devices is considered and given to morning reports.

■ *Bedside* and corridor or "hallway"[46] more or less formal *teaching* (i.e., teaching once the door to the patient's room is closed) and *floor rounds*.[47]

■ Within the specialty and interspecialty *grand rounds*[48,49] to clarify selected challenging topics in and beyond everyday practice and care.

■ Occasional and regular and structured *morbidity and mortality reports* in clinical practice.

■ Any *communication of an administrative nature*, business meetings, on-the-spot problem solving, exchanges of ideas between interested parties and decision makers (personal and material resources discussions and solutions).

■ *Clinical guidelines, clinical protocols*, and other standard procedures of development, implementation, and evaluation.

■ *Emergencies, outbreak* investigations and control, *errors and mistakes* in daily routines requiring surveillance and corrective measures to prevent *harm*.

■ Consultation and other exchanges of ideas, data, or information by *electronic communication device uses* (e-mail, messaging, texting, teleconferencing, etc.).

■ *Scut work* environment: a place for communication and learning?

Any of those ways of communication reflect argumentative processes, in part or entirety. Let us remember them as we move from one section to another in this book as a fundamental mode of reasoning and decision making, prone to fallacies in communication. An illustrative review of the latter follows in Section 5.4.

As pertains to communication methods beyond unstructured chats, with the exception of patient charts, all communication may involve other tools including simple orders, elements of pimping and other humiliating and psychological assaults, teaching by Socratic discourse, and evidence-based modern argumentation. Preferences regarding the types of communication already outlined above are clear.

Let us take an example of teaching and learning in surgery. Figure 5.1 illustrates in a simplified manner (for the sake of explicitness) that desirable attitudes, knowledge, and skills are acquired in various clinical and paraclinical environments and settings. In each, an array of communication methods is used, namely simple orders, the venerated "show me, watch me, do it after me" technique, and other ways of reasoning and communication as presented above in this section. All teaching tools, environments, health professionals, and their patients are potential breeding grounds for fallacies.

Passive teaching tools and environments involve lectures, textbooks, articles, web information, and hearsay. *Active teaching tools* consist of a much broader group of events and environments: bedside teaching (including chart-based analyses), floor events (rounds, morning reports), impromptu intramural chats (elevators, hallways, cafeterias), operating rooms, emergency departments, imaging (x-ray) and laboratory advice and consulting, provided and received specialty consults, technology and management assistance problem solving, post-discharge support and care (social services, prosthetic care, readaptation), specialty gatherings (conventions, workshops), and interactive continuing education programs.

Regardless of the way each communication method contributes, from one setting to another, to the acquisition of desirable knowledge, attitudes, or skills, they merit further practice and evaluation. All methods, types, and aspects of communication and their settings must be fallacy-free to attain the fully desirable assets of teaching, training, and practice.

Understanding and evaluating communication is a multielement and multidimensional problem, as illustrated in Figure 5.1. It cannot be dealt with all at once, but should instead be fractioned into more manageable pieces, "cube by cube," as shown in this figure.

All these events and their formats imply questions, answers, feedback, and other elements of argumentation shared by all parties involved. All participants should discuss the questions of common interest in a fallacy-free

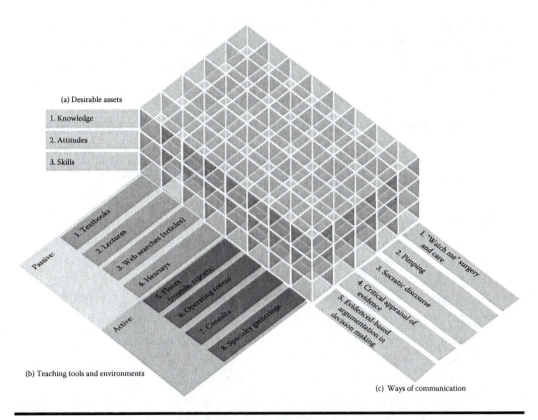

Figure 5.1 Matrix for understanding the evaluation of fallacy-free teaching, learning, and practice of surgery. (Based on Jenicek M. Evaluating Surgery. Uses of Clinical Case Reports and Case Series in Surgical Specialties. Draft document as reported at the *Balliol Colloquiums for Evaluating Surgery*, Jonathan Meakins, Chair. University of Oxford, Oxford, UK, September 6–8, 2007.)*

manner, in the same way as is required and expected for related scientific information in medical periodicals and other press. Such discussions cover not only the critical appraisal of bedside evidence and relevant external evidence but also connections between them and the reasoning toward better decision making.

---

* N.B. A clinical teacher who wants to evaluate freedom from fallacies by asking himself or herself *<if bedside and floors teaching based on Socratic discourse improves the knowledge and attitudes of students>* will base his or her evaluation on A1, A2, B4, and C4 teaching and learning elements. Evaluating *<how skills are developing through "watch me" surgery in operating rooms>* will involve elements A3, C2, and B5. Evaluating *<if surgeons acquire desirable knowledge based on literature from web searches focused on modern argumentation in decision making>* will consider elements A1, B2, C6, and so on. Fractioning the evaluation of teaching and learning in such a manner creates manageable pieces based on clear questions leading to a fallacy-free evaluation, understanding, and decision making process.

The teaching aspect is present in any communication of this kind, but its main purpose is to improve and offer a clearer guideline for understanding and what to do. This must be done between equals and made by equals in their understanding of the problem.

5.3.1 Patient Interviews: Admission and Opening Patients' Charts

Any communication with patients and between health professionals may be carried out in two ways:

1. In a *verbal, oral, or written manner* when we try to retrieve, convey, and retain information with its proper meaning and understanding to be shared reciprocally by all interested parties, patients, their physicians, and others. This is obviously the vital, ubiquitous, and most established approach.
2. *Nonverbal ways* of communication may be an important addition to verbal communication. They are not only complementary, but must also be considered where linguistic and cultural barriers exist. In some patients whose speech is impaired, sensorium and/or pathology, nonverbal communication may be the only way to establish communication and share the meaning of information to ensure proper care.

Let us comment briefly on both of them.

5.3.1.1 Verbal, Oral, and Written Communication

Any patient/doctor encounter is an exercise in communication coupled with physical examination, paraclinical (laboratory biochemistry and hematology), exploration of patient physiology and morphology by imaging techniques, and contextually expanded assessment (social, cultural, faith setting, and needs). The overall approach to such encounters[51–54] is well established, learned, and used at the beginning of the clinical experience and later on. From this larger framework, what is important for successful communication between the patient and his or her physician in order to provide the patient with the best possible care?

The comprehensive assessment of the adult patient includes the following: (1) identification of data and source of the history, (2) chief complaint(s), (3) present illness, (4) past history, (5) family history, (6) personal and social history and (review of systems).[55] Events are counted and must include their course in time wherever necessary and possible.

Once a patient–physician relationship is established (our references will tell the reader how and why), a mutual, common, and shared understanding about "what are we talking about" must be built. Different questions come into play:[51–55]

1. As a precondition, the physician must be ready to *define* in operational terms anytime and at any step of the encounter what he or she means when asking about pain and being comfortable, and when saying "this will hurt" or sharing with the patient the first impression of the patient's condition, and so on. This is easier for *hard data* (easy to measure, quantify, and categorize in the process of clinimetrics) such as bleeding or fever than for often challenging *soft data* such as pain or mood, values, and feelings, so important in psychiatry. Let us note that interviews in psychiatry,[53] if performed correctly, are also good examples of how soft data might be "hardened" for decision making purposes.

2. To optimize relationships, objectivity, and value assessments (for the patient, and for physician's diagnostic workup) of any information, encounters start most often with *open (open-ended) questions*: *What brought you here? What happened? How may I help you? How do you feel today?* Open questions reflect mostly deductive reasoning from which hypotheses are derived and formulated for further testing and uses. Open questions are hypotheses generators.

3. *Closed (closed-ended) questions* follow: *How does it feel when I touch your tummy this way? In this area? Does it hurt when I press? Does it change when I stop?* Closed questions initiate inductive reasoning and serve to confirm the hypotheses that are dependent on what we asked and saw. Closed questions are hypotheses testers.

4. *Directive (focused) questions* search for specific information like closed questions, but a more detailed one: *How does the pain in your tummy feel since it first appeared until now?*

5. *Double questions* simultaneously offer two options: *Do you have any pain in your tummy and do you have pain also in your chest?* Double questions asked rapidly seek potentially related information, but may be ambiguous and hard to understand by the patient. They are to be used with caution!

6. *Multiple choice questions* may be asked (without confusing the patient) to define the range of information sought: Do you have trouble concentrating, staying concentrated, concentrating on one problem or more, or with some other aspect of your mental functioning?

7. *"Yes or no"* questions are the most directional and restrictive form of closed questions. They may be needed in some instances for proper decision making.

8. *Leading questions* are meant to lead the patient to a particular conclusion. They are used sometimes in courts of law, but also in medical and psychiatric interviews: *You never used medication for your tummy pain, right? ... No? And you changed your dietary habits since having this problem? ... No? Or did you experience any other discomfort during this period? ... So, should we consider this a new problem?* More precise and more complete information usually cannot be obtained this way despite the somewhat Socratic character of such sequences of questions. They should be avoided.

9. At the end of the encounter, going *back to open question(s)* may bring additional valuable information for parallel and lateral thinking about other patient problems to be dealt with: *Is there anything else that we have forgotten? Is there anything else that bothers you? Is there some other way I can help you?*

Patient/physician dialogues should reveal the following:

■ *Information about independent variables* such as the causes of a disease or its cure *and dependent variables* in terms of disease occurrence and recovery. Any meaningful establishment of such cause–effect relationships and our reasoning about them depend on the interviews to obtain such information.

■ Once the phenomena of interest are identified, such as pain, bleeding, vomiting, or loose stools, a *dimension* must be given to them whenever it is important for diagnostic and/or therapeutic decision making and interventions. Frequency, amplitude, duration, localization, projection, episodes, and spells are of interest.[51-53,56] All phenomena of interest must be well defined and usable for categorization and classification if such categories are indicative of specific diagnostic approaches and distinct treatments and follow-up.

■ To give *meaning* to what we discover during the interview signifies making a diagnosis or giving direction in deciding what to do with the patient's complaints and the reason for the interview.

Any "impressions," our first working ideas about further exploration, diagnosis, and treatment, are already a set of claims or conclusions of some type of argumentative process:

1. *Grounds* are provided by the patient interview and completed by further clinical and paraclinical examinations and workups.
2. Such observations are supported or not by *backing* stemming from general and our personal past or present experience.
3. *Warrants* give a meaning based on the connection between grounds and their backing.
4. From this picture, we can see how certain we may be in our conclusions: such *qualifiers* as probabilistic expressions cannot always be satisfactorily quantified, given the biological nature of health problems with which we deal.
5. Ethical considerations, complications, adverse effects, multiple morbidities (comorbidities), and treatments both for the main problem and for the cotreatments of comorbidities may all underlie the *rebuttals* of our conclusions and recommendations.
6. Our diagnostic and therapeutic *conclusions* or *claims* resulting from the argumentative process represent either new hypotheses or their confirmation to which correct dialoguing with the patient must contribute.

Such argumentation relies heavily on our communication with the patient. This type of communication should also be a fallacy-free process. Some illustrations will follow in Section 5.4.

In any kind of communication with the patient, interviewing and communication relies on the a priori establishing of confidence and mutual understanding regarding how and why patient–physician interactions are created and what should be achieved by understanding and solving patient problem(s). Several ad hoc titles address very effectively this crucial element of clinical practice.[51–55,57,58]

Bickley and Szilagyi[51] recommend following these steps in the first physician/patient encounter:

■ From what you heard during the interview and saw at the physical examination, identify abnormal findings.
■ Localize these findings anatomically.
■ Assess the nature and quality of data (findings), their time–space relationship as webs of causes and webs of consequences.
■ Make hypotheses about the nature of the patient's problems.

- Test your hypotheses.
- Interpret the findings in terms of the probable process.
- Establish a working diagnosis.
- Generate the problem list.
- Develop a plan (concept maps may help).
- Make this plan agreeable and acceptable to the patient with all respect due to medical ethics.

This proposal of reasoning, assessment, and recording reflects a rather complex reasoning path consisting of a sequence of arguments covering a set of sequential steps in clinical work (risk assessment, diagnosis, treatment, prognosis, further expanded care) as already outlined in Chapter 3.

We often do not realize that each such step carries within it parts or the whole of an argumentative process and that our final words about each step represent statements, proposals, and conclusions of such argumentative processes. Both teachers and learners should be able to reconstruct and reproduce them on request if need be.

By the end of any patient interview, a review of mutual physician/patient understanding is worth considering: Did we talk about the same thing? Does all this mean the same for both of us? This is not always necessarily the case, even if contact with the patient was well established in mostly psychological terms of courtesy, comfort, and connection.[52]

5.3.1.2 Nonverbal Communication

The nonverbal process of communication refers to the sending and receiving of messages by ways other than speech: Visual messages, gestures, touch, body language, posture, facial expressions, eye contact, object uses (clothing, hairstyle, personal hygiene, etc.), "parlanguage" (voice quality, rate, pitch, volume, rhythm, intonation, stress).[59] Face-to-face interactions are the most frequent instances of nonverbal communication in clinical settings.

For example, even clothing may be part of a nonverbal message: White coats or scrubs or gowns convey and reinforce the professional meaning of what we do. Patient gowns convey the message of dependency, trust, or mistrust.

Physical space uses in communication (proxemics) may convey some meaning: Keeping a physical distance between communicating parties may reflect discomfort and may also affect the meaning of oral communication.

Time in communication (chronemics) means the organization and perception of time and reactions to it. The patient's time and that of the patient's caregiver may be precise, scheduled, arranged, and managed or not. Things may be done in a fluid or erratic way. Time may not mean only "money," but also "health."

Movement and body position (kinesics) are not only pathognomonic (characteristic or distinctive of disease and other condition) signs, but they also convey in a behavioral way a person's attitudes, values, or preferences. Posture and gestures are used, such as "thumbs up" if everything goes well or "thumbs down" if nothing works. A patient's "middle finger" may convey the patient's displeasure, lack of manners, intoxication, or mental state and disease.

Touching in communication (haptics) is more than an examination tool. Holding hands is a tool of sympathy and empathy; back slapping or "high fiving" are signs of comfort, relief, or success of care. Holding a child is an expression of affection and care. It is not simply a maneuver of care.

Eye gaze (oculesics) is not only of interest for ophthalmologists, neurologists, and psychiatrists as diagnostic tool and reflection of the progress of care. Interest, attention, involvement, mood, intimacy may be assessed by the length of gaze, glances, patterns of fixation, pupil dilatation, and blinks.

Cues of the voice (paralanguage, vocalics) such as tone, pitch, accent, and other voice qualities ("voice print") may affect the meaning of the words spoken by the patient and the health professional. An "uh-huh" or "hmm" may indicate that a person is listening, thinking about, and paying attention to another. Even health professional's comfort, competency, or decision certainty in specific situations may be reflected by cues of voice.

Artifacts like choices and preferences of clothing, jewelry, hairstyle and even art, or the patient's private and hospital space arrangements (furniture and other possessions, placement, visibility and accessibility of tools and instruments) may say a lot about the patient, the caregiver, and the health care environment.

The physical appearance of the patient and his or her caregiver is a nonverbal expression both for the physician (disheveled patients entering psychiatric care) and the patient (projection of professionalism, involvement, engagement, and devotion in providing health care by his or her physician or nurse).

The observation and evaluation of nonverbal communication are an important part of a psychiatric interview, the evaluation of the effectiveness of treatment and care.

Many clinical conditions and actions such as endocrinological disorders, obesity, premenstrual syndrome, stress and distress, surgical care, drugs prescribed and used, and others may affect patient's nonverbal communication and its interpretation by the patient's physician. It is also possible for the patient to misread a caregiver's nonverbal messages.

In the eighties, Waitzkin[60] drew our attention to the need for more structured training of health professionals in nonverbal communication with patients. Communication between health professionals themselves should not be forgotten either.

Since then, applications and methodology developments have evolved further. Not surprisingly, they often cover psychiatry, mental health, and diagnostic purposes.[61]

5.3.1.2.1 What Role Does Nonverbal Communication Play in Argumentation and Critical Thinking?

Practically speaking, nonverbal communication may play a role as part of an argument building block: A patient's sigh or pointing to where it hurts may be part of grounds in the diagnostic process. Grimacing may signal an adverse reaction to a drug or a rebuttal for further medical decision making. A V sign can be a conclusion or claim that treatment works. Thumbs down means the opposite.

However, nonverbal messages must be interpreted and used in a multicultural context and an increasing amount of literature is devoted to this topic. For example, an index—thumb O—sign does not always mean success or victory in activities, proposals, and consequently even patient care. In some countries, it can represent a body orifice where some suggestion of real or proposed activity belongs, if it is not appreciated by the messenger or receiver of this nonverbal expression.

More systematic, methodological development, uses, and evaluation of nonverbal and especially bilateral communication may be expected in the near future. For example, in the diagnostic domain, it may start by our better understanding of nonverbal messages and communication at any stage of the diagnostic process:

Global observation of a patient's nonverbal message(s) → isolation of the message of interest → description of the sign → its identification and dimension → its interpretation in terms of patient state → meaning, extrapolation, and categorization, hence diagnosis itself of which a nonverbal message is a part, either together with other messages and signs or sometimes as a single presentation.[62] We still do not know these well enough.

Let us remember again that nonverbal communication may be the only communication in patient–physician interaction where speech, senses, and sensorimotor activities are impaired or impossible whatever the underlying pathology might be. As such, we should know and use it better in the context of our communication and decision making in clinical settings.

5.3.2 Revisiting the Patient: Updating Opening Interview and Record through Bedside Communication and Progress Notes (SOAPs)

Bedside rounds, however limited they may be by other activities and time constraints in today's technology-oriented world, remain an essential opportunity for communication with patients and their other health providers.[63] Progress notes resulting from such encounters should reflect the physician's reasoning and delineate his or her assessment and plans for further patient care.[51] Only reviewing and recording additional information, data, and results from previous encounters is not sufficient.

Similar strategies apply to repeated encounters with patients in *ambulatory* or *family care*.

Progress notes usually follow some sort of SOAP format:

- **S**ubjective observations including all *symptoms* (subjective manifestations of ongoing disease and care) as conveyed to us by the patient. They should be informative enough to provide ideas regarding the location, directionality (radiation and expansion), quality, quantity and severity, timing, setting of the occurrence, remitting and exacerbating factors, alleviating factors and associate manifestations, and their evolving changes.
- **O**bjective observations and findings from our own clinical and paraclinical follow-up, new and repeated data, information, and findings. *Signs* are in focus.
- **A**ssessment encompassing our evaluation of changes in patient's clinical course based on the integration of both subjective and objective observations resulting in our updated view.
- **P**lan proposes what should be deleted, modified, or expanded from current care: medication, surgical care, restoration of functions, psychological and/or psychiatric care or social support, and home or ambulatory care. Any plan should follow the *patient perspective*:[51] His or her feelings (fears, concerns), ideas, and views of the nature and causes of his or her condition and evolution, impact on his or her life and functioning, his or her expectations based on past and present experience.

An increasing number of excellent guides, coordinated by Uzelac (Series Editor), are being published for various specialties such as obstetrics and gynecology, pediatrics, emergency medicine, family medicine, urology, dermatology, neurology, and internal medicine.[64] This series offers an introductory coverage for many of the most relevant and frequent reasons for patient visits to medical offices, outpatient clinics, emergency services, or admissions for more prolonged hospital care.

Thinking as arguers (practitioners of argumentation and critical thinking) in medicine, we find these elements in establishing our argumentative process: *conclusions* (plan), necessary *grounds* in subjective and objective information, and *backing, warrants* (understanding), and *qualifiers* in the assessment of the updated clinical situation. Our plan should mention *rebuttals* whenever they exist and specify our decisions and recommendations.

Bedside rounds and progress notes represent valuable opportunities not only to teach physical examination skills, but also to model skills in communication and professionalism.[64]

Bedside rounds are often expanded to hallway, elevator, or drinking fountain continuations of discussion by at least two physicians and other rounds attending health professionals, most often nurses. The same above-mentioned rules and comments apply.

5.3.3 Narratives and Clinical Case Reports

Accepting a new patient in family medicine or admitting a new patient in hospital care starts by patients telling us what happened, their stories in context, concerns, and expectations. We build the patients' own clinical case, charts, and records on the basis of such a guideline.

5.3.3.1 Clinical Consultations as Narratives

Telling stories is part of everyone's daily life. It is also the case in everyday medical practice: During the first encounters between physicians and their patients, when updating patient charts during subsequent visits and consultations, when a patient moves from one specialist or medical service to another, and so on, the patients tell us about themselves, we tell them about ourselves, within or outside the context of the case, to establish mutual confidence and meaningful communication, retention and use of health information. Such narratives are defined as *an orderly, continuous account of an event or series of* events.[4] In medicine, without narratives, there would be no meaningful communication between the patients and their physicians. Narratives most often precede clinical case reports (CCRs) and may be an initial part of them. For some, narratives, even less than case reports, "explain nothing" with regard to cause–effect relationships. However, that is where etiological research, clinical trials, and even simple descriptions of clinical events and their reporters find their ideas and directions for next steps. They must not be forgotten in today's technological world of medicine, but rather further structured, developed, understood, and used as they have already been in general and family medicine,[65–67] applied to surgery,[68] connected to ethics,[69,70] clinical case reporting,[71,72] and evidence-based medicine.[73–75]

The narrative serves to build a *relationship*, to *collect data and information*, and to reach a *mutual agreement on a management plan*.

In terms of general characteristics, narratives include the following:

- Cover a well-defined time period as a time frame for the event of interest.
- Include both the narrator and the listener viewpoints in the story; hence, bilateral communication is essential. Usually, the patient is the storyteller and the physician is the story interpreter and facilitator of mutual understanding.
- Concern not only individuals, but also the settings and circumstances that are relevant for their clinical care.
- Help doctors understand what patients really experience for the purpose of clinically caring for them.
- Are the starting point for research, as are CCRs. Hypotheses are generated and better defined. The design of research studies may be refined by such experience.

These are some of the reasons why a doctor "who listens" is so appreciated.

Taking a patient's history and giving advice in clinical consultation is an exchange of narratives. Patients tell us what is going on, we try to explain to them why we want to do what we want to do, and make them understand why they should comply with our recommendations. It is a two-way exchange of different narratives of different genres. In pediatrics, it even involves three partners: the child, the parent, and the health services professional.

Running, analyzing, and using narrative requires *narrative competence*, which essentially is communication competence. For Charon,[76] it is *the set of skills required to reorganize, absorb, interpret, and be moved by the stories one hears or reads*. *Textual skills* include identifying, adopting, and recognizing a story's structure, its multiple perspectives, metaphors, and allusions. *Creative skills* mean being able to make multiple interpretations, build curiosity, and consider multiple endings. *Affective skills* encompass acceptance of uncertainty throughout the story and entering the story's mood.

Narratives provide meaning, context, and perspective for information in medicine as well as an understanding of health problems that cannot be obtained by other means. They are an important teaching and learning experience such as through role playing that cannot be reproduced otherwise.[77]

If we define evidence in evidence-based medicine as any information or data necessary for understanding and making decisions about a health problem,[62] we may consider narratives and narrative-based medicine[78] as a part of and one of the tools to palliate some perceived shortcomings of the evidence-based medicine[79] and to complete it in an integrated manner.[71]

Montgomery[80] reminds us that when physicians who conduct research perform their clinical duties, they are no longer scientists, but clinicians, that is, physicians who take care of patients.

Narrative sequential presentations unfold the tactful, tactical development of knowledge and experience relevant to determining what is wrong with particular patients and deciding what action to take on their behalf. Case narratives supply a workable medium for representing knowledge that is time- and context-dependent. Once the diagnosis is made, physicians may say: "The patient's story is consistent with a myocardial infarction." Narrative, thus, is essential to thinking and knowing in clinical medicine.[81] We can consider it another example of pattern recognition.

5.3.3.2 Clinical Vignettes and Clinical Case Reports

Single clinical case reporting (CCR) and case series reports or presentations (CSRs) are perhaps the most frequent tools to communicate and share clinical experience. Cases are reported and briefly discussed at any time during the changing of teams on call, such as morning reports, when transferring patients to other services, consulting colleagues, or discharging patients home or to long-term care facilities. They must be meaningful for the purpose of interest and mutually understood.

As perhaps the oldest form of clinical communication, clinical cases are reported today for two major reasons:

1. Mainly as a *teaching* tool. Clinical vignettes serve this main purpose.
2. Mainly as a *research and knowledge* expansion tool. Single CCRs and case series reports (CSRs) are oriented this way today.

These terms are often used interchangeably across the literature; they should not be.

5.3.3.2.1 Clinical Vignettes

A clinical vignette is a concise presentation of an interesting or challenging patient encounter.[82] Clinical vignettes are descriptions of a clinical experience, usually with one clinical case, in a simple "title and author information, introduction (preferably with learning objectives), case presentation, literature review (sometimes), discussion, and summary."[83,84] At its core is a presentation of chief complaint, history, physical examination, laboratory and radiographic studies, assessment, and plan. A series of questions asked of trainees and their answers covering the core elements of the vignette are used as a tool to measure and enrich the trainees' knowledge and clinical reasoning. Presentation and its discussion are shaped to highlight either the natural history of a given health problem, a therapeutic relationship between clinician and patient, or patient management to improve knowledge and clinical skills.[82] A cornucopia of clinical vignettes examples was recently assembled by the Society for General Internal Medicine.[85]

In a written form, clinical vignettes and case reports are not essays. *Essays* are most often literary compositions usually covering a particular theme or subject from a limited or personal point of view. Clinical vignettes or case reports are more than that. Clinical vignettes and case reports are purposeful and structured presentations of a health problem with defined purposes and questions asked, answered, resolved, or guided to resolution.

A CCR is a structured presentation of a clinical experience with a single patient according to predetermined objectives and purposes for fact finding rather than education. It is used to exchange information about observed facts taking into account the improvement of practice in habitual clinical settings and tracing of possible directions in research of a health problem of which the patient is representative and other directions for further management of the problem and care.

CSRs are more than one case observations, descriptions, analyses, and explanation for better understanding and decision making about the medical and/or surgical management of the health problem and care represented by case series.

Objectives of CSRs include providing "numerators" of rates for clinical epidemiological research, prevailing characteristics of patients, sites, management or care, outcomes, constancy and consistency of findings, basis for a "meta-analysis of cases" whatever their limitations might be in these matters.

In research, single cases or case series as simple frequencies without denominators and control groups are considered by many as poor or low levels of evidence. This may be so in studies of cause–effect relationships and in other types of studies, especially of a descriptive nature. In hypotheses generation, they are important starting points and powerful idea providers. To fulfill this purpose, we consider the following:

- Reasons, objectives, and hypotheses must be stated in advance.
- All variables of interest must be well defined or provided on request to parties in communication.
- The structure of the case report must be clear.
- Conclusions must be explicated and discussed.

5.3.3.2.2 Reasons for Clinical Case Reporting and Discussing

Reasons to publish a CCR or case series study apply to medicine in its entirety, although some are of particular interest for surgery. Some of these reasons are as follows:[86]

For clinical cases, in general:

1. Obtaining leads as index manifestations to establish diagnostic criteria for a "new" disease
2. Unusual presentation of unknown etiology
3. Unusual natural history
4. Unusual natural or clinical course
5. Challenging differential diagnosis
6. Clinical failures, errors, and harm related to diagnosis and treatment
7. Unusual and/or unexpected effects of treatment (outcomes) or diagnostic results, whether good or bad
8. Diagnostic and therapeutic "accidents" (causes, consequences, remedies)
9. Unusual comorbidity (diagnosis, treatment, outcome)
10. Unusual setting of medical care (e.g., emergency or field conditions)
11. Patient compliance
12. Patient/doctor interaction (not only in psychiatry!)
13. Single case clinical trial ("*n*-of-1" study)
14. Clinical situations as valuable experience from an uncontrolled setting that cannot be reproduced for ethical reasons
15. Limited access to cases (economy, ethics, social reasons, patient choices)
16. Index case(s) of a potential or real outbreak (more cases expected to come)

17. Confirmation of something already known (only if useful for a systematic case report review and synthesis)
18. Solving a challenging problem in medical ethics
19. Economical aspects of the management of the case
20. Evaluation of the potential burden of the case (family, health services, work environment, social services, economy)
21. Detailed intimate information provided by qualitative research about the case (narratives)
22. Any set of cases allowing health administrators to assess and define needs and supplies in human, material, and organizational resources in order to respond adequately to individual and community needs
23. Operational research findings
24. Capture of rare cases

More specifically for surgical specialties:

1. New medical/surgical technology (use, outcomes, consequences)
2. Transfer of medical technology (from one disease, organ, or system to another)
3. Emergency, often heuristic management of a case with or without necessary evidence, data, and information
4. Technical challenges in the surgical management of the case
5. Operational research findings and considerations in this and other cases
6. Complications of surgery (adverse effects, rejections, other failures, intolerance of procedures)
7. Faith, cultural, and social considerations implicated in the case management and decisions
8. Legal aspects of the case management and its outcomes
9. Demonstrated or newer dexterities, ergonomics, ease, or technical and technological requirements for the surgery and management of the case
10. Generation and proposal of a hypothesis about biological and other mechanisms of the health problem relevant to surgery (often by way of qualitative research methodology; vide infra)
11. Presentation of "Black Swan" evidence (all swans are white, this unique black swan [a disease, its causes, and interventions] proves otherwise)
12. Tolerance of a procedure by the patient (equiv. Phase I clinical trial)
13. Ancillary interventions and care; that is, cotreatments for this and other health problems (comorbidity)

14. Medical and/or surgical error and its connection to potential and real harm
15. Medical/surgical harm and inquiries about its potential and real causes
16. Operational findings (again)
17. Medical humor (Use it sparingly and with care!)

Failures to communicate reasons for single clinical case or CSRs contribute to their misunderstanding and related actions underlying potential errors and eventual harm.

5.3.3.2.3 Content and Architecture of a CCR Presented in the Literature

In essence, any CCR is an exercise in argumentation and communication. Communicating a case report in a medical journal requires a structured presentation, usually in sections such as "Summary, Introduction to the case, Presentation of the case, Discussion of the case experience, and Conclusion" that may be drawn from such an experience. Elements of content of each CCR section may be summarized as follows[70] (N.B. Let us immediately recognize that any oral or written version of a CCR is limited in time and page space. A reporter, however, must have the following elements [which should also be part of the case research protocol] at hand and be ready to share them on request with any interested party):

1. In the Summary, four information elements usually appear:
   – *Motives* and reasons for the report "Why are we reporting this?"
   – *Background* to the problem "In what context?"
   – *Highlights* of the report "What have we found?"
   – *Conclusions* "What does this mean?"
   From the point of view of argumentation, claims (conclusions) of the argument about the case appear here together with the other most important building blocks.
2. In the Introduction, we should find the following:
   – The definition of the *topic* (problem, disease, clinical activity)
   – The general *context* of the topic (relevant knowledge, present clinical situation, and challenges)
   – A *question* that this report should answer, a gap in knowledge this report can fill
   – *Objectives* and justification of this report

– What is to be *evaluated*: Soundness, structure, process, impact, constancy, consistency?

3. The presentation of the case reflects the following:
   – *Situation, context,* and *triggering factor* of the report
   – Clinical and paraclinical *initial state* of the patient
   – *Evolution* of the clinical and paraclinical spectrum and gradient of the case
   – Diagnostic and therapeutic *acts*, care, and support
   – Expected and actual *results* of actions carried out or omitted
   – Unexpected results and events

   In terms of modern argumentation, grounds are presented in this section.

4. Discussion and Conclusion sections cover the following:
   – The *discussion of observations* and results preferably through modern argumentation
   – The *contribution* of the report to the fundamental knowledge of the problem represented by the reported case
   – The *proposals and recommendations* for practice (clinical decisions) and for research (new hypotheses generated by the case).

   The exercise of modern argumentation is found in this section, especially the warrant, qualifier, rebuttals, and the acceptance or refutation of the claim.

5. References are often a weak section of case reports. Only the most important are usually included, but they should clearly cover different elements:
   – The health *problem* and disease under study
   – The most important *past experience* for comparisons
   – Clinical and paraclinical *actions*
   – *Decisions* made and under consideration
   – *Methodology* and *techniques* specific to all the above

Even oral presentations of clinical cases should encompass, in a less structured and complete manner, the most relevant elements of written clinical case reporting.

Despite the limited role of CCRs and CSRs in causal proofs, when they are correctly done and interpreted in a nonexaggerated way, they are an important part of the methods and techniques used in clinical and field epidemiology.[87]

5.3.4 *Morning Reports*

Morning reports are summaries of events that occurred on the hospital floor, service, or department that the individuals and teams in charge communicate at the end of their shift to the individuals and teams who take over. They may be regular, formal and institutionalized, or informal as dictated by the reality of the practice.

Participants may be members of the house staff, residents, interns, attending physicians, nurses, and others.[88]

Newly admitted cases, progress in patients under current care, functioning of services, unusual events worthy of attention and care may be discussed. Led in informal language, they follow more formal information, as illustrated by Table 5.1 in this chapter (Section 5.2.6).

Cases are ideally discussed in the Socratic manner, as summarized in Section 5.1.6. Focused questions on problem formulation, diagnosis, and management of patients admitted through the emergency room and patients seen in the inpatient consultation services or in ambulatory clinics are addressed to the staff[89] and their understanding is reached through a mutual exchange of proposals and statements (premises) through the modern argumentation process.

In this context, morning reports go well beyond the ritual and are an important teaching tool during clinical training.[90,91] Amin et al.[92] offer a valuable review and explanation of the desired state of morning reports.

5.3.5 *Morbidity and Mortality Reports and Rounds*

Morbidity and mortality conferences and meetings represent a forum for faculty and trainees to explore the management details of particular cases.[93] When they are correctly executed, they contribute to patient care, medical knowledge, practice-based learning and improvement, interpersonal communication skills, professionalism, and problem-based learning and improvement.[90,93] The primary goal is to revisit errors without blame for their better understanding and prevention. Personal failures are not necessarily in focus.

Morbidity and mortality rounds are held less often, but still regularly throughout the year, and they may be offered to all health professionals. Such meetings are based on the analysis of a single case or of several cases by the Socratic method and argumentation. Multidirectional communication focused on equality and reciprocity of views exchange remains essential for their success.

Whether *Grand Rounds, Noon Rounds,* or *Academic Half Days* are applied to medicine, surgery, and psychiatry, these areas benefit from the morbidity and mortality review experience.[94,95]

Even if a live discussion with the patient and discussion with participants are part of rounds, communication between presenters and listeners is mainly a one-way experience. Participating physicians needs assessment, multifaceted intervention (rounds' ways of coverage of problems) strategies, logical order in presentations (sequencing), interaction, and commitment to change are not always easily fulfilled.[96]

5.3.6 *Journal Clubs*

Journal clubs are periodic, most often monthly sessions open to both learners (clinical clerks, interns, residents) and elders (staff). Topics and problems are presented by more senior learners followed by discussion. The basis for discussion may be the following:

- One or more original journal articles covering the topic of interest
- An issue of a reputed journal covering one or more important topics of the day
- A systematic review of the available relevant evidence of the problem of interest
- An unsystematic review of a clinical topic of interest

A journal club is summarized by an elder specialist in the domain and related fields.

Compared to rounds, a journal club offers more space for communication and exchange of ideas and a more active role for the learner. Students and juniors have an opportunity here to improve their professional communication.

At the core of presentations may be the following:

- A critical appraisal EBM style of original evidence (journal articles single studies) as partly outlined in Chapter 1 (Section 1.5).
- **Critical appraisal** as currently understood is the fundamental way to assess the internal validity, adherence to reporting standards, conclusions, and generalizability of a health problem presented in a medical article. Internal validity (how structured and interpreted the document is) is more in focus than contributions to the solution or advancement

of the health problem covered. Structured checklists concerning what to answer and not to miss are now available for physicians and other health professionals. The University of Oxford Centre for Evidence-Based Medicine offers online various appraisal sheets[97] as does the Ontario Public Health Libraries Association.[98]

- An analysis of the problem in an argumentative manner (see Section 2.1 in Chapter 2), that is, how the evaluated evidence is subsequently used in medical decision making.
- Presenting all the above in a Socratic manner where all important advanced statements are supported by the best evidence imbedded in a modern argument.
- Systematic review and/or meta-analysis of a chosen topic.
- Implementing other structural and organizational characteristics,[99] such as regular and anticipated events, mandatory attendance, defined clear short- and long-term purpose and objectives, leaders trained in paper selection and their discussion in journal club circulating papers among others.

All those ways should enable successful and formative presentations of journal club topics. The *interactive character* of journal clubs is essential and makes them distinct from many rounds.

Critical appraisal of medical evidence is also supported by a monthly feature of the American College of Physicians (ACP) and its Annals of Internal Medicine's *ACP Journal Club*[100] and *ACP Journal Club PLUS*,[101] which systematically review selected biomedical original studies and their systematic reviews.

Current evaluation still shows that journal club objectives are not always reached in terms of the learners participation, attitude and perception changes, knowledge and skills, behavioral changes, changes in organizational practice, and last but not least in more benefits to patients and other clients health and well-being.[102] Such a better and more complete evaluation only enhances the role of journal clubs in the acquisition of clinical experience.

5.3.7 Other Types of Rounds

Types of rounds may vary from one medical environment and culture to another. In the North-American context, communication opportunities may also include the following:

- Small groups and "academic half days"[103] (may be interdisciplinary)
- Journal clubs[103] (less focused discussion of selected journal issues or other updating information media)
- Grand rounds and clinical conferences[103] (periodical formal continuing education gatherings for updated topics often triggered by recent clinical experience at the institution)
- Lectures[103] (more formal presentations involving preclinical students and clinicians of all levels of training and experience)
- Workshops (more in depth, usually methodologically oriented coverage of selected topics implying guided multilateral communication and exchanges)
- "Post-take" or admission rounds[104] following on call periods
- Morning reports[104] (overnight experience exchanges)
- Daily work/working rounds[103] (daily for trainees)
- Review rounds[104] (by trainees and consultants held at the bedside)
- Social issues rounds[104] (interdisciplinary, administrative and social work reviews of patients' status, discharge plans, referrals, and post-hospital follow-up)
- Preceptor rounds[104] (teacher and learners developing and improving clinical examination and presentation skills)
- "Down time" or "dead space" uses[104] (already mentioned elevator, drinking fountain, and coffee sipping stand ups)

Some of these events may be regular, with fixed dates; others are organized and presented to try to answer the current events and needs of the moment. All of them, however, are subject to the same general rules of evidence management, argumentation, and communication, as outlined earlier.

5.3.8 Mostly One-Way Communication Vehicles: Consults, Referrals, Discharge Notes, and Summaries

A medical consult refers to the provision of expert opinion and recommendations by a senior specialist on request. (N.B. In the British Commonwealth and the Republic of Ireland, the title of consultant in medicine mainly recognizes the expertise of its holder. A consultant does not necessarily provide consults.)

A medical referral is the transfer of a patient from one physician's care to another.

A discharge summary or discharge note is a summary of a patient's clinical course over the period of time of defined clinical and other institutional care provided by a physician or other health professional. It serves to reiterate the chief patient complaint along with the final diagnosis, past and at discharge radical and conservative treatment and care provided. Finally, it includes recommendations for further treatment, care, and follow-up. Many of these elements may not be communicated in current discharge reporting.[105]

Further communication between providers of information and its recipients is not expected in most cases. However, it must be established on request. To be satisfactory, authors of consults must be ready to communicate and exchange explanations and additional ideas with the necessary best evidence at hand. They must also use it in an argumentative manner. All parties involved in the clinical dialogue must ensure that such vehicles are fallacy-free.

Developing clinical guidelines,[106,107] however, is the product of evidence-based argumentation arrived at by multilateral communication, understanding, and action guidance acceptable to all interested parties. *Following clinical guidelines* is mainly a one-way and passive communication.

5.3.9 Scut Work

Scut work is a necessary everyday activity for all healthcare providers in hospitals. It includes monitoring and maintaining patient vital functions and the related apparatus, intravenous canulation, wound care, drawing body fluids and tissues for laboratory analyses, establishing and maintaining updated written and electronic records about patient care and functioning, communicating with patient's relatives and other nonprofessional parties.

Scut work, which is often disliked both by freshmen and oldest elders, is also an opportunity to acquire many automated skills even if it does not offer a great deal of bidirectional communication. In fact, in scut work, unidirectional communication prevails. At the scut opportunity, communication with patients, their friends and families, and other health professionals in the hospital must be established (even in the most routine daily activities), achieved, and maintained according to the general rules of reasoning and communication outlined in this chapter. It may, but should not, be hampered by a ubiquitous clinical activity overload of all the parties involved.

"Scut" or "scut work" (scutwork) refers to the repetitive, minimally educational chores that are a major part of most residents' (and other juniors at the hospital) duties. They are frequently considered educationally irrelevant. However, even scut should provide the trainee with a learning experience and be educationally sound if a faculty mentor anticipates the trainees' activity, discusses clinical issues with the residents, and creates an educational opportunity from the task, conditions permitting.[108]

5.3.10 Formal (Magisterial) Lectures

Time-honored formal lectures, where a selected topic is presented by an experienced lecturer to specific groups of learners (medical students, residents, specialties, researchers) or interdisciplinary gatherings (all health professionals in the hospital, city or region, key note addresses at medical, nursing and other conventions), are not always appreciated if they are unstructured, not based on more bilateral communication (discussions), and relying solely on literature and other past experience reported secondhand.

How can lectures be made livelier, more motivating, and more grounded in reality for students?

An "action movie"-type experience can be adopted and adapted in the following manner:

- Topics can be introduced by a short dialogue with a live invited and consenting patient. Psychiatrists know all too well that such firsthand experience is often invaluable.
- If not, a "clinical scenario" can be presented as a second-hand experience and actualization (what happened to and with the patient).
- A "resolution of the clinical scenario" at the end of the lecture strengthens the usefulness and relevance of the lecture's fundamental message.
- Discussing any topic may be relegated to the end of the lecture or an experienced lecturer may insert pinpoint exchanges of views with learners at any moment of a formal presentation of the topic.

How can a lecture (or seminar) be structured to facilitate learner's understanding?

A lecture and its message structure should preferably be known to learners even before the lecture. Such lecture "programs" should include the following:

- Title (topic) of the lecture.
- Name of the lecturer or all other invited lecturers if more than one.
- Objectives in terms of knowledge, attitudes, and skills to be acquired.
- Contents: A short list of subtopics.
- Teaching methods to be used (see above): Oral presentations, discussion, illustrative medical article presentation and analysis, ad hoc exercises and problem solutions, invited debaters, other selected readings.
- Technical tools: electronic acoustic and visual media (perhaps interactive devices in the future).
- Key references.
- Additional readings.
- Optional: Evaluation to see if objectives were attained. Especially at the undergraduate level, learners always think, at least implicitly, of the kinds of questions waiting for them at various examinations (crediting the lecture, course or professional competencies, licensure) and that they will be expected to know the answers to them later on.

No, lectures do not need to be boring, as long as they remain as interactive as possible for the benefit of both teachers and learners. This way, even a lecture can enable shared and multilateral communication.

5.3.11 Medical Articles and Other Scientific Papers

In a medical article, an important writer–reader communication tool, we do more than present the results of original research, such as how a disease spreads in the community, what causes it, how to diagnose it, how to prevent and treat it, or what to do in this new perspective in the future. We communicate our findings and discuss them with readers. As readers, we judge their relevance and decide if we will put into practice what research shows.

We critically appraise them (see Chapter 1); that is, we evaluate if a medical article "makes sense" from a scientific standpoint and if it is in a larger sense a result of the application of the scientific method. We also must read and understand such scientific communication as an argumentative process leading to some conclusions, claims, and recommendations for practice and further research. A medical article must be "logical" in this latter sense.

> Most medical research articles are or should be seen and understood as one giant logical argument and exercise in critical thinking. They must be equally sound not only in clinical, epidemiological, and biostatistical terms, but also as an argument, and critically assessed.

A medical article reporting original research has a fairly standard form accepted by major medical journals as recommended by the International Committee of Medical Journals Editors and detailed as Uniform Requirements for Manuscripts Submitted to *Biomedical Journals*.[109] This is known as a SIMRAD (**S**ummary, **I**ntroduction, **M**aterial and methods, **R**esults, **a**nd **D**iscussion) format:

- A *Summary* reflects the sections of the article to come in an increasingly structured manner, summarizing (as do the *Annals of Internal Medicine*) "Objective, design, setting, participants, interventions, main results, conclusions."
- An *Introduction* defines the problem and often offers a related review of the literature (past experience).
- A *Material and Methods* section presents a technical framework of "how it was done."
- A *Results* section is a factual presentation of findings of the study.
- A *Discussion* section debates possible and real strengths and weaknesses of the study, missing information, and possible other completions and corrective measures.
- A *Conclusion(s)*, often coupled with Discussion, highlights the most important findings for the understanding of the problem and further decision making for research and practice.

In the above-mentioned article sections, we find more or less complete elements of modern argumentation somewhat hidden in the natural language of the article. We may find them, however, by reconstructing arguments from the natural language of written or spoken medical communication. *What did the author really want to say? Does all this communicated information support my decision to use it?*

The subsequent understanding of a medical article depends not only on how well it is executed and presented as an occurrence or etiological study or clinical trial, but first and foremost on how the problem is defined in terms of the following:[110]

- The topic, that is, the health problem that we try to solve, at least in part, through the intended research. Defining the topic also means "defining **definitions**" in the best operational terms of all entities and variables of interest.
- The research **objectives** as points we want to reach in a study. They can be either specific (to be reached by the study itself) or general (those of the broader set of activities into which the study falls).
- The research **hypothesis** as a proposition to be evaluated, accepted, or rejected by the research study and its results.
- The **research question** as an expression of doubt and uncertainty about the nature and solution of a health problem in their specific context (population, setting of care, community) to be discussed, solved, and answered by an intended inquiry.

These four points represent the essence of what is communicated. Without such clear formulations, the recipient of the message cannot understand what is covered in an article. The argument analysis depends on it.

An article written in natural language reflecting an argument format (problem in context, grounds, backing and warrant, support and rebuttals, qualifier, claim) shows the following:

Natural Language	Argument Building Block	Its Location
• As a subject of this study … We found that ….	Claim, Conclusions	Title, Conclusions
• Our original idea is (was) …	Problem in context	Introduction
• Here's what we have seen: …	Our own findings as grounds	Results
• How solid are our findings from our perspective …	Qualifier	Discussion
• What can we offer as an explanation for all this …	Warrant	Review of literature (Introduction), Discussion

• *How does it all look in light of past and present experience or some warrant (if available) ...*		Discussion, Conclusions
• *What is the balance between the supporting and negating elements in this argument ...*	Adducts (findings for), Rebuttals, adducts	Discussion
• *Once all this is brought together, what strength can we attribute to our findings ...*	Qualifier (as some kind of quantification of our conviction about the Claim)	Discussion, Conclusions
• *Yes, this is what we propose and may conclude ...*	Claim	Conclusions (as they also may appear in the Title)

In summary, the problem and backing may be found in the short review of the literature in the "Introduction" section of the article, the problem and possible rebuttals are in the "Methods" section, and the grounds are in the "Results" section. The claim appears and then the backing and rebuttals reappear in the "Discussion" ("Comment") section.

We already presented elsewhere[111] a detailed and concrete example of the application of this type of analysis of a medical article. Please expand your reading and understanding by consulting those sources.

So as logicians of medicine, how should we look at a medical article?

■ Does the message derive from simple intuition as noninferential knowledge or is it also a structured argument?

■ Is the message (description, observational analytical study, experimental study, or trial) acceptable from a clinical epidemiological and/or field epidemiology standpoint?

■ If it is acceptable from a clinical epidemiological or field epidemiology standpoint, examine the title to see if it leads to what will follow as (a) logical argument(s) to support it.

■ If it is not, is similar information made explicit in the introduction of the medical article? If not, is it possible to rebuild it from the available information that may eventually be spread across different sections of the article?

■ Try to understand if the discussion of results focuses on the same problem as stated in the introduction. The discussion itself should reflect the process of an argument and its resolution; that is, its path from the initial proposition to backing, warrant, grounds, support, rebuttals, qualifier, and ensuing claim (conclusion).

■ If this is not clear, reconstruct all relevant statements and arguments to obtain a message whose cogency would be more suitable for understanding, assessment, and interpretation from a logical standpoint.

■ Decide if the arguments are cogent, with justified premises, complete information, warranted inferences, and absence of rebuttals to the warrants.

■ Conclude if the whole message makes sense not only from a clinical, epidemiological, biostatistical, biological, and medical (decision making) standpoint, but also from the point of view of logic and critical thinking.

■ Attempt yourself to better explain and understand what the authors did not state clearly enough. You may hesitate between improving the "authors' homework" (in this case, you should have enough information and missing or incomplete building blocks of the argument at hand) or concluding that you do not have enough elements to put yourself in the authors' position and to improve the message in this sense.

■ Accept (with or without explicit and clear reserve), adopt, or reject the message of the paper.

As for medical articles as papers on original research or reviews, they present not only the state of science but also the state of art in logic and critical thinking. They must reflect the former as much as the latter.

Horton proposes to adopt Toulmin's model in medical articles,[112] and Gleischner suggests to use general journal articles as a base for learning critical thinking[113] and for improving further critical thinking in medicine and elsewhere. They are right. Beyond introductory pages, Huth's monograph on writing and publishing in medicine[114] is not only for authors. It is for you, the readers as well. Specifically for readers, Greenhalgh[115] puts the reading of medical papers in the context of evidence-based medicine.

To spread and share information by effective communication, medical experience remains not only a challenge, but also a subject of development, implementation, and evaluation of the new and still crystallizing domain of knowledge translation in medicine.

5.3.12 *Other Forms of Communication*

Other forms of communication that are not reviewed here and that are specific to a certain language, general and local medical culture, tradition, experience, and faith may be missed by some readers. Therefore, readers are encouraged to complete this section on the basis of their expectations, needs, and irreplaceable experience.

5.4 Illustrative Fallacies in Communication

Fallacies in communication may result not only from erroneous reasoning and decision making, but more than often, they are deliberate manipulations of messages and the ways they are conveyed.

The number of lists of fallacies increases over time, as applied to medicine[115] and other domains too.[117–122] Only some of them may and should be quoted here.

A valuable exchange of ideas with patients and nonhealth professionals and reaching a clear mutual understanding of health problems and related care are perhaps the most challenging aspects of communication. Knowledge, attitudes, values, and preferences vary from one patient to another, from one group of community stakeholders and decision makers to another. Health professionals communicating among themselves are more or less "on the same wavelength" (or they should be), but this is rather exceptional when dealing with patients and the community at large regarding health problems.

Communication in medicine may be hampered by several elements:

We have defined *fallacies in communication* as errors in reasoning and/or decision making by a health professional or produced through a health professional's communication with another health-interested party or in the interaction with another party in the understanding and/or solving of a health problem.[116] Perhaps less often, fallacies as poor reasoning are responsible for communication failures.

In communication, it is possible for flawless reasoning to be incorrectly used as *rhetorical ploys*, that is, often nonargumentative deficiencies in reasoning, intentionally misdirecting premises, proposals or claims to reach their proponent's goals as the art of mental trickery, and manipulation to a variable degree.

Let us then make a distinction between a fallacy as an error in reasoning by ignorance (conscious or not, often an unlearned error on the path from premises to conclusions of an argument) as opposed to conscious manipulations of an argumentation's components and path, such as non-argumentative or extralogical elements, language and not-explicated or implicit objectives of lateral thinking in the mind of the proponent of communication.

Whether "true" fallacies or rhetorical ploys are behind our interactions, they both fall under the common notion of *communication errors*. Here is a partial list of some illustrative examples. (Their full array can be found in the literature.)

In our practice, we encounter two kinds of patients:

1. Some expect that the physician will solve their problem for them and thus place themselves more or less blindly in the physician's professional hands, without questioning the physician's rationale. ("I am paying you to solve my problem. So, do it!")
2. Others with curious minds exchange views and ideas in an argument with their physician, trying in a participatory way to contribute to the solution of their health problem. These patients, argument-able laymen can, because of their intellectual abilities, experience, and judgment broader than the medical field, assist the physician by asking proper questions and providing other information to direct even better clinical decisions in their case.

Beyond the patient world and clinical environment, almost everyone in the community is concerned about health issues since they are not automatically well understood and correct solutions are not always applied to resolve them: Governments and civic administrations, other planners and providers of material (funding) and human resources (agencies, schools, higher academic institutions), lawyers and courts of law, security forces (police and army), electronic, print, radio, and television media, clergy and institutions of faith. The domains of politics, media, and entertainment are an even more fertile field for fallacies and remain wide open to rhetorical ploys of all kind. Especially, in these areas, reaching the absolute truth about a health problem is not necessarily an ideal and ultimate goal, objective, or claim to be reached by meaningful argumentation. In the struggle for the attention of recipients of messages and claims, their minds must be won for the proponent's causes. Very often, anything goes.

The following examples of fallacies in communication cover both physician ←→ physician and physician ←→ patient dialogues.

5.4.1 Slippery Slope Fallacy (Domino Theory, Argument of the Beard, Barefoot, Beard Fallacy, Domino Fallacy, Reductio Ad Absurdum, Slippery Slope Argument)

This fallacy presumes that *if* one event happens, *then* other events must/will also happen (without giving any other supporting reason for each cascading conclusion):

A physician to his or her patient: "... Your chemotherapy will immunosuppress you, weaken your immunity, you know ... you will then develop a cross-infection ... we will not be able to control it ... and you will die. ..."

"... If you do not become physically active, modify your eating habits and stop leading a stressful life, you will become more and more overweight. ... Once you are overweight, you will develop diabetes, ... coronary heart disease will follow and you will have a myocardial infarction. ... Coronary bypass surgery will have to be performed on you ... and your life expectancy will be dramatically reduced. ..."

N.B. A "competent layperson" (patient) may correctly ask the physician for his or her qualifier leading to his or her claims (conclusions): "... Doctor, how sure are you that all this will happen? What is the probability of such disquieting events? ... Does all this really apply to me?" Will the physician always be able to provide a proper answer to such questions?

5.4.2 Gambler's Fallacy

We commit this fallacy by ignoring that if events are statistically independent, any event in the sequence has an equal chance of occurring:

"... Doctor, why not try this drug again? ... If it did not work for others, it should work for sure for me! ..."

Gamblers believe that their luck will change after good or poor bets. This might also be true in medicine if the clinical course and the physician's skills were the same from one situation to another. However, the consecutive decision might be right if the situation, patient chances, and care outcomes are the same. A blind bet on the same chances in different situations leads to the gambler's fallacy and its uncertain outcomes.

5.4.3 Appeal to Consequences Fallacy (Wishful Thinking)

This fallacy occurs when we show the undesirable consequences of a belief by showing that this belief is false:

"…Failing this operation that I propose in order to solve your limping and hip pain can never happen to me. If I believed that it might happen, I would never forgive myself for bringing this kind of surgery to your attention. …"

The consequences of a belief have no bearing on whether the belief is true or false. Although a rational reason to believe is the evidence to be taken into account, it is replaced here by motivation.

5.4.4 Self-Evidence Fallacy (Mystical Assertion, Blind Conviction)

This kind of fallacy may also be seen as a rhetorical ploy: Statements, propositions, or claims are based on conviction only and they are unsupported by a valid argument, its premises, and other evidence-based argument building blocks. Qualities attributed to claims are ambiguous:

"…It is generally known that electromagnetic fields in some parts of the country cause cancer. …"
"…People using cellphones while driving cause accidents, it's obvious!…"
"…Everyone knows that drinking coffee helps the brain work better. …"
"…We keep seeing this same type of skin lesion in moisturizer users. …"
"…Observations speak for themselves! …"

Around 1910, Ambrose Bierce teasingly defined the adjective "self-evident" as "evident to one's self and to nobody else." More seriously, as a sole explanation of a given proposition, the French have an expression: "Ça saute aux yeux!" or "It jumps out at you." This type of fallacy is ubiquitous (in media, advertising, in courts of law, and even in medical writings and practice) and is committed both by professionals and their partners in argumentation, such as by physicians and their patients. The mystical shroud of impressive universality in the above-mentioned statements is not supported by evidence or this evidence is not made explicit enough to support in a valid way the proposed claims. However, claims may be right or wrong depending on the missing premises and the evidence they carry. The remedy to this fallacy is to support claims by best evidence-based valid arguments.

5.4.5 Appeals to Anything Other than the Best Evidence ("Low Instincts")

This kind of fallacy, most often a conscious rhetorical ploy, is based on uses of appeals to any irrational, unrelated, nonevidential states, entities, and issues instead of specific evidence in various building blocks of argument to justify its conclusions, claims, and ensuing recommendations.

In an *appeal to poverty (argumentum ad lazarum)* the position is considered to be correct because it is held by the poor: "… In our community, low income families appreciate our hospital services. Therefore, our hospital services are good. …"

In an *appeal to belief,* we are wrongly convinced that because many people believe in it, it must be true: "… Most Canadians believe that their health care system is the best. … Therefore, the Canadian health system is the best. …"

Other appeals are based and count on humor, flattery, emotions individualism, private motives, guilt, celebrity, and popularity and used in cases where there is no valid evidence in grounds, backing, and other building blocks of these arguments that would lead us to an evidence-supported claim. These so-called fallacies are rhetorical ploys because they are intentionally drawing away partners in argumentation from a valid support of argument conclusions and recommendation (claim) that would be the argumentation toward conclusions undesired by the proponent of the appeal.

The proponents of the *fallacy of one-sidedness* present only evidence favoring a conclusion (claim) and ignore and/or downplay evidence against it: "… You should note that 45 studies confirm the effectiveness of rubbing honey into your skin in the treatment of psoriasis…." (What about the other studies that show the contrary?) … "… I have seen first-hand that as long as patients see us often and regularly over a one-year period, blood pressure is reduced with none of the traditional side effects of drug therapy. …" (What about the other patients you saw whose blood pressure remained the same?)

Prejudicial language uses emotive terms to enforce the belief in one's proposition:

"… No reasonable person in this community would refuse to be immunized against this year's influenza strain. …," "… Any competent colleague in this Department would refuse to consider a knee replacement in any patient of this age. …"

Review the validity of such statements without prejudicial adjectives like "reasonable" or "competent" in the context of these examples.

5.4.6 Alternative Choice Fallacy

Any other option must be better: "… Standard management of multiple sclerosis fails to satisfactorily control this health problem. Neck vein surgery instead is a better and appropriate option. …" Alternative choice may be a worse choice or may produce the same results until proven otherwise.

5.4.7 Complementary Treatment Fallacy

If anything is added, the conjunction and combination of treatments or other procedures must be more effective and beneficial:

"… I was told to meditate during the entire treatment program established by oncologists for my cancer. Should I meditate then to improve my chances of nonrecurrence and recovery? …"

It may not cause harm. Or it may. Did anyone run a clinical trial of complementary treatment programs? In clinical medicine, combined treatments are tested against single treatments or other treatment combinations. Most often, different outcomes may be in focus (feeling well-cared for vs. stopping cancer growth and spread).

Put them all together fallacy lumps together several fallacies into the same statement (claim) or argument:

"… 90% of physicians in our survey are prescribing Cholysol to their patients to control high cholesterol blood level. Shouldn't you get a prescription for yourself too? …"

There is more than one fallacy hidden in this simple advertising statement seen on television. Physicians remain unidentified, a *reference (fallacy) to anonymous* (false to some degree) *authority* is made. From an unknown set of observations, an inference is made to a specific patient, you: a *fallacy of the general rule* (assuming that something true in a more general context and observation is true in every possible case). Because the drug is prescribed and used by many (*fallacy ad populum*) does not replace post-marketing studies, trials evaluating not only "clean" cases but also interventions offered ultimately to patients with multiple comorbidities and cotreatments for co-morbid states (i.e., other health problems, related, associated or not, besides the disease of principal interest, attention, and care). By not mentioning that an exception might exist in this patient, a *fallacy of accident* might also be committed.

5.4.8 Blinding with Science Fallacy

This communication error is based on using scientific jargon as a reflection of the prestige of science to pass one's assertions for something they are not, often instead of legitimate evidence:

"... Our team-based multiangulated analysis of current focused research involving a network of issues in the comparison of our new diet with some of its major alternatives shows as confirming the null hypothesis and the space and imperative for further tackling the problem through promising multivariable and multivariate analyses in a further experimental and observational analytical research. ..."

It is up to the recipient of such message to judge the magnitude of the verbal salad articulated by the transmitter. In other words, in plain English, most likely, it did not work. Using research jargon may hide poor evidence or unexpected and undesirable results or outcomes. For consumers of medication and health services, it offers a false reassurance that their problem is handled seriously. Advertising should be free of this kind of "dressing up" of facts.

Argumentum ad numeram fallacy relies on numbers in support of a statement and thus confounds numbers with the validity of the statement:

"... Yes, our diet plan is not cheap. But thousands of current users cannot be wrong! ..."

This fallacy is often preferred by advertisers, public orators, and other preachers. Numbers of adherents, users, or benefactors supplant evidence of effectiveness and benefits. Moreover, adverse effects and contrary evidence are often ignored.

Conclusion: From Patient Problem Solving Dialogue to a Broader Communication by Knowledge Translation in Medicine

Any meaningful communication in medicine has several prerequisites:

- A meaningful patient/physician or physician/physician psychological and otherwise facilitating contact must be established first as a basis for mutual understanding.
- The topic is clarified and clear for both parties.

- Semantics, definitions, formulations, and taxonomies are understood and acceptable for both parties.
- Definitions and taxonomies reflect biological distinctions between the entities compared, different epidemiological evaluations, and different clinical decisions or all of them from one discussed entity to another.
- Ways of reasoning and decision making are known and understood by both parties communicating.
- Modern argumentation and Socratic discourse are mutually perceived not as detrimental to mutual understanding, but as facilitating the opposite.
- The movement of ideas and statements is as fallacy-free as possible.

Teaching and learning medicine in their entirety are an exercise in communication of correct knowledge, attitudes, and skills. The transmitting party conveys his or her experience to the receiving party and both adjust their interaction to obtain the best results.

After the teaching and learning experience, physicians produce new evidence about treatment effectiveness, development and uses of new technologies, innovative surgery, disease prevention tools. Producing even the best evidence is not enough. Evidence must travel effectively from its producers to its users, reached users must use correctly right; patients and other individuals and communities to which it is applied must benefit from such a knowledge translation process. Knowledge translation relies heavily on effective and fallacy-free communication. Failures in communication may prove to be detrimental to the knowledge translation process and its results.

In the current generation, an expanded domain of *knowledge translation* is emerging.[123–128] It is, as a matter of fact, a "knowledge–attitudes–skills" translation and it is still defined in various ways. Its Canadian definition sees knowledge translation as "a dynamic and iterative process that includes synthesis, dissemination, exchange, and ethically sound application of knowledge to improve the health of Canadians, provide more effective health services and products, and strengthen the health care system."[126]

Even better, more simply and pragmatically, we may agree that it is "the science of conversion of current knowledge to patient outcomes."[127]

The process of conversion, however, is not as straightforward and simple as this definition.

"**Knowledge**" *itself* in the context of knowledge translation is defined as "a fluid mix of framed experience, values, contextual information, evidence interpretation, and expert insight that provides a framework for decision making, evaluating, and incorporating new experiences and information. It may be explicit and tacit, and individual or collective. In organizations, it often becomes imbedded not only in documents or repositories, but also in organizational routines, processes, practices, and norms."[128]

More generally, it is "the range of one's information or understanding of facts or ideas acquired by study, investigation, observation, or experience."[5,6]

"**Translation**" *itself*, surprisingly enough, has not yet been defined in the context of knowledge translation. Let us see it in this context as "multiple ways of moving experience, knowledge, facts, and their meaning from their original source and transmitters to their recipients or receivers in the framework of mutual understanding and followed by actions to change receivers' actions and care and health states of their expected beneficiaries."

Knowledge translation implies multidirectional, multilateral, and multiparty continuous communication between researchers, practicing physicians, other health professionals, patients, community, policymakers, pharmaceutical and other technology producers, and stakeholders in the health of individuals and whole communities.[123,124]

It has now its own array of terms (KT Terms in the literature) and a still developing methodology.[127,128]

There are two approaches to knowledge translation. One of them is to study "knowledge" and "translation" as separate but related entities to better understand how different ways of "translation" (moving knowledge from one person, place, or time to another) will change "knowledge" or its surrogate representation.

In this first case, epidemiologically speaking, in an "initial state → maneuver → subsequent state" model, "knowledge" is in essence the basic research design equivalent of a "state" (initial or subsequent) or dependent variable and "translation" is the basic research design equivalent to "exposure" (independent variable or "maneuver," see Figure 2.13 in Chapter 2) in a study of "maneuvers" as actions of noxious or beneficial factors. Subsequent states (after exposure; i.e., translation of knowledge) may not only be the knowledge itself, but also the possible consequences of such a knowledge change including its uses and desirable and other effects of a "translation acquired state." Hence, for example:

Being healthy (initial state)	→	Smoking or not (maneuver)	→	Developing cancer (subsequent state)
Having a certain type and degree of knowledge (initial state)	→	Translating or not translating knowledge (maneuver, results of which are to be tested)	→	Knowledge adopted, used, patient outcomes improve or not (subsequent state)

"Knowledge translation" can also be considered an entity, maneuver itself, or independent variable. This enables us to evaluate if "knowledge translation" changes health practices and care and ultimately the health of patients and community (dependent variables):

Current health practices and/or patients' and/or community health and disease(s)	→	Knowledge translation (its different ways, means, uses, arrays)	→	Change in health practices and/or patients' and/or community health and disease(s)

Both approaches may prove useful in the future of this rapidly developing domain.

So far, knowledge translation follows this general path:

Evidence-based innovation and production (knowledge) → potential adopters in their practice environment identification → implementation strategies → adoption of strategies to be implemented → outcomes of implemented knowledge in patients, practitioners, system, and/or community → evaluation of what was accomplished.

Failures in communication anywhere in this multistage process may be behind numerous cases of medical error and harm.[129]

Moreover, a considerable number of patients still do not get treatments of proven effectiveness or the information they need for their own decision making. They also get care that is not needed, and their physicians do not get all the evidence they need for their decision making. A better knowledge translation understanding and improvement should remedy this situation.

Medical communication is now more than a simple physician–patient contact or physician–physician exchange of ideas or facts as covered in this chapter. Both teachers and learners will also encounter communication as the basis of a larger framework of knowledge translation.

Medical communication may be seen by some as a simple interactive tool, but it also represents itself as a topic, having its own research questions, methodological challenges, and objectives.[130] Basic clinical communication as outlined in this chapter remains one of the core components of communication in health sciences, medical care, disease prevention, and health promotion. Current trends in "medical communicology" reflect this well.

References

1. Rodney Peyton JW. *Teaching & Learning in Medical Practice*. Silver Birches, Heronsgate Rickmansworth, Herts: Manticore Europe Ltd., 1998.
2. Spencer J. ABC of learning and teaching in medicine. Learning and teaching in the clinical environment. *BMJ*, 2003;**326**:591–4.
3. Wikipedia, the free encyclopedia. *Communication*. 11 pages at http://en.wikipedia.org.wiki/communication, retrieved October 25, 2010.
4. Gordon NE. *Communication. An Encyclopaedia Britannica Article*. 13 pages at ebcid:com.britannica.oec2.identifier.ArticleIdentifier?tocId=91096..., retrieved from Encyclopaedia Britannica electronic version on September 21, 2010.
5. *Random House Webster's Unabridged Dictionary 3.0*. Electronic edition on CD. Antwerpen: Random House Inc., 1998 and 2003.
6. *Merriam-Webster's Collegiate Dictionary*. Eleventh Edition. Springfield, MA: Merriam-Webster Incorporated, 2007.
7. Wikipedia, the free encyclopedia. *Semiotics*. 11 pages at http://en.wikipedia.org/wiki/Semiotics, retrieved April 8, 2010.
8. Air War College. Gateway to the Internet. *Communication skills*. 27 pages at http://www.au.af.mil/au/awc/awcgate/awx-comm.htm, retrieved April 18, 2010.
9. Lanigan RL. Communicology: Towards a new science of semiotic phenomenology. *Cultura. Int J Phil Culture Axiol*, 2007;**8**:212–6; http://www.international-journal-of-axiology.net/article/nr8/art14.pdf, retrieved February 14, 2011.
10. Lanigan RL. Communicology: Approaching the discipline's centennial. *Razon y Palabra, Numero 72*. 'Semiotica y Communologia: Historias y propuestas de una mirada cientifica en construccion', Numero 72. 15 pages at www.razonypalabra.org.mx/N/N72/Monotematico/8_Lanigan_72.pdf, retrieved February 14, 2011.
11. Eicher-catt D, Catt IE. *Communicology: The New Science of Embodied Discourse*. Danvers, MA: Rosemont Publishing & Printing, 2010. (See also <books.google.ca/books?isbn=0838641474>.)
12. Blackwell Reference Online. *International Encyclopedia of Communication*. http://www.communicationencyclopedia.com/public/tocnode?id=g9781405131995_yr20..., retrieved February 14, 2011.

13. American Association of Medical Colleges. *Report III. Contemporary issues in Medicine: Communication in Medicine. Medical School Objectives Project October 1999*. Washington, DC: Association of American Medical Colleges, 1999.

14. Professional Education Strategy, Curriculum Working Group, M. Talbot, Chair. *Talking Tools II. Putting Communication Skills to Work*. Ottawa: Health Canada, 2001. (Catalogue No:H39-509/2001-2E.)

15. Higgs J, Ajjawi R, McAllister L, Trede F, Loftus S. *Communicating in the Health Sciences*. Second Edition. South Melbourne: Oxford University Press, 2008.

16. Textbooks.com. *Communication in Medicine Textbooks*. 4 pages at http://text-books.com/Catalog/PM6/Communication-in-Medicine.php?s=1, retrieved June 24, 2010.

17. Brancati FL. The art of pimping. *JAMA,* 1989;**262**(1):89–90.

18. Wear D, Kokinova M, Keck-McNulty C, Aultman J. Pimping: perspectives of 4th year medical students. *Teach Learn Med,* 2005;**17**(2), 184–91.

19. Detsky AS. The art of pimping. *JAMA,* 2009;**301**(13):1379–81.

20. Jenicek M, Hitchcock DL. *Evidence-Based Practice. Logic and Critical Thinking in Medicine*. Chicago, IL: American Medical Association (AMA Press), 2005.

21. Lieberman SA, Trumble JM, Smith ER. The impact of structured student debates on critical thinking and informatics skills of second-year medical students. *Acad Med,* 2000 (No 10/October Supplement);**75**:S84–S86.

22. University of California, San Diego, Website designed by Thompson J. *A Practical Guide to Clinical Medicine. Clinical Decision Making*. 6 pages at http://medicine.ucsd.edu/clinicalmed/thinking.htm, retrieved March 30, 2005.

23. Wikipedia, the free encyclopedia. *Socratic method*. 6 pages at http://en.wikipedia.org/wiki/Socratic_method, retrieved March 20, 2010.

24. Hurst JW. *Four Hats. On teaching Medicine and Other Essays*. Chicago, IL: Year Book Medical Publishers, Inc., 1970.

25. Frits HW Jr. Are we Socratic teachers? *Trans Am Clin Climatol Assoc,* 1979;**90**:109–15.

26. Oh RC. The Socratic method in medicine—The labor of delivering medical truths. *Fam Med,* 2005;**37**:537–9.

27. The Critical Thinking Community. *Socratic Teaching*. 2 pages at http://www.criticalthinking.org/resources/articles/socratic-teaching.shtml, retrieved December 30, 2006.

28. Wikipedia, the free encyclopedia. *Socratic method*. 5 pages at http://en.wikipedia.org/wiki/Socratic_method, retrieved September 22, 2006.

29. Paul R. *A Taxonomy of Socratic Questions*. 2 pages at http://www.wolaver.org/teaching/socratic.htm, retrieved January 3, 2007.

30. Paul R. *Critical Thinking: How to Prepare Students for a Rapidly Changing World*, pp. 276–7. Santa Rosa, CA: Foundation for Critical Thinking, 1993.

31. Grahame-Smith D. (Education and debate.) Evidence-based medicine: Socratic dissent. *BMJ,* 1995(29 April);**310**:1126–7.

32. Carmichael C. (AETC National Resource Center.) *5 Models of Successful Clinical Consultation.* 2 pages at http://www.aidsetc.org/aidsetc?page=et-15-02-05, retrieved February 22, 2007.

33. AIDS Education & Training Centers National Resource Center, AETC Training Levels. *Level IV: Clinical Consultation.* 4 pages at http://www.aidsetc.org/aidsetc?page=tr-29-04, retrieved February 22, 2007.

34. Lang D. (Research and Training Opportunities at the National Institutes of Health, Clinical Electives Program.) *Pediatric Consult Service. Four Week Session.* 2 pages at http://www.training.nih.gov/student/cep/p_consult.asp, retrieved February 2, 2007.

35. Spickard A III, Ryan SP, Muldowney A, Farnham L. Outpatient morning report. A new conference for internal medicine residency programs. *J Gen Intern Med,* 2000;**15**:822–4.

36. Parrino TA, Villaneuva AG. The principles and practice of morning report. *JAMA,* 1986;**256**:730–3.

37. Shankel SW, Mazzaferri EL. Teaching the resident in internal medicine. Present practices and suggestions for the future. *JAMA,* 1986;**256**:725–9.

38. Harris ED Jr. Morning report. *Ann Intern Med,* 1993;**119**:430–1.

39. Kennedy CC, Cook RJ, Eggert CH, Krajicek BJ, Leenstra JL, West CP. *Developing a Blueprint for Morning Report.* 10 pages at https://www.im.org/AAIM/PUBS/Docs/2006TCMR/MorningReport.pdf. retrieved February 10, 2007.

40. Archer TP, Young JJ, Mazzaferri EL. *Morning Report. Internal Medicine.* New York and St. Louis: McGraw-Hill, 2000.

41. Marks AR (Editor in Chief). Physician-scientist, heal thyself … *J Clin Invest,* 2007;**117**:2.

42. Barbour GL, Young MN. Morning report. Role of the clinical librarian. *JAMA,* 1986;**255**:1921–2.

43. Sackett DL, Straus SE for Firm A of the Nuffield Department of Medicine. Finding and applying evidence during clinical rounds. *JAMA,* 1998;**280**:1336–8.

44. Schwartz A, Hupert J, Elstein AS, Noronha P. Evidence-based morning report for inpatient pediatric rotations. *Acad Med,* 2000;75:1229.

45. Houghtalen RP, Olivares T, Greene Y, Booth H, Conwell Y. Resident's morning report in psychiatry training. Description of a model and survey of resident attitudes. *Acad Psychiatry,* 2002;**26**:9–16.

46. Weinhlotz D, Edwards JC, Mumford LM. *Teaching During Rounds. A Handbook for Attending Physicians and Residents.* Baltimore and London: The Johns Hopkins University Press, 1992.

47. Lye PS, Simpson DE, Wendelberger KJ, Bragg DS. Clinical teaching rounds. A case-oriented faculty development program. *Arch Pediatr Adolesc Med,* 1998;**152**:293–5.

48. Myint PK, Sabanathan K. Role of grand rounds in the education of hospital doctors. *Hosp Med,* 2005;**66**:297–9.

49. Mueller PS, Segovis CM, Litin SC, Habermann TM, Parrino TA. Current status of medical grand rounds in departments of medicine at US medical schools. *Mayo Clin Proc,* 2006;**81**(3):313–21.

50. Jenicek M. Evaluating Surgery. Uses of Clinical Case Reports and Case Series in Surgical Specialties. Draft document as reported at the *Balliol Colloquiums for Evaluating Surgery*, Jonathan Meakins, Chair. University of Oxford, Oxford, UK: September 6–8, 2007.

51. Bickley LS, Szilagy PG. *Bates' Guide to Physical Examination and History Taking*. Tenth Edition. Philadelphia, Baltimore/New York/London: Wolters Kluwer Health/Lippincott Williams & Wilkins, 2009.

52. Partnership with Patients. Building a history, chapter 1, pp. 1–31 in: *Mosby's Guide to Physical Examination*. Edited by Seidel HM, Ball JW, Dains JE, Flynn JA, Solomon BS, Stewart RW. Seventh Edition. St. Louis, MO: Mosby/Elsevier, 2011.

53. Billings JA, Stoeckle JD. *The Clinical Encounter. A Guide to the Medical Interview and Case Presentation*. St. Louis/London/Toronto: Mosby, 1999.

54. Kurtz S, Silverman J, Draper J. *Teaching and Learning Communication Skills in Medicine*. Second Edition. Oxford and San Francisco: Radcliffe Publishing, 2005.

55. Robinson DJ. *The Psychiatric Interview Explained*. Port Huron, MI/London, ON: Rapid Psychler Press, 2000.

56. Feinstein AR. *Clinimetrics*. New Haven and London: Yale University Press, 1987.

57. Silverman J, Kurtz S, Draper J. *Skills for Communicating with Patients*. Second Edition. Oxford and San Francisco: Radcliffe Publishing, 2005.

58. Lloyd M, Bor R, Blanche G, Eleftheriadou Z. *Communication Skills for Medicine*. Third Edition. Edinburgh/London/New York: Churchill Livingstone, 2009.

59. Wikipedia, the free encyclopedia. *Nonverbal communication*. 15 pages at http://en.wikipedia.org/wiki/Nonverbal_communication, retrieved November 22, 2011.

60. Waitzkin H. Doctor-patient communication. Clinical implications of social scientific research. *JAMA*, 1984;**252**(17):2441–6.

61. Philippot P, Feldman RS, Coats EJ. *Nonverbal Behavior in Clinical Settings*. Oxford and New York: Oxford University Press, 2003.

62. Jenicek M. *Foundations of Evidence-Based Medicine*. Boca Raton/London/New York/Washington: The Parthenon Publishing Group/CRC Press, 2003.

63. Uzelac PS, Moon RW, Badillo AG. *SOAP for Internal Medicine*. Philadelphia/Baltimore/New York/London: Lippincott Williams & Wilkins (Wolters Kluwer), 2005.

64. Gonzalo JD, Chuang CH, Huang G, Smith C. The return of bedside rounds: An educational intervention. *J Gen Intern Med*, 2010;**25**(8):792–8.

65. Greenhalgh T, Hurwitz B. *Narrative Based Medicine*. London: BMJ Books, 1998.

66. Greenhalgh T, Hurwitz B. Why study narrative? *BMJ*, 1999;**318**:1848–50.

67. Shapiro J, Ross V. Applications of narrative theory and therapy to the practice of family medicine. *Fam Med*, 2002;**34**:96–100.

68. Pearson AS, McTigue MP, Tarpley JL. Narrative medicine in surgical education. *J Surg Educ*, 2008;**65**(2):99–100.

69. Jordens CFC, Little M. 'In this scenario, I do this, for these reasons': narrative, genre and ethical reasoning in the clinic. *Soc Sci Med*, 2004;**58**:1635–45.

70. Hudson Jones A. Narrative based medicine: Narrative in medical ethics. *BMJ*, 1999;**318**:253–6.

71. Jenicek M. *A Physician's Self-Paced Guide to Critical Thinking*. Chicago, IL: American Medical Association (AMA Press), 2006.

72. Jenicek M. *Clinical Case Reporting in Evidence-based Medicine*. Second Edition. London and New York: Arnold and Oxford University Press, 2001.

73. Reis S, Hermoni D, Livingstone P, Borkan J. Integrated narrative and evidence based case report. Case report of paroxysmal atrial fibrillation and anticoagulation. *BMJ*, 2002;**325**:1018–20.

74. Greenhalgh T, Worrall JG. From EBM to CSM: the evolution of context-sensitive medicine. *J Eval Clin Pract*, 1997;**3**:105–8.

75. Greenhalgh T. Narrative based medicine in an evidence based world. *BMJ*, 1999;**318**:323–5.

76. Charon R. Narrative and medicine. *N Engl J Med*, 2004;**350**:862–4.

77. Skelton JR, Hammond P. Medical narratives and the teaching of communication in context. *Med Teacher*, 1998;**20**(6):548–51.

78. Kalitzkus V, Matthiessen PF. Narrative-based medicine: Potential, pitfalls, and practice. *The Permanente Journal*, Winter 2009;**13**(1):8. http://xnet.kp.org/permanentejournal/winter09/narrative medicine.html, retrieved December 8, 2010.

79. Charon R, Wyer P. Narrative evidence based medicine. *The Lancet*, 2008;**371**(9609):296–7.

80. Montgomery K. *How Doctors Think. Clinical Judgment and the Practice of Medicine*. Oxford and New York: Oxford University Press, 2006.

81. Toulmin S. Knowledge and art in the practice of medicine: Clinical judgment and historical reconstruction, pp. 231–49 in: *Science, Technology, and the Art of Medicine*. Edited by C Delkeskamp-Hayes and MA Gardell Cutter. Dordrecht: Kluwer, 1993.

82. International Training & Education Center on HIV (I-TECH). *Structured clinical vignettes: What are they and how they are used?* An I-TECH Clinical Mentoring Kit. 5 pages at The University of Texas Medical Branch (UTMB). *Clinical Vignettes.* 2 pages at http://www.utmb.edu/aim/vignettes.htm, retrieved October 6, 2011.

83. American College of Physicians (ACP). *Presenting a Clinical Vignette: Deciding What to Present.* 3 pages at http://www.acponline.org/residents_fellows/competitions/abstract/prepare/clinvin_pres.htm, retrieved October 6, 2011.

84. American College of Physicians. *Writing a Clinical Vignette (Case Report) Abstract.* 2 pages at http://www.acponline.org/residents_fellows/competitions/abstract/prepare/clinvin_abs.htm, retrieved October 25, 2011.

85. Society of General Internal Medicine. *Clinical Vignettes. J Gen Int Med*, 2004 (April);**19**(s1):23–83. See also 241 pages at http://www.ncbi.nlm.nih/gov/pmc/articles/PMC1492602/, retrieved October 6, 2011.

86. Jenicek M. Clinical case reports and case series research in evaluating surgery. Part II. The content and form: uses of single clinical case reports and case series research in surgical specialties. *Med Sci Monit*, 2008;**14**(10):RA149–RA162.

87. Albrecht J, Bigby M. Case reports and case series, pp. 134–6 in: *Encyclopedia of Epidemiology*. Edited by S Boslaugh and L-A McNutt. Los Angeles/London/ New Delhi/Singapore: SAGE Publications, 2008.

88. Wikipedia, the free encyclopedia. *Morning report (medicine)*. 1 page at http://en.wikipedia/org/wiki/Morning_report_(medicine), accessed March 6, 2011.

89. Department of Medicine, University of Ottawa. *Morning Report*. 1 page at http://www.med.uottawa.ca$internalmedicine/residencyprogram/eng/ morning_report.html, accessed March 6, 2011.

90. Parrino TA, Villanueva AG. The principles and practice of morning report. *JAMA,* 1986;**256**(6):730–3.

91. Schiffman FJ. Morning report and work rounds: Opportunities for teaching and learning. *Trans Am Clin Climatol Assoc,* 1995;**107**:275–86.

92. Amin Z, Guajardo J, Wisniewski W, Bordage G, Tekian A, Niederman LG. Morning report: Focus and methods over the past three decades. *Acad Med,* 2000;**75**(10):S1–S5.

93. Kravet SJ, Howell E, Wright SM. Morbidity and mortality conference, grand rounds, and the ACGME's core competencies. *J Gen Intern Med,* 2006;**21**(11):1192–4.

94. Goldman S, Demaso DR, Kempler B. Psychiatry morbidity and mortality rounds: Implementation and impact. *Acad Psychiatry,* 2009;**33**(5):385–8.

95. Kuper A, Zur Nedden N, Etchells E, Shadowitz S, Reeves S. Teaching and learning in morbidity and mortality rounds: An ethnographic study. *Med Educ,* 2010;**44**:559–64.

96. Van Hoof TJ, Monson RJ, Majdalany GT, Gianotti TE, Meehan TP. A case study of medical grand rounds: Are we using effective methods? *Med Educ,* 2009;**84**(8):1144–51.

97. University of Oxford, Centre for Evidence-Based Medicine. *Critical Appraisal*. Variable number of pages at http://www.cebm.net/index.aspx?o=1157, retrieved May 6, 2011.

98. Ontario Public Health Libraries Association. *Critical Appraisal of Research Evidence 101*. 16 pdf pages at www.health.gov.on.ca/english/proviers/ program/.../caore.pdf, retrieved May 6, 2011.

99. Deenadayalan Y, Grimmer-Somers K, Prior M, Kumar S. How to run an effective journal club: A systematic review. *J Eval Clin Pract,* 2008;**14**:898–911.

100. *ACP Journal Club*. Variable number of pages at http://www.annals.org/site/ acpjc/index.xhtml, retrieved May 6, 2011.

101. McMaster University Health Information Research Unit. *ACP Journal Club* Purpose and Procedure. 4 pages at http://hiru.mcmaster.ca/acpjc/Pplong,htm, retrieved May 6, 2011.

102. Harris J, Kearley K, Heneghan C, Meats E, Roberts N, Perera R, Kearley-Shiers K. Are journal clubs effective in supporting evidence-based decision making? A systematic review. BEME Guide No, 16. *Med Teacher,* 2011;**33**(1):9–23.

103. Sackett DL, Richardson WS, Rosenberg W, Haynes RB. *Evidence-Based Medicine. How to Practice and Teach EBM*. New York and Edinburgh; Churchill Livingstone, 1997.

104. Straus SE, Richardson WS, Glasziou P, Haynes RB. *Evidence-based Medicine. How to Practice and Teach EBM*. Third Edition. Edinburgh/London/New York: Elsevier/Churchill Livingstone, 2005.

105. Laine C, Taichman DB, Mulrow C. Trustworthy clinical guidelines. (Editorial) *Ann Intern Med*, 2011;**154**:774–5.

106. Hill J, Bullock I. A summary of the methods that the National Clinical Guideline Centre uses to produce clinical guidelines for the National Institute for Health and Clinical Excellence. *Ann Intern Med*, 2011;**154**:752–7.

107. Kripalani S, LeFevre F, Phillips CO, Williams MV, Basaviah P, Baker DW. Deficits in communication and information transfer between hospital-based and primary care physicians. *JAMA*, 2007;**297**(8):831–41.

108. Hayward RSA, Rockwood K, Sheehan GJ, Bass EB. A phenomenology of scut. *Ann Intern Med*, 1991;**115**:372–6.

109. ICMJE: *Preparing a Manuscript for Submission to a Biomedical Journal.* 8 pages at http://www.icmje.org/manuscript_1prepare.html, retrieved March 12, 2011.

110. Jenicek M. The four cornerstones of a research project: health problem in focus, objectives, hypothesis, research question, chapter 3, pp. 27–34 in: *Biomedical Research. From Ideation to Publication*. Edited by G Jagadeesh, S Murthy, YK Gupta, and A Prakash. New Delhi/Philadelphia/London: Wolters Kluwer Health/Lippincott/Williams & Wilkins, 2010.

111. Jenicek M. Writing a 'Discussion' section in a medical article: An exercise in critical thinking and argumentation, chapter 27, pp. 457–65 in: *Biomedical Research. From Ideation to Publication*. New Delhi/Philadelphia/London: Wolters Kluwer Health/Lippincott/Williams & Wilkins, 2010.

112. Horton R. The grammar of interpretive medicine. *CMAJ*, 1998;**159**:245.

113. Gleischner JA. Using journal articles to integrate critical thinking with computer and writing skills. *NTCA J*, 1994;**38**(4 December):34–5.

114. Huth EJ. *Writing and Publishing in Medicine*. Third Edition. Baltimore, MD: Williams & Wilkins, 1999.

115. Greenhalgh T. How *to Read a Paper: The Basics of Evidence-Based Medicine*. Fourth Edition. Oxford and Hoboken, NJ: John Wiley & Sons Ltd and BMJ Books, 2010.

116. Jenicek M. *Fallacy-Free Reasoning in Medicine. Improving Communication and Decision Making in Research and Practice*. Chicago, IL: American Medical Association (AMA Press), 2009.

117. The Nizkor Project. *Fallacies*. Evolving number of pages at http://www.nizkor.org/features/fallacies/, retrieved March 14, 2011.

118. Thompson B. *Bruce Thompson's Fallacy Page*. Evolving pages (including other related subsites) at http://www.cuyamaca.net/bruce.thompson/Fallacies/intro_fallacies.asp, retrieved November 1, 2006.

119. Curtis GN. *Fallacy Files*. Evolving number of pages (including sub-sites) at http://www.fallacyfiles.org, retrieved March 14, 2011.
120. Wikipedia, the free encyclopedia. *List of cognitive biases*. 10 pages at <mhtml:file://F:\List of cognitive biases—Wikipedia, the free encyclopedia. mht>, or http://en.wikipedia.org/wiki/List_of_cognitive biases, accessed March 14, 2011.
121. Wikipedia, the free encyclopedia. *List of fallacies*. 10 pages at http://en.wikipedia.org./wiki/List_of_fallacies, retrieved March 14, 2011.
122. Downes S. *Stephen's Guide to Logical Fallacies*. Evolving number of pages at http://www.fallacies.ca/new.htm, retrieved March 14, 2011.
123. Canadian Institutes of Health Research (CIHR). *Glossary of Funding Related Terms*. 14 pages at mhtml:file://Glossary of Funding Related Terms—CIHR.mht, retrieved March 15, 2011. See also http://www.cihr-irsc. gc.ca/e/29418 html.
124. Yeoh MJ. Knowledge translation, chapter 34, pp. 235–41 in: *Patient Safety in Emergency Medicine*. Edited by Croskerry P, Cosby KS, Schenkel SM, Wears RL. Philadelphia: Wolters Kluwer/Lippincott/Williams & Wilkins, 2009.
125. Public Health Agency of Canada. *Glossary*. 19 pages at http://cbpp-pcpe.phac-aspc.gc.ca/glossary/all_terms_eng.html, retrieved December 17, 2009.
126. Harrington A, Beverley L, Barron G, Pazderka H, Bergerman L, Cleland S for Alberta Health Services—Alberta Mental Health Board, Alberta Mental Health Research Partnership Program (2009). *Knowledge Translation: A synopsis of the literature 2008*. Edmonton, AB: Alberta Mental Health Research Partnership Program, 2009. See also 27 pages at www.mentalhealthresearch.ca/.../ Knowledge%20Translation%20review_FINAL.pdf, retrieved March 15, 2011.
127. What is KT. *KT Terms*. Variable number of pages at http://whatiskt.wikispaces. com/KT+terms, retrieved January 10, 2011.
128. Straus S, Tetroe J, Graham ID. *Knowledge Translation in Health Care: Moving from Evidence to Practice*. Oxford and London: Wiley/Blackwell/BMJ Books, 2009.
129. Jenicek M. *Medical Error and Harm. Understanding, Prevention, and Control*. Boca Raton/London/New York: CRC Press/Taylor & Francis/Informa/ Productivity Press, 2011.
130. Kurtz S, Silverman J, Draper J. Forewords my J van Dalen and FW Pratt. *Teaching and Learning Communication Skills in Medicine*. Second Edition. Oxford and San Francisco: Radcliffe Publishing, 2005.

Chapter 6

Conclusions (with a Short Recapitulation): Welcome to the World of Reasoned and Evidence-Based Medicine

Learn in order to teach and to practice.

Talmud, first–sixth century AD

The physician ought to know literature
to be able to understand or to explain
what he reads. Likewise also rhetoric,
that he may delineate in true arguments
the things which he discusses; dialectic
also so that he may study the causes and
cures of infirmities in light of reason.

Isidore of Seville, 570–636 BC

It is necessary that a surgeon should have a
temperate and moderate disposition. That he
should have well formed hands, long slender
fingers, a strong body, not inclined to tremble,
and with all his members trained to the capable
fulfillment of the wishes of his mind. He should

be well grounded in natural science, and should
know logic well, as to be able to understand what
is written; to talk properly, and to support
what he has to say by good reasons.

Lanfranc of Milan, d. 1315

I am still learning.

Michelangelo, 1475–1564

An able and dextrous Chirurgion is a great
Treasure in the Army, and cannot be
valued enough, especially if he consults in
all dangerous cases with the understanding
Physitian. These two, Physitians and
Chirurgions, are to be intimate friends
together, assisting one another without
envy and pride, for the better relief and
the greater safety of their Patients.

Raymund Mindererus, 1620

The foundations of medicine are
reason and observation.

Duro Armano Bagliavi, 1668–1707

One of the chief defects
in our country's education plan is that we
give too much attention to developing
the mind; we place too much stress on
acquiring knowledge and too little on
the wide application of knowledge.

William James Mayo, 1933

Are you sure, Dr. Mayo?

Knowledge is acquired when we succeed
in fitting a new experience into a system
of concepts based upon our old experiences.
Understanding comes when we liberate

ourselves from the old and make possible
a direct, unmediated contact with the new,
the mystery, moment by moment,
of our experience.

Aldous Huxley, 1956

Critical and evidence-based reasoning, structured, focused, and pragmatic decision making, and balanced multilateral communication, together with knowledge, experience, and the best possible sensorimotor skills, remain crucial for good practice, care, and research. Fallacy free, they make medicine and clinical care as a whole more effective and warrant patient safety.

As we have seen in this book, we believe that medical reasoning, decision making, and communication are three methodological and execution-distinct entities. They are also somewhat interfacing and complementary and should be used in an integrated manner in conjunction with other clinical skills.

Patient life cannot be twitted; it must be shared and lived in its entire reality and complexity. Web traffic–generated social grooming or creating peripheral awareness may tell us only where problems are. The rest takes place at the bedside and on hospital floors. Using and over-relying on electronic communication media is not a sign of a physician being up to date or modern. Even worse in some cases, anyone uncomfortable with person-to-person communication may hide and isolate himself or herself behind Bluetooth devices, earphones, or earplugs. This is not a sign of sophisticated communication skills. It may be more than useful, however, in many situations and activities in emergency medicine and surgical specialties. Newer educational techniques (simulation-based techniques) such as using standardized patients or mannequins (patient dolls) should also help. However, standardized patients talk (and argue if they are trained for it), whereas mannequins do not (yet). As we saw in Chapter 5, communication with patients and health professionals is more than passing words from one person's mouth to someone else's ears electronically, sotto voce, or through a whisperer's whispers.

Let us emphasize again: Absorbing the largest possible volume of knowledge and information and successfully learning necessary sensorimotor clinical skills is not enough. Reasoning well, developing sane clinical judgment, or mastering evidence-based structured decision making is not enough either. All the aforementioned must be integrated. That is why learning medicine is such a long process.

Building and using a clinical decision tree will always be more tangible than inserting a catheter. However, the decision to use the catheter precedes its successful execution and more favorable patient outcome. "… Did I do it right? …" is one question learners correctly ask. "… What led me to do it? …" and "… what will it give? …" are some other equally important questions.

Any clinical newcomer must know in advance what awaits him or her besides rules for the best possible clinical routine, the nature and quality of tools, and protocols of instrumentation. Uncertainty is perfectly understandable. Clinician reasoning, decision-making rules, and communication might seem overwhelming at first, but learning them is a more than rewarding experience. Mastering some content of this book may lead to a heartwarming thought "… ah, that's why they are saying so! …" or "… yes, this is really important for me …."

Medical technologies, drugs, management of care, and health administration will change all the time. Essential ways to handle them intellectually will not.

We live not only in a world of uncertainties, probabilities, wrong, missing, and almost never complete but required information. We also live in a world of errors, which may lead to harm to patients. Our mistakes in reasoning, decision making, and communication should not contribute to such often dramatic events for patients and their physicians. We must think as correctly as possible.

Whatever we do relies first on often forgotten rigorous semantics and pragmatic understanding and decision-oriented taxonomy for health problems of interest and their beneficial or noxious causes. We must correctly define and categorize in this sense what interests us, what we intend to do with it, and to whom all this should apply. Our strategies regarding cardiovascular disease, cancer, psychiatric problems, social well-being, and even a newly emerging domain of "spiritual health" depend on it.

The fervor of evidence-based medicine has gripped medicine in many parts of the world. Good old clinical epidemiology remains at its core. It is not enough, however, to produce, grade, and otherwise evaluate the best evidence available. We must also use it in the best way possible. Critical thinking, structured reasoning, and argumentation are essential for this purpose. Modern argumentation lies behind the acceptance of any criterion of cause–effect relationships be they noxious factors generating disease or beneficial ones such as treatment underlying cure and recovery. Modern argumentation is a learned experience now like other more traditional ways to perform medicine.

Rational medical thinking through argumentation cannot be limited to cause–effect relationships, however relevant, primordial, important, and vital for medicine they are. It also supports, as we saw in Chapter 3, every step of clinical work.

Modern argumentation is also a meaningful way of answering questions raised in the Socratic dialogue. Any discussion of a clinical problem or reviewing specific patient care benefits from it. To succeed, learners must know how their teachers reason. Teachers must know how and why learners react and interact.

In Chapter 4, medical decision making follows our understanding of the clinical problems that we face and are asked to resolve. Reasoning in the decision-making domain requires the mastery of additional methodology in the gnostic domain. Whatever may be the transition and interface between knowing and deciding, these two distinct entities remain complementary.

Mutual understanding, based on the use of best evidence in rational argumentation and decision making, relies on a third element, that is, communication, as discussed in Chapter 5. Opportunities for communication are much wider than in person-to-person exchanges within the patient–physician world. Rounds, reviews, bedside or hallway discussions, consults or administrative and other operational summaries, and reports are all subjects of rational thinking, judgment, and decision making.

Even the simplest "why?" question raised by any learner should be answered in an argumentative way, grounded in the best available evidence. The learner should recognize elements and good building blocks of argumentation as proposed by the teacher.

Moreover, to produce, read, understand, and apply clinical, fundamental, and operational research findings, we must argue about health problems in a way that defines topics, objectives, research questions, and subsequent methodology of epidemiological, biostatistical, operational, administration, or other nature. Research problems defined first must also be presented as an argument. Their entire methodology depends on it. Results of research are discussed and conclusions made about them in light of the argumentation outlined at the beginning of the research work. This is one of the ways to prevent, avoid, or forget the unrelated "technobabble" that often seeps into medical articles. For example, is there any other better way to run a journal club?

The young learner will be exposed sooner or later to large-scale health policy and program development, making, and evaluation. From the point of view of reasoning and argumentation, their general rules are similar to those used in individual or group patient care. The desirable productivity of health professionals in a given health system should not suffer either.

Doing all this correctly should give us the priceless rewarding feeling that we are making sense and that our good intention to arrive at meaningful results has succeeded: Our patients and communities are healthier, safer, and unharmed; research money, energies, and human resources are well invested. Good will in itself will not succeed. Together with acquired knowledge and mastered sensorimotor clinical skills, the integrative ways of producing and using the best evidence in our reasoning, decision making and communication should contribute to the best possible results in health care. Let us give all this a chance by adopting the message presented in the pages of this introductory reading.

What about teaching and learning clinical reasoning and decision making in the future? Assuredly, we are already doing so in our courses on epidemiology, clinical epidemiology, biostatistics, preventive medicine and public health, formal and clinical teaching in family medicine and clinical specialties, and in other forms of sharing clinical and community medicine expertise. Perhaps, sooner or later, we will succeed in integrating, absorbing, and harmonizing all these crucial contributions to our professional knowledge and competency into a framework of understanding, decision making, and communication in health professions as outlined in the broadest of terms in the preceding pages. The monumental experiences and contributions of past and present generations, which pave the way for modern health sciences, would then appear under an even better "it makes sense" light. The well-being of our communities and patients would benefit from it that much more.

Dear Samantha, John, Claudette, Pierre, Izzy, Hans, Henrik, José, Luis, Mahmoud, Kwang Ho, Munira, Hiroko, and everyone else, your journey to discover how the clinical environment works is now over. Let us hope that you enjoyed it and found it useful. Welcome now to the hospital starting gates. The race is about to begin.

Glossary: Preferred Terms and Their Definitions in the Context of This Book

Unless otherwise specified in our chapters, this glossary is based on the literature quoted in the text, our own definitions and formulations, and the following key references:

- Dorland WA Newman. *Dorland's Illustrated Medical Dictionary*. 30th Edition. DM Anderson, Chief Lexicographer. Philadelphia, PA: Saunders/Elsevier, 2003.
- *Encyclopedia of Epidemiology*. Edited by S Boslaugh and L-A McNutt. Los Angeles/London/New Delhi/Singapore: Sage, 2008.
- *Encyclopedia of Biostatistics*. Edited by P Armitage and T Colton. Chichester, NY: Wiley, 1998.
- *Routledge Encyclopedia of Philosophy*. Edward Craig, General Editor. London/New York: Routledge, 1998.
- *Encyclopedia of Communication and Information*. Edited by JR Schement. New York/London/Munich: Macmillan Reference USA, 2002.
- *Encyclopedia of Cognitive Science*. Lynn Mandel, Editor-in-Chief. London/New York/Tokyo: NPG (Nature Publishing Group), 2003.
- *A Dictionary of Epidemiology*. Fifth Edition. Edited by M Porta. A Handbook Sponsored by the I.E.A. Oxford/New York: Oxford University Press, 2008.
- *A Dictionary of Public Health*. Edited by JM Last. Oxford/New York: Oxford University Press, 2007.

- Reese WL. *Dictionary of Philosophy and Religion. Eastern and Western Thought*. Expanded Edition. Amherst, NY: Humanity Books/Prometheus Books, 1999.
- *The Cambridge Dictionary of Philosophy*. Second Edition. R Audi, General Editor. Cambridge/New York: Cambridge University Press, 1999.
- Everitt BS. *The Cambridge Dictionary of Statistics in the Medical Sciences*. Cambridge/New York/Melbourne: Cambridge University Press, 1995.
- Vogt WP. *Dictionary of Statistics and Methodology. A Nontechnical Guide for the Social Sciences*. Newbury Park/London/New Delhi: Sage, 1993.
- *Wikipedia, the free encyclopedia*, various entries in the current electronic version.

And our own glossaries and definitions in

- Jenicek M, Hitchcock DL. *Evidence-Based Practice. Logic and Critical Thinking in Medicine*. Chicago, IL: American Medical Association (AMA Press), 2005.
- Jenicek M. *Foundations of Evidence-Based Medicine*. Boca Raton/London/New York/Washington: Parthenon/CRC Press, 2003.
- Jenicek M. *Fallacy-Free Reasoning in Medicine. Improving Communication and Decision Making in Research and Practice*. Chicago, IL: American Medical Association (AMA Press), 2009.
- Jenicek M. *Medical Error and Harm. Understanding, Prevention, and Control*. A Productivity Press Book. Boca Raton, FL/London/New York: CRC Press/Taylor & Francis, 2011.

This glossary defines terms as they are used and understood in the spirit, context, and content of this book. How did we compile this glossary?

1. Two criteria were used for inclusion: (1) operational quality or adequacy for practical use (inclusion/exclusion criteria, measurability, and taxonomy suitability), and (2) compatibility with prevailing meaning and terminology in mainstream clinical epidemiology, evidence-based medicine and uses of evidence in reasoning, critical thinking, understanding, and decision making in medicine and allied health sciences.
2. Additional attention was paid to the overlapping of various definitions. Such instances were avoided as much as possible.

3. Whenever more than one definition is quoted, it is because of the definitions' complementarity and convergence rather than because of their differences and ensuing controversy.

The following list of definitions, established with beginners in mind, is therefore proposed. This list can never be complete. For additional definitions within the book and its chapters, the reader is encouraged to consult the index.

Abduction: A form of reasoning in which one reasons from observed phenomena to a hypothesis (proposition) that would explain them. Abductive reasoning usually shows only that the hypothesis (proposition) is a possible explanation; further observation, experiment, and/or reasoning are required to determine whether the hypothesis (proposition) is justified. Together with induction and deduction, abduction is considered one of three basic forms of inference.

Accident (in medicine): An unexpected, specific, identifiable, unusual, and unintended (unplanned) event that occurs at a particular time and place of medical care, originally without an apparent or deliberate cause but with marked effects.

Active error (human, medical): An error or failure resulting from human behavior, made by a health professional (operating surgeon, prescribing internist, consulting psychiatrist, nurse at floors or in the operating room, etc.) who, in a health establishment, provides direct clinical or community care, acts, or services; it may be knowledge based, rule based, or skill based.

Additive effect: An arithmetic sum of the effects of a set of factors (such as drugs or pollutants).

Adduct: A common term for rebuttals and all major supporting and/or weakening elements related to conclusions (claims) of an argument.

Adduction (to adduce): In the context of this book and philosophy, the process of offering an example, reason, or proof in discussion or analysis.

Advocacy: A tool using language strategies to justify beliefs and actions to others.

Algorithm in medicine: A graphical representation (flowchart) of a set of rules to solve a clinical problem by setting down individual steps in a sequence of actions and their results; each action step depends on the result of the preceding one. Therefore, as opposed to a decision tree, an algorithm is an unequivocal direction-giving tool.

Argument (in general): As a vehicle of reasoning, an argument consists of various statements or propositions (premises) from which we infer another statement or conclusion. A connected series of statements or reasons intended to establish a position, that is, leading to another statement as a conclusion.

Argument (in medicine): A connected series of statements originating from a live situation, experience, or research in medicine intended to establish a position (another statement as conclusion) in medical problem solving, understanding, and decision making. In a medical argument, a position or conclusion may be the diagnosis, patient admission, or treatment decision, or an error and/or harm that occurred. As an exchange of ideas, views, or opinions, it may focus on problem solving in an individual, specific patient (should the patient undergo surgery or not?), or it may be directed toward finding the best solution to a more encompassing problem and toward more general strategies to find the best way to manage them (prevention and control of nosocomial infections or medical errors in a hospital or in a broader medical care system).

Argumentation (in general): A discussion between two or more people in which at least one advances an argument. It is the methodological use or presentation of arguments.

Argumentation (in health sciences): A process of shared reasoning about a health, disease, or well-being problem.

Argumentation (medical): The methodological use or presentation of medical arguments to solve a problem in medical practice or research.

Argument-based error: Misusing or omitting valid argument components (grounds, backing, warrant, qualifier, rebuttals, conclusions, or claims) or using inappropriate arguments and linking them poorly in medical decision making.

Argument-based medicine: The research and practice of medicine in which understanding and decisions in patient and population care are supported by and based on flawless arguments using the best research and practice evidence and experience as argument and argumentation building blocks in a structured and fallacy-free manner.

Art (in general): Skills directed toward the work of imagination, imitation, or design, or gratification of the esthetic senses.

Art of medicine: The systematic application of sensory skills, creative imagination, faithful imitation, innovation, intuition, and knowledge in speech, reasoning, or motion in the care of the health of patients and communities.

Attending (adjective): A health professional, most often a physician, who as authorized and plenipotentiary decision maker has primary responsibility and authority over a patient and care from his or her staff position in an accredited hospital. A form of "attending function" may be found in any other health profession such as nursing, respirology, readaptation, physiotherapy, and others.

Attitudes: A part of the affective domain that can be viewed in this context as learned tendencies to act and decide in a consistent manner with regard to a particular object and situation. It means having in the decision making process the capacity to sense and recognize the situation, and to act in a controlled, predictable, and consistent manner relevant to the problem requiring a decision. The decision maker's attitudes must be appropriate for the task to avoid errors in decision making.

Attributable risk: The difference between the rate of events in a group of interest (subjects exposed to a factor) and a control group (nonexposed group).

Backing (in modern argument): The body of experience and evidence that supports the warrant and grounds in modern argument and argumentation.

Bedside manner(s): Ways in which health-care professionals and providers and their patients communicate and interact. These include the mastery and execution of verbal and nonverbal (sensorimotor) communication skills as well as behavior to create empathy, provide information, and establish mutual understanding, will, and compliance in view of the best possible care.

Bias in medicine: A nonrandom, *systematic* deviation from truth, or a well-defined "reality." Caveat: Bias, cognitive error, and cognitive bias are often considered synonyms.

Case–control study: A type of study of cause–effect relationships based on a single comparison of exposure to a potentially causal factor in groups of potentially factor-produced diseased individuals (cases of disease) and noncases.

Case fatality rate: The occurrence of death in individuals suffering from a specific disease. Used as an expression of disease severity.

Case series study or case series report (clinical): A detailed description and analysis of series of cases that explain the dynamics, pathology, management, and/or outcome of a given disease (including error and harm).

Case study: An in-depth examination, analysis, and interpretation of a single instance or event such as the occurrence of error or harm.

Categorical syllogism: A classical, Aristotelian form of argument consisting of three elements (building blocks): (1) A general statement (major premise), (2) a specific (about a particular case) statement, and (3) an inference indicators–related conclusion.

Cause: In general, an event without which some subsequent event would not have occurred or because of which it occurred. It is an agent or act that produces some phenomenon (the effect). In clinical medicine and public health: Contextual factors that produce changes such as the occurrence of a disease or its cure. In courts of law: Each separate antecedent of an event. Something that in some manner is accountable for a condition that brings about an effect or that produces a cause for the resultant action or state.

Chain of causes: A sequence of events in time in which each possibly related event follows (and may be caused by) another.

Claim: A conclusion that we arrive at through our reasoning supported by the argument at hand.

Clinical case report: A structured form of scientific and professional communication normally focused on an unusual single event (patient or clinical situation) to provide a better understanding of a case and its effects on improved clinical decision making.

Clinical clerk: A medical or other health sciences undergraduate (nursing, dentistry, physiotherapy, imaging technology, etc.) working with patients under the supervision and control of an instructor. Clerkship is usually scheduled in the second part of the medical undergraduate curriculum and is an unpaid activity. See "extern."

Clinical context: A set of case-related established clinical practices, healthcare providers, patients, and physical environments (technologies included), which apply to a particular case such as a patient, strategies of care, or teamwork and which influence meaning, understanding, and decision making about the case.

Clinical decision analysis: An application of decision analysis in a clinical setting. It has three main components: (1) Choices available to the patient, his or her physician, or both; (2) chances as probabilities of outcome for each choice; and (3) values of treatment options and their outcomes for interested parties. It represents any activity, systematizes (organizes) decision making, clarifies decision making, and leads to the "correctness" of decisions.

Clinical epidemiology: The science and method of studying and making optimal decisions in clinical medicine, while taking into account the epidemiological characteristics of the patient and the patient's outer clinical environment, the pathology concerned, and the factors and maneuvers to which the patient is exposed in his or her clinical environment, especially medical actions. The application of epidemiological knowledge, reasoning, and methods to study clinical issues and improve medical and other decisions when dealing with individual patients and groups of patients and to improve overall clinical care (N.B. and its outcomes). Also, using the experience acquired in groups in reasoning and decision making in the care of individuals.

Clinical judgment: The capacity to make and choose data and information to produce useful (true or false) claims in clinical practice and research. It also means critical thinking in the practice of medicine based on the "patient/evidence/setting" fit. Together with elements of knowledge and experience, it relies on the process of integrating meanings and values of clinical and paraclinical observation and data into the making of conclusions and decisions derived from such an integration.

Clinical practice guidelines (CPGs): A set of systematically developed evidence and other elements-based statements to assist practitioners' and patients' decisions about the best possible health care for specific clinical and community medicine circumstances. As opposed to clinical protocols, clinical practice guidelines are not prescriptive; they are only proposals regarding what to do.

Clinical protocols: Structured and organized step-by-step activities prescribed to be followed in a given health structure, setting, and situation. As opposed to clinical practice guidelines, critical protocols are prescriptive; they must be followed in the framework of a given clinical activity.

Clinical reasoning: A context-dependent way of thinking and decision making in professional practice to guide practice actions. It involves the construction of narratives to make sense of multiple factors and interests pertaining to the current reasoning task. It occurs within a set of problem spaces informed by the practitioner's unique frames of reference, workplace context, and practice models, as well as by the patient or client contexts. It utilizes core dimensions of practice knowledge, reasoning, and metacognition and draws on these capacities in others.

Clinical trial: An experimental procedure based on the scientific method to evaluate if some health interventions such as drug treatment, surgery, or other types of patient or community care produce expected results. Randomization of patients into groups that are compared, blinding of patients and clinical trialists themselves, and other methods of arriving at unbiased information are just some of the ways of making a trial as objective as possible.

Clinical vignette: A teaching case of patient history, state, and clinical course in view of building, developing, and improving the medical care relationship between a clinician, his or her knowledge and clinical skills, and his or her patient. It is used as a tool to measure and improve a trainee's knowledge and clinical reasoning.

Clinimetrics: The definition, measurement, classification, validation, and evaluation of clinical observations such as symptoms and signs, indices and scales, and other distinct clinical phenomena to make them as reproducible and meaningful as possible. The domain concerned with qualification, counting, measurement, and categorization of clinical observations, data, and information.

Closed (closed-ended) questions: Questions requiring direct answers. They initiate inductive reasoning and serve to confirm hypotheses as hypotheses testers.

Cognition: The human faculty of processing information and creating, changing, and applying knowledge and preferences. Mental functions and processes (thought, comprehension, inference, decision making, planning, learning, abstraction, generalization, concretization, metareasoning, knowledge, preference, intentions, and others) in view of the development of new knowledge and concepts culminating in both thought and action.

Cognitive error (bias): A pattern of deviation in judgment that occurs in particular (in our context) in medical and clinical situations or in medical research reasoning and conclusions. In medicine, it is a pattern of deviation in judgment that occurs in particular, within our area of interest, in medical and clinical situations or in medical research reasoning and conclusions. Caveat: Bias as it is used currently across the medical literature has multiple meanings including almost any flaw in reasoning and decision making, especially in medical research (research design, execution, and evaluation).

Cognitive science: An amalgamation of disciplines including artificial intelligence, neuroscience, philosophy, and psychology. Within cognitive science, cognitive psychology is an umbrella discipline for those interested in cognitive activities such as perception, learning, memory, language, concept formation, problem solving, and thinking.

Cohort: A group of subjects studied by repeated examinations over a defined period of time from their entry under observation until the end of a period of interest including follow-up.

Cohort study: A study of two or more groups of individuals over a defined period of time allowing the establishment of a causal association between exposure to a factor of interest and the occurrence of disease, its good or bad outcomes, or its prevention.

Communication in medicine: Imparting or interchanging thoughts, opinions, or information about a health problem through speech, writing, or signs. It is a process by which information is exchanged between health professionals, patients, and other stakeholders in health through a common system of symbols, signs, or behavior. A transactional process in which messages are filtered through the perceptions, emotions, and experiences of those involved. As such, interpersonal communication remains the linchpin of medical practice.

Communicology: The science of human communication between individuals and communities (groups). It is based on the critical study of discourse and uses the logic-based research methods of semiotics and phenomenology to explain human consciousness and practice in the context of other people and their environment. Communicology is developing currently in medicine, psychiatry, and nursing.

Community: A group of patients bearing particular characteristics (demographic, hospital settings where they are treated, requiring similar clinical care), such as residents of an area, a socioeconomic and/or ethnic group, or a group of faith. It must be always well defined.

Community medicine: The practice of medicine at the community (beyond individual) level and setting, having as a purpose identification of health problems and needs and the means by which these needs may be met, and evaluation of the extent to which health services meet these needs.

Comorbidity: A clinical condition (disease, a state requiring additional care) existing simultaneously and most often independently with another condition, which is the main subject of ongoing attention and care, and which alters and/or expands current understanding and care decisions regarding a patient.

Compassion: The feeling of understanding, sympathy, and sorrow experienced by a health professional for his or her patient or community, accompanied by a strong desire to alleviate the patient's or community's suffering and state.

Complication (clinical): A disease or injury resulting from another related disease, health state, and/or health-care intervention.

Concept map: A visualized time–space drawing of interrelationships of causes, consequences, interventions, outcomes, and other person/time/space characteristics of both patients and their caregivers.

Craft (in general): A practical and utilitarian art, trade, or occupation requiring special manual skill and dexterity.

Craft (in medicine): Sensorimotor and behavioral skills in patient–physician interactions, surgery, and medical care.

Critical appraisal: More generally, the systematic evaluation of a process, service, research design, and so on, consisting of the detailed scrutiny and logical analysis of all phases of the process with the aim of ensuring that it conforms to acceptable standards, or, if it does not, identifying the shortcomings of the service, process, research design, and procedures. More specifically, critical appraisal is the application of rules of evidence to a study to assess the validity of the data, completeness of reporting, methods and procedures, conclusions, compliance with ethical standards, and so on. The rules of evidence vary with the circumstances.

Critical thinking: The intellectually disciplined process of actively and skillfully conceptualizing, applying, synthesizing, and/or evaluating information gathered from or generated by observation, experience, reflection, reasoning, or communication as a guide to belief and action. A "purposeful, self-regulatory judgment" that results in interpretation, analysis, evaluation, and inference, as well as in the explanation of the evidential, conceptual, methodological, criteriological, or contextual considerations upon which that judgment is based. Reasonable reflective thinking that is focused on deciding what to do or believe.

Decision analysis: A systematic approach to decision making under conditions of uncertainty. A derivative of operations research and game theory to identify all available choices, and potential outcomes of each, in a series of decisions that have to be made (e.g., about aspects of patient care such as diagnostic procedures, preventive and therapeutic regimens, and prognosis). Epidemiological data play a large part in determining the probabilities of outcomes following each potential choice.

Decision making in medicine: A process of reasoning and judgment in the path from recognition of the health problem to be solved to its formulation, generation of alternatives, information and evidence search, selection, and action.

Decision theory in medicine: A set of quantitative methods for reaching optimal decisions in medical and health care.

Decision tree: A space–time organized structure (flowchart) of clinical options, decisions, actions, their outcomes, probabilities, and values used for the choice of the best possible clinical care and public health actions, which are most beneficial for the patient and other involved parties. As opposed to an algorithm, a decision tree is a direction-searching tool.

Deductive reasoning: A type of reasoning in which the conclusion (findings) is *definitely true* if premises are true.

Deductive research: A type of research in which a general principle or hypothesis is used as a starting point for data collection, analysis, and interpretation in order to confirm or refute a preestablished hypothesis. Deductive research often leads to deductive reasoning in which the conclusion (findings) is definitely true if premises are true. Deductive research provides (at least theoretically) *absolute support* for study findings and their conclusions.

Definitions: Formal statements of the meaning and significance of entities of interest (variables, tools, conditions, settings, etc.).

Delphi method: A method for reaching a consensus about a given clinical or other problem based on the progressive repetitive exclusion of the least important opinions from an array of choices to solve the problem. An iterative circulation of the problem discussion by a panel of expert health professionals (ideally, mutually anonymous) during which questions and responses are refined in light of responses to each preceding round of questions. The number of viable options and solutions is reduced to ultimately arrive at a consensus judgment preventing any participant from dominating the process.

Disease: An anomaly in health as defined and seen by a qualified health professional. For example, "This patient has anemia." See "illness" and "sickness."

Disease gradient: A directional expression of different grades of disease according to the severity of disease manifestations and outcomes.

Disease spectrum: The range of different systematic manifestations of a disease.

Disposition: A right state of mind and inclination regarding something. The natural or prevailing aspect of one's mind as manifested in behavior and relationships with patients and peers. A disposition is an acquired state, a habit, a preparation, a state of readiness, or a tendency to act in a specific way.

Distilled clinical judgment: A judgment that encompasses and integrates knowledge of facts, evidence, experience, intuition, common sense, and gut feeling in understanding and solving medical problems and related decision making.

Effectiveness: Beneficial and other results under "ordinary," prevailing, or customary conditions and for ordinary, prevailing, or customary patients. An answer to the "does it work?" question.

Effectiveness/efficiency/efficacy triad: An evaluation of the impact of medical, clinical, or community interventions (error and harm control included) in habitual conditions (*effectiveness*), in ideal conditions (*efficacy*), and in relation to the cost (material and human means) invested in health interventions (*efficiency*).

Efficacy: In health economics, a beneficial result under ideal conditions. An answer to the "can it work?" question.

Efficiency: Effects of the end results in proportion to the effort (human and material resources, time) invested in the health-care activity. An answer to the "what does it cost for what it gives?" question.

Empathy: The intellectual identification of a health professional with a patient's state, feelings, thoughts, or attitudes. It may also be seen as the patient's understanding of his or her physician and the physician's rationale in the management of the patient's problem.

Enthymeme: The simplest form of argument consisting of one reason (statement, proposition, premise) leading to (connected to) a claim (argument conclusion, recommendation, orders).

Epidemiology: The study of the occurrence and distribution of health-related states or events in specified populations, including the study of determinants influencing such states (causes), the ensuing decisions and the impact of such intervention decisions on individuals, groups of individuals, communities, diseases of interest, their treatment, and the health of those under scrutiny. The direction of its reasoning is from multiple observations of individuals to the applications to communities and the health problem as a whole. Epidemiology may be subdivided into clinical epidemiology, field epidemiology, and fundamental epidemiology (see separate entries for these terms).

Epistemology: The branch of philosophy concerned with the nature and extent of human knowledge (*episteme* means knowledge, *logos* means theory, hence epistemology means theory of knowledge).

Equity: In health economics, the fairness and impartiality of health-care activities such as access to health care as a possible cause or effect of a health-care activity. Equity seeks to answer the "how well are costs and benefits distributed?" question.

Error (in general): An act of commission (doing something wrong) or omission (failing to do the right thing) that leads to an undesirable outcome or significant potential for such an outcome.

Error (medical): An inaccurate or incomplete assessment of a patient's risks and diagnosis, conservative or radical treatment, prognosis, follow-up and care, including disease, injury, syndrome, behavior, infection, and other subjects of care. It usually reflects a deficiency in the system of care.

Essay: A short literary composition on a particular theme or subject, usually in prose and generally analytic, speculative, or interpretative, most often from a limited or personal point of view.

Etiological fraction: The proportion of events in exposed subjects that is due to the factor of interest from the web of potential causes of the health problem under study.

Evaluation (in medical lathology): A process that attempts to determine as systematically and objectively as possible the relevance, effectiveness, and other characteristics of activities, programs, and policies to prevent and control medical error and its consequences as well as the impact of such activities, programs, and policies in light of their objectives. The systematic assessment of the activity (medical or other) and/or the outcomes of such an activity, program, or policy compared to a set of implicit or explicit standards as a means of contributing to the improvement of the activity.

Event (medical): Something that happens to or with a patient and/or a health professional or any other person or technology involved in health care.

Evidence (in general): Any piece of information or data needed, required, and used either to understand a problem or to make a decision about it.

Evidence (in law, in relation to medicine): Any type of proof of facts in court: **Real evidence** (defective medical instruments), **direct evidence** (photographs, prescriptions, patient records, oral testimonies), **circumstantial evidence** (circumstances under which a medical error occurred), **hearsay** (third-party information quoted by the health professional), **confession** by the defendant, **dying declarations** (made prior to death by a patient), other statements that prove to be relevant at the hearing (records of some routine observations), **declarations against interest** (information showing the motive of a health professional's actions), connected events proving design or intent (repeated past events contradicting an isolated happening), or evidence as to the character of the defendant (health professional or patient). Their admissibility is decided by the court. The term "evidence" in this context has a broader meaning than in medicine.

Evidence (in medicine): Any data or information, whether solid or weak, obtained through experience, observational research, or experimental work (trials). This data or information must be relevant and convincing to some (best possible) degree to enable understanding of the problem (case) or the diagnostic, therapeutic, or otherwise care-oriented clinical decisions made about the case. Evidence is not automatically correct, complete, satisfactory, and useful. It must first be evaluated, graded, and used based on its own merit.

Evidence-based error: Using poor or inappropriate evidence in argumentation and decision making in clinical practice and research.

Evidence-based medicine (EBM): The practice of medicine in which physicians find, assess, and implement methods of risk assessment, diagnosis and treatment, prognosis on the basis of the best available current research, their expertise, the needs, values, and preferences of the patient, and medical ethics considerations in a specific setting of practice and society.

Expertise: Special skills and knowledge acquired by a person (a health professional in the context) through education, training, and experience.

Extern: A qualified or in-training person connected with the health care institution or organization, but not residing in it, such as a physician or medical student at a hospital.

Factoid: An apparent fact that is not a fact.

Fallacy (in general): A mistake or flaw in reasoning or argument. In the broadest of terms, it is a violation of the norms of good reasoning, rules of critical discussion, dispute resolution, and adequate communication.

Fallacy (in medicine): Any error in reasoning pertaining to a health problem and its supporting evidence pertaining to the handling of evidence in our reasoning and throughout the process of argumentation interfering with the best possible understanding and decision making in the task of solving a health problem.

Field epidemiology: The practice of epidemiology in the community, commonly in a public health service. (N.B. sometimes termed "**shoeleather** epidemiology" given its on-foot door-to-door practice of inquiry and services delivery.) Uses of experience gathered from individuals when dealing with health and disease at the community level.

Flaw: Any characteristic, deficiency or inadequacy in technology, operation, human reasoning, and decision making contrary to expectations from the expected function, task, and outcomes of a health-care event. This term denotes any variable that may be considered a possible (often yet to be proven) causal factor or marker related to the domains of risk and prognosis in the domain of medical error and its consequences.

Flowchart in health sciences: A graphical representation of the progress of a system for the definition, analysis, and solution of health care problems. Both algorithms and decision trees are flowcharts.

Fraction (relative frequency): Two related numerical entities (frequencies) as expressions between them. Rates, ratios, and odds are fractions.

Frequency (absolute frequency): A simple number of events or entities of interest.

Fundamental epidemiology: The development and testing of basic manners of reasoning and decision making in epidemiology through various domains such as philosophy, epistemology, logic and critical thinking, quantitative methods (biostatistics), and/or qualitative research in dealing with health and disease at the group of individuals and community levels.

Fuzzy theory (logic): A paradigm of perceiving phenomena without precise borders; everything is a matter of degree such as obesity, being conscious, being dehydrated, and such situations where bivalent thinking (it is or it is not) corresponds to the multivalent reality of phenomena under consideration.

Gradient of disease: See "disease gradient."

Grounds: The basis from which we reason. In medicine, they are most often fundamental data, information from various sources, and/or our own findings.

Guts (in clinical medicine): Cheeky, intuitive, and sometimes arrogant-appearing claims in clinical problem understanding and especially decision making. Having the courage or nerve to make reflex-looking propositions for patient management or community care problem solving. Courage, nerve, or emotions may be associated with even the best rational and argumentation-based problem-solving processes underlying often speedy decisions. It may be seen as a part and trait of heuristic medical problem solving.

Harm (in general): Injury or damage to people, property, or environment.

Harm (medical): A temporary or permanent physical impairment in body functions (including sensory functions, pain, disease, injury, disability, and death) and structures, as well as suffering and other deleterious effects due to a disruption of the patient's mental and social well-being. Unintended physical injury resulting from or contributed to by medical care (including the absence of indicated medical treatment) that requires additional monitoring, treatment, or hospitalization, or that results in death. Such injury is considered medical harm whether or not it occurred within the hospital. Some errors do indeed result in medical harm, but many errors do not; conversely, many incidents of medical harm are not the result of any errors. See also "medical harm" (vide infra).

Hazard (in medicine, biostatistics, lathology): A biostatistical broader term for probabilities studied in the domain of prognosis; a theoretical measure of the probability of occurrence of an event per unit time of risk. Elsewhere, it is a factor or exposure that may adversely affect health or disease. Used sometimes as a synonym of risk.

In epidemiology, hazard means the inherent capability of an agent or a situation to have an adverse effect. Risk is the probability of disease occurrence in terms of incidence or mortality densities, whereas hazard refers to probability in the field of prognosis usually as a function of mortality, although any outcome other than death can also apply. In lathology, hazard is an error capable of causing harm; a potential source of harm. Any threat to safety, for example, unsafe practices, conduct, equipment, labels, and names.

Healthcare (health-care, health care): Services provided to individuals or communities to promote, maintain, monitor, or restore health, including self-care. Those services may be provided by physicians (medical care), all other health professionals (clinical care or community care), and/or civic bodies (in public health) either in hospitals, clinics, medical/health offices, or communities at large. It also refers to services provided to individuals or communities by agents of the health services or professionals to promote, maintain, monitor, or restore health. Health care is not limited to medical care, which implies action by or under the supervision of a physician. The term is sometimes extended to include health-related self-care.

Health promotion: Policies and processes, mostly at the community level, that enable people to increase control over and improve their health. Communities' behavior and their environment are generally highlighted.

Health protection: Steps taken to eliminate as much as possible the risk of adverse consequences on health attributable (most often) to environmental and other hazards.

Heuristics: Quick and "dirty" mental shortcuts to understanding and decision making used to simplify our thinking in order to arrive at a solution for a problem, reduce the complexity of a task, and save time, memory, attention, and other requirements of problem solving. Making diagnosis at the bedside or in an emergency setting or clinical decision making regarding what to do under the pressure of the conditions of the clinical workplace are often heuristic processes.

Hindsight: A way of reasoning and drawing conclusions about an event after it has happened.

Hindsight bias: The tendency to judge events leading up to an accident as errors because the bad outcome is known; the more severe the outcome, the more likely that the decisions leading up to this outcome will be considered errors. Judging the antecedent decisions as errors implies that the outcome was preventable.

Human error (in general): The failure to complete a planned action as it was intended or when an incorrect plan is used in an attempt to achieve a given aim. All occasions in which a planned sequence of mental and physical activities fails to achieve an intended outcome, and when these failures cannot be attributed to the intervention of some chance agency. Failures committed either by an individual or by a team of individuals.

Human error (in medicine): An operator's error in reasoning, understanding, and decision making about the solution of the health problem and/or in the ensuing sensory and physical execution of a task in clinical and/or community care.

Humanities (medical): An interdisciplinary field, which includes humanities (literature, philosophy, ethics, history, and religion), social science (anthropology, cultural studies, psychology, sociology), and the arts (literature, theater, film, and visual arts) and their application to medical education and practice.

Hypothesis(es): Propositions to be evaluated, accepted, or refuted in light of clinical experience with a case or problem or by a research study.

Iatrogenic illness: The adverse effect of preventive, diagnostic, therapeutic, surgical, and other medical, sanitary, and health procedure(s), interventions, or programs attributable as resulting from the activity of a health professional. It also includes other harmful occurrences that are not natural occurrences of the patient's disease. It does not automatically imply the culpability or responsibility of the physician or the hospital, or that the illness was necessarily preventable.

Illness: An anomaly in health as perceived by the health problem sufferer himself or herself: "I feel tired and I look pale, I must be ill?" See "disease" and "sickness."

Incidence: The frequency of *new* cases of disease or other health event occurring over a defined period of time and community. It is usually presented as a rate.

Incidence density: An incidence rate that uses as a denominator, not only the number of individuals of interest, but also the duration of observation, follow-up, or exposure of each of those individuals one by one. An average of person-period of time is obtained, which is also called "force of morbidity." For example, 10 new cases of disease over a 5-year period per 100,000 person-years of risk is an expression of incidence density or force of morbidity. Used when periods of time of interest vary considerably from one individual to another.

Incident (in general): An event, process, practice, or outcome that is noteworthy by virtue of the hazards it creates for subjects, or the harm it causes. All accidents are incidents, but not all incidents are accidents.

Incident (in medicine): An event, process, or outcome that is noteworthy by virtue of the hazards it creates for patients, or the harm it causes to them.

Inductive reasoning: In philosophy, research-producing premises that bring only some degree of support to conclusions (findings from the study).

Inductive research: A type of research based on using existing information and data (whatever the purpose of their collection might be) to generate and/or confirm a hypothesis. A hypothesis is generated by preestablished fact, data, and information.

Inference indicators: Natural language words identifying premises and conclusions in reasoning and arguments.

Inference (in general): The process of logical reasoning that combines observed phenomena with accepted truths or axioms in order to formulate generalizable statements. **Statistical inference** applies such a process to a series of observations and calculates degrees of uncertainty in comparison with various data sets. **Causal inference** refers to the thought process and methods that assess or test whether a relation of cause to effect does or does not exist.

Informal logic: A branch of logic that uses methods and techniques to identify, analyze, interpret, and evaluate reasoning and argument as it happens in the context of natural language used in everyday life. Contrary to formal logic, it is nonsymbolic and nonmathematical.

Inquiry: A process leading to the finding of appropriate beliefs and actions.

Intern: A graduate of a medical school serving and usually rotating in a hospital in order to be eligible for a license to practice medicine. Depending on the health system, the intern may reside or not at the hospital.

Intuition: The direct perception of truth, fact, falsity, or decisions independent of any reasoning process.

Journal club: A periodical interactive meeting of learners (clinical clerks, interns, residents) and elders (professional and academic staff) to critically review selected topics or arrays of topics of the day communicated by medical periodicals and other electronic media.

Judgment (clinical): See "clinical judgment."

Judgment (in general): The act or faculty of affirming or denying a proposition, whether based on a direct comparison of objects or ideas or derived by a process of reasoning. It is the evaluation of the nature and soundness of some information, giving it a value for subsequent decision making.

Knowledge: A part of the cognitive domain that encompasses both retention of data and information about the subject and the capacity to apply them to specific tasks. Errors occur if the operator's knowledge, especially evidence based, is deficient and insufficient. Used in the context of knowledge translation (vide infra).

Knowledge (in the context of knowledge translation): A fluid mix of framed experience, values, contextual information, evidence interpretation, and expert insight that provides a framework for decision making and evaluating and incorporating new experiences and information. It may be explicit or tacit, and individual or collective. In organizations, it often becomes embedded not only in documents or repositories, but also in organizational routines, processes, practices, and norms. More generally, it is the range of one's information or understanding of facts or ideas acquired by study, investigation, observation, or experience.

Knowledge translation: A dynamic and iterative process that includes synthesis, dissemination, exchange, and ethically sound application of knowledge to improve the health of a defined community, provide more effective health services and products, and strengthen the health-care system. Knowledge translation implies a multidirectional, multilateral, and multiparty continuous communication between researchers, practicing physicians, other health professionals, patients, community, policy makers, pharmaceutical and other technology producers, and stakeholders regarding the health of individuals and whole communities.

Lapse (in lathology): Failures of memory that do not necessarily manifest themselves in actual behavior and may only be apparent to the person who experiences them.

Lapse (in medicine): A memory-based error; a memory-generated failure (e.g., forgetting a patient's allergy to an antibiotic).

Lathology: The study and management of error and harm occurring in clinical and community medicine and care (error and harm caused by medical or any other health professional and working environment in the context of this book). "Lathology" is derived from the Greek words *lathos*, which means error and *logos*, which means study.

Learning curve: The description of the development and acquisition of a new surgical or medical skill in the search for moments, levels, or stages of reaching a potential for lower-than-expected success rates or higher-than-expected error, complication, and/or harm rates. Learning curve study and analysis is used increasingly in the evaluation of health professional training progress.

Likelihood: A state of being likely or probable, or the probability that an event that has already occurred would yield a specific outcome. It differs from probability, which refers to the occurrence of future events.

Likelihood ratio (in the domain of diagnosis): The probability that a given test result would occur in a person with the target disorder divided by the probability that the same result would occur in a person without that disorder.

Logic in medicine: A system of thought and reasoning that governs understanding and decisions in clinical and community care, research, and communication.

Malpractice: Improper or unskillful conduct on the part of a medical practitioner that results in injury to the patient. It generally describes professional misconduct or negligence on the part of a person delivering professional services.

Medical decision: The choice of the best option in assessing risk (explanatory decisions), in treating patients (managerial decisions), or in making prognosis (both explanatory and managerial, if treatment decisions are involved).

Medical decision making: A process by which one arrives at a given medical decision, the latter being the result or end point of such a process.

Medical error: An individual and/or system failure resulting from human behavior of a health professional (e.g., operating surgeon, prescribing internist, consulting psychiatrist, nurse at floors or in the surgical or office setting) who, in a health establishment or community setting, provides direct clinical or community care, acts, or services. It may be knowledge based, rule based, or skill (execution) based. Error unintentionally being wrong in conduct or judgment in medical care. Medical error leads often (but not always) to medical harm: These two entities, however, must not be confused. In other words, medical error is a reasoning- and decision making–based inaccurate or incomplete assessment and management of a patient's risks and diagnosis, choosing and executing radical or conservative treatment, making prognosis, and extending and widening patient and community care. Such faults fall into the category of fallacies, biases, and cognitive errors. Medical error is also a human or system error in health care and community medicine, and medicine-related public health.

Medical harm: A temporary or permanent physical impairment in body functions (including sensory functions, mental functioning, social and occupational functioning, pain, disease, injury, disability, and death) and structures as well as suffering that disrupt a patient's physical, mental, and/or social well-being. Some errors result in medical harm, but many errors do not. Conversely, many incidents of medical harm are not the results of any errors. Reasoning, deciding, or acting poorly lead to medical errors and harm.

Medical humanities: See "humanities (medical)."

Medical logic: See "logic in medicine."

Medical propaedeutics: A preliminary instruction, introductory course, or preparatory teaching preceding and pertaining to clinical training and care.

Medicine: The art and science of diagnosis, treatment, and prevention of disease and the maintenance of good health.

Meta-analysis in medicine: A mostly statistical integration of original research studies focusing on a similar problem and question, leading to a largely quantitative summary of pooled results. Looking this way across studies helps us better understand whether health interventions work or whether other causal relationships exist beyond an original study. It is a quantitative component of research synthesis; systematic review is its qualitative component.

Metacognition: A reflection about the thought processes that led to a particular diagnosis or other clinical or scientific decisions in order to consider whether biases or cognitive shortcuts may have had a detrimental effect.

Metaevaluation: An evaluation of evaluations.

Mistake (in general): A deficiency or failure in the judgmental and/or inferential processes involved in the selection of an objective or in the specification of means to achieve it, irrespective of whether or not the actions directed by this decision scheme run according to plan.

Mistake (medical): An incorrect reasoning, problem solving, and/or decision making or sensorimotor action in clinical care. Inappropriate planning of knowledge-based and rule-based actions resulting in errors in clinical care or in medical research. A commission or omission with potentially negative consequences for the patient that would be judged wrong by skilled and knowledgeable peers at the time it occurred, independent of whether there were any negative consequences.

Mixed methods research: Any kind of research that uses and combines methodology and findings usually obtained separately by quantitative or qualitative research. Such a new mixed method research should bring additional information and insight as opposed to information produced either by isolated quantitative or by qualitative research only.

Modern (Toulmin's) argument: An argument consisting of six elements (building blocks), such as grounds, backing, warrant, qualifier, rebuttals, and conclusion.

Morbidity: The occurrence of disease in a defined community; usually presented as a rate.

Morbidity and mortality reports and rounds: Conferences and meetings representing a forum for faculty and trainees to explore the management details of particular cases and expand such details into the broader understanding of problems they reflect. They are expected to contribute to the improvement of patient care, medical knowledge, communication skills, professionalism, and problem-based learning and improvement.

Morning report: A summary of events that happened at the hospital floor, service, or department to the individuals and teams in charge during the working period (shift) and that is communicated to the individuals and teams who take over.

Mortality: The occurrence of deaths caused by a specific health problem in a defined community.

Narrative: An orderly, continuous account of an event or series of events. Clinical care reports and case series reports are often narratives or preceded by narratives.

Nomogram: A graphical representation that enables its users to establish the value of a variable of interest at its scale from an intersection of the values of two other determining variables read on their respective scales. The two variable scales are used to predict a third one.

Nursing: A health profession based on assisting individuals and groups of individuals under medical or other health professional care, whether sick or well, in the performance of those activities which he or she could not accomplish independently, thus contributing to health and its recovery and gaining independence. (This is a North-American perspective.) Nursing is the use of clinical judgment in the provision of care to enable people to improve, maintain, or recover health, to cope with health problems, and to achieve the best possible quality of life, whatever their disease or disability, until death. (This is a British paradigm.) Medical, surgical, pediatric, psychiatric, and public health nursing are among its specialties.

Objectives: Points to be reached in practical clinical problem solving or research, either specific to the problem or in general, encompassing a broader context into which the problem belongs.

Odds: The ratio of the probability of occurrence of an event to that of non-occurrence of the same event in another set of observations. They are fractions having an event in the numerator and a nonevent in the denominator. It is the ratio of the probability that something is one way to the probability that it is another way.

Odds ratio (synonyms: cross-product ratio, relative odds): A ratio of two odds.

Open-ended questions: Questions offered to multiple answers, such as "how does it feel?" They reflect deductive reasoning from which hypotheses are derived.

Operational research: A research encompassing a wide range of problem-solving techniques and methods applied in the pursuit of improved decision making and efficiency. Often used synonymously with operations research (vide infra).

Operations research (synonyms: operational research, decision science, management science) in medicine: A multidisciplinary science based on mathematics, probability and statistics, computer science, modeling, simulation, path exploration, optimization, and other approaches that are devoted to the analysis of a process of operation used in making decisions. A maximum profit for the price of a minimum loss decision is sought. Not to be confused with surgical operations, which may or may not be the subject of operational research as defined previously.

Orismology (medical): The study, uses, and evaluation of definitions in medical practice and research. "Orismology" is derived from the Greek words *orismos*, which means definition and *logos*, which means study.

Outcome: The product, result, or practical effect of health care in terms of patient health and associated costs. "What happens" when acting on patient (or community) health and disease. The health status of an individual, a group of people, or a population that is wholly or partially attributable to an action, agent, or circumstance.

Outcomes research in health sciences: Research that seeks to understand end results of particular health-care practices and interventions; effectiveness and better ways to monitor and improve the quality of care are its objectives. The ability to function, quality of life, mortality, and other clinical events serve as outcomes.

Patient safety: Reduction and mitigation of unsafe acts (and their undesirable consequences) within the health-care system through the use of best practices shown to lead to optimal patient outcomes.

Pattern recognition: The mental process of finding characteristics of a health problem corresponding or identical to a previously lived and/ or learned experience. Particularly important not only to diagnosis but also to surgery and execution and evaluation of sensorimotor skills.

Philosophy (in general): A systematic analysis and critical examination of fundamental problems and the nature of being, reality and thinking, perception, values, and causes and choices underlying principles of physical and ethical phenomena. Its fundamental branches are meta-physics, epistemology, logic, and ethics.

Philosophy (in medicine): The uses and application of philosophy to health, disease, and medical care. It examines the methods used by medicine to formulate hypotheses (like questions about diagnosis and treatment) and directions on the basis of evidence (what to do), as well as the grounds on which claims (diagnoses, treatment decisions and effects, prognoses made) about patients and health problems may be justified.

Philosophy of medicine: Philosophical considerations of the nature of medicine's own additional contributions to philosophy in general such as the experience from clinical trials or other studies of cause–effect relationships; the focus is on the advancement of the theory of medicine.

Pimpee: A junior clinical clerk who is the unfortunate target and recipient of pimping (vide infra).

Pimper: An attending or resident quizzing subordinates on minutiae and medical trivia during rounds or class as a questionable test of a junior's knowledge.

Pimping: A clinical practice where persons in power and entitled to decision making (attending, seniors) ask questions of their junior colleagues (medical students, residents) with often blurred and infre-quent expectations in order to correctly execute assigned tasks. It is the quizzing of juniors with objectives ranging from knowledge acquisition to embarrassment and humiliation; it may be positive or negative. Pimping is done by barraging juniors with seemingly ran-dom and topic-/problem-unrelated or unanswerable questions to which the juniors most often do not have answers, which leads to humiliation regardless of the conscious intention of the attending or resident asking the questions. Thus, it creates a feeling of "I do not know" in the face of peers and those who know better.

Potentiation of effect: The combined effect of multiple causal factors (drugs, pollutants, etc.), which is more than the arithmetic sum of the effects of each.

Practice (in general): The action or process of performing or doing something.

Practice of medicine: An action, sensorimotor or other, in the domain of health and disease resulting from critically thinking about a problem and decisions regarding what to do. Recognition, treatment, and prevention of disease are emphasized.

Predictive value of a negative test result: The probability that an individual who tested negative really does not have the disease of interest. It shows how many individuals from among all who tested negative really do not have the disease in question.

Predictive value of a positive test result: The probability that an individual who tested positive for a disease really has it. It shows how many individuals from among all who tested positive really do have the disease of interest. The clinician's certainty before action is sought.

Premise: A statement or proposition that leads (most often with other premises) to the conclusion of an argument. An argument is drawn from such premise or premises.

Presumptions: Positions or argumentative grounds available until some sufficient reason is adducted against them.

Prevalence: The frequency of disease or other health event in a defined community (patients, community at large) at a given moment (point prevalence) or over some time interval (period prevalence). Usually presented as a rate.

Prevention (disease prevention): Policies and actions to eliminate a disease or minimize its effect. Actions that control disease occurrence by preventing new cases (primary prevention), lowering disease prevalence, usually by shortening the duration of cases (secondary prevention), minimizing the severity and sequelae of cases beyond primary and secondary control (**tertiary** prevention), or actions to limit iatrogenesis (quaternary prevention).

Primary prevention: Actions and measures to reduce the incidence of disease by personal and communal factors.

Primordial prevention: Actions and measures to minimize hazards to health and that hence inhibit the emergence and establishment of processes and factors (environmental, economic, social, behavioral, cultural) known to increase the risk of disease. In this context, there is an obvious overlap with the definition of health protection.

Probability: Quantification of uncertainty.

Problem (topic) in focus: The health problem to be solved in practice or research.

Process (in health-care evaluation): A course of action or sequence of steps, including what is done and how it is done. A "how does it work" characteristic of an activity or system within which errors occur. All that is done to patients in terms of diagnosis, treatment, monitoring, and counseling.

Prognosis: An assessment of a patient's future (based on probabilistic considerations of various beneficial and detrimental clinical outcomes as causally or otherwise determined by various clinical factors, biological and social characteristics of the patient) and the pathology under study (disease course) itself.

Prognostic factors: Causally related characteristics or health events once the individual has the disease of interest, which can be modified, and then possibly the outcomes of the disease of interest.

Prognostic markers: Causally or otherwise related characteristics or health events once the individual has the disease of interest, which cannot be modified, however related they might be to the outcomes of the disease of interest.

Propaedeutics (in general): The knowledge that is necessary or useful for understanding or practicing an art or science, or that explains its nature and extent, and the method of learning it.

Propaedeutics (medical): A way of acquiring the basic preparatory knowledge, attitudes, and skills required for further full learning and training, but which is not enough in itself for necessary and sufficient proficiency in understanding, decision making and actions and their evaluation in a particular clinical or community medicine setting and domain.

Public health: A society's organized efforts, structures, policies, and programs to protect, promote, restore, and improve health and prolong the life of the community.

***P* value:** In biostatistics, the probability of obtaining a result as extreme as, or more extreme than, the one observed if the dissimilarity is entirely due to variation in measurement or subject response, that is, if it is the result of chance alone.

Qualifier: An expression in argumentation, often a single word or number, somehow quantifying our certainty about our claim in light of the preceding argument blocks and the links between them.

Qualitative research: A method of inquiry, without statistical descriptions and analyses, which aims to gather an in-depth understanding of human behavior and the reasons governing such behavior. Qualitative methods, based on an in-depth study of cases that may be either individuals or situations (events), focus on the why and how of understanding and decision making. Quantitative methods focus instead on what, where, and when. In medicine, its subject may be professional practice, environmental issues affecting health, treatments, or health-care economics among others. Making sense of cases and interpretation and discovery of meanings are emphasized. Any kind of research on error and harm that produces findings not arrived at by means of statistical procedures or other means of quantification. It is research about a person's lived experience with health events and problems and related behaviors. It also includes organizational, functional, social, or interactional relationships between health professionals and their patients and community.

Quality of health care: The degree to which health services for individuals and populations increase the likelihood of desired health outcomes and are consistent with current professional knowledge. The extent to which a health-care service or product leads to a desired outcome or outcomes.

Quantiles: Divisions of a directional (from smallest to biggest, etc.) distribution into equal, ordered subgroups. Deciles are tenths, quartiles are quarters, and centiles (percentiles) are hundredths.

Quantitative research: A mainstream type of research referring to the systematic empirical investigation of quantitative properties and phenomena and their relationship. Biostatistical and epidemiological methods focus most often on cause–effect relationships such as phenomena related to disease occurrence or its cure.

Quaternary prevention: Actions that identify patients at risk of overdiagnosis or overmedication and that protect them from excessive medical intervention.

Rate: A quantitative expression that relates and includes both events (like becoming ill, dying, recovering, being born, and so on) and non-events (like staying healthy or alive, etc.). The coupling of a set of observations (events) in the numerator (A) and some additional ones, such as non-cases or non-events (*B*) together with non-events (others) in the denominator create an expression of rate: *A/A + B* (and multiplied by a convenient coefficient, usually some power of 10). A rate has a different meaning here then the expression of "speed" elsewhere.

Ratio: A relationship between two different entities (sets of observations) in the numerator (*a*) and the denominator (*b*) in a fraction: *a/b*. The value obtained by dividing one quantity by another. It is a relationship between two separate and distinct quantities, neither of which is included in the other.

Rational medicine: A precursor of evidence-based medicine defined in the 1960s as "the practice of medicine based upon actual knowledge" without making distinctions between actual knowledge and evidence.

Reasoning (clinical): See "clinical reasoning."

Reasoning (in general): Thinking leading to a conclusion. Making judgments or inferences from facts, observations, and/or hypotheses. A tool to form conclusions, judgments, or inferences from facts or premises. It is a methodological employment or presentation of arguments.

Rebuttals: Conditions or circumstances under which a claim stemming from an argument does not apply. In medicine, differential diagnosis and/or exclusion criteria in diagnosis and/or decision making are often used as rebuttals.

Relative risk: A ratio of two risks. A fraction relating the incidence of events in one group to the incidence of events in another group.

Research question: An expression of doubt and uncertainty about the nature and solution of a health problem in its specific context (population, setting of care, community) to be discussed and solved by an intended inquiry and its authority. Research questions are questions regarding a health problem to be solved, which specify (in various combinations and completeness from case to case) the population under consideration, condition of interest, intervention, controls when comparisons are made, outcomes, setting, and time frame.

Research synthesis: Answering, confirming, or rejecting research questions and findings through the linking and integration of scientific information available from multiple sources, activities, and experience. It has a quantitative component (meta-analysis of findings) and a qualitative component (systematic review of evidence). It is "an epidemiology of research findings.

Resident: A graduate and licensed physician residing in a hospital, usually pursuing training in a specialty of his or her choice.

Rhetorical ploy: A nonargumentative deficiency in reasoning containing misdirecting premises, proposals, or claims to reach their proponent's goals (often unrelated to the question) as the art of mental trickery and manipulation to a variable degree.

Risk: The probability that a health event will occur. (N.B. "To be at risk" is often not limited to noxious factors.) It is most often related to persons who still do not have a disease of interest. The probability of danger, loss, or injury within the health-care system. In epidemiology: The probability that an event will occur, for example, an individual will become ill or die within a stated period of time or by a certain age. (N.B. Usually, an unfavorable outcome or event is in focus, but probabilities of other events (even beneficial ones) may be quantified as risk.)

Risk factors: Causally related characteristics that *can be modified* (e.g., overeating in obesity).

Risk markers: Causally related characteristics that *cannot be modified* in their possible causal relationship, such as age or gender (e.g., age or sex in disease etiology).

Root cause: A causal factor that, if corrected, would prevent the recurrence of an incident. In lathology, it is derived from several contributing causes of error and harm such as system deficiencies, management failures, performance errors, and inadequate interpersonal and/or organizational communication.

Root cause analysis: A structured retrospective inquiry in lathology to identify triggering causal and contributing factors in chains of events leading to adverse events and other critical incidents.

Rounds (clinical): Bedside, floor, or formal classroom meetings, or other less formal encounters between health professionals, often including patients, to discuss the cases under current care, and expanded further into a learning experience about broader clinical problems underlying patients (cases) under current care.

Science (in general): The study of the material universe or physical reality in order to understand it.

Science of medicine: Organized reasoning, discovery, implementation, use, and evaluation of evidence in understanding human health, disease, and care decisions, and their evaluation based on the scientific method. A structured and organized way of using probability, uncertainty, and facts in preventive medicine and clinical care to best benefit the patient and the community. It is a logical and systematic approach to exploration, organization, and interpretation of data from initial observations to clinical decisions and final conclusions concerning problems of interest. The latter are defined, measured, analyzed, and interpreted with a satisfactory degree of reproducibility.

Scientific method: A way and direction of conducting research from currently available experience and evidence, formulating hypotheses and research questions, and conducting observational and experimental studies to analyzing results, driving conclusions, and reporting the entire experience.

Scientific theory: A plausible and consistent explanation for observable phenomena. In the sciences, it comprises a collection of concepts, including abstractions of observable phenomena expressed as quantifiable properties, together with rules (i.e., scientific laws) expressing relationships between observations of such concepts. Such a proposed explanation of empirical phenomena is made in a way consistent with the scientific method.

Screening: A presumptive diagnostic test, technique, or procedure whose purpose is not to establish a definitive diagnosis and prescribe treatment but to lead patients with positive results to a more complete diagnostic workup, evaluation, and treatment, as required.

Scut work: A daily hospital and floor chore of clinical trainees that consists of the repeated execution of necessary basic and general clinical care acts such as the establishment and maintenance of patient charts, vital functions surveillance, and providing medications or wound care.

Secondary prevention: Actions and measures to reduce the prevalence of disease by shortening its duration. Most clinical medicine falls into this domain.

Semiotics: The science or study of the relationship of signification between three concepts: (1) sign, (2) object, and (3) mind. In health sciences, communication with patients and peers are subjects of semiotics.

Sensitivity: The property of a diagnostic test to detect cases of disease from all cases existing in a given clinical and community setting. It shows how a test works in diseased subjects. The clinician does not want to miss cases that should be treated.

Set: A defined, categorized, and enumerated group of observations such as patients' exposure to noxious or beneficial factors and otherwise related to other events, which is distinguishable from another group.

Set of causes: A defined, categorized, and enumerated set of observations with *no* specific time, space, and any other interrelationships between them.

Sickness: An anomaly in health as perceived by a third person, a health professional or not: "Boy, this young lady looks thin, pale, and tired. She looks sick to me." See "disease" and "illness."

Side effect (in medicine): An effect, other than that intended, produced by a preventive, diagnostic, or therapeutic procedure or regimen. It is not necessarily harmful.

Significance (in general): Something that is meaningful from a clinical standpoint and/or from public health, scientific, statistical, social, emotional, or political view(s). It may abide by probability, judgment, anecdotes, emotions, and other considerations that, depending on the context, may be as important or significant, if not more, than associations unlikely to occur by chance (see significance in biostatistics).

Significance (biostatistics): A significance that follows the laws of probability. A characteristic of a health phenomenon or an observation that is unlikely to have occurred by chance. In biological sciences, an event is often considered significant if it is unlikely to occur by chance more often than 1 time in 20; that is, with a probability $p < 0.05$, or less than 1 in 100 ($p < 0.01$). See "p value."

Significance (clinical): The importance, relevance, or meaning for individuals involved in clinical care, patients, health professionals, and specified others. The importance of medical decisions and other considerations does not mean the degree of statistical significance. Statistical significance may sometimes be a prerequisite for other considerations of significance.

Skills: A part of the psychomotor domain defined in general as expertness, practical ability, facility in doing something, dexterity, and tact. In the decision making domain, they are abilities to apply structured decision making methodology to the solution of problems in practice. Errors may occur if the decision maker's skills are inadequate for the successful execution of a task.

Skill-based errors: Slips and lapses; errors in execution of correctly planned actions, encompassing both action-based errors (slips) and memory-based errors (lapses).

Slip (medical): An inappropriate action and execution or the incorrect execution of a correct action sequence due to competing sensory or emotional distractions, fatigue, or stress. Failure in schematic (often learned and mastered) behavior due to distractions rather than professional qualification and experience. May be related to execution (goals, intention, action specification, execution itself) and/or evaluation (perception, interpretation, action evaluation). Action-based error centered on attention or perceptual failure of an action, such as the dispensing of an elevated dose of medication and other failures.

Socratic dissent, debate, dialogue: A negative method of hypotheses elimination, in that better hypotheses are found by steadily identifying and eliminating those leading to contradictions. Its form consists of the following: statement of the question, answer to the question, exploration of objections to the answer, revised answer that avoids these objections, and exploration of objections to the revised answer. The successful dialogue reaches its end when the answer stands up against all objections.

Specificity: The property of a diagnostic test to confirm by its negative result that healthy individuals effectively do not have the disease of interest. It shows how the test works in nondiseased individuals. A clinician's certainty to do nothing (needlessly treating a nondiseased patient) is sought.

Spectrum of disease: See "disease spectrum."

Spheres: Collections of people in the process of interacting and making decisions.

Standard of care: A set of steps that would be followed or an outcome that would be expected. A level of measure, rather than a rule or policy.

Structure (of a health activity or system): The supporting framework of essential parts including all elements of the health-care system that exist before any actions or activities take place. The "consisting of what and how is it organized" characteristic of an activity or system within which errors occur. The setting in which care occurs and the capacity of that setting to produce quality. Structural measures such as credentials, patient volume, and academic affiliation.

Structure-process-outcome triad: The triangular evaluation of the quality of clinical and community care. Such a view of quality depends on what is part of care, how the care is delivered, and what is its impact, that is, favorable outcomes in patients or members of the community.

Survival: In epidemiology, it does not mean merely "avoiding death," when death represents the disease outcome of interest. It is a broader term for a state inception until the occurrence of some event or outcome of interest. It can be any discrete event such as a relapse, recovery, disease spell (well-defined), or any other change of disease course. The term "survival" is used here because of its persisting use, although it represents "time-to-event," "survival time," or any prognostic function of interest.

Survival curve: A curve that starts at 100% of the population and shows by time increments or intervals the percentage of the population surviving as long as the information is available. Survival here is a misnomer of sorts, because phenomena other than death can be illustrated and studied this way: disease complications, freedom from disease, and other phenomena related to treatment, prognosis, and exposure to noxious or beneficial factors and their covariates.

System (in general): A set of interacting and independent entities, real or abstract, forming an integrated whole. A set of relationships that are differentiated from relationships of the set to other elements and from relationships between an element of the set and elements not part of the relational regime. Systems have a structure that is defined by their parts and composition. They have behavior that involves inputs, processing, and outputs of material, information, or energy. Various parts of a system have functional as well as structural relationships with each other.

System (in health care): A set of interdependent components interacting to achieve a common claim. System characteristics include complexity and coupling.

Systematic review of evidence: The uniform application of (mostly qualitative) strategies and the qualitative overview of original studies of a given health problem to improve information, limit bias in the assembly, perform critical appraisal, and synthesize available (preferably all) relevant studies of the same specific topic. It is also a kind of epidemiology of research results across the available information.

Tertiary prevention: Measures aimed at softening the impact of long-term disease and disability, and handicap; minimizing suffering and maximizing potential years of useful life. The severity, spectrum, and gradient of the disease are emphasized rather than its duration.

Theory (in general): A coherent group of general propositions used as principles of explanation for a class of phenomena. A particular conception or view of something to be done or the method of doing it. It encompasses interrelated constructs (variables), definitions, and propositions that present a systematic view of phenomena by specifying relations among variables, with the purpose of explaining natural phenomena.

Theory of medicine: The body of principles of the science and art of medicine as distinguished from the "practice of medicine," or the application of those principles in actual practice. Colloquially speaking, it is anything that happens in the head of the physician, researcher, or practitioner of medicine before orders by word or stroke of the pen are given and an action by hand or other technological tools are taken.

Thesis: A proposition in medical research and practice, stated and put forward for consideration, especially one to be discussed and proved or to be maintained against objections.

Thinking: A mental action, which, if verbalized, is a matter of combining words in propositions.

Thought experiment: A proposal for an experiment that would test a hypothesis or theory but cannot actually be performed due to practical, ethical, or other limitations (cultural, value, etc.); instead, its purpose is to explore the potential consequences of the principle in question. A device of the imagination used to investigate the nature of things.

Threshold knowledge: Core concepts that, once understood, transform the perception of a given subject.

Time-to-event analysis: An analysis of intervals between two events and the meaning of such intervals in relation to the nature of events and relationships between them. Used in clinical trials, prognosis, survival studies, lathology, and elsewhere. In the broadest sense, it also includes analyses of incubation periods of diseases and generation time in the infectious disease domain.

Translation (in the context of knowledge translation): Multiple ways of moving experience, knowledge, facts, and their meaning from their original source and transmitters to their recipients or receivers in the framework of mutual understanding followed by actions to change the receivers' actions and the care and health states of their expected beneficiaries.

Uncertainty (in general): Any situation where probabilities of different possible phenomena or outcomes are not known due to our poor knowledge of them, whatever might be the reason for such imperfect knowledge. Probability refers to the quantification of uncertainty.

Uncertainty in medicine (clinical uncertainty): Incomplete knowledge of a clinical or community health problem as an entity and of its etiology, controllability, prognosis, and natural and clinical course.

Understanding in medicine and other health sciences: The successful sense making or accurate synthesis of health- and disease-related information pertaining to an entity (a patient, a health problem, or clinical and community care) that allows a justified explanation of the characteristics, behaviors, and events (their occurrence, evolution, and changes) associated with the entity. Proper understanding is a prerequisite for rational decision making in health promotion, health protection, disease prevention, and clinical and community care.

Warrant: In general, a warrant is something that serves to give a reliable and formal assurance of something, guarantee, pledge, or security. In argumentation, a warrant is a general rule or experience, as well as understanding of the nature of the problem under study that allows us to infer from, and in light of, the argument building blocks to its claim (conclusions).

Web of causes: An enumerated set of observations with specified time, space, and other interrelationships between causes and their consequences.

Index

A

Abduction, 45
Abductive reasoning, 52
Absolute risk reduction, 92
Academic half days, 245
Accident (in medicine), 187, 240, 260
Active error (human, medical), 16, 48, 72, 76, 133
Active teaching tools, 226
Actuarial judgment, 157
Actuarial method, 149
Additive effect, 81
Adduction (to adduce), 48
Adducts, 63, 143, 156, 181
Adducts (in argumentation), 63
Advocacy, 46
Algorithm in medicine, 183, 185
Allopathic medicine, 132
Alternative choice fallacy, 260
Ambiguity effect fallacy, 195
Appeal to belief, 259
Appeal to poverty, 259
Argument, 47, 50–52, 55, 212
   building blocks, 67–68
Argumentation, 45–46, 212
   claim, 220
   communication, 219
      nonverbal, 234
   components in physician's natural
      language, 218–219
   diagnosis as subject of, 127
   elements of, 226–227
   medical article as exercise in, 60–61
   modern, 276, 277
   prerequisite considerations, 216–217
   process, 71
   prognosis as subject of, 153–154
   risk as subject of, 117
   step-by-step evaluation of, 72
   structured critical thinking and, 216
   tools for, 50
   Toulmin's argumentation in
      communication, 210
   Toulmin's model of, 68–69
   treatment as subject of, 140–141
Argument-based error, 71, 72
Argument-based medicine, 45, 50
Argumentum ad numeram fallacy, 261
Argumentum ad verecundiam fallacy, 129
Art (in general), 9
Art of medicine, 7–11, 22, 188
Ascertainment bias, 127
Attending (adjective), 129, 143, 157, 213, 214, 221, 225
Attitudes, 167
Attributable benefit fraction, 91, 93
Attributable (etiological) fraction, 93
Attributable risk, 92, 93, 138
Attributable risk percent, 91
Availability fallacy, 128

B

Backing, 56, 58, 180
Backing (in argumentation), 58
Base rate neglect fallacy, 128
Bayes fallacy, 128

Milos Jenicek—A Biographical Sketch

Milos Jenicek, MD, PhD, LMCC, FRCPC, CSPQ, Canadian citizen, is currently a professor (part-time) in the Department of Clinical Epidemiology and Biostatistics, Faculty of Health Sciences at McMaster University, Hamilton, Ontario, Canada. He is also professor emeritus at the University of Montreal and he holds an adjunct position of professor in the Faculty of Medicine at McGill University, Montreal, Quebec, Canada. In 2009, he was elected fellow of The Royal Society of Medicine, London, United Kingdom.

Milos contributes to the evolution of epidemiology into a general method of reasoning and decision making in medicine. Supported by the University of Montreal to further enhance his teaching and research, he has committed himself to short sabbaticals and study visits to Harvard, Johns Hopkins, Yale, Tufts, North Carolina at Chapel Hill, and Uniformed Services at Bethesda Universities. Later on, his lecturing, professional expertise, visiting professorship, and other professional initiatives brought him to academic, governmental, and professional institutions mainly in Western Europe, North Africa, and on the Pacific Rim.

During his term as the acting chairman of the Department of Social and Preventive Medicine at the University of Montreal (1988–1989), he founded the graduate teaching of clinical epidemiology at the University of Montreal, his core course being also part of a similar program at McGill University. Until 1991, he was a member of the Board of Examiners of the Medical Council of Canada (Committee on Preventive Medicine). In 2000, he was invited by the Kuwait University as an external examiner for its final-year medical students.

In addition to numerous scientific papers and other collaboration with leading medical journals, Milos Jenicek has published 13 textbooks, which reflect the best of his national and international initiatives: *Introduction to Epidemiology* (in French, 1975); *Epidemiology: Principles, Techniques, Applications* (in French with R. Cléroux, 1982, and in Spanish, 1987); *Clinical Epidemiology: Clinimetrics* (in French with R. Cléroux, 1985), and *Meta-Analysis in Medicine: Evaluation and Synthesis of Clinical and Epidemiological Information* (in French, 1987), by the James Lind Library recognized as the first textbook of meta-analysis and systematic reviews in medicine. The book *Epidemiology: The Logic of Modern Medicine* (EPIMED International, 1995) was also published in Spanish (1996) and Japanese (1998). His sixth book, *Medical Casuistics: Proper Reporting of Clinical* Cases (in French, 1997), is again produced jointly by Canadian (EDISEM) and French (Maloine) publishers. *Clinical Case Reporting in Evidence-Based Medicine* (Butterworth Heinemann, 1999) appears as an expanded second edition in English (Arnold, 2001), Italian (2001), Korean (2002), and Japanese (2002). His *Foundations of Evidence-Based Medicine* was published in 2003 by Parthenon Publishing/CRC Press. His 10th book, *Evidence-Based Practice: Logic and Critical Thinking in Medicine* (with DL Hitchcock), was released by the American Medical Association (AMA Press, 2005) as well as *A Physician's Self-Paced Guide to Critical Thinking* (AMA Press, 2006) and *Fallacy-Free Reasoning in Medicine: Improving Communication and Decision Making in Research and Practice* (AMA Press, 2009). His *Medical Error and Harm: Understanding, Prevention, and Control* was published by CRC Press/Taylor & Francis in 2011. This monograph, *A Primer on Clinical Experience in Medicine: Reasoning, Decision Making, and Communication in Health Sciences*, is his 14th book.

His current interests include development of methodology and applications of logic, critical thinking, decision making and communication in health sciences; enhancement of evidence-based medicine and evidence-based public health, health policies, and program evaluation; and decision-oriented (bedside) clinical research.

Contact by e-mail: jenicekm@mcmaster.ca
Contact by telephone/fax: (519) 856-1324